W9-ABZ-229

Nice Work
If You Can Get It

my life in rhythm and rhyme

Nice Work
If You Can Get It

my life in rhythm and rhyme

MICHAEL
FEINSTEIN

HYPERION *New York*

This book is dedicated

to Peace, Healing, and

the Divine Spirit

Chapter 7 originally appeared in the New York Times *in slightly different form.*

Part of Chapter 8 originally appeared in the Washington Post *in slightly different form.*

Photo and song permissions and credits appear beginning on p. 402.

Library of Congress Cataloging-In-Publication Data
Feinstein, Michael.
Nice work if you can get it : my life in rhythm and rhyme /
by Michael Feinstein.
p.   cm.
ISBN 0-7868-6093-6
1. Feinstein, Michael.   2. Singers—United States—Biography.
3. Popular music—United States—History and criticism.
ML420.F332A3   1995
782.42164'092—dc20   95-2165
[B]   CIP
MN

Designed by Karolina Harris

First Edition
10 9 8 7 6 5 4 3 2 1

acknowledgments

Writing a book is definitely *Nice Work If You Can Get It,* and this book was made infinitely nicer thanks to the assistance and dedication of many people. They *all* have my deep gratitude and appreciation, but some must be singled out.

First, to Peter Occhiogrosso for his tireless contribution to this book in body and most definitely in soul. To inspiring friends like Rosemary Clooney, Page Cavanaugh, Eppie Lederer, Donald Smith, Ed Jablonski, Sharon Gerber, Marcia Lopez, Mark Sendroff, Jack Larson, and Max Wilk. To Bob Kimball for his unstinting dedication and desire to help me set the record straight. To Shana Alexander for taking time out from her own book to help me with mine. To my parents, Mazie and Ed Feinstein. For special help: Robin Siegel, Mary Ellin Barrett, Frank Military, Tita Cahn, Michael Kerker, and Steve Allen. To two giant songwriters: Marshall Barer and Jimmy Webb. To two of Ira's former nurses: Craig Siemens and Dwayne Ratliff. To my literary agents: Jim Stein and Dan Strone. To Sharon Weisz for her loving attention. To Baldwin Pianos: Danny Riscili and Myron Martin. To Buddy Morra, darling Barbara Mero, Ken Fritz, and Pam Byers. To Pat Mulcahy, Bob Miller, and the staff of Hyperion—you are all wonderful to work with. To Sarah Paris, Phyllis Werlin, and a particularly wonderful and tireless dynamo—Michon C. Stanco. To all those who helped with clearances and permissions too numerous to mention yet too important to forget. And finally—to June Levant: You started it all and I'll always remember.

author's note

$\mathcal{I}$n the years I spent with Ira Gershwin, he often retold stories that had appeared in his book, *Lyrics on Several Occasions,* as well as many other events and anecdotes mentioned in Jablonski and Stewart's *The Gershwin Years,* Kimball and Simon's *The Gershwins,* Deena Rosenberg's *Fascinating Rhythm,* and Max Wilk's *They're Playing Our Song,* among others. Sometimes Ira's account differed from another version of the same event presented in one of those books. In most cases, I have gone with Ira's version, even when it differed from one which appeared in print, if his felt more credible to me. I should add that my book is not intended to be in any sense a definitive biography of Ira or George. For those readers interested in finding more detailed descriptions and explanations of their lives and work, I highly recommend all the books above.

Nor is this book meant to be an exhaustive account of the great songwriters of the Golden Age of American popular song. You may ask why, in choosing to write in detail about a number of legendary songwriters, I've had less to say about the brilliance of so many others—Frank Loesser, Dorothy Fields, Harold Arlen, Arthur Schwartz. The only reason is that I ran out of space. And this won't be my last book, so stay tuned.

contents

IN THE MAGIC CAVE

*M*y life is music. It has always been music and it will always be music. Sometimes a little out of tune, maybe. Sometimes too plaintive and often at entirely the wrong tempo. In fact, it occasionally feels more like heavy metal or lite FM than like the classic American popular music that's my mainstay. But music in one form or another has been my constant companion from my earliest childhood (when I began playing piano by ear at the age of five) through my years of obsessively collecting records, books, sheet music, and photographs (the older and dustier, the better) on into a career playing and singing the music I love.

Although the music was always there and always inseparable from my sense of who I am, I'm not so sure I would be doing exactly what I'm doing today if I had never met Ira Gershwin. As I write this, I realize that, although Ira changed my life, although he did more to shape my future than anyone besides my parents (and my accountant), his name is hardly a household word these days. Even in his heyday, writing lyrics for a string of Broadway and movie musicals in the 1920s and '30s, he was often overshadowed by his brilliant younger brother George. So who exactly is Ira Gershwin and why am I dedicating such a large portion of a book about my life and career to an account of the six years I spent working for him? The best way to answer that question may be to feel my way back through the mists of memory to the time when he had just entered my life, a time when, as a naive twenty-year-old, my life itself was in a sense just beginning.

One of Ira Gershwin's greatest lyrics runs through my head now as I recall a day very early in our relationship when the fortunate nature of my situation began to hit me with the force of just the kind of waking dream he once wrote about: "Long ago and far away / I dreamed a dream one day— / And now that dream is here beside me." Although the memory of how I met Ira and of my years spent working for him now comes to mind with the clear inevitability of logic, at the time I was filled with the most delightful disbelief that any of this was happening to me at all. I had only recently escaped from the loving but decidedly uncozy confines of Columbus, Ohio, and had come to dip my toe into the enormous pond of Los Angeles. I had grown up thrilling to the music of George and Ira Gershwin—along with that of Irving Berlin, Cole Porter, and a few dozen other members of the charmed inner circle of great American popular songwriters of their era—and I wanted only to get a little closer to the music and to some of the magical people who created it. If I could somehow make a living at the same time, that would be gravy.

I would have given almost anything to meet someone of Ira's stature and, to be honest, I did everything I could to try to bring that meeting about. But when, through a series of apparent coincidences and fortuitous connections, I actually found myself in his employ, I was sometimes overcome by feelings of unreality. I'd been hired ostensibly to help Ira catalogue his invaluable collection of rare, private Gershwin recordings, but I had also been taken into his confidence rather quickly and to a degree that frankly surprised me. Even now, in the middle of what I hope will be a long career playing and singing the music of the Gershwins and many of their contemporaries, I still look back on the six years and one month I spent with Ira with a profound sense of having lived a dream. Calling up those memories is a bit like watching old home movies of a charmed childhood too impossibly happy and strange to have belonged to me. Can that half-frightened adolescent with the shy grin on his face and the reverential tone in his voice, sitting across the table from Ira Gershwin, really be me? Even though I can see the images so clearly that they might as well *be* home movies playing on a screen in front of me, I have to look twice to be certain it's not some actor, some impostor, playing my part.

But when I look again, the image remains as luminous as it has always been. Ira is still smiling that generous smile I remember so well. He is dressed in one of his custom-made flowing wool shirts, the purple one with his initials embroidered on the pocket, and with a silk ascot tied at the neck lending him the air of a genial Buddha, serene and welcoming. The right eye droops a little, a remnant of Bell's palsy he had suffered from some ten years before. His face, so familiar to me from countless photographs in the Gershwin books I've collected over the years, is adorned with a small mustache that he grew to cover up the effects of the palsy, which had slightly disfigured his upper lip. Unless Ira gets carried away about something, his voice is soft, the voice of a diminished man. When I comment that he doesn't have a New York accent, he replies that he does, but that it's hard to hear anymore because his voice is so weak and raspy. As always, he apologizes for his voice, prompting me to say, as always, "Well, Mr. Gershwin, I guess you'll have to cancel your appearance at the opera tonight."

Having turned eighty some months ago, Ira shows none of the vitality so apparent in the home movies of the Gershwins taken in New York and California when George was still alive, or even later, at gatherings of Ira's successful songwriter friends in his Beverly Hills home. The sad truth is that Ira has become so infirm that he can barely walk without the help of his omnipresent canes and walker, which lie at the ready behind him, and round-the-clock shifts of sturdy male nurses. (He had a female nurse for a while but she made him too uncomfortable.) His hands are small and he keeps them folded in his lap, one on top of the other, similar to the way Fred Astaire used to hold his hands. Astaire always thought his hands were too big, so when he danced he tucked the thumbs under his other fingers to make them look smaller.

Ira's face begins to grow animated as he talks about an episode in George's early days as a burgeoning songwriter. It has become clear to me since I began working for Ira some weeks ago that he loved his brother more than any other person in his life—more than his parents, more than his wife of over fifty years—that he loved George for his energetic spirit and amiable personality as much as for his genius as pianist and composer. And, of course, Ira loved the joy of collaborating with George on songs and shows as he had done with few interruptions from the early 1920s until George's death in 1937. "Of all the composers I worked with," he has said, implying a list that includes Jerome Kern, Harold Arlen, Sigmund Romberg, Harry Warren, Kurt Weill, Burton Lane, and Vincent Youmans, "George is the only one I consider to be a true genius."

As Ira talks about George, his face fairly beams with the recollection of that love, and his infirmity and all the years of loneliness without George seem to slide away for the moment. More than anyone who knew George in the early 1920s when he was just beginning to make his mark in American music and theater, Ira believed in George's gift and genuinely reveled in being close to it. He always claimed with pride that he was the first to recognize the vast extent of his brother's abilities, and he became his most fervent booster. After George's death, Ira's house became so filled with objects and artifacts belonging to or relating to George that it has taken on the air of a shrine, with George's manuscripts, recordings, letters, photographs, art collection, and George's own paintings everywhere to be seen.

At the moment, Ira is telling me the story of one of George's encounters with Jerome Kern, thirteen years George's senior and the great wizard of show music of his day. Having studied piano and composition in New York and Heidelberg, Kern was a masterful musical presence who exerted a major influence on the modernization of musical theater in America, and so the world. By the time George arrived on the scene, Kern had already written songs for nearly fifty stage shows, including more than two dozen complete shows of his own, sometimes as many as four in one year. As the reigning king of Broadway, Kern was initially beguiled and swept away by George's exuberant young talent, graciously making of him an early protégé. But the master later began to feel threatened by the upstart, as well he might have been.

Ira is humorously recounting the pivotal moment in Kern's changing perception of George. Until that time, he says, Ira had practically been the only one to recognize the true scope of George's genius, but the word was beginning to get around. Ira, who happened to be in the room that day, repeats the story in such vivid detail that he makes me feel as if I'm there in the room with him and George. It seems that George was sitting with a bunch of his songwriter cronies from Harms Incorporated, one of the powerhouses of the era whose name still appears on countless pieces of sheet music by all the greats. The office belonged to Max Dreyfus, the legendary head of the publishing company and a renowned talent spotter. Balding, very thin, always neatly groomed and quite reserved, Max was intelligent but also well suited to the hard-nosed nature of the music business. Most of all, he was gifted with an exceptional ear for musical ability. If Max took a liking to you, he could shape your rough talent into a career of extraordinary proportions, since he provided all the top-drawer composing talent to theatrical producers. (His only lapse was failing to pick up on Richard Rodgers when Rodgers first played his songs for Max in 1922.) And so Max's office was a favorite hangout for the most promising young composers of the day.

Jerome Kern had come in with a new lyric that he was working on for one of his shows, and George was sitting at the piano as usual. George was, of course, not only a rising composer but also a fluent and energetic pianist, as we know from the recordings and piano rolls he made in the '20s; he liked few things better than sitting at the keyboard and playing his tunes for whomever would listen, and there were plenty who would. In an attempt to belittle George, Kern thrust the lyric on the piano in front of him. "Let's see what you can do with that," the master said.

George took one glance and immediately started to set it, spinning out melody and harmony at the piano almost as fast as he could read the lyric. After Gershwin had played about eight bars, Kern snatched the lyric sheet away. "That's enough!" he barked, and strode from the room. Not long after that, Jerome Kern turned on George and took under his wing Lewis Gensler, another promising songwriter—although, as history has proven, not nearly so fulfilling of that promise as his predecessor. Kern had contracts with different producers to write a series of shows, including the Princess Theatre Shows, named for the theater where they were regularly staged in the teens. "I'm going to retire soon," he had told George, "and when I do, I'm going to give you all the contracts for all my shows. I want you to take my place and be my successor." George had been delighted. "But if you get any offers," Kern had added, "you come to me for advice and I'll take care of you."

George did get an offer in 1919 to do *La-La-Lucille!* with a producer other than the one Kern worked with; but Kern wasn't around and George accepted the offer without asking Kern's advice. No doubt sensing George's emergent self-confidence and independence, Kern was angered and dropped George as protégé and promised successor. The next time they met, in a room full of theater people, Kern had Gensler in tow and was introducing the young man as his new protégé. Pointing across the room to George, Kern announced in a voice for all to hear, "There's George Gershwin, who once showed a lot of promise."

Ira wasn't there this time, but he was still awake when George came home fuming. When he told Ira what had happened, Ira responded, "Yeah, you should have said, 'And there's Jerome Kern, who once promised a lot of shows.'"

Alone in the room with Ira now, I'm taking in every word. As one of the few remaining masters of the Golden Age of classic American popular music, Ira is not only relishing the story but also, it seems, consciously passing on a tradition that he wants to see preserved. I have the sense that his stories are coming to me on a direct pipeline, like the anecdotes of a piano teacher who can trace the lineage of his own teachers back to Chopin or Beethoven. Ira knows me well enough by now to know that I already understand the setting and that he doesn't have to explain the significance of Max Dreyfus or Jerome Kern or the Princess Theatre shows. Or, in fact, the irony that despite Kern's talk of retiring, he was only at the beginning of a great career and would not write *Show Boat* for another eight years or so. If there were something Ira thinks I may not know, he very gently and kindly explains it to me, never in a condescending way. We share a sense of joy at these exchanges—Ira at being able to talk about his brother again, and I because I am hearing it all for the first time. I can see him blossoming, coming alive as he tells the story, partly from the satisfaction of passing it on and partly from the sheer pleasure it gives him to feel again his enormous pride in George's genius.

This kind of exchange has begun to happen more frequently of late, with Ira sharing some almost forgotten recollection that has just popped into his mind, perhaps spurred by a record or a chance comment about some obscure figure from that era. At these moments I try to pay close attention, but I can't help being distracted by thoughts of how unlikely it all seems. This is the man everyone has told me was incapacitated, too infirm even to greet strangers, completely inaccessible. And yet, here I am in his presence, not just as a momentary visitor but in a position of some trust. In a very short period of time, I've begun to feel like family in Ira's household.

My reference to family is not arbitrary or fanciful. What I seem to have with Ira and his wife Leonore is indeed a kind of family relationship—later, at times, perhaps a dysfunctional one, with all the ramifications of what we now understand that to mean, but family nonetheless. Ira and Leonore and I are to become a very peculiar yet cogent family unit. By virtue of the plain fact that I am in the house on a daily basis, talking and working with Ira for hours at a time, Ira has more contact with me than with any of his relatives, including his brother Arthur, to whom he never speaks, or his sister, Frankie, with whom he speaks only occasionally despite his great affection for her. (When I later meet Frankie's son Leopold, almost the first thing he asks me is, "What is my uncle like?")

Without doubt I enjoy being so close to someone I've admired from a distance for so long. But at the same time, part of my mind is swimming in a thick fog. This continues to the point where I feel lightheaded, almost dizzy. It's a kind of joyous dizziness, but still a bit discomfiting, like a mild bout of hyperventilation. As Ira finishes his story, I'm fighting to refocus my full attention on what he is saying, but all the time my mind is racing. Although I'm being paid to do a job—something I'd gladly do for free—on another level I feel as if I've found the entrance to a magical cave and am now seated before the teacher for whom I've been searching all these years. Nor is "cave" an entirely inappropriate metaphor, since Ira has become so reclusive that he has achieved an existence similar to that of certain mountain solitaries, inaccessible to all but a persistent few.

The feeling of lightheadedness at times becomes so intense that I can barely concentrate on what Ira is saying. I wonder if something is physically wrong with me. Then I take a few deep breaths and the dizziness begins to dissipate. I realize that it is probably just a manifestation of my extreme excitement at having arrived somewhere that I have wanted to be for a long, long time—not consciously knowing exactly what or where that was until it crystallized in this moment. For many years, I've had a longing for something without being able to define it, not certain what I was doing with my life—playing in piano bars and feeding my love for Gershwin music without knowing where it was taking me. For years I've been thinking, Okay, so what? Why am I doing this? And what's it all about, Alfie? I've been thinking, Someday it'll come along, the job I love. Nice work if you can get it. But those have just been fantasies—haven't they?

Now it feels like the major piece of the puzzle is falling into place. Suddenly, so many disparate experiences are making sense. I can begin to glimpse a line that my life may actually be following—a line that reaches back to my early days in Columbus, Ohio, when I first heard *Rhapsody in Blue* and started collecting every Gershwin record I could lay my hands on. A line that leads through Oscar Levant, the gifted but eccentric pianist and composer who was part of the Gershwin circle and who has led me, in spirit at least, to Ira. A line, finally, that stretches off into the indeterminate future, and that may yet take me into the world that George and Ira helped so intimately to create. Sitting here with Ira, I can't quite see it all yet. I can't fully imagine myself making a career of preserving and interpreting the music not only of the Gershwins but of all the other great composers of classic popular music, people like Irving Berlin and Richard Rodgers and Lorenz Hart and Burton Lane and Jule Styne and Sammy Cahn and Harold Arlen and Yip Harburg and Dorothy Fields and Frank Loesser and Cole Porter and Betty Comden and Adolph Green and Johnny Mercer and Jerry Herman and Stephen Sondheim and Harry Warren and countless others. But surely the seed is there. Surely some transformation is beginning to take shape even as I sit here trying to stay calm and forget my momentary confusion.

And Ira is the conduit; he is the door. No matter that his productive days are well behind him, that he no longer has the clarity of mind needed to put together a single lyric, or that, on a physical level, he is virtually helpless. More than anyone I have known or will know, he will be responsible for my gaining access to the world of song that will change my life forever. He will have such a dramatic effect on my life, in fact, that I can divide it into two segments: Pre-Ira and Post-Ira. He will infuse my life not only with the knowledge and insight bred of his long experience in the music world but also with a connection to the great lineage of the Golden Age of American popular song, directly introducing me to Harry Warren, Burton Lane, Comden and Green, and so many others that I would otherwise probably never meet and come to know personally. Through Ira I will meet his good friend Vincente Minnelli and Minnelli's daughter, Liza—Ira's goddaughter, named for the great Gershwin song—who will spur my career as few others could. Ira's next-door neighbor Rosemary Clooney will become a kind of spiritual mother to me, another source of aid and inspiration in my work. All this will happen without Ira's ever leaving his house or barely even getting out of his chair. He is like the queen bee, sending out energy and making life possible in the rest of the hive without ever appearing to do much of anything.

Ira is smiling as he settles back in his swivel chair, his storytelling done for the moment. The underlying feeling of depression or sadness that so often suffuses him has dissipated as it always seems to do when he starts talking about George, about the days that were the most exciting and precious in his life. And, for all the days that stretch ahead of me in my own life, the days he is talking about appear exciting and precious to me, too. The great burst of creativity of those joyful and turbulent times has left us with a virtually inexhaustible supply of great songs on which to draw. It's a resource that will fuel my entire life and career, not only financially but also emotionally and spiritually, and one to which I will dedicate most of my energy.

Sitting face to face with Ira now, though, I have to wonder how I got here in the first place, contemplating the string of seeming coincidences that in retrospect appears to have been guided by some force I would be hard put to identify. I say guided because I don't think that anything that has happened to me was accidental, beginning with my childhood back in the bland, unsympathetic world of Columbus, Ohio, with the parents who I'm certain transmitted their passion for music directly to me.

WHY, OH WHY, OH WHY, OH, WHY DID I EVER LEAVE OHIO?

*"Now listen, Eileen, Columbus was frightening.
We just couldn't wait to get out of the place."*
—*My Sister Eileen*

The city where I was born, Columbus, Ohio, was not exactly a hotbed of musical activity, especially for the kind of show music that I quickly became interested in. Musical shows that played Columbus had a pretty tough time of it. They frequently had trouble drawing full houses and more often than not lost money. Even when the legendary concert pianist Vladimir Horowitz played Columbus in the mid-'70s, the house was only three-quarters full on an otherwise sold-out tour.

So where did *my* musical influences come from? Family, of course. My father loved to sing—still does—and when he was growing up, he sang with local amateur bands in Columbus. He always adored music.

When he was a young boy, he sold newspapers on a corner outside a bar that had a jukebox playing, and he still remembers clearly the words and melodies of all the songs from the mid-'30s that he heard drifting out of that jukebox. Whenever I have trouble remembering a lyric or melody line, I can call him up and he'll usually know it.

My dad used to take me to the meetings of the barbershop quartet he sang in. He belonged to SPEBSQSA: the Society for the Preservation and Encouragement of Barber Shop Quartet Singing in America. When I was six, I already knew how to say SPEBSQSA, and at their meetings I harmonized with the guys. My mother was and still is a tap dancer and, like my dad, has great passion for music. She was always the live wire of our family, and when I was a kid she used to tap dance around the house and entertain us at family gatherings. One of her best bits was a Charlie Chaplin routine performed to a 78 rpm record of Joe "Fingers" Carr playing a song called "Down Yonder," rinky-tink silent film music that perfectly matched her routine. At home, she used to take a feather duster and go around the house dusting everything like Charlie Chaplin. Dad often sang when I played the piano, so he was the first person I ever accompanied.

My parents were both born and raised in Columbus, where they met through B'nai B'rith shows at the Jewish Community Center. Mom danced in the shows and Dad sang. For a while before Mom started dating Dad, she dated a man named Aaron Cohen. He later changed his name to Artie Kane and became a prominent Hollywood pianist and composer who wrote the scores for a number of different movies. He made a record of two-piano arrangements of Gershwin with Ralph Grierson, and he was known for his interpretation of *Rhapsody in Blue.* My mother finds it ironic that she almost married Aaron, who, to put it mildly, doesn't like to be called Aaron anymore. But it wouldn't have worked out, anyway. Artie has been married many times now—so many times in fact, that I once saw a bumper sticker on a car in Hollywood that said, "Honk if you've been married to Artie Kane."

My father's name is Edward Feinstein; by coincidence, my mother's older sister Sylvia was dating a man named Meyer Feinstein. Sylvia used to say, "Gee, wouldn't it be funny if we both married Feinsteins?" My mother said, "Forget it. I'm not going to marry Ed." And in fact, when my father proposed to my mother, she said no. He was so devastated by her refusal that he started crying. Realizing in that moment how much he loved her, she changed her mind and agreed to marry him.

We moved several times while I was growing up. My parents liked to buy houses, fix them up, and sell them. I recall one house in particular that had a basement with painted cinder block walls but otherwise was in a raw state. My father built all the walls and put in plumbing and electricity and everything else and moved us in before the building inspectors got wise. He knew instinctively how to do all those things, and I used to watch him in amazement because I never had any talent in the construction field. That was their passion: Dad built and fixed things up and Mom decorated. I lived in that house for my last couple of years of high school.

My father was a salesman for Kahn's Meat Company, which had been started in Ohio in the 1850s. Their slogan was "The Wiener the World Awaited," and their logo was an American Beauty rose. It's ironic that Dad was involved with meat, because at a certain age I stopped eating meat on a doctor's advice, and we had friendly arguments about it. Eventually my father was diagnosed with heart trouble and had to have balloon therapy. He had to stop eating meat, too, and that put him in a real bind because one of his jobs was to assess the quality of different kinds of meat by tasting them. Not long after that, he retired. Now my father is about as strict as anyone could be in his dietary habits. I've never seen anybody more dedicated to eating a nonfat diet. If something has just a couple of grams of fat, he won't touch it.

Dad had started out as a butcher and owned his own grocery store before working for Kahn's. But the grocery store was located in a bad part of town, and he lost the business in part because of all the theft. He had mixed feelings about that; on the one hand he was angry about it, but on the other hand he realized people were stealing food because they were hungry. And he was a pushover; when people came in and begged for milk for a little kid, he would give it to them because he couldn't stand to see anyone go hungry. One of the reasons he was a successful salesman—at Kahn's he was always winning awards for selling more meat than anyone else—is that he believed in what he sold; he could ingratiate himself with people without ever being dishonest. He always let them know exactly what he was trying to sell. I think that is an amazing skill, especially since I can't sell anything. One of the reasons I voted against Richard Riordan for mayor of Los Angeles is that my father once had business dealings with him and pronounced him very unsavory. "He's a bad guy," my father said. So I listened.

My mother and father both claim that I began humming songs when I was still a babe in arms. My father in particular says that I hummed songs I could not have heard at that tender age. He certainly does not believe in reincarnation or anything like that, yet he swears that these melodies came out of my mouth, and who am I to dispute Dad?

When I was five years old, my parents took me shopping for a piano. They had recently bought a home, and they had a choice of buying a piano or buying furniture; they couldn't afford both. My mother said, "Let's buy furniture," but my father opted for the piano. For some reason—I'm still not sure why—they took me to Grave's Piano Store on Broad Street in downtown Columbus and asked me if I saw a piano that I liked. Maybe they had discerned that I had some sort of musical ability, although this was before I had begun playing the piano. I pointed to the biggest piano I saw, a huge white grand over in the corner. "No, no, honey," Mom said. "We have to buy something a little more economical."

They bought a spinet that was on sale for $500 and a couple of days later I literally sat down and started playing the piano. My mother came into the room because I wasn't just picking out notes with one finger but was playing with both hands. The song I was playing was "Do Re Mi" from *The Sound of Music,* which I must have heard on a record since the movie didn't come out until I was a bit older. I have no memory of ever playing a piano prior to that time. "When did your father teach you that?" Mom asked me.

My father could play three songs on the piano: "Heart and Soul," "Chopsticks," and "Midnight in Moscow." I said, "Dad didn't teach me this. He can't play this."

"Of course, he had to teach you!" she said. "Somebody had to teach you!"

"No. Nobody taught me."

So she sent me to my room for lying, and I didn't get dinner. When my father came home that night, they realized that I was playing by ear. They sent me for piano lessons, and I got started on the Michael Aaron Piano Course, Book 1. The teacher played an exercise for me and then asked me to play it. I simply listened to what she played and copied it. I wasn't reading the music. One day, after about two months, she opened the book to a new page and said, "Okay, play this."

"I can't," I said.

"Why can't you?"

"Because I can't read that."

"Why not? You've been reading all along, haven't you?"

"I've been listening to what you do and I've just been copying it."

She went out in the hall. "Mrs. Feinstein," she said, "I need to talk to you." When my mother came in, she said, "Did you know that your son has been playing by ear?"

"Yes," Mom said. "Didn't *you* know?"

After that, I stopped taking piano lessons. I told my parents that I wanted to play on my own, and they allowed me to. I was the youngest of three kids, and my theory is that my brother and sister had broken my parents down in a certain way so that by the time I came along, they had learned to go easy. My mother says she recognized that I was a very sensitive kid and so she wasn't as demanding and didn't have as many rules with me. When I was in elementary school, about the fourth grade, a visiting music teacher named Glen Harriman used to teach us once a week for forty-five minutes. Harriman was an imperious, impossible man who was always putting together orchestras of young children and then getting exasperated at how poorly everyone performed. He seemed perennially angry and frustrated, and I always wondered why he did what he did. The kids disliked him because of his attitude; he never seemed to smile. But at one point, we were all given a musical aptitude test. Mr. Harriman met with my parents afterwards and said, "Your son has extraordinary musical ability, and he should be playing an instrument."

They told him that I already played the piano, but he suggested that I take up some other instrument. Since my father had a violin, I started playing it. His parents, who were quite poor, had scrimped and saved to buy him a violin when he was a kid. I now inherited that violin, a beautiful but fragile instrument, slightly worn but with a mysterious feeling to it. I started to take lessons, but that lasted only about a month. When I discovered that I couldn't play it naturally, as I could play the piano, I gave it up. It sounded so sparse compared to the richness and range of a piano, and its tone didn't sound at all encouraging or sympathetic. I didn't have the same connection with the violin, and both the instrument and I knew this. In the meantime, my brother studied trombone for a short while, which was a disaster. Then my sister tried to take up the violin and that didn't work any better. Neither of them became musicians, though they both love and appreciate music from afar.

Besides Mom's dancing and Dad's singing, I picked up a lot of music from the movies and musicals we went to. And we always watched the *Lawrence Welk Show* and *Sing Along with Mitch,* which acquainted me with much of the music that I later embraced, even though I instinctively knew that the song performances were hokey. The few live shows available to me as a kid were mainly summer stock, such as the Kenley Players shows with Mitzi Gaynor, Paul Lynde, Carol Lawrence, Mimi Hines, Jane Powell, or John Davidson. They did productions of *Music Man* and *Damn Yankees* and *I Do, I Do* that were exhilarating if not terribly profound or classic. Who knew from Broadway? I was happy with summer stock. As I said, Columbus was notorious for its inability to sustain audiences for the arts. My great-uncle Hymie Gates, who worked as a property man on Broadway since the teens and is now in his nineties, told me that in the '40s and '50s, Columbus was always considered the death city.

Since Uncle Hymie was my first direct connection to the Broadway theater world, I owe him a few words here. Uncle Hy is one of the last of the Gates brothers, from my mother's mother's side of the family. He worked at the Morosco Theatre for so many years and was so well known that he was called the Mayor of 45th Street. He was one of the best-loved property masters—commonly known as prop men—on Broadway, but to my family, Hymie was always the uncle in show business in New York. He was prop man for *Of Thee I Sing* at the Music Box Theatre in 1932 and he also worked in Yiddish theater with Paul Muni. He told me that he gave Joe Papp his first job in theater, hiring him as a stagehand. If you brought up Papp's name to Uncle Hy, he invariably exclaimed, "I gave the bum his first job!" Hymie talked like that all the time. I once mentioned Cab Calloway and he said, "The bum owes me twenty dollars!" Cab has since died, but Hymie is probably still compounding the interest.

Uncle Hymie came to Columbus periodically for family weddings or bar mitzvahs. I can remember being eight or nine years old, sitting in my grandmother's living room and being carried away by his stories—stories about doing the lights for a George Gershwin concert at some hotel, or being a stagehand at a Leonard Bernstein recording session with the New York Philharmonic. I couldn't believe that I actually had a relative in show business. Of course, the stories he told were from the perspective of a prop man. If he talked about a particular show, he would say, "Oh, we had great props for that show!" He told me once about working on a show for which they needed a mahogany desk. Hymie took an old pine desk and covered the whole thing in contact paper to make it look like mahogany. Uncle Hy was extremely proud of being able to do things like that.

The first time I ever set foot in New York, in my early teens, I was dropped off in front of the Morosco Theatre on West 45th Street to meet Hymie. He introduced me to some of the other prop men who worked at the other theaters. Through him I met a prop man named Paul Biega, who later took me backstage at a show that Liza Minnelli was appearing in called *The Act* (1977), and he got me Liza's autograph. I thought that was about as close as I was ever going to get to rubbing elbows with anyone involved with Broadway, not dreaming that a decade later I would be playing there.

One time when we were walking down 45th Street, Uncle Hy pointed to the Music Box Theatre and said, "What's unusual about that theater?"

"I don't know," I said.

"It was built without a box office. The architect designed the theater and forgot to put a box office in! They had to add one after it was finished."

I have never met any veteran stage actor who didn't know Uncle Hymie. *The Shadow Box,* which was Mandy Patinkin's first Broadway show, ran at the Morosco. Mandy used to sit backstage with Uncle Hy for hours listening to him tell his stories, and Mandy still talks about doing a show based on Hymie's life. When Uncle Hy and Aunt Blanche had their sixtieth wedding anniversary, it was pretty much an intimate family gathering, but Mandy and his wife were there, having become good friends with Uncle Hy—even though Hy still calls him Mandy Potemkin. Mandy does a wonderful vocal impression of my Uncle Hy. In fact, his voice of the character he played in *The Princess Bride* is virtually Uncle Hy's voice. I found out about this when Jonathan Schwartz was interviewing Mandy on television and asked him to do the voice from *The Princess Bride*. Mandy started doing the voice, but suddenly he burst out laughing. "What's so funny?" Schwartz wanted to know.

"I'm really doing this guy Hymie Gates, and he was such a stitch that just thinking about him cracks me up."

Uncle Hy also talked about working on the 1921 show *Bombo*, starring Al Jolson. He claimed that even though Jolson's father was a rabbi, Jolson himself could not read Yiddish. When an article about him ran in one of the Yiddish papers, Hy had to read it for him. But Jolson's dark side overshadowed everything else about him. According to Uncle Hy, Jolson used to be so terrified of going onstage that he often hid before the curtain went up. One time they found him literally hiding in a big garbage can. I had never heard that about Jolson, but it fit with other stories I had heard relating to Jolson's unbalanced state of mind. Hy also confirmed more familiar stories, like Jolson holding the curtain because he was downstairs in a crap game with the stagehands.

Milton Berle's late wife, Ruth, was very good friends with Jolson's last wife, Erle, during the five or six years she was with him. Erle told Ruth that whenever she complained about a headache or was not feeling well, Jolson would put on a show of great concern. "Oh, you've got to lie down," he would say, "maybe you're pregnant—wouldn't that be wonderful!" But Erle discovered after Jolson died that he had had a vasectomy and wasn't able to procreate. He was so convinced that she was cheating on him that he kept hoping she would get pregnant so he could catch her.

Jolson's jealousy and anger at the success of other performers was legendary. If Jolson was on a bill with other singers and he started to hear applause while he was backstage waiting to go on, he had his dresser turn on the water faucet to drown out the sound of the applause. Jolson wasn't the only performer who suffered from irrational jealousy, of course. Barbara Cook repeated a story she had heard from a cast member of a 1960s musical called *Foxy*, starring Bert Lahr and featuring, among other supporting players, Larry Blyden. Every time Blyden got a big laugh onstage when Lahr was backstage, Bert became so disturbed and even enraged by the sound of laughter that wasn't for him that he too would turn on the faucets to drown it out. And Harry Warren told me that when Fanny Brice was in his show *Sweet and Low,* she followed a singer named Hannah Williams who introduced the Warren/Ira

Gershwin song "Cheerful Little Earful." Every night, Hannah got a tremendous hand and Warren said that Fanny felt so threatened by it that she always walked onstage immediately after the applause started, just to squash Hannah's ovation.

Jolson's egomania, though, dwarfed most other performers'. Burton Lane tells the story about the 1940 show *Hold on to Your Hats,* in which Ruby Keeler starred with Jolson. They were separated at the time but not yet divorced, and Jolson, who had never shared the stage with Ruby, felt that if she did a show with him she would be so impressed that she would come back to him. Burton had written the music for the show and was traveling with it for out-of-town tryouts before going to Broadway. But when the show left Chicago, Burton stayed behind because he couldn't bear to watch Jolson's cruelty to his fellow performers. (When I met Patsy Kelly many years later, for instance, she talked about how mean Jolie could be. On Broadway in *Wonder Bar,* there was a scene where Jolson shot Patsy and she did a dying swan routine, floating all over the stage until she dropped dead. One night as a gag, Jolson put buckshot in the gun, and when he shot her, she said, "I was in such pain that I did leaps that couldn't have been done by Pavlova.")

While *Hold On* was in Chicago, something happened that may have been a first for American musical theater. In the middle of one scene with Keeler, Jolson broke character and said, "You know, Ruby, we'd still be together if your mother hadn't walked into the kitchen that day." Burton said that Ruby walked off stage, walked out of the theater, and left Chicago. The understudy finished the show and Keeler was barely heard from again. The show went on to Broadway, where it was an SRO smash, but as soon as Jolson recouped his investment, he closed the show, claiming he was sick. He disappeared, but his coproducer had him photographed at a racetrack in Florida and went to court with the evidence. Jolson wasn't sick—he was just in love. He was forced to reopen the show, but by then audience interest had flagged.

Jolson had a habit when doing shows of coming onstage after the final curtain and saying to the audience, "Folks, you ain't heard nothin' yet." Then he would undo his tie and proceed to sing all his old hits, effectively eradicating the audience's memory of the new songs in the score. To circumvent this behavior for *Hold on to Your Hats,* Lane and lyricist Yip Harburg created an opening number in which Jolson got to do just that—sing a medley of all his biggest hits—before going on with the show. But when the curtain rang down at the end of the show, Jolson came out, undid his tie, and sang all the same hits over again. That was Al Jolson.

W HEN Uncle Hymie wasn't around to liven things up, I'd spend hours at a time playing the piano or reading. Sometimes I'd listen to the stacks of 78s I had started to collect or watch an 8mm silent film of Abbott and Costello or Laurel and Hardy. Anything but the real world, thank you. My mother worried about me because I was very shy and kept to myself. She often asked if I wouldn't rather go out and play or go see some friends. I never wanted to. I was a lonely child with few friends, and I wasn't close to my siblings. My sister is four years older than I am, and my brother, six, which seemed like an unbridgeable chasm when I was growing up. I didn't get along at all with my brother, who was the kind of person who would change the rules at Monopoly as he went along. I don't have any memory of how my sister treated me or how I treated her. I did like her, though. I remember only that when she started taking piano lessons, I was able to duplicate whatever she practiced on the keyboard, and she practiced very diligently. At one point she was practicing "Malaguena" over and over again. As soon as she finished, I could sit down and play the piece, because I had heard it enough times. It used to make her nuts. She would go in the kitchen and cry and say, "Mom, make him stop!"

I always wanted to hang around with people who were older than I was, never with kids my own age. I hated school. When I was in first grade and we were taught to read, I learned very quickly. The teacher divided us up into groups: the best readers, the average ones, and the worst ones. Because I was so quiet, she put me in the lowest group, thinking that I wasn't very good. That upset me so much that when my turn came to read, I read very quickly and as eloquently as I could to show her that I was better than she had pegged me. Then she put me in the best group. But although I was able to learn quickly, I hated the idea of learning. My parents hadn't instilled a sense of discipline in me, and I resisted and resented school. I did as much as I had to do to get by, but I never had any real ambition. Years after I graduated from high school, they put my picture in the showcase of notable students; I wasn't especially notable when I was there, of course, but I suppose they forgave me.

My parents seldom bought classical records, but they did buy a multirecord set put out by Columbia Special Products called *Andre Kostelanetz Plays the World's Most Beautiful Melodies*. From that five- or six-record set I learned much of the basic repertoire of great European music. Years later, when I met Kostelanetz, I told him how I had been influenced by his recordings and he responded with enormous grace and gratitude. It was one of the first of many opportunities I have had to thank people who have influenced me over the years. The record set, which featured excerpts of great classics, was the prototype of all those "best of" sets hawked nowadays on TV by people with fake British accents. You know: "Not *one* unwanted or unneeded musical passage!" It was the sort of package that's easy to make fun of because it provides only excerpts, not complete works, but it served me as a primer in classical music: the first movement of the Grieg Piano Concerto, the first movement of the Tchaikovsky Piano Concerto, the third movement of the Rachmaninoff Second Piano Concerto, the last movement of Gershwin's Concerto in F, and the famous final andante portion of *Rhapsody in Blue*. One record had a lot of Strauss waltzes and ethnic pop like the Pizzicato Polka.

After that, I started listening to classical radio stations and haunted used-book stores for books about music. Anytime I heard something that attracted me in any way, I went searching for recordings of it. My parents had a collection of old 78s in the basement of our house, and I delved into them. At that time, I didn't know the difference between classical and popular, so it all seemed fine to me, but in retrospect the selections were peculiar, to say the least. There was Beatrice Kay singing "Hello, My Baby" and the Glenn Miller Orchestra with "Little Brown Jug," an Andre Kostelanetz record of "Yesterdays," a recording of John Philip Sousa's "Washington Post March," and the famous third movement of *Sheherazade* by Rimsky-Korsakov. Whatever show albums we had were for the most part those dime-store knockoffs that had covers trying to approximate the original cast album cover art, but they were all studio casts and they sold for ninety-nine cents. So I didn't know from Mary Martin; it was Marni Nixon for me.

My parents did have a set of 45s of *Finian's Rainbow,* which was the first original cast album I ever heard. I remember putting them on the changer and listening to them over and over again. I was fascinated with Ella Logan's voice when she sang "How Are Things in Glocca Morra?" with that Scottish brogue that was her trademark. I was captivated by that music and started playing those songs on the piano. When my Uncle Henry learned about my fascination for this music, he gave me his collection of some six hundred 78 rpm records. That's when I discovered Bing Crosby and Al Jolson. I listened to a Decca set of 78s called *Al Jolson Singing Songs He Made Famous* that included "Swanee," "April Showers," "Mammy," "Toot-Toot-Tootsie," "Carolina in the Morning," "Sonny Boy," "Golden Gate," and "California, Here I Come." Suddenly, I was running around the house singing "Swanee." *Mwahhh!* And no, I didn't get down on one knee.

I occasionally heard other music on the radio—early rock 'n' roll, Motown, and R&B—but for the most part, I wasn't very aware of it. My sister, Randi, played Carole King's *Tapestry* album over and over again. My brother had Lenny Bruce's Berkeley concert and a lot of Rolling Stones LPs, none of which appealed to me. I had seen the Beatles on *Ed Sullivan* but hadn't liked them a whole lot. My reaction at the time was probably similar to that of my parents—I felt ill at ease with their music and their look. Now I feel differently about them—maybe not as nostalgic as most of my generation, but at least a fleeting sense of connection with a lost time in my life.

I had very few friends when I was growing up, and I don't remember ever listening to music with any of them except my friend Celia, with whom I listened, over and over again, to "Puff the Magic Dragon." My abiding fear is that one day my agent will book me in a land called Honah Lee. By junior high and high school, I began to feel very clearly that I was from another planet. Acknowledging my difference from other kids, my father used to take me to Goodwill Industries, where you could buy 78s for a nickel apiece, and let me randomly pick out records. I didn't know what I was buying; sometimes they were dance band recordings from the '30s and '40s, sometimes much older than that. I was consciously trying to find records with older-looking labels because I was intrigued by older recorded sound. I've always been fascinated by the idea of capturing and preserving sound, and even then I wanted to hear what had come earlier.

When I was seventeen I came across an album called *Starring Fred Astaire,* which contained Astaire's original recordings with Johnny Green, Leo Reisman, and Ray Noble of the classic songs he introduced by the Gershwins, Berlin, and Kern. At that point I started to pay more attention to the lyrics; before that, the melodies had been the primary attraction for me in their music. When I did hear contemporary pop songs on the radio, the lyrics didn't bother me so much as the melodies, which just weren't as appealing as the older songs. I started collecting sheet music—song sheets and songbooks—and began learning complete songs, music and lyrics.

· People have often asked me why I like old music and old films so much. Obviously I feel a deep connection with that world, but I don't have any rational answer to the question. I was too young to have been into "nostalgia." I think there can be very little dispute that the music of the era I'm interested in is of a better quality and certainly more interesting than a lot of what came afterwards. As a kid, I could very easily turn off the radio and put on an old 78. There was no question about what I wanted to hear, which was the music that affected me. When I listened to Top 40 radio, I had no emotional reaction, only boredom.

I never had guides who introduced me to this stuff. I did it on my own. My parents never told me what to listen to or what not to buy. Occasionally my father commented on a Bing Crosby record that I brought home, reminiscing about him, but we never sat down and talked at length about any of this music. We did have sessions at the piano that were enormously enjoyable, during which I played and Dad sang, but that was the extent of it.

George Gershwin was the first modern composer whose name I became aware of. When I was fifteen, I saw a movie on television called *Rhapsody in Blue,* an all but fictitious biography of Gershwin released in 1945, only eight years after his death. The producers had to create some sort of dramatic tension in George's life, because he didn't have an especially controversial or conflict-filled career. Gershwin pretty much knew what he wanted to do from an early age and, what's more, he was successful at it almost from the beginning. The producers and screenwriters contrived various conflicts of their own, making it appear that George was torn between writing popular songs and classical music and could never make up his mind. In fact, Gershwin enjoyed doing both and used his popular music successes to finance the time to write his longer orchestral pieces and his opera, an arrangement that could only make most of today's "serious" composers envious. The only tragic element in George Gershwin's life is that he died at the age of thirty-eight, in his creative prime, which is how the film ends.

I was deeply affected by *Rhapsody in Blue* when I first saw it, and I decided I had to find every piece of music that had the name George Gershwin on it. Naturally, I began with *Rhapsody in Blue.* This particular composition did things to my insides that had never happened before. Hearing the *Rhapsody* for the first time was a transcendent experience, and one that was repeated no matter how many times I listened to it. I felt a connection, a sense of finding something to which I belonged that was unique in my life to that point. Gershwin was able to express in musical notes exactly what I was feeling inside but couldn't possibly communicate. I was hooked.

Compulsive by nature, I plunged into learning as much as I could about the man and his music. Norm and Betty Wasserman, friends of my parents who lived down the street, lent me a complete recording of the *Rhapsody* played by Leonard Pennario with Felix Slatkin conducting the Hollywood Bowl Symphony Orchestra. (Many years later, I became friendly with Pennario and helped to get him reengaged at the Hollywood Bowl after years of silence enforced on him by a personal vendetta conducted by one of the directors of the Bowl. The Bowl was also where I first played the *Rhapsody* in 1987, commemorating the fiftieth anniversary of the death of George Gershwin.)

The Wassermans also lent me the Decca original cast recording of *Porgy and Bess,* and I was off and running. I started to haunt all the thrift shops and used-record stores around town in search of Gershwin recordings. Around the same time I found a biography of George, written for teens, at a musty bookstore downtown. The store carried publishers' overstocks and closeouts, so the $2 they wanted for the hardcover book was within my means. I also got some books from the public library, but, already exhibiting dangerous signs of collector's mentality, I found that borrowing the books was not enough—I had to own them.

I became obsessed with Gershwin's music. I knew I had some connection with George Gershwin that was special to me. I wasn't sure why, but I didn't question it. I didn't know where it would take me, although I doubt that I could have imagined then, even in my fantasies, that it would lead me to that house on Roxbury Drive.

By the time I was twelve or thirteen, I'd discovered that other kids thought I was weird because of the music I listened to. The first classical record I bought was Rachmaninoff's Second Piano Concerto, played by Pennario, and I left the record store hoping that I wouldn't run into anybody I knew. It was a terrible thing to have a record by Rachmaninoff when I could have had the Beatles or Bob Dylan. My brother and sister listened to all of the pop music on the radio, and I heard a lot of that music, but it didn't affect my insides, my *kishkes,* the way other music affected me. And that other music—both classical and classic American pop—began to change my young life. I discovered that music had the ability to alter my mood. Subsequently I have seen how it can change an emotion, can heal, and can actually transform people's lives. Whether we are aware of it or not, we are affected deeply by music—even by the Muzak we hear in the grocery store or background music we hear subliminally on the radio or television.

I started listening to particular kinds of music when I was in a particular mood to see how it might affect me. I did occasionally hear things on the radio that I enjoyed. Thanks to Randi's repeated playings, I grew to like Carole King's *Tapestry* and some of Steely Dan's recordings; I was tickled when I discovered that their album *Pretzel Logic* contained a note-for-note transcription of a late-'20s Duke Ellington record called "East St. Louis Toodle-oo." I pointed this out to several schoolmates but, of course, they couldn't have been less interested.

My earliest memory of performing in public was when I played "Fly Me to the Moon" in the assembly room in elementary school. I started singing in choir in junior high school and I loved the music classes. I learned for the first time about certain pieces of classical music, like Menotti's *Amahl and the Night Visitors* and Grofé's *Grand Canyon Suite.* Our music teacher also played some contemporary music and taught us about Henry Cowell and John Cage. I was kicked out of choir in my senior year of high school because during a musical aptitude test I gave an answer to a classmate. The teacher saw me and, since he had always thought I was a snot-nosed know-it-all anyway, he used that as an excuse to expel me from all the music classes. But he couldn't keep me away from music altogether. I got involved with the drama club and became president of the Masquers, and when I helped put on their variety shows, I played the piano in them.

Already I had started to develop a snobbism about music, especially when it came to singing. Certain things just sounded like junk to me and I hated singing them. Before I was kicked out of the choir, we had learned an elaborate choral arrangement of "Hey, Jude," and we ended a junior high concert with that long repeated coda: "Nah, nah, nah, nah-nah-nah-nah." It went on for about twenty choruses as everybody slowly filed up and out of the auditorium. It was one of the really cool moments in our concert, but even then I can recall feeling a little funny singing a Beatles song, thinking, I don't like this as much as I like the show music—even though I don't think I identified it as show music.

One of the ways I expressed myself in high school was by creating little recorded spots for the public address announcements in the morning. Among other things, these took the form of song parodies. To announce the prom, for instance, I used the tune of "The Rain in Spain" from *My Fair Lady*: "The prom is on / The twenty-fourth / Of May." I sang those parodies with a stable of performers that I assembled. I also wrote a six-part soap opera that was on every day for about a minute and a half. In some ways I had become a class clown by that time, trying to get attention because I was so lonely and enjoying the laughter that I seemed to be able to evoke with ease. At one point, the school newspaper asked me to create a contest, the prize being a subscription to the paper. I put together an ambitious contest asking the students to identify various voices. But the voices I asked them to identify were Bing Crosby, Al Jolson, and Fanny Brice—and of course nobody won the contest or could identify a single voice. It hadn't occurred to me that nobody else would know who they were. Those voices were already so much a part of my world, but it was a world none of my schoolmates shared. Even some of my teachers didn't know who the voices belonged to or who Fanny Brice was.

By the time I graduated from high school, I was voted best actor even though I had acted only a little and wasn't particularly good. Maybe the other kids were trying to acknowledge the fact that I had a unique way of expressing my creativity. One of the roles I had played in tenth grade was the Rabbi in *Fiddler on the Roof*. In retrospect, that seems like perfect casting because I was such a serious type and because then and now my approach to music begins with the role of the scholar, the archivist. Oy.

More to the point, perhaps, I created the sound design for several shows, selecting the music that was played and putting together whatever sound effects were called for. I knew how to splice tape. I had a reel-to-reel tape recorder at home and had been playing with it for several years. For one of the variety shows, a group of dancers performed the prologue from *West Side Story*. They needed to edit a section that is repeated but didn't know how to cut it in half. I took my reel-to-reel, cut the tape, and synchronized it perfectly, much to the amazement of everybody, including myself.

Despite all my dabbling in comedy, theater, music, and recording technology, I didn't seem to know what I wanted to do or who I wanted to be when I grew up. I loved music, but I didn't see any way that I could make a living from it. When I was fifteen or sixteen, I got an offer from someone in the neighborhood to play at a bar mitzvah, and I was stunned. I couldn't believe that somebody would actually pay me $25 for playing the piano. After that, I took out an ad in the *Ohio Jewish Chronicle* and started playing locally. I graduated from high school in 1974 without a clue about what I was going to do next. A guidance counselor told me, not very delicately, that she didn't think I was college material. My parents never brought up college. All my friends were taking college entrance exams and the SATs, but nobody ever said a word about college to me. Finally, I went to my mother and rather angrily said, "Aren't you going to ask me if I'm going to college?"

"You never said anything about it," was her answer, "so we figured you didn't want to go." That was the end of it. I don't have any regrets about not going to college, but I still feel fundamentally ignorant about a lot of basic literature I've never read. Not to mention all the campus drinking and brawling, a form of camaraderie that seems as strange to me as water polo.

In high school, I started to play at a place called the Dell, which was a sort of theatrical hangout where the Kenley Players held their cast parties. People involved with community theater came in, waiters got up and sang, and I accompanied them on Kern and Romberg and whatever musical theater bits were current. After graduation, I worked as a dance accompanist at Ohio State University for a year, mainly for the jazz and modern dance classes. At one point, I had to fill in for a ballet class, and I improvised some Chopinesque stuff, which was fun. I still didn't read music then. I was asked to play in unusual rhythms—say, in the count of five or seven. I played the famous theme from *Candide,* which I discovered was in seven. It was fun to invent things, but a lot of the time I was traumatized by trying to come up with something I could play in the count of whatever. I prayed that I wouldn't lose count. When I did, the effect was like the climax of an old Keystone Kops comedy. Then the teacher would glare at me, make an effort to regain her composure, and say in an unnaturally calm voice, "OK. Let's take it again. . . ."

By then, I had started collecting sheet music of old songs. When people came into the Dell and requested a particular song, I tried to play it. If I didn't know how it went, I would ask my father that evening, but sheet music was becoming more and more essential. I also became involved in community theater and portrayed Chico Marx in the Players Club's production of *Minnie's Boys.* They expanded the part so I could do more shtick at the piano at the end—that bit where Chico runs his index finger over the keyboard, then swats a particular note. I was pretty good at that.

*W*HEN I was twenty, I decided to move to Los Angeles independently of my parents, who also moved there. I was old enough to have lived by myself, but I was too scared to go out in the world on my own, so when I arrived in L.A., I ended up moving back in with them. I didn't learn to drive until I was eighteen, out of fear that I might get into some kind of accident or create problems for other people on the road. The fact that everyone else routinely learned this skill didn't help me get over *my* fear. As I grew up, I seemed to be increasingly inundated by fears and repressions; the more scared I felt of the outside world, the more I retreated into my inner world of music. As long as I could hum the melody, that felt like the safest place for me.

As part of turning inward, I started to read books about spirituality and metaphysics. I used to go outside at night, look up at the heavens, and try to get some sense of a greater power or spiritual center. I felt so alone and so disconnected that I often asked for some sign that there was *something* outside of myself. While I was still living in Columbus and playing at the Dell, I met a chorus dancer named Bill with the Mitzi

Gaynor show. Bill told me about a friend of his who was a spiritual master in California. "How do you become spiritual?" I asked.

"The first thing is to have a desire for awareness," Bill said. "You just have to keep asking over and over again. You have to keep saying as you go to bed every night, 'I do want to be aware. I do want to be aware.' "

So every night when I went to bed, I asked for awareness. I probably sounded like Bert Lahr: I do believe in spooks. I do, I do, I do. . . . But now I realize that it was the best thing I could have done, because when we ask for something, we do get it; when we open ourselves up to something, it comes into our lives.

One of the reasons I believe that concept so firmly is that I've always had the ability to manifest things in my life by my desire for them. When I started collecting records in Columbus, for example, I looked for fantastically rare recordings and they materialized with surprising ease and frequency. When I became obsessed with George Gershwin and his music after hearing *Rhapsody in Blue,* I began collecting the rare 78s that were listed in the appendix of the Robert Kimball and Al Simon book *The Gershwins.* Some of them were original cast recordings from 1920–1923, and I eventually found all of them in Columbus—no small feat. Many Gershwin recordings are extremely rare because they go back to the early days of recorded sound and were issued in limited quantities, compared with the millions of discs that are sold today. The success of a song was not measured in terms of record sales but by sales of sheet music; records were secondary. As I started to search for the rarer Gershwin recordings listed in various discographies, I found that some of the more obscure ones were turning up at a surprising rate.

The records also began to manifest in unlikely locations. When I worked with a community theater group once, I had an impulse to look in the basement of the building, as if something was drawing me there. I found a cache of old records, which the director of the theater group eventually gave to me. Of course, some records were harder to come by than others. In 1973, even some of the more recent Gershwin releases were hard to locate, as many were out of print. For example, it was very hard to find a recording, any recording, of the Second Rhapsody. I kept searching in vain for either the 1949 Oscar Levant/Morton Gould version or the later Leonard Pennario disc, to no avail. But while I was on a trip to Norfolk, Virginia, I wandered into an old shop containing piles of mint-condition recordings from the '50s and there I found the Pennario Second Rhapsody.

The earliest Gershwin original cast recording (of a song from the *George White Scandals of 1920*) dates from 1920 and is among the rarest of the rare, not having sold many copies. It was a rather forgettable piece titled "Songs of Long Ago," sung by a man named Lester O'Keefe and issued on the Brunswick label, an early competitor of Columbia and Victor. Shortly after becoming aware of the existence of the disc, I started to visualize it as part of my collection, and it suddenly turned up in a box of 78s I had purchased without knowing it was included in the sale. I would have gladly paid for that single disc what I paid for the entire collection. I also found Jolson's 1920 recording of "Swanee" and Paul Whiteman's 1922 recording of "I'll Build a Stairway to Paradise." It was as if they were being hurled through the universe at me.

I don't consider it an unusual ability to be able to manifest something after visualizing and contemplating it mentally. Many people who collect things tell similar stories. Nowadays, I hear talks about manifestation all the time. It's the principle behind spiritual groups such as the United Church of Religious Science, Unity, and A Course in Miracles. These groups and others like them are based on the belief that the power of the brain is a scientific reality, that if we pray, or "treat" (they prefer the word "treatment" because of the stigma attached to the word "prayer"), in a particular way, we will always get the same result. I accept most of that philosophy in principle, but I believe fully in the laws of manifestation because they have been constantly demonstrated to me.

When I met Rosemary Clooney many years later, I asked her if there were any recordings she had made that she didn't have. She told me that when she was singing with her sister Betty in the Tony Pastor Orchestra, they had recorded a series of songs from the Disney movie *Song of the South*—a total of six sides that were never released. Rosemary told me how much she wished she had those recordings. A couple of weeks later, I was in the San Fernando Valley getting my car repaired, and, with nothing to do for a few hours, I took a walk up the block and went into a secondhand store. They had boxes of 16-inch acetate and vinyl transcriptions from the '40s, and I started leafing through them. There in the pile were two discs containing the complete recordings of the songs from *Song of the South* that Rosemary and Betty had made with Tony Pastor. In the same pile was an acetate of Rosemary by herself singing "I've Got My Love to Keep Me Warm." There couldn't be more than a handful of these recordings in existence, and I was happy to give them to Rosemary on her birthday the following month. Her reaction as she looked at the discs in wide-eyed amazement was more reward than I needed. Just finding them was a big enough thrill for me. But when she showed them excitedly to all of her kids—exclaiming "Look what he found! I've wanted these my whole life!"—I felt fortunate just to have been the conduit.

I have also frequently experienced what Jung called "synchronicity," which he defined as "the occurrence of meaningful coincidences which, in themselves, are chance happenings, but are so improbable that we must assume them to be based on some kind of principle, or on some property of the empirical world." After the composer Milton Ager died, for instance, I was asked by his wife, Cecelia, to catalogue his musical effects. Milton was a friend of the Gershwins; he wrote "Happy Days Are Here Again," "Ain't She Sweet?" and "Hard-Hearted Hannah," and his daughter is the author Shana Alexander. While working on his effects, I came across a song he had written in the teens called "China, We Owe a Lot to You." It's a very silly song, so silly that it's now funny. Milton had rewritten it later when Nixon went to China, thinking—ever the song plugger—that maybe he could revive it. That night, when I got home, I discovered that a neighbor had slipped a piece of music under my door with a note that said, "Michael, found this old sheet music and thought you'd get a kick out of it." It was a copy of "China, We Owe a Lot to You." About a week later, I was in a Goodwill store and asked, as I always do, if they had any old records. The man said "Oh, there's a few of them, but they're in pretty bad shape." He had a stack of about twenty or thirty 78s, very old and dusty. I started going through them and found a cracked but playable recording of "China, We Owe a Lot to You," which I bought for a quarter.

At home, I discovered that the record had extra lyrics, a second release, or bridge, that wasn't published in the sheet music. I thought to myself, I guess I'm supposed to sing this—and I actually did the song for a number of years. It goes:

China,
Way out near Asia Minor,
No country could be finer,

Beneath the sun.
You gave us silk to dress our lovely women,
'Twas worth the price,
And when we couldn't get potatoes,
You gave us rice.

It wasn't my biggest hit, but some friends still request it.

Over the next few years, I continued to have experiences like that, not only with records and sheet music but also with certain rare books. This happened in particular with a figure from the Gershwin era who was to provide a crucial transition from my youthful experiences to my professional involvement in music.

Oscar Levant was a brilliant concert pianist who was a close friend of George Gershwin's. He made a few movies for different studios, wrote three witty and acerbic books, and was a composer in his own right with many popular songs (but only a couple of hits) and a number of symphonic compositions to his name. Yet he stopped composing songs in 1939 and symphonic works as of 1940 because by that time, he had been so overwhelmed by the output of George Gershwin that he decided there was no need for him to compose. In *A Smattering of Ignorance,* published in 1940, Levant speaks about his growing friendship with Gershwin with equal parts wry, self-deprecating humor, unbridled admiration, and ruefulness. Explaining his sudden abandonment of composing, Levant writes,

> Once I had been admitted to George's friendship, I took so much pleasure in the things he was writing and doing that I did nothing of my own. I got so much, vicariously, out of his ability and creativeness that whatever latent talents I had were completely submerged. In consequence I had no formative period as a composer. Listening to him improvise and play were enough for me. He had such fluency at the piano and so steady a surge of ideas that any time he sat down just to amuse himself something came of it.

Gershwin apparently expressed everything that Levant wanted to say musically. It is unfortunate that Oscar felt that way, because he might have had more significance as a composer if he had kept at it.

For reasons not entirely clear to me, Levant had a great influence on my life as a child. I had seen him playing himself in the film *Rhapsody in Blue,* which impressed me at the time, not knowing then all the inaccuracies it purveyed. I was further intrigued by Oscar's persona in *An American in Paris* and I was quite taken with his pianistic interpretations of Gershwin, recognizing even at my young age his unique style and his ability to interpret that music in a jazzy fashion without making it sound classical or clinical. I read *A Smattering of Ignorance* when I was still in junior high school, and loved its witty, ironic tone. I was working in a private study session with a teacher who encouraged students to read on their own, and when I told her that I'd become intrigued with Oscar Levant, she asked if I had read all of his books. "I've always found," she said, "that you have to read all of the works of a particular author, because you might discover in the last book something so different that it will change your whole opinion about his or her body of work." Properly chastened, I went out and found Levant's other two books, *Memoirs of an Amnesiac* and *The Unimportance of Being Oscar.* I did discover an alarming escalation in Levant's eccentricity quotient in those books as he began to talk quite openly about his obsessive-compulsive behavior and his deepening dependence on powerful prescription drugs.

I even wrote a letter to Levant which he never answered. Having become well acquainted with his personality through his books, I certainly didn't expect him to. In fact, I was probably a little relieved that he didn't answer, feeling I had in all likelihood escaped a potential skewering.

Because of Levant's close connection with the Gershwins, I started to look for his music as well. By the time he died in 1972, I had started collecting his recordings both of Gershwin and of contemporary classical music, including some pretty obscure composers like Jelobinsky, Honegger, and other names that are still largely unfamiliar. By visualizing Levant's works, I constantly found things connected with him—not only his recordings but also objects that had belonged to him. Once when I was trying to locate an unusual Gershwin book, I spotted among several volumes on the top shelf of a used-book store a book that drew my attention even though I couldn't read the title. I just knew I wanted to see this book. I got a ladder, climbed up, and pulled the book off the shelf. It turned out to be *Songs My Mother Never Sang* by Harry Ruby, a great songwriter who wrote comedy songs for Groucho Marx. I opened up the book and discovered that it was inscribed to Oscar Levant. I went up to the guy at the desk and asked, "Did you buy Oscar Levant's book collection?"

He looked at me with a vacant expression. "Who's Oscar Levant?"

This kind of thing happened continually. In perhaps the strangest manifestation of this connection with Levant, I was in an old music store on Santa Monica Boulevard one afternoon when I was overcome by a feeling that somebody was watching me. I looked around and saw no one. I tried to shrug off the feeling but couldn't. Finally I glanced up— and way, way up at the top of the very high-ceilinged building was a photograph of Oscar Levant! I talked the owner of the store into selling it to me. Later I went into an old sheet music store on Western Avenue in Hollywood. In reality, it was just a house owned by an old man who lived there with sheet music piled up everywhere—under his bed, in the bathroom, in every nook and cranny. The house was a real fire trap. The classical music was very well organized, but the popular music was a mess. "Do you have any songs from the '20s and '30s?" I asked.

"Oh yeah, they're in the back."

I went into the back room, where mountains of music were strewn about helter-skelter. I felt there was something I was supposed to find, and I spent about an hour going through the piles of sheet music, but without finding anything of Levant's. Finally I decided to look in one more pile. I picked up half a stack and moved it to my right, and the first piece of music on top of the remaining pile was an artist's promotional copy of a song Levant had written in 1938 that I didn't own.

After innumerable incidents of this sort over a period of years, I had amassed all of Oscar Levant's records except his last album, which was a real rarity. There's a store in Hollywood called the Record Collector, a scary-looking place, dusty and heavy with gloom, run by a man who, if he knows you really want a record, will quickly add ten or fifteen dollars onto the price. Gritting my teeth, I walked in and asked if he had the album *Oscar Levant at the Piano*. "No, we don't have that record," the clerk barked, "but we have some records that used to belong to him."

"Really?" I said. "Could I see them?"

He took me in the back room and showed me a stack of musty

acetates. Acetates are individually made records that were often recorded as air checks—disc recordings made to preserve radio broadcasts before the advent of audiotape. The stack included recordings Levant had made going back as early as 1934 and some unreleased tracks from his last commercial recording session in 1958. It was an extraordinary collection, with many compositions he had written himself that weren't available in any other form. "Where did you get these recordings?" I asked.

"We bought them at an auction of the Levant estate by Sotheby's," the man said. I borrowed $150 from my father to buy those records. It was a lot of money at the time, but a shrewd investment, since those recordings eventually led me to Ira Gershwin.

By that time, I had started playing in a restaurant in the San Fernando Valley called Mother's, a kind of Mafia hangout run by a guy who talked like Humphrey Bogart. In April 1977, a waitress there asked me if I had ever been to see a psychic. When I said I hadn't, she told me about an especially interesting one who charged $25 and recommended I go to her. I figured for $25, what could I lose? The psychic's name was Carol Dryer. (Years later I came across a picture of her in Tina Turner's autobiography, and I once met Tina at a party at Carol's.)

"I see a man around you who wears a rumpled blue suit and chain-smokes," Carol said. I immediately recognized her description.

"That must be Oscar Levant," I said. The name didn't seem to register with her.

"Did he play the piano?" she asked blankly. If she knew anything about Levant, she certainly didn't let on. But at that and subsequent sessions, she told me that his spirit was very strongly around me. Naturally I was intrigued because of all my experiences of finding things of Levant's and because of the feeling of being watched by that photograph on Santa Monica Boulevard. You could probably say that I was skeptical but open to the idea, and I wondered if she was just reading my mind. But many of her later predictions turned out to be too accurate to be mere coincidence. A couple of years later, for instance, I went back to Carol for another reading. "Levant's spirit is leaving you," she said at that time. "He's moving on now."

"If he's leaving," I joked, "I want a going-away present." Carol laughed. "You'll get it."

I had compiled a complete discography of Levant's recordings by then, acquiring take sheets from Columbia—the only label he regularly recorded for—listing everything he had done in the studio. About a week later, I was in another secondhand store, going through a stack of records that included V-discs, special records made for servicemen and never sold commercially. Among the V-discs, I found one recorded by Oscar Levant that contained unreleased versions of the Second and Third Gershwin Preludes and, on the opposite side, a portion of the Gershwin Concerto in F. So I got my going-away present all right, a record of which I had been previously unaware. I quickly added it to my discography. (That recording was not only rare but rather peculiar because it contained Levant's recording of the Concerto in F that he had made for the soundtrack of the movie *Rhapsody in Blue.* Toward the end of the film, Levant re-created on the soundtrack the two moments in the performance of the concerto when George Gershwin faltered at the piano, which turned out to be the first symptoms of his brain tumor. This V-disc included the two fumbles without explanation; it must have sounded incongruous to the servicemen listening to a record with two obvious clams in the middle of the concerto.)

But before Oscar's spirit moved on, my peculiar connection to him continued to grow as I acquired more of his books and recordings, and I even started affecting some of his wisecracks, much to the bemusement of my family and friends. I came to understand that as a pianist he was a great artist but that he had been frequently undermined by his own fear and nerves and would have been more highly regarded except for his problem with nervousness. Years later, when I was working for Ira Gershwin, Andre Kostelanetz came to visit Ira one day. Kostelanetz recounted recording the Concerto in F in 1942 with Levant at the piano and told just how nervous Oscar was. At that time, they did takes in four-and-a-half-minute segments because of the time restrictions on 78 rpm records. Levant played one chord wrong during one of the takes and Kostelanetz said, "Should we go back and do it again?"

"No, no, no," Oscar said. "It's fine, it's fine." He was such a nervous wreck that they left it. So what is considered today one of the finest recordings of the concerto still has a funny chord because Levant was too nervous to go back and redo it. Levant's last public appearance, at the Hollywood Bowl in August 1958, also involved playing the Gershwin concerto with Kostelanetz. Andre told me that after the completion of the first movement, Levant went over to him, said, "I'm leaving," and started to walk offstage. Kostelanetz immediately gave the downbeat for the next movement and Levant sheepishly returned to the piano and brilliantly concluded the performance.

The critical opinion of Levant during his day ran the gamut from those who considered him to be one of the great interpreters of concert music to those who viewed him as a hack. The fact that he acted in movies and wrote popular songs did not help his image in the eyes of highbrow critics. Worse yet, he played himself in the movies, not so much as a pianist but as a character, and a rather cynical one at that. One movie critic, after seeing a film in which he appeared, said, "Oscar Levant was, well, Oscar Levant." And yet at one time, Levant earned more money for his concertizing than Horowitz or Rubinstein.

Levant had always wanted very much to be a concert pianist, but recognition was rather slow in coming. To survive, he started taking jobs with dance bands in New York and played in radio orchestras. He had all but given up the idea of being a serious concert pianist when, toward the end of the '30s, he appeared on a radio show called *Information Please*. The program was perfectly suited to Levant's persona, allowing him to show off his encyclopedic knowledge—impressively vast even though he was not well schooled. More important, it gave him the opportunity to play snippets of classical themes on the piano. From that exposure, he obtained offers to concertize and went on to become one of the biggest concert artists of the '40s. He was known first and foremost for his interpretations of Gershwin, which was a very personal matter to him because of his friendship with George. As other pianists started to interpret Gershwin and Gershwin became more integrated into the mainstream concert world, Levant was traumatized emotionally. He felt as if part of his personal world were somehow being taken away from him, as if he were being deprived of an important connection and strangers were treading on his personal ground.

Oscar stopped playing piano professionally in 1958, but he appeared frequently as a panelist on the television quiz show *Who Said That?* between 1948 and 1955. In Levant's last appearances on TV, on the *Jack Paar Show,* Paar inevitably coaxed him to go over to the piano and play. But Levant appeared clumsy because of his lack of practice. He had become addicted to drugs by that time and probably didn't feel good about what he did, but he always got enthusiastic responses from the audience on the strength of his reputation. That must have nettled him.

The pianist Stan Freeman told me that when he met Levant in the '40s, he was struck that Levant asked him what his fingering choices were in interpreting *Rhapsody in Blue*. This was a piece that Levant had played thousands of times, yet he was so insecure that he wanted to know how a relative newcomer like Stan played it. Acclaimed concert pianist Leonard Pennario said that Levant once phoned him and asked for piano lessons. Pennario thought it was a gag at first, but then he realized that Oscar was serious. "I couldn't teach the great Oscar Levant how to play," he said.

"Take my number anyway," Levant replied, "in case you change your mind."

Levant had just as low an opinion of his own music as he did of his piano playing. Nevertheless, judging from the recordings of his work that I have listened to, I think he was a much better composer than he ever wanted to admit. One of his problems was that he couldn't settle on an idea; his manuscripts at the USC library show how he revised and reworked pieces ad infinitum. One of his most moving compositions is a dirge he wrote to the memory of George Gershwin, which he introduced with the Pittsburgh Symphony (Pittsburgh being his hometown). At my suggestion, the work was revived for a performance by Michael Tilson Thomas in 1982. In the last couple of years, a few pieces of Levant's have been recorded, including his Caprice for Orchestra and Piano Sonatina, the latter of which has been recorded commercially at least twice and is slowly gaining recognition. However, his most prominent composition is a piano concerto that was introduced during the Second World War by the NBC Symphony conducted by Alfred Wallenstein. Levant, who had been studying with Schoenberg, described it as a mingling of Schoenberg's twelve-tone system and boogie-woogie. Indeed, it is a very strange piece of music that, as a whole, doesn't quite succeed. It was so poorly received that Levant reported getting a telegram from one friend who said, "Not since Pearl Harbor have I heard such sounds." Oscar may have made that up, but the concerto was played only a few more times before he permanently retired the score and parts to a closet shelf in his home.

Levant also wrote the score for the films *Nothing Sacred* and *The Awful Truth,* but the film music of his that I enjoy most is an opera sequence he wrote for the 1936 movie *Charlie Chan at the Opera.* I sometimes play the soundtrack recording for opera buffs—especially arrogant ones who claim to know everything—and have them try to guess who the composer is, knowing they cannot possibly come up with the answer. Levant had one stipulation, that he be able to use the word *silenzio* in the opera sequence, just because he had always wanted to. So at the beginning of a tenor aria, you hear "*Silenzio!*" (According to Shana Alexander, Oscar's other favorite word was *désolée*.)

Levant frequently subverted his own opportunities for having his compositions played by making wisecracks about them. When conductors told him that they wanted to perform one of his pieces, he often talked them out of it. One story has it that the conductor Otto Klemperer said to Oscar, "I understand you've written a piano concerto. I'd like to hear it."

"All right," Levant said. He sat down at the piano and started playing "Chopsticks" and other frivolous pieces of music. Then Harpo Marx joined him, and Klemperer stormed out of the room. (Erratic behavior appeared to run in his family. The lyricist Irving Caesar once told me a story he had heard from Oscar about the time Levant's uncle arrived late for a concert by the great Toscanini in Pittsburgh. As custom decrees, Oscar's uncle had to wait to be seated until after the first number was over. When the doors were finally opened, he rushed down the aisle and pointed his finger accusingly at the maestro. "You wop son-of-a-bitch," he yelled, "don't ever do this to me again!")

For all his self-destructiveness, Oscar was a very insightful man. On one occasion, he did send a piece of music to a conductor in hopes of having it played, and the two had a meeting a couple of weeks later. The conductor began the conversation by saying, "You are a very talented man, Mr. Levant."

"Then that means you're not going to play my piece," Oscar responded.

"How did you know that?" the conductor asked.

"It's easy," Levant said. "When someone's going to play your music, they say, 'I've arranged a concert for next May,' or they immediately start talking terms. When they begin the conversation by talking about your talent, you know that you're sunk."

Like so many in the Gershwin circle, Levant was a great wit. Liza Minnelli contends that Oscar was the first person to say, "Death is nature's way of telling you to slow down." However, my favorite quip of his that

I've never seen in a book was something he said on his local television show in Los Angeles. "They Can't Take That Away from Me" was nominated for an Academy Award as the best song of 1937. George had already died by the time the song became famous, and so a lot of emotion had become attached to it before the awards ceremony was held in March 1938. It was the only time George was ever nominated for an Oscar and the first time Ira was nominated. Nevertheless, the song lost to "Sweet Leilani" (from the movie *Waikiki Wedding*), which was popularized by Bing Crosby and was a huge hit. It was written by Harry Owens, who had a band called Harry Owens and His Royal Hawaiians, and the Oscar itself was presented by Irving Berlin. Levant was so angry that the Gershwin song lost that he quipped, "I'd like to say something about Harry Owens: His music is dead, but he lives on forever." When Owens finally passed on a couple of years ago, my only reaction was one of irritation; what nerve to ruin a perfectly good anecdote.

AFTER my family and I had moved to California in the fall of 1976, I decided that I should get a "real" job because I didn't think I would be able to make a decent living playing the piano. Playing in piano bars was all well and good, and I enjoyed it, but I also figured that in twenty or thirty years I might still be playing in piano bars, only by then I would probably have a drinking problem, back trouble from sitting on hard benches, emphysema from all the smoke-filled rooms, and a serious Pavlovian disorder brought on by the requesting or playing of "Happy Birthday." It didn't look good. So I started demonstrating pianos at a store in the San Fernando Valley called Finnegan's Pianos, but I discovered that, unlike my father, I was a lousy salesman. People loved the way I demonstrated the pianos, but I could never close the deal. The owner, Bill Finnegan, couldn't play the piano, but he sold hundreds of them. One day a lady came in and said she loved Richard Wagner. Bill pointed to a piano and said, to my astonishment, "This was Wagner's piano. Yes, it was! He wrote 'Ride of the Valkyries' on this." And he sold it right there. I couldn't do that.

Bill had also gotten involved in a business deal with Liberace, selling something called Liberace's Hot Nuts—a piano with a bowl in the center for heating nuts. Some of the models were fitted with a cassette player so you could put in a tape of Liberace playing some kind of honky-tonk music. Liberace always admonished Bill not to tell anyone it was him playing because the music was so cheesy.

Eventually, I sold several pianos that should have earned me a commission of about $200. When Bill refused to pay me the two hundred dollars, I quit. I had to file a claim with the labor board to get my commission. When I went back to the store to pick up the check, Bill said, "I'll see that you never work again." That was the first time I heard that line. Every once in a while I think about calling Bill to let him know that I'm doing all right in spite of the Finnegan curse.

Before I quit, though, a secretary at the store who seemed to want to help me out and who knew that I had purchased those rare Oscar Levant acetates said to me, "Why don't you call his widow, June Levant, and find out why she got rid of them at the estate sale?"

I shrugged. "I'd love to do that," I said, "but I don't know her phone number, and I wouldn't want to bother her anyway."

"I can get you her phone number," she said. "I have friends at William Morris who used to represent Oscar." Just like that, she got me June's phone number and I called her up.

"Hello," I said hesitantly when Mrs. Levant answered, "my name is Mike Feinstein. I've recently moved here from Ohio, and I just bought some records that belonged to your husband. I want to ask you why you got rid of them."

"Who is this?" she asked indignantly. "What are you talking about?"

"I bought some records from a man who said they came from a sale of Levant memorabilia."

"Oh, no, no!" she said. "I have all of my husband's records. There must be some mistake. They must have come from someplace else."

I don't know where I got my nerve, but I was insistent. "No," I said, "I think they came from Oscar Levant because there was a letter tucked in the sleeve of one of the records addressed to him." I read her the letter and she recognized its author as an executive from Columbia Records. There was a long pause. "Call me back in two hours," she said, and abruptly hung up.

When I called her back, she said, "I think I have all of my husband's records, but I'm curious about this. Can you come over and bring the records with you?"

"Okay," I said. "I'll come over, but I don't think I should transport the records because they're acetates and they're too fragile." The early acetates were glass discs coated with acetate, and they had a habit of breaking if you just looked at them askance. I went over to meet her without the records, and I could see the shock in her eyes as she watched a twenty-year-old kid walk through her door. I don't know what she expected, but it certainly wasn't me. She introduced me to a man she said was her lawyer. Later, I found out he was just a friend of hers named Sam Marx, a former MGM exec; not knowing what she was getting into, she wanted to have some kind of protection. She offered me a drink and invited me to sit down and we started talking. "Why are you interested in my husband?" she asked.

"Because I love his music."

"Music?" She seemed puzzled. "You mean his *songs?*"

"Yeah, right."

"Nobody knows his songs."

"Well," I said, "I do." I started naming song titles, but she didn't recognize some of them because Oscar didn't like his songs and never played them. I sat down at the piano and played a song of his that she was not familiar with, and then she started telling me stories about Oscar. Every story she told, I already knew. "Do you know *this* one," she began each time, only to be foiled when I revealed the ending. "Point killer!" she finally said in exasperation.

It turned out that the records did belong to Oscar Levant. When June had moved from her home on Roxbury Drive to a condominium, she had designated some things to be saved and some things to be sold at an estate sale. She knew she had to get rid of some of Oscar's effects since it was too painful for her to continue being surrounded by those memories, and she didn't go to the estate sale for the same reason. By mistake, the records were split into two groups, and one of the groups was accidentally sold. Those were the records I had bought with my borrowed $150, and now I was sitting in her living room telling her about it. "You can keep the records," June told me, "as long as you make me a tape of them and don't do anything commercial with them."

In that way, we became friends. I helped her catalogue the remainder of her husband's record collection, and when I was done she wanted to pay me. I told her that I didn't want to be paid but that I'd love for her to introduce me to Ira Gershwin. She had talked about Ira and, even though she had said he was infirm and not open to having visitors, I hoped there was still a chance.

"I will if I can," she said. In the meantime, June started taking me out to dinner and to parties, introducing me as her protégé. I played the piano at these parties and, because of the circle she moved in, I started to acquire a bit of notice in Beverly Hills. Suddenly I had entrée to the homes of the stars. On New Year's Day 1977, June took me to a big bash at Sam Goldwyn Jr.'s home. Sam had just moved back into his father's old house, the home he'd grown up in. At the party I saw people like Alan Pakula, the film director, Jean Howard, who was one of the great Beverly Hills hostesses and who later wrote the book *Travels with Cole Porter,* the director William Wyler, Sam Marx, and Dorothy McGuire, all under the gaze of a fabulous collection of Matisses, Picassos, and Degas. That was pretty exciting. George Christy, the columnist, was there and wrote a little item about me in the *Hollywood Reporter.*

That was the first notice I ever got in print. June introduced me to Goldwyn—they called him Sammy, although now they call him Sam— who asked me if I'd play. I sat down and played some Gershwin songs. He asked me if I knew "Love Walked In" and I played it for him. "You know," he said when I finished, "this is the piano on which George Gershwin first auditioned that song for my father when he was working on *The Goldwyn Follies."* I didn't have the heart to tell him that I had read an account in one of the Gershwin books of how demeaned George had felt by that very event. "I've spent my whole life in music," Gershwin complained later, "and I have to sit and audition songs for Sam Goldwyn." He was already ill by then and feeling disillusioned with the whole Hollywood system.

Then there was a party at the studio of Tony Duquette, the great scenic designer for MGM. That was the first large-scale gathering of celebrities I ever attended—all venerable Hollywood types like Ann Sothern and Dolores Del Rio—in a studio filled with old movie props and artifacts. When Duquette asked me to play the piano, he said, just before I struck my first chord, "This is the piano that Horowitz and Levant played many times." I was sitting with Charles Higham, the author of all those controversial Hollywood biographies and a talented poet, who is quite an acerbic character. After Tony asked me to play the piano, I turned to Charles and said, "Well, maybe if I play 'Ramona,' Dolores will sing it." Del Rio had sung "Ramona" in the 1928 talking film of that name. Higham looked at me and snapped, "Some dreams do not come true!"

But at one point when Dolores was rather close to the piano, I did start to play "Ramona," whereupon she suddenly swept around with a grand gesture of her hands, exactly like something out of a silent movie. She took a very deep bow, acknowledging my acknowledgment of her, and it was as if forty years had evaporated and she was back in the glory days of Hollywood. Then she smiled and turned back to her conversation, but that moment left me with a profound impression of the power of music to transform people, however briefly. (Vincent Price was very good friends with Dolores Del Rio, incidentally, and when people asked him for an autograph he would frequently sign her name. One day Roddy McDowall asked him, "Why do you always sign 'Dolores Del Rio'?" "Well," Vincent said, "right before she died she turned to me and said, 'Don't ever let them forget me!' ")

Thinking over how I came to be playing piano in a room full of stars, I was struck by how magical it seemed. I had gone from collecting rare records to gaining entrée into the rarefied world of Beverly Hills society, all through a string of apparently innocent coincidences. In the midst of this good fortune, I didn't forget Carol Dryer, the psychic who had recognized Oscar Levant as being in my life. Although psychics have served me well over the years, I have to admit to sharing at least some of the popular skepticism about them. When I asked Carol, for instance, whether George Gershwin's spirit was around the way Oscar Levant's seemed to be, she told me that I had been in the operating room when they were operating on George right before his death—that I was there in spirit, not in any bodily form. According to Carol, I had made some sort of pact with George's soul that I would come into Ira's life at a future time to help Ira and to help perpetuate their music. My gut feeling as I repeat that story is one of disbelief. Yet at the time, I wanted to believe it. I was trying to find ways to explain my connection with the Gershwins. One can go to any number of well-respected psychics and each will have a different perspective. I've come to regard much of what psychics have told me, especially about reincarnation and specific past lives, as symbolism. It's not important to me whether I actually lived a particular life they are talking about. I've lost interest in reincarnation because I think it's another means of avoiding reality.

Nonetheless, I felt reinforced enough by what had already happened to go back to see Carol again. Now she told me that Oscar Levant was going to lead me to somebody who would be very important in my life. She went on to say that I was going to meet Ira Gershwin. I couldn't conceal my disbelief. I knew that June Levant was a friend of Ira's, but she had told me that Ira was very ill and bedridden a good deal of the time. She had said he was quite reclusive and rarely saw anybody. Besides, it was something I wanted so much that I probably couldn't believe it would actually happen. But Carol was adamant about it. She spent most of that session talking about how I was going to meet Ira and how it was going to change my whole existence. Convinced finally, I left the session in a state of great high spirits and immediately ran to see a friend of mine, almost yelling out, "I'm going to meet Ira Gershwin!"

One day not long after that session, June Levant had lunch with Leonore Gershwin and Emily Paley and began talking me up to Lee. Emily was Lee's sister; their maiden name was Strunsky. Emily was born in 1897, three years before Lee, so she was Ira's age. Both sisters were born in San Francisco. Emily met and married a schoolteacher named Lou Paley, a wonderful literary fellow who loved Gilbert and Sullivan and shared that passion with Ira. Emily and Lou used to have regular Saturday night gatherings in Greenwich Village, which George and Ira attended along with Howard Dietz and many of the names that became associated with the Gershwins as they became famous. It was at one of those gatherings that Ira first met Leonore. Lou even wrote a number of early songs with George Gershwin—nothing that was terribly popular but a couple that were mildly successful. He kept his day job of school-teacher, though, and everybody adored Lou.

As adorable as Lou was, Emily was more so. George once wrote a letter to Emily that said, "A warm day in June could take lessons from you." She was the most delightful, gentle, and kind person I ever met, which makes it all the more extraordinary that Emily and Leonore came from the same family. They were so diametrically opposed and seemed to be that way from the beginning. Emily, for instance, would never say anything bad about anyone. The only time I heard her speak ill of Leonore was after Leonore got angry at her for some ridiculous reason and stopped talking to her. Venting some of her rage for the first time, Emily told me that when Lee was a little girl, she would do things like pull the tablecloth off the table with all the dishes on it. Lee was apparently always an unhappy person trying to get attention.

For her part, Leonore resented Emily because Emily was so universally adored. One day in a fit of anger, Lee said,. "My sister Emily is adored by everybody, but she hasn't had to put up with what I've had to put up with. She hasn't gone through what I've gone through." At the time I met June, of course, I had no idea about all these sibling dynamics, although I was soon to find out more than even I wanted to know.

During her lunch with Lee and Emily, June discovered that the gentleman who worked for Ira, Eddie Carter, was quite ill. He had cancer, and it was only a matter of time before he would no longer be able to continue his work. Leonore told June that they might need some assistance as Eddie became less able to function. June explained the situation to me and suggested I could be the one to help Eddie out.

June was not particularly friendly with Lee Gershwin, and their relationship always seemed rather tenuous. June was a woman who readily spoke her mind and, as I was to find out, Leonore didn't like people who spoke their mind because they inevitably would say something in opposition to what she felt. And to Lee, anyone holding an opinion contrary to hers quickly became persona non grata. In the '20s, for instance, Lee had a friend named Golly who got drunk one night in a club; because of that one night's excess, Lee never talked to Golly again. (Ira was inspired to write a song in 1925 because of Golly. While sitting in a nightclub, Golly became impatient that nobody was acknowledging the wonderful band and kept repeating, "When do we dance?" That song was a minor success in *Tip-Toes*.)

June was also good friends with Emily, who came to California every summer to spend a couple of months with Lee and Ira. Emily later said that it wasn't until she spent those summers in California that she realized what a strange, angry, and manipulative woman her sister was. Whenever June wanted to have lunch with Emily during her summer visits, Lee insisted on coming along, even though June would have much preferred to spend the time alone with Emily. It was at one of those lunches that June learned about the situation with Eddie Carter.

"That would be wonderful," I said when June told me about the possible job. "I'd love to help out Mr. Gershwin with his records, and I know I could do a great job."

"Then the next time I have lunch with Mrs. Gershwin," June said, "I'll ask her about Eddie."

Carter was a wonderful fellow who had been Raymond Chandler's literary agent and, in his later years, started working for Ira mainly because they were such good friends. He was Ira's secretary and right-hand man for almost ten years. A couple of months had gone by when I learned from June that Eddie had died and been replaced by a man named Walter Reilly. Leonore had evidently been looking for somebody for a while, and a mutual friend knew about Walter needing work. This plunged me into an extreme depression because I felt my one and only opportunity of meeting and working for Ira Gershwin had passed. I was certain that this was the specific situation that Carol had predicted, and yet somehow things hadn't panned out as she had said they would. I called her up and complained. "You told me that I was going to work for Ira Gershwin," I moaned. "I want my money back! You know, you can't just tell people things like that and get away with it."

"Okay," she said. "Come back in. I'll give you another reading—on the house. Let's talk about this."

When I went back, she asked me if I had told many people about her prediction. "Yes, as a matter of fact I told quite a few," I said. "I told all my friends I was going to meet Ira Gershwin." I had also bragged to the Bogart imitator who ran Mother's that I would soon be working for the great Ira Gershwin. To my chagrin, he had started ridiculing me in front of patrons. "Ah, you think you're gonna work for Ira *Gershwin?* What kind of a *putz* are you? Why would Ira Gershwin be interested in somebody like you?"

"You'll see," I had responded lamely, like the Elisha Cook Jr. character in the Bogart movie this guy thought he was in. "I *am* going to work for him, you'll see."

"You dispersed the energy!" Carol said. "When something like this is in formation, you can't tell a lot of people, because everybody takes a little bit of the energy and it becomes diffused, killing the charge of the situation."

"Okay. Is there some way to bring it back?"

"Yes, there is." She said I had to do meditations, lighting candles and visualizing myself meeting Ira. She had been right about Oscar Levant and her explanation seemed credible, so I decided to follow her advice. I began doing the visualizations daily. About two months later, June called me. "I just had lunch with Mrs. Gershwin," she said excitedly, "and she's dying to meet you."

"Really?"

"Yes. She's a very touchy woman, so you have to be very careful how you talk to her. But she sounds like she's really crazy about meeting you." June cautioned me that Leonore must be addressed formally, as she was a woman in her seventies. She also said that she had found an autograph of Oscar's for me. I thanked her profusely for what she had done. She said I should call her and let her know what happened.

June had told Leonore about my cataloguing Oscar's phonograph records for her and mentioned in passing that I knew all about Gershwin and Levant and their work. Leonore was the type of person who, if June had something, she wanted it too. June's mentioning the phonograph records probably brought to Lee's mind her concern about her husband's phonograph records sitting disorganized in their closet. She was constantly getting ideas in her head that this or that needed to be done, and then it often became a huge project to which she would devote massive amounts of time and money and energy and effectively fill up her days. But it might also have been a simple matter of Lee's just wanting to use someone whom June had been using.

June gave me Leonore Gershwin's number and I called her. "Oh, I'm so glad you called," she said immediately. "June says you're just a treasure, and we can't wait to meet you! When are you available?"

"Tonight," I said. "Tomorrow. You name it, I'm available."

"Do you know where we live?"

Of course I did. I knew exactly where they lived. I used to drive by the house, hoping I'd see somebody, maybe even catch a glimpse of Ira. We made arrangements to meet Friday at one o'clock. Five minutes later, the phone rang. "Hello, dear"—in a British accent—"it's Lee Gershwin. I'm afraid Friday's a bummer for me."

She was trying to relate to me, the young kid. I had probably never used the word "bummer" in my life. We rescheduled for Monday. At one o'clock on the afternoon of July 18, 1977, I pulled up in front of 1023 Roxbury Drive, the house just east of the one belonging to Ira and Leonore Gershwin. At about the same time, a silver Rolls-Royce with a vanity plate that read LSG pulled into the driveway at 1021 Roxbury. Later I decided it should have been LSD, because Leonore Strunsky Gershwin was such a psychedelic force of nature. Lee got out of her car and came toward me. "Oh, hello, darling," she said. "So nice to meet you. Right this way."

As I followed her to the front door, she asked me how I knew about cataloguing records. I explained that the job was simple enough. I also talked briefly about my musical background and mentioned that my father used to sing "barbershop." Lee was thrilled by that. She put her key in the front door, the door swung open, and I saw Ira Gershwin sitting at a card table with Emily Paley, sorting his mail. Leonore took me over to them and introduced me first to Emily and then to Ira.

I was shaking as I began to realize what was happening. I knew that some illness kept Ira confined to bed most of the time, so I hadn't even been sure that I would see him when I arrived, nor did I know how coherent he would be. But Ira looked much better than I expected. A small white mustache was the only element on his face that I wasn't familiar with from dozens of photographs I'd seen. In the background, I noticed his painting *My Body,* a portrait he had done of himself in yellow underwear. It was fascinating to me that Ira saw himself in yellow underwear while George painted himself in top hat and black tie. The difference between the two brothers was expressed succinctly in those two paintings. A collection of medals and other paintings decorated the hallway. I went over and shook his hand.

"Pardon me for not getting up," Ira said. Behind him were his walker and canes. He was autographing an album called *Ira Gershwin Loves to Rhyme.* "Oh," I said, "I have that record." It was an album put out by George Garabedian on Mark 56 Records. Mark 56 was a small record company located in Anaheim, and these were home recordings of Ira singing demos with Kurt Weill and Burton Lane. The album was a limited edition issued at the insistence of friends and purchased mainly by hard-core aficionados.

"You have it?" He looked at me curiously. "You're the first person I've met other than a friend or relative who has that record. Why do you have it?"

"Because I'm very interested in your work and know a lot about it." Then we sat there and kind of smiled at each other.

Ira later expressed amazement that somebody would actually want to put out a record album with him singing, because he felt that his voice was impossible to listen to. It was not a pleasant voice, although there is something about hearing a songwriter perform his own works that usually transcends vocal quality. Not always, of course. There's a famous story about Irving Berlin recording "Oh, How I Hate to Get Up in the Morning" for the movie *This Is the Army,* in which he appears singing that song. At the recording session, one of the engineers turned to a colleague and said, "Jesus, if the fellow who wrote this song could hear this guy singing it, he'd turn over in his grave."

Ira asked me again why I had bought his record and I told him that it contained much material that was never commercially recorded. The next record he picked up to autograph was the Houston Opera cast album of *Porgy and Bess,* which was the second truly complete recording of *Porgy.* I mentioned that I liked the Houston Opera recording better than the Cleveland recording. Ira said he liked it better, too. As Ira autographed the albums, he asked me what the date was and I told him.

Ira and I continued talking, and I was pleased to find him quite coherent. As he was reading *Variety,* he mentioned that a woman named Schulenberg, the wife of a famous man, had died. Leonore quickly said that Mrs. Schulenberg had had a full life. That, I later discovered, was a ritual. Ira read the obituary page every day, often noting that some famous personage or former colleague of his had died. Lee invariably responded, "He had a very full life Ira, a wonderful life. We mustn't be sad for him."

That kind of comment was also typical of Lee because she refused any show of emotion or tears. She was absolutely steel-willed in that way; even when George died she hadn't allowed anybody to cry. I think the reason Lee hadn't wanted any show of emotion then was that she had been so mean to George during his illness, believing it was psychosomatic and thinking he was feigning it to get attention.

Making a reference to her favorite childhood book, *The Water Babies,* Lee asked whether I wanted some water, which I needed badly. Then she took me across the hall, opened a door, and led me into a huge closet filled with old phonograph records, some of which went back almost to the turn of the century. The closet was concealed, coming into view only after she pushed a part of the wall until the door slid open. The whole room was made of something Lee called wormwood chestnut, which by the '70s was a very rare variety of wood. Termites had eaten away part of the wall and the Gershwins were never able to get more chestnut to replace the part the termites had eaten—I guess the new termites had done a more thorough job than the old ones. Ira had an ancient sound system with an old speaker built into the wall, which he later informed me had been installed by Rudolph Valentino's nephew.

"We want you to organize these records," Lee said. "June says you organized hers. Can you do this?"

I took a gander, and I couldn't believe what I saw. There were multiple copies of everything including the Decca original *Porgy and Bess* recordings, all in perfect condition. There were also private recordings, acetates, test pressings, and rows of home recordings, some of which went back to 1916 or so. Lee then told me that even though I had done the work for June Levant for free, they wanted to pay me. "How much money would you want?" Lee asked.

Money? I was ready to pay *them!* I told her that I'd have to think about it. Not having any idea of how long it would take me to do the job, I said that maybe I should ask my father. "What a brilliant idea!" she said. "Talk to your father!"

The issue of money put aside for the moment, I informed Lee that I would have no trouble organizing the records. "But I need to know how you want them organized," I said. "Do you want them by artist, by song title, chronologically, by category?"

"Ask Ira," she said.

Ira replied that he wanted all the shows in order, which sounded simple enough. But later he told me he wanted everything cross-referenced so that any record could be found any way, and that's what I ended up doing. "How long do you think it will take you to do that?" he asked.

"I'm not sure. Maybe a couple of months."

Out of the blue, Lee said to Ira, "You don't have any of the pre-1930 discs, do you?" Ira replied that he thought he did. I mentioned that I had a 1920 disc of Gershwin songs with a medley from the show *La-La-Lucille!* After thinking a few short moments, Ira correctly identified the two songs in the medley. "One is 'Tee-Oodle-Um-Bum-Bo,' " he said, "and the other must be 'Nobody but You.' "

"That's right!" I said. Lee laughed, looked at Emily, and said, "Hah! He's saying to Ira, 'That's right!' " I realized later how absurd I must have seemed to them at the time. I was so delighted to find someone who knew this music as well as I did and who felt as close to it as I did, that I almost forgot that he was there when it happened.

Although I felt it would take me only a couple of months to organize the records, once I got into it I realized that it was going to take quite a bit longer. Eventually, after consulting with my father, I agreed to accept a flat fee for my services, somewhere in the neighborhood of $500. It was a very low amount given the volume of work, but I was afraid to ask too much for fear they wouldn't hire me.

As I was leaving, I shook Ira's hand and said, "I'm sure I'll be seeing more of you, Mr. Gershwin." Leonore put her arm around me as she led me out and said she would tell everyone that I would be coming and going as I pleased. She said that their day started around nine in the morning and to feel free to call her anytime. I asked her if Mr. Gershwin would mind my bringing a few things for him to autograph. She said to bring just two things because of his condition, indicating that today had been one of his better days. "He's been through a lot these past few years," she said, "but thank God, he's still alert."

"Goodbye, Mrs. Gershwin," I said.

"Are you going to call me Mrs. Gershwin for the rest of your life?" she said. I told her that I would call her what she wanted me to call her. She said, "Lee would be fine."

I told her I played the piano by ear and was learning to read. "I'm glad to hear that, because it's so much harder to play by ear. Don't you think so?"

Although I really didn't think so, I agreed because it seemed so important to her. I was later to discover that her casual addendum of "Don't you think so?" was never just a rhetorical question. Lee expected complete agreement on everything, part of a difficult, darker side of her nature that I would not appreciate fully until I was deeply ensconced at the Gershwin household. But for the moment I felt nothing except a kind of giddy joy at my good fortune.

And so, for the second time, Carol had proven to be prophetic. Or was it just that she had planted the idea in my head and I had manifested Ira as I had the rare books and records? By that time, I didn't particularly care. I was too excited about my new job. The next day, I started working for the Gershwins, not realizing that this, too, was only another step along the way.

ONCE THERE WERE TWO OF THEM

*I*f Ira was surprised to find that I knew about some of his private recordings, I think he would have been astonished to learn just how much I knew about his life, and George's, on the day I went to work for him. That knowledge grew and compounded over the years I worked for Ira, partly from reading books but more extensively from talking with Ira, Leonore, and all the friends and acquaintances they introduced me to. I learned quite a bit by osmosis, just from being surrounded by people who had been instrumental in the development of American musical theater, and from spending so many hours every week in the Gershwin home, becoming in effect part of the household. But before I go on with the story, I ought to explain what had made Ira a figure of such importance in the realm of popular music and, in passing, to say a few words about George, their relationship, and the world of musical theater on which they had such an irreversible impact.

Ira was born December 6, 1896, the eldest of four children, on the Lower East Side of Manhattan. His parents, Morris and Rose Gershovitz (nee Bruskin), were both Russian immigrants from St. Petersburg, and the family name went through a number of permutations, changing from Gershovitz to Gershvein, Gershwein, and eventually Gershwin. Morris frequently switched from one business to another, running various restaurants, bathhouses, bakeries, and a cigar store and pool parlor in Midtown. Ira said that they lived in twenty-eight different residences before he was twenty—most of them in Manhattan at a time when it was obviously a lot easier to find an apartment there. When George was born in 1898, the family was living in the East New York section of Brooklyn, but they soon moved back to the borough that so indelibly marked the Gershwin spirit.

Ira's father was by all accounts a lovable man whom Ira adored, but he liked to live close to where he worked, and he changed jobs frequently. Not that the family ever starved; they lived decently, and although they didn't have a great deal of money, they generally did better than most. Rose Gershwin boasted that they were never without the services of a maid, and Ira talked about living in a building that had an elevator when he was ten years old. It was quite an extraordinary thing to have an elevator in 1906, a sign of their relative means. Morris Gershwin spoke with a very thick Jewish accent, yet even after George and Ira had become great successes and were often feted at glittering parties given by the likes of Elsa Maxwell and Jules Glaenzer of Cartier, George always introduced his father with great pride and felt no embarrassment about his being a greenhorn.

If Ira took after his father, George was much more like his mother in temperament. Rose Gershwin was not particularly emotional; she was ambitious and a little tough and expected things to be done for her. Leonore told me that only a week after George died, Rose started wearing her jewelry again. When the movie *Rhapsody in Blue* opened in 1945, Rose Gershwin was at the premiere. In the film, of course, George dies at the end, and after the movie was finished reporters gathered around Rose and asked her what she thought of it. "Sveet," she said. "Very sveet."

Morris was a very different piece of work, a sweetly jovial man with a whimsical sense of humor who spouted frequent malapropisms. He referred to "Fascinating Rhythm" as "Fashion on the River." Ira loved to tell stories about his father, and as he told them he would start to laugh so hard that he had trouble finishing them. One day at the height of George's success, it seems that a ladies' group was at the Gershwin penthouse viewing the different works of art in George's collection. Morris started following behind them, listening in. When there was a lull, he turned to them and said, just to make conversation, "Tell me, ladies. Whatever became of 'Oh, Fudge!'?" Morris may have had trouble remembering Ira's lyrics and song titles, but he was well aware of George's melodies. Ira told me that in the early days, when George played the piano, Morris sat outside and listened and if there was silence for ten or fifteen minutes, Morris would knock on the door. "George," he would say, "the last thing you played was. . . ." And then he'd whistle it. "Does that help you?"

Once when Morris was out driving, he was stopped by a cop for speeding. In a thick Jewish accent that made "George" sound like "Judge," he told the cop, "You can't gif me a tigget—my son is Judge Goishvin!" The cop thought he was saying his son was a judge and didn't write him up. Ira was devastated when his father died of lymphatic leukemia in 1932, yet, strangely, in his dressing area he kept a picture of his mother, not his father.

Ira was very studious and quiet and kept to himself, and like most introverts he had a retentive memory. Once he told me in great detail everything he did—even what he was reading—on his tenth birthday, which also happened to be the day his sister, Frances, was born. He remembered, for instance, that he was reading *A Study in Scarlet* by Conan Doyle on that day, and when I asked him how he could remember that, he said, "It was the first hardcover book I had ever read." He was impressed that he was reading a hardcover book instead of some kind of pulp.

Although Ira was a better student than George, he eventually dropped out of college after two years. Still, in those early days, he was considered the learned one in the family compared with George, who was a rough and tumble kid and never finished high school. The family evinced neither musical talent nor any great interest in reading and books, and it's hard to say where those interests and abilities on the part of George and Ira came from. Nor was it a religious family. On the Jewish holidays, Ira and George asked their parents to pull down the curtains so the neighbors wouldn't see that they were not observing the holidays. Ira was given a bar mitzvah ceremony at age thirteen, but neither of his brothers got one. He launched into his bar mitzvah speech and promptly forgot it. His aunt Kate yelled the words that he had forgotten across the synagogue to him and he picked it up and got through the rest of it. Ira always adored aunt Kate after that.

The third Gershwin child was Arthur, who was born in 1900, followed by Frances in 1906. Arthur later became a songwriter, which most people would have characterized as sheer chutzpah. He did write a couple of mildly popular songs in 1936 and '37, including one I like, called "After All These Years." In 1945, he wrote a Broadway show called *A Lady Says Yes*. But the audience said no; it closed after eighty-seven performances. His biggest success was a song that was recorded by Ella Mae Morse around 1946 called "Invitation to the Blues." Arthur's son, Marc, gave me an opportunity to meet Arthur and I declined, because I knew Ira wasn't close to him and would have felt betrayed in a certain way. I regret it now.

One of Ira's last trips to New York was in 1968. He saw Arthur, for the first time in many years. Arthur played a few of his melodies for Ira, who told me, with complete surprise in his voice, "You know, some of them were really good!" Ira felt that they were good in "a Sigmund Romberg operetta" kind of way, which at least meant that Arthur had the good sense not to imitate George. Eventually Arthur got involved in stocks and the financial world. He lived very well after George died, of course. Even though Rose still controlled the purse strings then, she took good care of Arthur because Arthur had given Rose the thing she most wanted, a male grandchild.

Ira's sister, Frances, or Frankie as everyone called her, married a man named Leopold Godowsky, Jr., who coinvented (with Leopold Mannes) the Kodachrome process of color photography and whose father was the renowned concert pianist who died in 1938. As a result, Frankie's children can boast a father who invented Kodachrome, a grandfather who was considered one of the greatest concert pianists of his generation, and uncles named George and Ira Gershwin. Not a bad lineage, all things considered. I've always been fond of Frankie. She's a darling woman and a fine painter. She was less successful when she recorded an album in 1973, singing Gershwin songs in a sweet but unexceptional voice. Ira loved her in his own quiet way, in spite of Lee's objections. Once when she visited him in Beverly Hills, we played a recording of a live performance of hers and Ira sweetly smiled and nodded approval, concerned as ever about his kid sister's feelings.

Ira was the first person to recognize the genius inherent in his brother George. He recalled for me the time he first became aware of George's inclinations. Before the Gershwin family owned a piano, George came home one day and announced that he had played in the school assembly. "I didn't know you could play the piano," Ira said.

"I didn't know I could, either," George replied. He had picked it up by practicing on a neighborhood friend's player piano. In the days before phonograph records, almost every family that could afford a piano had one in the parlor; it was rapidly becoming a middle-class status symbol. And so in 1910, Morris and Rose decided that the Gershwin family should have a piano, too. When the newly purchased instrument was hoisted up and lowered in through the front window of their Second Avenue apartment, George, who had still had no formal training, sat down and began to play a popular song of the day. As Ira remembered it, George not only played the song correctly but played with great skill and accomplishment, already throwing in the kinds of rhythmic and melodic effects that vaudeville pianists were using. The first clipping in the Gershwin scrapbook that Ira assembled over the years is rather telling. It's an article about a youth orchestra with a photograph of the orchestra and the names of all the people in it, dating from around 1913. When I first came across the clipping in Ira's scrapbook, I scoured it very carefully trying to find some mention of George or Ira, but there was none. Then I took the scrapbook upstairs to Ira and asked him why this article was in it. "Look," he said and pointed to a character standing next to the piano in the photograph. "That's George."

"So why isn't his name listed in the orchestra?" I asked.

"Because he wasn't *in* the orchestra," Ira said. "He just loved the music and he was hanging around there the day they took the photograph."

As the oldest, Ira was given lessons by a neighborhood piano teacher and got up to page thirty-two of *Beyer's Piano Method* before he stopped. By that time, the family realized that George was the one with the real talent, so George took over and started playing. Later in life, Ira could still hum those exercises from *Beyer's*, but that's as far as he ever got. But if he never learned to play the piano, Ira had an extraordinary musical memory. If you hummed a melody to him only a couple of times, he could remember it, perhaps the result of years of working with George and having to remember melodies to write lyrics for.

Ira had started writing light verse at a very early age and showed an ability for writing lyrics independently of George. George achieved success before Ira did, though, George's first song having been published in 1916, Ira's not until 1920. But it was "Swanee," which George wrote with lyricist Irving Caesar in 1919 and which Al Jolson made into a huge hit the following year, that propelled George into the forefront when he was barely twenty-one years old. Caesar had suggested they capitalize on the success of the popular one-step (a fast dance tune) "Hindustan" by writing a one-step of their own. (Like so many lyricists of the time, he chose to write about an exotic southern locale he had never visited. Some years later, Caesar actually rode across the famous Swanee River, which looked no grander than a muddy stream in Caesar's recollection, causing him to remark that it was a good thing he hadn't seen it earlier or he might never have written the song.) Caesar's idea—and Gershwin's music—proved golden, as "Swanee" reputedly sold two and a half million copies of sheet music alone, a height no other single Gershwin composition was ever to match. Ira's biggest hit was "Long Ago (and Far Away)," written with Jerome Kern; it always haunted him that his biggest hit wasn't written with George.

Ira had written a song with George in 1918 that was not published until 1958. Titled "The Real American Folk Song (Is a Rag)," it was sung by Nora Bayes in a show called *Ladies First*. But his first published song was "Waiting for the Sun to Come Out" from *The Sweetheart Shop* in 1920. When that first song was published, shortly after "Swanee" had become a hit, Ira used the pseudonym Arthur Francis, combining the names of his other brother and sister, because he didn't want people to accuse him of cashing in on the already prominent Gershwin name.

Ira tried his hand at writing lyrics for some melodies by Gus Edwards, who was famous for "School Days" and for his vaudeville children's troupes that included George Jessel and Eddie Cantor as child performers. Ira also wrote some songs with Al Sherman, who later wrote "Now's the Time to Fall in Love" and "No, No, a Thousand Times No!" and hung around Tin Pan Alley trying to get a job as a lyricist. Some of Ira's light verse was published in Franklin P. Adams's witty "Conning Tower" column and a number of other outlets. But most of the time he got rejections. He tried his hand at short fiction, including a short story called "A Harlem Idyll." About three years before he died, I found it in his files and showed it to him. "Oh, this is terrible," Ira said upon seeing it, and then he ripped it up, much to my regret.

Ira struggled for quite some time because he was resolute about not cashing in on George's success. From 1920 to 1924 they did write a number of songs together (Ira under the name Arthur Francis), including "(I'll Build a) Stairway to Paradise," which was George and Ira's first hit song written together (Buddy DeSylva collaborated on the lyrics). After that, Ira began to do pretty well and collaborated with composers Louis Silvers (who had written "April Showers"), Lewis Gensler ("Love Is Just Around the Corner"), and a number of other names that are pretty obscure now. In 1921, before "Stairway to Paradise," Ira wrote the lyrics to a show called *Two Little Girls in Blue,* with music by Vincent Youmans, that produced some notable songs, giving him his greatest success up to that time—still as Arthur Francis.

But the Gershwins' success as a team really began in 1924, when Ira, under his own name, collaborated with George on *Primrose* (for which he cowrote lyrics with Desmond Carter) and *Lady, Be Good!,* which became George's first big Broadway success and served as the major Broadway introduction of another pair of gifted siblings, the song and dance team of Fred and Adele Astaire. Fred and George had met when Fred was a juvenile working in vaudeville and George was still a song plugger. They often spoke of one day doing a show together, and Fred was to become the inspiration for quite a few great Gershwin songs. (Toward the end of his life, George wrote two film scores for Astaire, *Shall We Dance* and *A Damsel in Distress.*) Ira started using his own name because by then everybody knew who Arthur Francis was anyway. He had also discovered that there was a British lyricist named

Arthur Francis, so he dropped the name for good. From that point on, Ira began to come into his own as a distinctive lyric writer. From 1924 through the 1930s, his regular collaborator was George. To this day Irving Caesar, who besides "Swanee" had written a number of lyrics for George's earliest songs, still expresses anger about the fact that George dropped him to collaborate regularly with Ira.

Ira was very proud of a letter he received from Lorenz Hart in 1925 after he wrote *Tip-Toes* with George. Hart wrote, "May I take the liberty of saying that your rhymes show a healthy improvement over those in *Lady, Be Good!*" Hart was just coming into his own around that time, having written songs like "Manhattan" and "Sentimental Me" for the 1925 show *Garrick Gaieties*.

I've already told the story about Jerome Kern taking on George as his protégé for a time and then dropping him. Kern's anger and jealousy toward George continued long after that. When Ira was collaborating with Kern on the movie *Cover Girl* in 1944, Kern asked Ira if he had read the recent David Ewen biography of him. According to Irving Drutman's account of the exchange, Kern asked, "Did you read about your brother George standing outside my window when he was a kid, listening to me composing?" Ira pointed out that at the time in question, Kern was living on an upper floor in a tall building and George couldn't have heard him if he'd wanted to. Kern didn't care. "It says so in the book," he insisted. By 1919, Kern was already extraordinarily famous, yet almost all of the songs for which we remember him were composed long after that. *Show Boat,* for instance, with "Ol' Man River" and "Bill," didn't appear until 1927.

One of the reasons Kern may have been jealous of George was George's amazing facility at the piano. In fact, while Ira made ends meet by working at the local steambaths, George went to New Jersey to cut piano rolls on a regular basis, creating them for five dollars apiece, or six for twenty-five. Of the 125 rolls he cut, 22 were of his own tunes, including his first published song, "When You Want 'Em You Can't Get 'Em, When You've Got 'Em You Don't Want 'Em," "Swanee," and his own arrangement of *Rhapsody in Blue.* Before stopping in 1926, he also recorded songs by Berlin, Kern, and Walter Donaldson, among many others. Later, as George and Ira's Broadway shows became increasingly successful, George would occasionally step into the orchestra pit during intermission to play duo pianos with his friend William Daly, dazzling the audience with a medley of his hits.

George's abilities as a pianist stood him in good stead early in his career, as he was generally in demand at parties. Only too happy to oblige, George played plenty of his own compositions, often drumming up interest in them. "Swanee" had gone nowhere for several months, despite having been interpolated in the Capitol Theater Revue where, according to Irving Caesar, it was played by Arthur Pryor's band and danced by sixty girls with electric lights in their shoes for four shows a day. "We didn't sell five copies," Caesar recalls, "and the publisher was going to drop it." That is, until George happened to be at a party given by Al Jolson at Bessie Bloodgood's House of Fame—a high-class brothel. Buddy DeSylva, who had been writing songs for the stupendously popular Jolson, brought George as his guest and generously suggested that George play his new song for Al. Jolson immediately decided to put "Swanee" into his show *Sinbad* the following week, and soon after, the publisher was flooded with requests for the sheet music from all over the country. Tourists returning to their hometowns couldn't get the song out of their heads and had to have the music.

Despite George's reputation as an exciting pianist always eager to perform, Harold Arlen, who knew him quite well, tells an enlightening anecdote in his preface to Ed Jablonski's book *George Gershwin*. Arlen was impressed by George's naturalness and ease playing piano at gatherings of Hollywood songwriters that included the likes of Irving Berlin, Arthur Schwartz, Yip Harburg, and Harry Warren. One night he approached Gershwin and said, "George, you always seem so comfortable at the piano. Don't you ever get nervous?"

After a moment of silence, George replied bluntly, "Of course—but I never let on."

The sudden popularity of "Swanee" early in 1920 made George a hot commodity on Tin Pan Alley and, better still, opened the door for him to begin writing for Broadway shows. Likewise, the stunning success just four years later of his orchestral *Rhapsody in Blue,* written in a matter of weeks after Paul Whiteman had announced in the papers that Gershwin would be contributing a composition to his now famous Aeolian Hall concert of 1924, confirmed Gershwin's status above and beyond that of mere Tin Pan Alley songsmith or Broadway composer. George's career sped forward virtually nonstop from those first successes through a string of Broadway shows and Hollywood movies, which, if not always commercially successful, almost invariably produced a number of memorable songs. While his songs played on Broadway stages and movie screens across America, he enjoyed a parallel career as a composer of "serious music" (a term I dislike), including two rhapsodies and one concerto, *An American in Paris, Porgy and Bess,* and other early works for string quartet and for solo piano, a few of which have, unfortunately, disappeared.

Ira was always proud of George's achievements and used every opportunity to sing his brother's praises, almost as an excuse not to talk about himself. He knew that his own achievements were good, yet he didn't consider himself nearly as important as his brother in the scheme of things. Ira clearly suffered from an inferiority complex all his life, and he probably developed the unique sense of irony and whimsy in his lyrics as a kind of defense. On rare occasions, when I put on a recording for him and he listened to a particular lyric he had written, he might say, "Listen to this. Listen to this rhyme." When he could get caught up in the pleasure of his own work this way, he lost his self-consciousness and reveled in the joy of what he had created. But those were the exceptions.

There's a lot of talk these days about how most of the American popular songwriters had Jewish backgrounds and how they were influenced by Jewish music. Ira always vehemently denied this, saying that George was not any more influenced by Jewish music than he was by black music or Caribbean or Italian or any of the other cultures that made up the American melting pot. Yet there is definitely something to the Jewish influence on George; so many of the major Tin Pan Alley and Broadway musical composers of that era were Jewish, and many of Gershwin's melodies are rooted in a folk music sound. It was much less of an influence on George, though, than on Irving Berlin, who wrote a number of truly Jewish-flavored songs in the early days, like "Yiddisha Nightingale" and "Yiddle on Your Fiddle (Play Some Ragtime)" and "Sadie Salome—Go Home," all Yiddish dialect songs with melodies that sound a lot like folk music.

Burton Lane once told me a story about Cole Porter going to see George Gershwin early in his career. Porter had not had any successes yet and he asked George, "What am I doing wrong? Can you give me some advice?"

"You have to write more Jewish-sounding music," George said.

"What do you mean?" Porter asked.

"Write a few songs that sound a little more like Yiddish folk music," George said. Then Porter wrote "What Is This Thing Called Love?" and "Love for Sale," which, like a lot of his early songs, have a folksy sound to them. To me, Porter's most Yiddish-sounding song is "My Heart Belongs to Daddy," which is almost like something a cantor might sing in the synagogue.

Irving Caesar pointed out one day that the introduction to "Swanee" on the Gershwin piano roll is a traditional introduction for Yiddish musical theater songs of that era. Caesar also said that all folk music sounds alike, and he's right in that it is all music of lament. For one thing, most folk songs are in minor keys. If you play a Jewish melody and an African melody, they are going to sound somewhat alike. As the musical historian Deena Rosenberg pointed out in her book *Fascinating Rhythm,* both Jewish liturgical music and African American blues make extensive use of the blue note. Technically, a blue note is usually a flatted third or seventh in the well-tempered European musical scale. But in fact, Jewish immigrants and black Americans were incorporating aspects of Middle Eastern and African scales when they played klezmer music or sang the blues. Flatted thirds and sevenths were the closest the tempered scale could come to approximating these sounds, which were more like quarter-tones than half-tones. George was wild about a Hoagy Carmichael song called "Hong Kong Blues," which Hoagy sang in a manner that approximated the quarter-tone scale by bending the vocal line appropriately.

Although Ira went to Yiddish theater occasionally, he didn't think of his and George's life as being particularly Jewish. And yet, since they lived in neighborhoods peopled by other Jews who were more ethnic and more observant than their family, you could say they were Jewish by osmosis. What is unquestionable is that both George and Ira traveled to all parts of the city as young men, absorbing not only Jewish culture but also Harlem nightlife, the rough and tumble of the West Side docks, Chinatown, and the varied Irish-Italian-Jewish culture of the immigrant neighborhoods where they grew up. As George was maturing musically, he spent many nights listening to the great black pianists of his day playing in Harlem, from Eubie Blake to James P. Johnson. But he also listened to white pianists, to European concert music, and to just about anything else he could go and hear.

Of course, you can always create enough examples to prove any theory. In one chapter of his poorly researched and rumor-laden book *Gershwin, His Life and Music,* Charles Schwartz juxtaposes melody lines from Jewish liturgical music with Gershwin songs, trying to prove that the one somehow derived directly from the other. The Australian-born composer Percy Grainger often insisted that George was greatly influenced by Edvard Grieg, and he wrote an article to prove his point. Abram Chasins, who for years was the director of classical music at WQXR, used to speak privately but frequently about how Gershwin had stolen themes for his concertos from works of Rachmaninoff and about how outraged Rachmaninoff supposedly was. Vincent Youmans, who wrote "Tea for Two," "I Want to Be Happy," and "Without a Song" and who collaborated with Ira in 1921, claimed that Gershwin had stolen certain rhythmic ideas and phrases from him. Youmans was notoriously paranoid in this area, as many popular composers were, but there is in fact a great similarity between Youmans's "Oh Me, Oh My, Oh You" (with lyrics by Ira) and "Funny Face." Yet all of these supposed borrowings are questionable and of no more merit than the notion of a potent Jewish influence other than by cultural osmosis.

The question of subconscious or unintentional borrowing can be endlessly debated in almost any creative realm, including song lyrics. Ira's former secretary, the author Lawrence Stewart, once alerted Ira to the following passage in Isadora Duncan's autobiography, *My Life:* "October loomed cold and dreary. We had our first taste of a London fog, and a régime of penny soups had perhaps rendered us anemic. Even the British Museum had lost its charm." That was published in 1927, ten years before Ira wrote "A Foggy Day (in London Town)" with the now famous lines

I viewed the morning with alarm.
The British Museum had lost its charm.

Should Miss Duncan's estate have sued the lyricist? Or is this just another case of Jungian synchronicity in action? When Stewart asked Ira about the book, he said that he had never read it. I leave it to the reader to decide.

*M*uch has been said about George's active love life, including speculation that he was gay—an assertion for which no convincing evidence exists. But we do know quite a bit about his relationship with one extraordinary woman who was by many accounts the great passion of his life—after music, that is.

Kay Swift was a highly cultured and gifted woman who was also one of the great beauties of the 1920s. She was a composer at a time when women were unwelcome in the music world except as singers or chorines. Yet she eventually created the music for George Balanchine's first ballet choreographed in this country, *Alma Mater*. She met George Gershwin in 1926, around the time he was writing *Oh, Kay!* "At that time," Kay said, "I was rather stiffo about popular music." But one day shortly after they met, George sat down at the piano and played popular songs for her for hours, extolling the virtues of Irving Berlin. After that single session, Kay suddenly changed her opinion about pop music and by the late '20s she had started to write popular songs herself. She created the standards "Fine and Dandy," "Can't We Be Friends?" and "Can This Be Love?"

At the time she met George, Kay was married to James Warburg of the Warburg banking family and had become a well-known party giver and socialite. She was best friends with the likes of Libby Holman, the famous torch singer later equally famous as a suspect in the murder of her millionaire husband, of R. J. Reynolds tobacco fame. But Kay soon became romantically involved with George and they had a long and passionate affair during which Kay divorced her husband in hopes of marrying George. When George wouldn't commit to marrying her, she suggested that he go for psychoanalysis—which he did, for many years, five days a week in the beginning. The analysis eventually backfired on Kay; many observers feel it was ultimately responsible for breaking up their relationship.

As Ira told it, the story of their romance was very simple. Kay had everything that George wanted but she also had something he didn't want—children. He loved her three daughters but he didn't want to be responsible for them; in fact, George had trouble forming a lasting commitment with anybody. Carol Koshland, who dated George after her divorce from the composer and bandleader Johnny Green, described George as one of the most oversexed men she ever met. She said he was constantly coming on to women and making eyes at them. (On one date together, George asked Carol, "What do you want to do tonight? We can go to the fights or we can see *Porgy and Bess.*" It was one of the show's final performances but to nettle George, who clearly expected the obvious answer, Carol replied, "The fights." And that was where they went on what turned out to be their last date.) If George had been able to overcome his fears of commitment, though, Kay was the woman he most likely would have married. George seemed to be attracted primarily to Gentile women, and in Kay's case he was also able to share with her his obsession with music.

I once asked Kay blatantly how George was as a lover. Without hesitating, she said, "He was the best lover I ever had." That story conflicts with some of the other stories about George. He once went to a whorehouse in Paris, where his friends watched through a keyhole and later described him as a very mechanical lover. Still, it all makes sense if you consider that Kay Swift was a woman with whom he experienced both physical attraction and intellectial companionship; otherwise he apparently looked at sex as something to get out of the way so he could get back to the music.

Larry Adler, the mouth organ virtuoso, once related a story to me about Simone Simon, the famous French actress of the '30s. In Hollywood at that time, Adler had made some home recordings at Simon's place with George at the piano. When Larry went to Paris in the late '60s, he contacted Simon and asked if she had these recordings. She didn't, but as they were discussing George, she told Larry about accompanying George on a trip to Washington for what turned out to be one of his last concerts in the last year of his life. They traveled together from Hollywood to D.C. but when they got into bed, George never touched her. "I think he was strange," she said.

"What do you mean?" Larry said. "You're not suggesting that George was a homosexual."

"Well, what else could I think?" she said. I suspect that there was just something about Simon that kept him from touching her, perhaps something about her that reminded him of his sister, about whom George was apparently very prudish.

Among her abundant talents, Kay had a phenomenal musical memory and many years later was able to reconstruct several of George's songs for which the music had been lost. When the lost manuscripts were eventually discovered, her reconstructions turned out to be note perfect. Kay was also psychic and very much involved in spiritualism, and said she knew when George died even though she was in New York at the time. When I went to see her, she often talked about feeling George's presence. She did not believe that physical death was the end and felt that she had a connection with George that transcended the physical state. After George's death, Ira returned all the personal letters that George had received from his friends, except in the case of Kay Swift, who wrote a letter to Ira asking him to destroy all of her letters, which he did. Similarly, Kay destroyed all of George's letters to her. Leonore Gershwin intensely disliked Kay, which follows if you accept the premise that Lee was in love with George and Kay was the woman for whom George felt the most intense romantic connection.

It must have been difficult for both Kay and Lee when Kay was working so closely with Ira on organizing George's unpublished music after his death. One day when Lee returned home from shopping, a pile of manuscripts they had been working on lay on a chair beside the piano. Lee promptly sat down on the music. "For God's sake, Lee," Ira said, "don't sit on the manuscripts."

"Oh," she said, refusing to move, "I like to sit on trash and manuscripts and things like that."

Ira always claimed to know very little about George's personal life, but I have to wonder if he knew more than he was letting on. Ira was well aware of George's numerous affairs with women; not only was it common knowledge, but among the things that Ira kept secured in his private locked filing cabinet was George's black book with the women's phone numbers. I believe that George Pallay and Emil Mosbacher were George's primary suppliers of women and I doubt that Ira wanted to know much about that since he was embarrassed by it. Ira distanced himself from George's personal life, even though they spent so much time working together. It has been suggested by their biographers that because George and Ira's parents left them free to roam the city and because Rose herself was emotionally distant, neither George nor Ira was able to form lasting emotional attachments and instead turned their energies to their creative work.

It seems an extraordinary coincidence that the family produced two geniuses in two separate areas of expertise who happened to work so well together. They had an unspoken communication whereby George could sense the kind of tune Ira wanted for a particular lyric and vice versa. For example, Ira talks in *Lyrics on Several Occasions* about writing "A Foggy Day" with George, noting that after they had written a chorus, Ira said, "George, how about an Irish verse?" George "sensed instantly the degree of wistful loneliness" that Ira wanted, and then played a strain that became the opening phrase of the verse, a very wistful, Irish-sounding tune. Ira once told me about the time that George played a tune for him that eventually became "They Can't Take That Away from Me." At that point, there were three long notes preceding the downbeat of the chorus, roughly corresponding to the present lyrics "The way you . . . hat." As George played it for him, Ira said, "It's a beautiful tune, but if you'll give me a few more notes in the introduction, I have an idea for a lyric that I think will amplify the effectiveness of the tune." George then played a similar melodic figure but with six notes now instead of four, and Ira wrote, "The way you wear your hat." They constantly worked on those kinds of ideas together. George would play a fill on the piano and Ira would come up with a lyric for it.

Ira could speak in the most oblique terms or with a wave of the hand, trying to convey something, and George communicated in the same unspoken way. Ira very deeply felt the emotions expressed in George's music and understood the underpinnings of sadness in much of it, how the rhythms and the musical figures could be used in connection with the lyrics. George's theatrical sense allowed him to comment readily on Ira's lyrics, saying when they needed to move a phrase or improve the singability of a certain line. It was the combined work of the two, the way they fed off each other, that made them so extraordinary. Ira often remarked on the closeness of their collaboration and what pleasure it gave him, and yet their personalities couldn't have been more different. George, outgoing and extremely social, often stayed out at parties until after midnight, while Ira enjoyed burying himself in his books. Even after they moved out of their parents' home, George and Ira always lived in close proximity to each other. They once owned adjoining pent-houses and at another point shared a five-story house in which Ira and Lee occupied one floor and George another. Typically, George might arrive home at one A.M. to find Ira still up and reading, and the two of them would engage in one of their late-night work sessions. Perhaps the fact that they complemented each other emotionally and tempera-mentally made it possible for them to collaborate so successfully and for so long—from 1924 until George's death in 1937.

In fact, you could easily make the case that the unique genius of the Gershwin collaboration stems from the complementarity of opposites. George's passionate exuberance, so clearly expressed in the energetic syncopations and rhythmic vitality of his music, was somehow perfectly suited by the introverted, intellectual wit and vernacular of Ira's lyrics. The whole of their songs was more than the sum of those parts, just as the very act of combining a musical form with a literary form in the pop-ular song creates a third entity that is very different from either a musical composition or a piece of rhymed poetry.

Despite the fact that Ira lived another forty-five years or so after George died, and wrote actively for almost thirty of those years, roughly sixty percent of his work was written for George because they worked so intensively and so frequently. The projects that Ira worked on in the years after George's death were sporadic assignments. George had been more consistently, almost compulsively, productive, constantly turning out shows and songs. Ira was always trying to keep up with his brother, who would write a tune and say, "Come on, Ira. Where's the lyric?" Ira often said that if it hadn't been for George, he wouldn't have achieved as much as he did because he was not driven the way George was.

George and Ira's style of collaboration is all the more striking when compared with the way most songwriters work together. A composer typically writes a melody that pretty much stays the same as the lyricist works to fit words to it. Of course, a lyricist may occasionally make sug-gestions, and writing any song requires very close collaboration; in some cases, a lyricist may present lyrics for the composer to set, but those are the exceptions. In most instances, the tunes are left alone. Burton Lane, for example, told me that when he worked with Frank Loesser, he played his tunes for Loesser, who then went away and came back a week or two later with a completed lyric. Loesser never made one sug-gestion to him about the music. (That's what made it so astonishing to

Burton when Frank Loesser later wrote both music and lyrics for *Guys and Dolls*, he had no inkling that Loesser had that level of musical ability. "You know," Loesser used to say to him, "someday I'd like to write a musical comedy, and I'd like to try writing the music myself." Burton wished him luck, but couldn't have predicted that Loesser would create *Where's Charley?* and *Guys and Dolls* and *The Most Happy Fella,* which borders on opera.) Compared with that kind of collaboration, there was an unusual amount of participation on Ira's part in the creation of the music—not in the actual composition of it, but in his suggestions that spurred George on to further ideas.

For example, in the Second Rhapsody there's a beautiful slow theme, the equivalent of the Andante in *Rhapsody in Blue,* that is rather unusual in that it goes on for a certain number of bars and then reaches a point where one would logically think that the theme is over. But then the theme is extended and goes into another theme that is part B. Ira told me that he suggested that George continue that theme and amplify that section of the music, just as he had suggested putting a slow theme in a certain part of *Rhapsody in Blue.* Those were extraordinary suggestions and Ira's musical memory was very keen. Because they both understood theatrical sense so well, they were able to create expressions of emotion that were unusual in musical comedy, like *Of Thee I Sing.* The pure collaboration not only of George and Ira but also of George S. Kaufman and Morrie Ryskind, who wrote the book, created a transcendent work. When I asked Ira why *Let 'Em Eat Cake,* the sequel written two years later, was a dismal flop, he said, "Sometimes things just fall into place and everything goes smoothly. With *Of Thee I Sing,* we definitely had that feeling. But with *Let 'Em Eat Cake,* everything was off from the start. It was going along all right, but there wasn't that feeling that the thing is absolutely right." In 1934, Ira was brought in to work on *Porgy and Bess,* George's opera about southern black life, and to my mind the greatest opera of the twentieth century. DuBose Heyward, on whose book the opera was based, wasn't comfortable writing conventional song form with the rhymes in the right place. At the beginning of George's work on *Porgy and Bess,* Ira had busied himself on other projects, not expecting to have anything to do with the opera. But as it turned out, Ira's participation was essential to *Porgy* because he added that theatrical sense.

In a more subtle example, when "Someone to Watch Over Me" was written for *Oh, Kay!,* the melody was originally conceived as a fast-paced dance number. It had a rhythmic trick in it that would be hard to describe in words but that was later incorporated into another dance number entitled "Fidgety Feet." In essence, a series of four-note phrases was cut off prematurely and repeated. But as George was playing that music for Ira one day, they began talking to each other and, as they were talking, George unintentionally began playing the melody slower and slower. Finally they both realized that the melody would work very nicely as a ballad. That's when they got the idea to turn it into what became the hit ballad of the show, and one of the great ballads of all time. To my way of thinking, it's no accident that such a significant transformation took place not while George was working alone at the piano but while he was in direct contact with Ira, talking to him in the same room. Even though Ira didn't suggest anything, his very presence may have created a form of "energetic" collaboration.

Ira may have been the more intellectual or bookish of the two, but George was also highly intelligent and Ira loved to point out that in all the letters written by George, he had never seen a grammatical or spelling mistake. That always amazed Ira, considering that George had quit high school at age fifteen to become the youngest song plugger on Tin Pan Alley.

Ira's deep love for George was always apparent to me and, indeed, to many others who knew the two of them personally. When the director Rouben Mamoulian went to hear George and Ira perform *Porgy and Bess* for him, George playing the piano with Ira singing and George occasionally joining in, he was struck by the way Ira stood over George "like a guardian angel" or put his hand on George's back and as if to say, "Isn't he just wonderful?" It was a physical demonstration that was unusual for Ira yet flowed naturally from his being so overcome with the joy of what they had created together.

George clearly had a better self-image than Ira did, yet he also suffered from what he referred to as his "composer's stomach," a nervous condition characterized by attacks of nausea, chronic constipation, and insomnia. His psychological problems have never been clearly articulated or explained to an extent that satisfies me. After George went to a psychiatrist for a while, his sister, Frankie, said that he did become more generous in certain ways. But he remained obsessed with his music and it's easy to understand how Ira became the most important person in his life, since Ira was part of that music.

In the period that I knew Ira, he was so sedentary that it was hard to imagine him in any other condition. He would lie in bed and shake his fist at the ceiling and ask God why He had done this to him. That's why it was so much fun for me to look at their early home movies, taken in the '30s, because they show Ira swimming and moving about and being very physical. I find it amazing that with Ira's intelligence he never grasped the idea that if he had exercised and continued being active he wouldn't have been in that state. I wonder if that's just the way he looked at life, that certain things happened and you couldn't do anything about them. He was so keenly insightful and understood so many things because of his sensitivity, yet was blind to his own eccentricities—like most of us.

Contrariwise, George was always very physical. He had a gym and a trainer and even near the unexpected end in California, he went running on Mulholland Drive every day. He took very good care of himself and, if not for the brain tumor, might have lived a long life and changed the course of American music even more than he did.

The theories as to how George developed his fatal brain tumor still abound today. When he was in Chicago in the early part of the '30s, there was a fire in his hotel, and he hit his head trying to get out. He also told his friend Rosamund Walling about an incident in his youth when he got caught in a feud between Irish and Jewish youth gangs and escaped on roller skates into an apartment house under construction—where he fell down an elevator shaft and landed on his head.

The composer Harold Spina was on the Goldwyn lot before George and Ira came there to work on *The Goldwyn Follies* and was always complaining about the horrible, drafty room he had to work in. Spina described it as being dark and almost foreboding, as if something awful was bound to happen there. When asked if he would give up that room so George and Ira could have it as their work space, he was only too happy to vacate. Spina insisted that that was how George caught the pneumonia that eventually killed him. He still thinks that George died of pneumonia, even though pneumonia had nothing to do with it. This reminds me of the story Lillian Gish once told me about giving George a device that kept him from going bald. "And do you know," she said, "that when George died, he still had a full head of hair?" She went on and on about how wonderful it was, overlooking the fact that the only thing that prevented George from going totally bald was his untimely death. The actor and writer Jack Larson told me that he had heard that George had contracted syphilis from a famous Hollywood actress, and the syphilis had killed him. As Oscar Levant once said in the '40s, "Even the lies about George Gershwin are being distorted."

George did go for a checkup in early 1937. With a certain test then available, it might have been possible to detect the beginnings of the tumor, but his doctor didn't give him the test because he didn't feel it was necessary. Gershwin spent the last ten months of his life in California, where he had begun developing headaches. Everybody thought that it was just a psychosomatic reaction to being in Los Angeles, and so his symptoms were ignored. In February 1937, he played a concert with the Los Angeles Philharmonic, and while playing the Concerto in F, he fumbled a passage at the very end of the second movement containing four notes that the piano plays as a solo, and later he fumbled another passage.

"What happened, George?" Oscar Levant joked after the concert. "Did I make you nervous or did you think Horowitz was in the audience?"

George replied, "I suddenly smelled burnt rubber, and I blacked out for a minute."

The symptoms got worse, including severe daily headaches and dizzy spells associated with olfactory hallucinations, but repeated physical examinations by several doctors revealed no abnormalities. Nonetheless, his family and friends were increasingly convinced that something was seriously amiss. In June 1937, about a month before he died, he stayed in a friend's guest house a couple of blocks away from his busy home on Roxbury Drive. He had to have the room blackened because bright lights intensified his severe headaches. He had moments when he felt better and could start to work again, but the headaches inevitably recurred. He was admitted to Cedars of Lebanon Hospital in Los Angeles on June 23, but after three days of tests and X-rays revealed nothing abnormal, he was released with the final notation on his record reading, "most likely hysteria." Not until his collapse and readmission on July 9 did the doctors finally discover what was wrong with him. They tried to fly in two brain specialists, including Dr. Walter E. Dandy, one of the leading neurosurgeons of the day, who was picked up by the Coast Guard while vacationing aboard a private yacht on Chesapeake Bay. But there wasn't enough time for him to fly to Los Angeles, and they finally had to operate with Dr. Dandy staying in touch with the proceedings by phone from Newark Airport. The surgeons removed the tumor, and the operation was considered a success, but George never regained consciousness and died at 10:35 the next morning, Sunday, July 11, 1937. Even had he survived the operation, George Gershwin most likely would have suffered from recurring tumors that would have taken him within a year anyway. According to Dr. Dandy, "It would have been a slow death."

I believe that Ira loved George more than he loved anybody else, ever. Even in his eighties, his passion and enthusiasm when he talked about George often seemed to revitalize him. After George's death, Ira's house became a shrine to George, so much so that it often felt as if George were still living there. When George died, Ira was truly numb and didn't cry at first. It wasn't until Fred Astaire came over to the house and, as they were sitting together, burst into tears that Ira finally broke down and sobbed. That wasn't so surprising, though, because Lee would not allow any display of emotion in the house. That was a terrible thing to deprive Ira of, but she insisted, just as she refused to have children. Lee knew, rightly, that she would not have been a very good mother, but she also didn't want to bother with kids. It's a shame, because considering how gentle and compassionate Ira was with me and with others around him, I think he would have been a wonderful parent.

At the time of George's death in 1937, they were working on the film *The Goldwyn Follies*. George and Ira had been rushing to finish their songs for the movie so that George would have the next couple of months free to work on a ballet for the star Vera Zorina. They had finished most of the songs but George died before completing "Love Is Here to Stay," which turned out to be the last song they worked on together. A good deal of controversy still surrounds the completion of this song, but here is the sequence of events as Ira told them.

George had just sketched a lead sheet consisting of nine bars of the melody line, nothing more. Fortunately, Oscar Levant had heard George play the song so many times that he was able to write down the entire body of the chorus from memory. Ira had started on the lyrics but had not finished and was in no condition to work. He was in shock, having believed, perhaps naively, that George was going to survive the emergency operation.

And so Ira had to pull himself together to finish the song for the studio deadline, and it turned out to be a cathartic experience as he wrote the verse of "Love Is Here to Stay," both lyrics *and* music. He came up with the melody in his head and Vernon Duke wrote it down for him. Duke later claimed credit for it. I once asked Ira if Duke had written the verse and Ira replied with characteristic self-effacement: "It's so undistinguished, isn't it obvious that I wrote it?" The words of that verse are always very poignant to me because they seem to express Ira's personal feelings about the loss of his brother. And yet, through Ira's consummate craftsmanship, they are also perfectly appropriate to the refrain, counterpoising the permanence of love against the evanescent nature of the phenomenal world:

> The more I read the papers,
> The less I comprehend
> The world and all its capers
> And how it all will end.
> Nothing seems to be lasting,
> But that isn't our affair;
> We've got something permanent—
> I mean, in the way we care.

After George died, Ira was in a deep, deep depression for a long time and many of his friends doubted that he would ever work again. Harold Arlen and Jerome Kern tried to get him to write by sending him home recordings of melodies (which I later came across in Ira's closet). One day in a stupor he stumbled over to the phonograph and put on one of the records that Johnny Green had recently made with his dance band and Fred Astaire of the songs from the movie *Shall We Dance*. They included what were to become some great Gershwin hits: "They All Laughed," "Let's Call the Whole Thing Off," and "They Can't Take That Away from Me." As Ira listened to the music, the vitality of the songs and the performances went to his heart; that was the first time he started even in a small way to feel better. Hearing those recordings was the thing that most helped Ira to assuage his grief.

Even so, he did very little work over the next three years. He moved out of the house on Roxbury to a temporary home on Beverly Drive, and was not able to be creative at all. I don't think he could conceive of working with anybody else after having written for so long and so closely with George. He made a half-hearted attempt at writing seven or eight songs with Jerome Kern and a few with Harold Arlen, but without a plot or a character to create for, the songs, in Ira's words, "didn't mean much"—even though some of them, like the paired songs "Once There Were Two of Us" and "Now That We Are One" are quite lovely all on their own.

But in 1940, Ira received an offer from Kurt Weill to do *Lady in the Dark,* and Moss Hart persuaded him to work on the show. It was based on Hart's experience with psychoanalysis—the original treatment was titled *I Am Listening.* Apparently, whenever Moss lay down on the couch to begin a session, his psychiatrist would say, "I am listening." I was once told that Moss Hart's psychiatrist was Dr. Gregory Zilboorg, who had also treated George. At the time of George's death, some people blamed Zilboorg for not having diagnosed George's brain tumor earlier; they claimed that some of the symptoms George supposedly reported in the course of psychoanalysis were actually symptoms of his tumor. Whether George actually reported physical symptoms to Zilboorg has neither been proven nor disproven, though it sounds a bit farfetched to me. Yet when I met Peg Zilboorg, Gregory's widow, a number of years ago and told her I had worked for Ira Gershwin, she launched into a defense of her husband, assuming that I knew about the accusations.

A couple of years before Ira died, he listened to a radio show narrated by Miles Kreuger in which Kreuger interviewed many Gershwin friends for a documentary about George. When Ira heard his old friend Yip Harburg describe George's death in great detail, he became depressed for several weeks. That was very disturbing to me, because I hadn't realized how deeply he still needed to heal that part of his life. In the end, he never did; he never got over his brother's death.

Ira's guilt in connection with George took many shapes. For example, he had a tremendous feeling that he should be doing more with

George's unpublished work. Through the years, he slowly published a few of the unknown Gershwin songs, but most of them remained in his possession because he was afraid to let go of them. They were the last representations of his brother's work, and he was deeply concerned that, if they were not properly presented, they might actually tarnish George's reputation. Several times a week, we had sessions during which we went through these unpublished songs, making notes about them and making plans to publish them. But then, just as we were getting ready to print them, Ira would say, "Let's wait a while."

I also discovered something extraordinary around that time: Ira talked to George in his sleep. Ira did not believe in God, and he certainly didn't believe in life after death or anything approximating it. However, when he was asleep, he often carried on rather lengthy conversations with his brother. They were often filled with anger, centering around Ira's desire not to stay here on earth and George's insistence that he stay. As far as I can tell, Ira didn't have any remembrance of these things when he was awake—or else he didn't want to. But one day I was sitting in the library adjoining his bedroom when I heard him yelling. "George! George!" he screamed. I ran into the bedroom and found him dazed but awake. "Ira," I said, "what's the matter?"

"Where's George?" he asked quite seriously.

"George is dead."

He looked at me in shock, and it took him some time to come back to the reality that his brother had been dead for almost fifty years. Then he sort of shrugged and self-consciously pulled himself together. About five or six months before Ira's death, after witnessing a number of these incidents and hearing many more recounted by one of Ira's nurses, I asked him if he ever had a feeling of George still being around.

"I'm going to tell you something that I've never told anybody," Ira said. Why he chose to tell me, I'm not sure. He certainly was very uncomfortable talking about this, and spoke in a hushed voice. "Not long after he died," Ira continued, "I went upstairs and passed George's workroom. I looked in—and he was sitting on the sofa, smiling and nodding to me. It terrified me. I wasn't drinking. I wasn't drunk. But I saw him."

Ira was so scared by that experience that he had never told a soul about it in all these years, not even his wife.

Not long after the radio program that so depressed Ira, as I was looking through some color transparencies that George had taken in Mexico
in 1935, I discovered two photographs of George. They were significant
because they turned out to be the only color photographs ever taken
of him. One was a shot of George sitting in profile in front of a wall
and the other was of him with two other people, a woman friend and
the artist Diego Rivera. In an effort to cheer Ira up, I had the transparencies color corrected and had prints made which I showed to him.
I asked if the colors were accurate and he replied that George's skin
had been a little pinker than that.

"See how thick his beard is?" Ira said. "George had a very heavy
beard and had to shave twice a day." Then he paused and grew very
quiet. "See how youthful and vital he looks," he finally said. "Can you
believe that somebody who looked like that, so healthy, died so young?"

Ira became very melancholy in a way I had never seen in him before,
and went on talking about George in a stream of consciousness. Then
he became quiet again, went upstairs, and was depressed for the next
week. That was the clearest indication to me that he had never really
dealt with George's death. The combination of Leonore's not allowing
any show of emotion and Ira's being quiet and repressed by nature con-
spired to make it very difficult for him to come to terms with this water-
shed event in his life.

Not only was Ira never able to accept George's death, but he felt
guilty about it because he couldn't understand why fate would take
George and allow him to live. He would gladly have volunteered himself if there were any way he could have gone in George's place. I think
that vexed him the most. Not *Why me?* but *Why him?*

So much has been written about George Gershwin's music that it
would be difficult to say anything that hasn't already been said. The stories about his early years—his rough and tumble youth on the streets
of New York, his propensity for "fighting just to be fighting," his innate
ability as a pianist and composer—are well documented. Much more
difficult has been the attempt to define the essence of George's contribution that has made him perhaps the most popular composer in the
history of American music—probably more so than Ellington, Copland,

Bernstein, or any of the other names that might legitimately vie for that distinction. Remarkably, George accomplished that in less than half the span of years of each of those composers. To begin with, every composer has a recognizable style or sound. At least every great composer does; the mediocre ones also have a recognizable style, but it's not their own. Without trying to analyze the Gershwin sound technically, I can say that it is a distinctive, highly energetic, jazz-infused sound rooted in the '20s and '30s but timeless to me. I've encountered people who are largely unschooled in music but who, when they hear certain chord progressions, say, "Oh, that's George Gershwin, isn't it?" The fast, rhythmic, jazzy sections of *Rhapsody in Blue* in particular, although born out of the energy of the '20s, have remained fresh and distinctive; when we hear that music today, or hear it echoed or evoked by modern composers, in movie scores or even in television commercials, it doesn't come across as dated.

The perennial question with Gershwin, though, is where it all came from. The answer that most people give is from the streets of New York with their various ethnic influences: black, Jewish, Italian, Caribbean, Russian. There is a certain superficial truth to that explanation, of course. But I say that it came from God. It had to come from a divine spark that passed through this man, because there's no other satisfactory explanation for the way all those elements were synthesized by George's musical imagination. In his music, black and Jewish influences met and were filtered through the thoroughly Anglo medium of musical theater, with its roots in Gilbert and Sullivan and Victor Herbert. We know that George was fully steeped in the jazz ethos of his day and spent countless hours listening to and absorbing the great black pianists such as Luckey (short for Luckeyeth) Roberts, James P. Johnson, Eubie Blake, and later Art Tatum. But apart from the obvious influences of ragtime and Harlem stride piano in his playing, Gershwin also spent years as a song plugger and piano accompanist, absorbing elements of vaudeville and other predominantly white styles of popular music, and we know he studied classical forms as well. By his own account, the first major influence on his musical imagination occurred when he was standing outside a 125th Street penny arcade at the age of six, barefoot and in overalls, listening to an automatic piano playing and replaying the Melody in F of late-nineteenth-century Russian composer Anton Rubinstein.

Perhaps because he was so thoroughly immersed in the jazz of his day, Gershwin's songs lend themselves to jazz interpretations better than the works of many other songwriters of the era. Whatever the reason, the literature of jazz attests to Gershwin's adaptability by the sheer volume of his compositions that have been played and recorded by the greatest jazz musicians—whether Art Tatum improvising endlessly on "Liza," Lester Young and Teddy Wilson duetting on "Love Is Here to Stay," Charlie Parker soaring through "Embraceable You," or the countless versions of "I Got Rhythm" and other jazz standards based on that song's harmonic structure (or chord changes).

Other composers besides Gershwin were writing syntheses of black and white music similar to what George was doing, namely Rube Bloom, Ferde Grofé, and Louis Alter, and even black composers William Grant Still and James P. Johnson, among others. But Gershwin's integration of those elements has a more organic feel, which is why his work survives after the others have faded. Some of the Grofé works may have been technically better crafted, but they don't have the spark of nervous energy that characterizes Gershwin's best work. In later years, Grofé was angry that he was not better acknowledged for his own music. Most of his major compositions, such as the *Mississippi Suite*, which was played by Kostelanetz, and the *Death Valley Suite,* were largely ignored. His *Grand Canyon Suite* was popular and was even played and recorded by Toscanini, but he never became world-renowned. It must have been very upsetting to him to see someone like Gershwin, who had little early formal training, achieve such fame when Grofé himself continued to be known primarily as an arranger and conductor. Rube Bloom, who wrote "Don't Worry 'Bout Me," "Fools Rush In," and a wonderfully imaginative instrumental piece called "Soliloquy," was jealous of George in much the same way.

A favorite refrain of many composers was, "What's the big deal about George Gershwin?" Plenty of other folks were writing songs with blue notes and longer compositions in that jazzy style. Yet Gershwin's synthesis was not some kind of theoretical exercise; he knew how to assimilate all the ethnic influences he had been exposed to on the streets. When he wrote *Porgy and Bess,* he went to South Carolina with DuBose Heyward and studied the songs and folk music of the Gullah Negroes among whom the story is set. George sat in on one of their music-making sessions during which the Gullahs were engaged in what they called "shouting." "This is a complicated rhythmic pattern beaten out by feet and hands as an accompaniment to the spirituals and is indubitably an African survival," Heyward wrote later. "I shall never forget the night when, at a Negro meeting on a remote sea-island, George started 'shouting' with them. And eventually to their huge delight stole the show from their champion 'shouter.' I think that he is probably the only white man in America who could have done it." So on top of everything else, George may have been the original funky white boy.

What may have made his white contemporaries even more jealous was that they lacked Gershwin's impressive range. Not only was George a great composer, but he also understood the workings of musical theater and knew how to make a song theatrical for the performer. Ira said that because George understood the limitations of musical theater of the time and knew how creaky the plots were, he put unifying factors into the songs themselves so that the listener subconsciously felt that the songs came from the same score. Ira once pointed out four songs in *Oh, Kay!*, for example, that he could identify as having the same melodic idea, an approach that was rather ahead of its time. Deena Rosenberg has examined shows like *Lady, Be Good!* and *Funny Face* and come to much the same conclusion. That kind of composition required the broader musical perspective more common among composers of long-form classical pieces. Other popular songwriters occasionally tried their hand at longer compositions, perhaps dogged by Gershwin's example, but without much success. Hoagy Carmichael wrote his *Johnny Appleseed Suite* and another larger-scale piece, neither of which was particularly acclaimed. Johnny Green wrote symphonies. Richard Rodgers wrote *All Points West,* a sort of symphonic poem with a narrator/singer, and Jerome Kern turned out a rather undistinguished *Mark Twain Suite* in 1942, though it does contain one superb melody that lacks an ending. Ellington was probably the most masterful at it, with pieces like *Black, Brown and Beige* in 1943 and later his various suites and sacred concerts, although some musicologists might argue with the designation of Ellington as a composer of popular music. He did write several shows (*Jump for Joy, Beggar's Holiday, Pousse Café, Queenie Pie*), and one would have to consider songs such as "Sophisticated Lady" and "Satin Doll" popular in the broadest sense of the word. But his major contribution was clearly in the realm of short jazz instrumental compositions, at which he was both unparalleled and extremely prolific.

Gershwin was originally going to write an opera based on *The Dyb-buk,* a story by S. Ansky based on a Jewish folk legend. He started to compose some themes but it turned out that an Italian composer had already purchased the rights to the story and George could not obtain them. I believe he was also looking at American Indian music but found it rhythmically uninteresting and didn't feel that it had contributed to popular music the way African American music had. He was looking for the true roots of American popular music, and that's when he decided to write *Porgy and Bess.*

Todd Duncan, the powerful baritone (and Howard University music professor) who was to play the lead role in *Porgy and Bess,* commented in a letter after hearing part of the score performed for him by George and Ira, "You have plunged into the core of an intensely interesting Negro philosophy with vision." He went on to call George's work "astounding" and to predict that it would "create epoch-making history of American music." He had worked on his vocal craft for years, he said, "waiting for a serious work like this, open to the serious Negro artists." George's intuitive feel for black culture always amazed Duncan, not only because of the way other white songwriters had consistently demeaned black life in their "coon" songs and minstrel shows and even in popular songs contemporary with George, but also because many black composers like Scott Joplin and others who came before Gershwin had not tried to do what George did. They were going in the other direction, searching for a more dignified fusion of African and European music.

In the introduction to *George Gershwin's Songbook* of 1932, George talks about the different piano stylists who influenced him. "The evolution of our popular pianistic style really began with the introduction of ragtime just before the Spanish/American War," he writes, "and came to its culminating point in the Jazz Era that followed upon the Great War. A number of names come crowding into my memory: Mike Bernard, Les Copeland, Melville Ellis, Luckey Roberts, Zes Confrey, Arden and Ohman and others. . . . To play American popular music most effectively, one must guard against the natural tendency to make too frequent use of the sustaining pedal. Our study of the great romantic composers has trained us in the method of the legato, whereas our popular music asks for staccato effects for almost a stenciled style. The rhythms of American Popular Music are more or less brittle. They should be made to snap and, at times, to crackle. The more sharply the music is played, the more effective it sounds. Most pianists with a classical training fail . . . in the playing of our Ragtime or Jazz because they use the pedaling of Chopin when interpreting the blues of Handy. Romantic touch is very good in a sentimental ballad, but in a tune of strict rhythm it is somewhat out of place."

Of course, that's precisely the problem that many pianists have in playing Gershwin even today: they overromanticize the music. The stiff interpretations of the classical singers in *Porgy and Bess* are yet another problem; it was written as an opera but was not meant to be performed in strictly operatic style. Liberties had to be taken—intelligently chosen liberties. Michael Tilson Thomas has pointed out how Gershwin interpolated the grace notes and embellished notes of jazz and blues into popular music and into his longer pieces such as *Rhapsody in Blue,* letting them remain jazzy.

George once asked the famous music teacher and composer Nadia Boulanger to give him lessons and she politely declined. Charles Schwartz mistakenly claims that Boulanger dismissed him. Not so. According to Mabel Schirmer, who was present during the encounter, Boulanger didn't feel that she could contribute much to his education, just as many of the classical greats of that time felt there wasn't anything that they could add to Gershwin. When George expressed a desire to study with Igor Stravinsky, the great pioneering composer asked, "How much money do you make a year?" George named a rather extraordinary figure, causing Stravinsky to reply, "Then perhaps I should take lessons from you." When George approached Ravel with a similar notion after meeting him in 1928, Ravel reportedly said, "Why become a second-rate Ravel when you're already a first-rate Gershwin?" In retrospect, Oscar Levant agreed; when George revealed his interest in studying with Ravel, Levant remarked that Ravel's Piano Concerto, premiered in 1931, showed signs of being influenced by Gershwin and that if George studied with him he might be moving backwards. I asked Ira about George's musical education and he said that George wanted to learn everything from everybody. He wanted to study with anyone who had a new musical idea or system, even if it was just for one or two lessons. Consequently, a number of people were able to say, "George Gershwin studied with me." When he was still quite young, perhaps in 1919, George decided to study with Rubin Goldmark, Aaron Copland's teacher and a composer in his own right; he had been taking lessons for about six weeks when he brought in a string quartet that he had composed the previous year. Goldmark studied the music and then declared, "See how quickly you're learning with me!" George never returned for another lesson.

Gershwin's style became more dense and complex as the years progressed. Yet the first time I heard "Blue Monday," which he wrote in 1922, I was struck by the richness of the music, which sounded quite different from the popular songs that he was writing at that time. When I asked Ira about it, he said that George always could write in two different styles. The songs were one thing, but the larger-scale works allowed him to express ideas in a greater language, a wider forum. When you listen to "Blue Monday" and then to "I Found a Four Leaf Clover," written for the same show in which "Blue Monday" appeared, you can't believe they were written by the same person. Ira felt that to a certain extent George's symphonic or "classical" ability was largely developed on an instinctive level and that his continuing musical education merely allowed him to amplify what he already knew. For example, when George started studying composition in 1932 with Joseph Schillinger, the music theorist who applied mathematical principles to composing, he was learning techniques that he largely did not need to learn. A good deal of what Schillinger taught was how to extend musical sections, how to come up with musical ideas when a composer might not have been as inspired as he wanted to be. Kay Swift talked about George pointing out certain sections of *Porgy and Bess,* like the Storm Music, that used the Schillinger system, taking one phrase and putting it through the professor's permutations of formulaic composition. But Gershwin didn't need Schillinger so much as he was interested in finding out what was going on in the wider musical world.

One of the clippings from the family scrapbook that Ira maintained shows George playing on a rather peculiar-looking keyboard, which the photo caption identifies as a quarter-tone keyboard. The year was 1933 or '34 and the caption went on to say that Gershwin had composed a piano piece for this quarter-tone keyboard. Ira knew nothing of such a composition, nor have I ever found any reference to it anywhere else. But it does seem indicative of Gershwin's restless musical soul. By the time of his death in 1937, George was in the middle of several new and challenging projects. In addition to the ballet for *The Goldwyn Follies,* he was writing a string quartet that he had finished in his head but had not fully committed to paper. He frequently played the themes for friends, but he had not gotten around to writing it all down. When his close friend Merle Armitage, who later produced *Porgy and Bess,* heard that George had died, the first thing he did was to call Harold Arlen, not wanting to bother Ira, and ask if George had written down the string quartet. They couldn't find even one scrap of paper that had any of the themes on it. It simply died with George. A very early Gershwin manuscript turned up a few years ago that was a viola part for a string quartet, but that's all we have, apart from an 8-minute quartet he wrote as an exercise and that Ira later titled "Lullaby." George was also planning to write a symphony.

But if George's premature death was both startling and saddening, Ira's long life was cause for celebration, especially to me. The fact that George had died so long ago and that Ira had lived through the entire history of American musical theater, from George M. Cohan to Stephen Sondheim, endowed Ira in my eyes with almost mythic status. It was as if I had suddenly been introduced to some figure out of history who had lived through, say, Vienna in the time of Mozart and Beethoven, or France during the rise of Impressionism, and could give me intimate details of the lives and work habits of some of the greatest artists of an era, most of whom he had known personally and had collaborated with. I could almost hear Walter Cronkite's venerable voice intoning in the background, "You are there!"

chapter 3

BEGINNER'S LUCK:
WORKING FOR THE MAN

*A*nd there I was. The inner sanctum had been opened to me. I was free to walk in and have a look around. Ira's home was large and well appointed, and everywhere to be seen were objects and images relating to George's and Ira's lives and their work together. Over the years, I got to explore most of the house and examine its many treasures. But in the beginning, at least, my focus was entirely on getting to know the man who was responsible for all those glorious artifacts.

When I began working for Ira, he was spending most of his time upstairs in bed, and as time progressed he was to become more and more sedentary. Since he didn't come downstairs until noon to have his breakfast, I tried to arrive around 11 or 11:30 each morning. His appearance was usually heralded by a slow, thumping sound as he slowly descended step by step with the help of a male nurse. By the time he reached the foot of the stairs, I could hear the *huhh, huhh* of his labored breath. He would walk to the table and settle into his chair with a loud gasp of "Uaaaah! Thank God!" For a time, he used two canes to walk, later progressing to a walker, which was sturdier for him.

Ira may have been a semi-invalid, but he always appeared meticulously dressed. He wore shirts that were specially made for him in a toga style in a variety of colors (his favorite was purple) with his initials on one side. Ira had received an honorary doctorate from the University of Maryland, whose symbol is a terrapin, so he always wore a little gold turtle pinned to his shirt. This was one of many things that disappeared after he died, probably swallowed up by one or another member of the staff, of which there were plenty around the house: a cook, a maid, a laundress, several gardeners, a secretary, and three nurses dividing eight-hour shifts around the clock. I realized the truth of a statement Leonore made to me around that time. "It's really the help," she said, "that runs all the homes in Beverly Hills. They're the ones who have the power."

After I'd been working there for a while, I was given a key so I could come and go on my own, and when they installed an alarm system I was given the code. (We had to come up with an abort code for the alarm system in case it was triggered inadvertently, so I suggested the word *rhapsody.*) I entered the house through the side door that opened into the kitchen. Richard, the cook, invariably buttonholed me as I came in; Richard always complained about his heart problems, and I was obliged to talk to him for a few minutes before I could get into my area. He disappeared less than a year after I arrived and was replaced by another cook, whose name was René Crouch (the cousin of André Crouch of Gospel music fame); unfortunately, René talked more than Richard.

Once I made my way past the cook, I went straight to the record closet in Ira's music room and began the daily labor of pulling out and organizing the multitude of discs. Sitting at a beat-up mahogany desk with my back to the sliding glass doors that faced the backyard, I took out the records piecemeal and recorded information about them on index cards. The closet contained mostly phonograph records along with copies of Ira's book, *Lyrics on Several Occasions,* and other weird odds and ends. One of the odder was a painting that Irving Berlin had given to Ira. Berlin had taken up painting in his later years—thank God, he never tried it earlier, because he was a terrible painter. The painting was of a man's face, which Berlin had told Ira was George Gershwin but which looked more like E.T. It was sort of square and didn't look human; if it bore a resemblance to anyone, it was Berlin himself. But when Ira had the occasional visitor, he loved to pull the painting out of the closet to show. "Guess who painted this?" he asked with evident pride. "Irving Berlin!" There's a story that Berlin's grandson was asked by a teacher to tell the class what his grandfather did and the boy replied, "He's a painter." The kid only saw Grandpa painting and didn't have any idea that he was a songwriter.

Ira's audio equipment was ancient and included an old, old reel-to-reel tape recorder. I asked Lee to upgrade the audio equipment so I would be able to play the recordings to identify them. Ira resisted buying a new stereo at first because he didn't see the sense of it, and, despite his evident wealth, he hated to spend the money. But after I started to play records for him, he perked up, and listening to music became a part of his day. It may sound odd for someone whose entire. life was devoted to writing songs, but at that time Ira had very little music in his days. (Even after the new stereo receiver was installed, it was hooked up to the single speaker that was built into Ira's wall, so the system remained effectively mono, although with markedly better fidelity than before. Tony Bennett told me that he once asked Ira if he had a stereo and Ira replied, "I don't need stereo. I've got two ears.")

Because Ira was so introspective, he rarely asked for anything for himself even when he was desperate. Nor was this something that developed only later in life. Ira had been painfully shy since childhood. He once told me about the time he was swimming in the East River when he was quite young and he suddenly became exhausted and started to drown. A lifeguard saw him, jumped in, brought him to shore, and revived him. But as Ira had started to go under, he said, he was so embarrassed to be drowning that he just let himself sink. "You mean you didn't call for help or anything?" I asked, incredulous. "What would have happened if the lifeguard hadn't come?"

"I would have drowned," he said matter-of-factly.

That's the way Ira was. He was so insecure that he didn't even feel he could bother somebody to pull him out of the water. For much the same reason, he never learned how to drive. Alan Jay Lerner once asked him why, and Ira said, "Suppose somebody honks at me?"

One day I had the thrill of discovering an old address book of Ira's in the closet. It was in pristine condition, yet it contained the phone numbers and addresses of many people who had long since died, people like Judy Garland and Ferde Grofé. Bing Crosby was still alive at that time, but his listing was obsolete. I used to thumb through that book and think, God, if I could only call these people. But most of the closet space was taken up by records, including some large sixteen-inch transcription discs that I wasn't able to play because Ira had gotten rid of his transcription turntable years before.

In that music room—so named for tax purposes when it was built during a remodeling of the house in the '50s—was a large glass table surrounded by four white swivel chairs that had been made for Ira so he could catch everything that was going on around him. Ira always sat in the swivel chair that was closest to me but with his back to me, facing the front door as he read the *New York Times* and whatever other publications interested him, tearing subscription cards out of the magazines and depositing them in the nearby wastebasket. One day after I'd been there for a couple of weeks, I was sitting at my desk cataloguing records and whistling the verse of a song called "Beginner's Luck," which was sung by Fred Astaire in the movie *Shall We Dance*. Ira was sitting in one of the swivel chairs, and he had his *New York Times* up, covering his face, and his back to me as usual. As I continued writing on the file cards and whistling, Ira suddenly froze, lowered the paper, and swiveled around with his feet, taking little baby steps until his chair was facing me. "Mike!" he said. "That's the verse of 'Beginner's Luck.' I wrote that with George in 1936 for *Shall We Dance!*"

"I know," I said.

"How do you know that?"

"I know a lot of your songs," I said. "I know a lot about your work."

I had told him before that I knew his work, but it hadn't really registered. Now he began asking me questions, looking at me quizzically. He wanted to find out exactly how much I *did* know. He played a record of "Someone to Watch Over Me" and asked, "What's wrong with this recording?"

"The singer messed up the interior rhyme on the bridge," I told him. "She held the first syllable too long."

"It's a trick rhyme," he said happily. The singer had sung:

Although he may not be the man
Some girls think of as handsome.

But Ira had written:

Although he may not be the man some
Girls think of as handsome.

Ira played another version of the same song and said, "Now listen and compare this one with that one." We spent hours listening to music together. As this went on, he began to realize that I knew a great deal about his world. I should have—I'd been studying it for years. Later Ira came to acknowledge, somewhat grudgingly at first, that in some areas I knew more about his life than *he* did. One day, for instance, Ira and I had an argument about a date in connection with *Girl Crazy*. He insisted the show came out in 1932. "No," I said. "It was 1930, because *Girl Crazy* tried out in Philadelphia in September 1930 and then opened on Broadway that October." He had probably confused it with the first movie version, which did come out in '32.

"No, no, no," Ira said.

"I'll show you," I said, and I went to his shelf and pulled out a book and showed him the date.

"Yeah, that's right," he said. "Well, you have an advantage over me."

"What's that?" I asked.

"You've thoroughly researched my life. I've only lived it." I understood what he meant, because memory doesn't always serve accurately. But after that day Ira treated me in a different way and we gradually grew closer. While I was cataloguing the records, we sometimes spent hours just sitting and talking. Soon he started autographing items to me—a piece of sheet music or a record sleeve. He was more forthcoming with his anecdotes because he realized that I genuinely wanted to hear them. Around that same time, I began playing the piano for him. At first I just improvised. I played a Gershwin song in the styles of different composers, like Beethoven or Mozart, something I used to do with an improvisational comedy group called Tuba City that I was in briefly.

Ira was delighted. After I finished with the improvisations, he said, "What can you do with 'I Got Rhythm'?" I suddenly felt intimidated. "Not much," I said. I hadn't practiced that and it wouldn't have been as good as what I'd just done. Even then I had performance anxiety. As if I weren't intimidated enough, Ira explained to me that George had written most of *Porgy and Bess* on the piano that I was playing, which had been George's favorite. I gently lifted my fingers off the keyboard as if someone had just told me that a knickknack I'd been handling was actually a rare Chinese porcelain. When George and Ira came to California in 1936, George had left that piano in New York and gotten another one. After he died, Ira disposed of the newer piano. But when Ira bought the house on Roxbury Drive in 1940, he had the piano from New York sent out. It was a Steinway, a gleaming seven-footer with an ebony gloss finish. A very nice man named Mr. Monk used to come and tune the piano, leaving little pamphlets about Jesus in his wake. "Have you heard about the Lord?" he would ask sweetly.

"Yeah," I would reply. "Have you heard about Porgy and Bess?" I wondered if Mr. Monk would have been so keen about tuning the piano if he knew Ira's lyrics to "It Ain't Necessarily So," with its rather cynical debunking of beloved Bible stories.

Within weeks Ira began inviting me to stay for dinner, and during that time a remarkable change came over him. He had been in a deep depression after his friend Eddie Carter died. In 1968 Eddie, who was originally from Russia, had retired and was looking for something to do. Leonore had just fired Ira's longtime secretary and assistant Lawrence D. Stewart, who had cowritten *The Gershwin Years* with Ed Jablonski. I never met Lawrence, but I know he was very bitter at the way his relationship with Ira ended. He never forgave Ira for not standing up to Lee when she fired him. In any event, Eddie Carter got the job and Ira came to adore him. When Eddie learned he had cancer, he let Ira know. Lee, in her typically insensitive fashion, was concerned only about how she was going to replace Eddie. Early in 1977, she brought in Walter Reilly, took him downstairs, and said to Eddie, "Show him what you do." As simple as that, because she didn't know how else to handle it. Lee remained friends with Eddie's widow, Lily, although Lily never completely forgave Lee for her behavior.

Walter had been working for Ira for about six months when I arrived on the scene; he was doing mainly secretarial chores, even though they might not have called him a secretary because that would have been a demeaning title for him. Whether Lee was aware of it or not, they needed someone to continue the work that Lawrence Stewart had been doing, and I wasn't equipped to do secretarial work anyway. Stewart not only was Ira's assistant as secretary, but also catalogued the Gershwin memorabilia for many years. He was an English professor and very well educated; he had annotated all the Gershwin material and helped Ira catalogue it before it was sent to the Library of Congress. I was constantly finding notes in Lawrence's hand about this or that, but there were still a lot of things that he hadn't done. The phonograph records had been organized at one time but had never been thoroughly catalogued. Walter continued doing Lawrence's work as I set to work on the phonograph records.

When Eddie Carter had finally succumbed to cancer in 1977, Ira became very depressed and retreated to his bed. Ira didn't handle death well, and he remained in this funk for four or five months. But from the day he heard me whistling "Beginner's Luck," he perked up and began to change. (Was it mere coincidence that "Beginner's Luck" was also one of the songs, recorded by Fred Astaire and Johnny Green, which had such a salubrious effect on Ira's spirit when he listened to them while still mourning George's death?) Ira's sudden regeneration may be a little hard to understand, but I believe that the mere fact that someone of my age knew so much about Ira's work had a subtle effect on his state of mind. As I played the piano for him and started spouting my knowledge about him and George, I saw him transformed from a mostly solemn character to a rather bubbly one. He began to come downstairs early and wait for me to arrive. I believe he knew that he could talk to me and that I would understand him and care about his world. He may have felt a sense of continuity, of his and George's work having been embraced by a new generation, and this may have given him a sense of the work's immortality, if not his own. I also increasingly became his lifeline to the outside world, which he had effectively shut out with Lee's complicity.

Ira asked me how many other people my age knew his work, and I fudged a bit and said that I thought a lot of us did but that I couldn't give the figures. "All of my friends know about you!" I said. That was true, of course. But when I told my friends that I worked for Ira Gershwin, their first response was usually, "Isn't he dead?" At least I made them aware that he was still alive and I let them know what he had accomplished.

As time went by and Ira became more lively during my visits, Leonore began to insist that he go upstairs by 4:30 or 5:00 at the latest so that he could rest before he came downstairs again for dinner. Lee liked to be abusive with Ira, and if he was having too good a time she often sent him upstairs. I later came to believe that she was jealous of my relationship with him and became more jealous as it intensified. But in the beginning, at least, she was grateful that I was there because she could see what was happening with Ira. One day she sat me down and said, "I want to talk to you."

That caught me off guard and I became nervous, thinking maybe she was going to fire me. "You've changed my husband's life, dear," she said as I swallowed with relief. "You've really given him a new life in many ways. I know that you are going to have to leave us one day and go on and do many things in your life, but I'd like to ask you to stay in this house as long as you can, because we need you. Ira needs you. I don't care what you do here, as long as you keep yourself busy and you keep him happy."

I thanked her, and after that, Lee put me on regular salary. She also told me that I was going to be famous one day, which made me laugh. "No, dear," she said, "you will. But for now I want you to do whatever you can to keep Ira happy." She told me that she was going to open up "every closet and drawer" in the house for me to do whatever I wanted; in fact, she gave me carte blanche.

$\mathcal{F}$ROM my point of view, cataloguing Ira's collection of recordings was a wonderful way to spend time with him talking about his lyrics and about all the great composers he had worked with, most notably, of course, his brother George. But by any realistic way of reckoning things, there was no pressing need to catalogue his phonograph records. Ira never listened to the records in his closet and so the idea of having them cross-referenced so that he could quickly find a particular song by a certain performer was, to say the least, unnecessary. Like many things in

Ira's life, they existed more in his memory than in reality. He hadn't actually been inside the record closet for years and he remembered things being arranged in it the way they had been many years ago, although they had long since been moved and rearranged. The same was true of many of his other closets and storage areas. One day he said to me, "Did I ever give you a copy of the signed limited edition score of *Porgy and Bess?*"

I said he hadn't. "There are several in the closet off the bedroom library," he said. "Go take one." I got the key and opened the closet for the first time. With trembling hands, I searched for a pristine copy of that rare volume, only to discover them all gone; Ira had given the last copy away some years ago to his lawyer, Ron Blanc. Every time I went to Ron's office, I saw his copy of the score lying casually on its side on top of some other books, quietly mocking me as I carried on my business. Its taunting proximity was one reason that I finally purchased my own copy years later. (Ron was a fine lawyer but had only a passing knowledge of George and Ira's music. One day when I was playing part of Tchaikovsky's First Piano Concerto for Ira, Ron walked in and asked, "Is that Gershwin?")

But such disappointments and the general confusion were minor off-notes in what was in large measure a blessed opportunity. In retrospect, it was almost as though the universe were creating an excuse for me to sit at the feet of the master and learn as much as I could from him. On a less cosmic level, of course, there were simple explanations for Lee's hiring me, principally that she loved hiring people to do things around the house. She liked to have projects going on that she could oversee. Lee might just as easily fixate on a tree in the yard and decide that it was dying or had to be removed for some reason. Suddenly, her life would be about that tree, and she would hire workmen to take care of it.

As for Ira's records, Lee probably opened the closet one day, looked in, and said, "Oh, they're all out of order! What am I going to do?" Or it may have happened spontaneously over lunch that June Levant told Lee and Emily that she had just had some of Oscar's records catalogued. However Leonore got the idea, Ira went along with it, as he generally did. It may have seemed like a good idea to him, but he also knew that he couldn't oppose Lee. If he disagreed with her on any matter, she simply screamed and yelled until he finally said, "I don't care. Do what you want." As Ira grew more infirm, he complained more frequently about how she never used to interfere with his business in any way in the early days but had virtually taken it over in later years. "She never used to be like this," was his occasional battle cry. But that's as far as it went.

The day I met Ira, he told me that he wanted the records cross-referenced in every way, so I devised a system with different letters denoting different categories: One letter stood for original cast albums that contained all Gershwin songs, another for albums of George and Ira's songs as performed by, say, Mel Tormé or Ella Fitzgerald, or songs from *Funny Face* played by the Barbara Carroll Trio, or Cy Walter playing Gershwin piano solos. Then there were albums on which only one or two Gershwin songs appeared. So, for example, we could look up Fred Astaire and find any album on which he sang a Gershwin song. Or we could look up a song title and see exactly how many recorded versions Ira had in his closet and whether there were duplicate versions of the same song. We could look up "Love Is Here to Stay" and see that Ira possessed more than twenty versions, with the same performing artist sometimes listed multiple times for different versions. We could also look up a show title and find the original cast recording, if one existed, or an album of, say, selections from *Treasure Girl*.

I had a natural affinity for the work involved, not only because of my own experience collecting records, but also because, from an early age, I had been fascinated, I would almost say obsessed, with recorded sound. Just being able to hear the voices of Al Jolson and other singers who are gone, being able to preserve that moment in time, seems magical to me. So to find myself suddenly handling hundreds of rare and vintage recordings of music that moved my heart so strongly was enormously exciting. For Ira's collection, I denoted the difference between commercially recorded and privately issued discs, whether they were on a 78, a 45, a 33, a 16-inch transcription, or a reel-to-reel tape or cassette, which I also numbered and catalogued. The 16-inch transcriptions were of special interest to me. They dated mostly from the '30s and stood out because of their odd size and extreme rarity. Even though most radio was live in its early days, movie studios sometimes created fifteen-minute promotional programs for radio advertising for their latest film. They put the program on a 16-inch disc that played at $33\frac{1}{3}$, a slower speed used for that purpose. Until 1948, most commercial records were at 78 rpm or somewhere in that vicinity—some were actually a little slower or faster. But 33⅓ transcriptions were created for radio so that fifteen-minute programs could be broadcast over the air devoid of the scratches and noise that were inherent to the 78. The biggest advantage was that fifteen minutes of material could be broadcast without having to change sides, since the longest 78 rpm record played a maximum of only four and a half minutes.

The 12-inch, 33⅓ records that most of us grew up with can hold up to thirty minutes of music with good sound quality, but that was a relatively recent development in recording technology, perhaps as radical in its implications as the compact disc was when it first appeared. In 1948, Columbia Records issued the first long-playing record, or LP, which used a smaller needle and a narrower groove called "microgroove"—a term that shows up on some of the older LPs. The 33⅓ records that had come out in the '30s then became known as "standard groove" because they used the same wide groove as the old 78s. Columbia was the first company to have success with LPs. RCA Victor actually issued some 10-inch and 12-inch LPs from 1931 to 1933, but they were standard groove and played only twelve minutes to a side. To get fifteen minutes or more on a side with standard groove technology, therefore, you needed a 16-inch disc.

But there was still a problem on those early long-playing records: The grooves were too close together, and sound would bleed through from one groove to the next. Because the tone arms on phonographs were so heavy, they wore out the grooves very quickly. Recording didn't change much until after the Second World War, when the Allies brought home tape recorders that they had confiscated in Germany; then the commercial use of tape recording began to spread in America.

Having lived through the era when advances in recording technology were being hammered out, Ira had examples of almost every kind of recording in his closet. It was quite an adventure for me to search through them and see and hear the different approaches that were taken back then. Much of the time, though, I simply played records for Ira. In the process of cataloguing, I sometimes played one to learn a particular bit of information or just to hear what was on it. In this way, Ira got to hear recordings he hadn't listened to for many years, which thrilled him. He hadn't heard some of the air checks of radio broadcasts from the 1940s since the time they were made, such as the songs from *The Firebrand of Florence,* a flop musical he wrote with Kurt Weill in 1945, based on the life of Benvenuto Cellini—a surefire idea for a musical if ever there was one. Ira never thought the show would work, and since most of those songs were never commercially recorded, he had not had an opportunity to hear them in all the years since the show closed. That was great fun for him, as it was exciting for me to observe his reaction. Having played the piano myself in convalescent homes from a very early age and having seen the reactions of the people there, I've believed for a long time that music is a healing force. For Ira to hear not only music but also something he had created years before proved to be extraordinarily revivifying.

And so I divided my time each day between sitting at my desk, searching through all the closets and drawers, and going through those records. Ira must have owned a couple thousand records all told, including 45s and 78s and special recordings. I loved the work because I learned an enormous amount; for instance, I discovered one song that existed only on an acoustic recording from the 1920s, called "I Can't Realize," written by George Gershwin and Buddy DeSylva. It's an instrumental with no vocal, and it doesn't exist anywhere else aside from this phonograph record—not on sheet music, not in the Library of Congress.

I learned a great deal about Ira, too, by playing those records. Often they jogged his memory and he began telling me stories that related to them. The old 78s in particular, some of which he hadn't heard in fifty years, brought back a flood of memories—records like "Song of the Flame" by Tessa Kosta, the beautiful Broadway singer of the teens and '20s, from a musical on which George Gershwin collaborated with Herbert Stothart, Otto Harbach, and Oscar Hammerstein II. On the flip side of one Gershwin 78 was a song that was written by Buddy DeSylva, Bud Green, and Ray Henderson. The famous songwriting team of the late '20s, of course, was DeSylva, *Brown*, and Henderson. DeSylva and Henderson probably collaborated at least once with Bud Green (I know they wrote "Alabamy Bound" together), and when Ira looked at the label, he deadpanned, "Look, they've got the wrong color." We listened to 78s that Judy Garland had recorded in the '40s for *Girl Crazy*, and some songs she had recorded from *The Shocking Miss Pilgrim*, the 1947 Fox film for which Ira supplied posthumous melodies of George's. The lead was originally intended for Judy Garland, but when MGM would not loan her to 20th Century-Fox, Betty Grable got the part. Garland recorded three of the songs, two as duets with Dick Haymes, and listening to those particular recordings Ira remarked how quavery Garland's voice sounded. "Judy didn't have good days and bad days," he said. "Instead, she had long periods when her voice sounded peculiar or quavery and then she would enter another phase when it sounded good."

There were all sorts of treasures in that record closet, especially for someone who was eager to learn all he could about the mysteries and minutiae of the recording process. Ira had acetates of the daily takes from *Ella Fitzgerald Sings the George and Ira Gershwin Songbooks*. Norman Granz, who was producing the recordings, would send or bring them over for Ira to hear at the end of each day's session. Among those sessions we discovered the song "Cheerful Little Earful," which was mistakenly recorded for the *George and Ira Songbook*—it has Ira's lyric but Harry Warren's music, and was later issued on another album. There was a version of Ella singing that song in a Betty Boop kind of voice, which Ira had no memory of and was delighted by. A couple of months later, I was on a radio show in L.A. with Ella and brought the recording for her to hear. She listened to the first sixteen bars and insisted that it was not her voice—until she listened further and realized that it was.

I had learned to appreciate Fred Astaire as a singer before I started working for Ira. When the album *Starring Fred Astaire* came out sometime before I graduated from high school, I listened to it over and over again. But Ira had in his closet a multiple-record set that Astaire had recorded in 1952 produced by Norman Granz, called *The Astaire Story*. On it, Astaire sings songs associated with his career going back to the '20s, accompanied on the piano by Oscar Peterson. I was not familiar with those recordings and I listened to them with Ira for days at a time. Anytime I came across a multiple set of something, we would listen to a bit of it every day. With *The Astaire Story*, we listened to maybe one or two sides a day until we'd gone through the whole set. It was a real education for me to hear how Astaire's style had changed from the '30s to the '50s and how he interpreted some of the same songs quite differently through the years. Most people prefer the later recordings because they don't sound so old-fashioned or hokey, but I still like the earlier ones better. I collated a number of home recordings from 1938 that Ira loved hearing and made a tape of them, which we sent to some of his close friends. About two months later, a copy of that tape arrived at Ira's house from the musician Saul Chaplin with a note saying, "Ira, I don't know if you've heard these. They were sent to me by Steve Sondheim and I thought you might get a kick out of them." In two months they'd made the rounds of all the musical theater collectors and found their way back to Ira.

I came to recognize that Ira loved Astaire and Ella because both singers enunciated the lyrics so clearly. I also learned that he didn't like some of Sarah Vaughan's '50s recordings of Gershwin because she did vocal tricks with the notes—much less so than she did later, of course. He found her last Gershwin recording, which she did with Michael Tilson Thomas, unlistenable. Ira was so dismayed by hearing those interpretations that he could get through only part of the first side before I had to take it off.

In the course of our daily explorations, I played Ira a recording of "My Cousin in Milwaukee." I said, "This is very untypical-sounding Gershwin to me." And Ira said, "I think it's very *typical*-sounding Gershwin." We then went through the song and he explained why he felt that way about it. He could not speak about music in technical terms, but that was fine with me because I couldn't converse fluently in that language either. Yet Ira was eloquent at conveying feelings and allusions to other songs. I didn't always agree with Ira, and still don't in some regards. For example, on Ella Fitzgerald's recordings of Gershwin with Nelson Riddle's arrangements, I did not like it that many of Riddle's charts took away some of the essential punch of George's harmonies. On the recording of "Love Is Here to Stay," Riddle uses a repeating blues figure after each vocal phrase. That figure recurs all through the song, and although it was not a cliché at the time, and the way Nelson used it was not a cliché, it became a cliché in the late '50s because it was copied so much. I loved the genius of Nelson Riddle but I would have much preferred hearing some of those Gershwinesque harmonies that were not in certain arrangements. Ira liked the imagination Nelson had used and the things that Nelson had changed, and so I understood his perspective. Even our disagreements deepened our sense of a developing teacher-student relationship.

Over the months that followed, Ira became more forthright in expressing his feelings. Although he denied it, his greatest outlet for his emotions was his song lyrics. He claimed that writing songs was "work," which was true enough, but it also revealed more about himself than he realized.

Early in my relationship with Ira, I felt free to ask him dumb questions. In the song "They All Laughed," the lyric refers in one place to "eating humble pie." I asked Ira what humble pie was and he very patiently explained it to me. Another time, Ira asked me if I knew what the reference to "olive oil" meant in the song "The Babbitt and the Bromide." The song is a duet and, at the end of the chorus, the two characters say to each other, "Ta! Ta! Olive oil! Good-bye!" I said, "Sure, Olive Oyl was the character in the Popeye cartoons."

Ira became hysterical. "No, no, no!" he said. "Olive oil was what we used to say in the '20s instead of au revoir." (I still like Popeye better.)

I always knew that Ira had a very droll way of looking at life because he expressed it in his lyrics, but now he gradually began to exhibit some of that wry sense of humor in our daily interactions. Alan Jay Lerner said that Ira Gershwin was the only man he could call "cute," and he was. One day, I was hanging out with his next-door neighbor Rosemary Clooney, whose son Gabri had come back from Japan with one of the first Sony Walkman machines. I asked Rosemary if I could borrow it and play it for Ira because whenever Leonore came home, she always told us to turn down whatever music we were listening to, even if it was playing at whisper volume, which used to make Ira crazy. When I put the headphones on Ira and played a tape, he responded enthusiastically to the brilliance of the sound. After I took them off, I asked Ira if he would like me to get him a Walkman. "No," he said, "but get my stockbroker on the phone." And he bought stock in Sony.

Ira's business consultant was Nico March, a darling man who used to come over often to visit. Nico took some photos of Ira one day, one of which caught him with a rather sly expression on his face. Ira called it his Mona Lisa look. He inscribed the photo to me, "What Ira Gershwin is really like," apparently feeling that the photo revealed some kind of sly inner nature that was not otherwise evident.

After Rosemary Clooney recorded an album of Ira's lyrics, she asked me to get a quote from Ira to put on the jacket. Ira was reluctant to give a blurb, though, because he felt it might seem blatantly commercial to endorse an album of his own songs. When I played him a demo tape of the album, he started laughing. "What did you think?" I asked, sensing that a quip had come to his mind.

Ira said, "I loved every word."

When I suggested he give Rosemary *that* line to use, he demurred. He wasn't going to write anything at all for the album until finally he wrote her a brief note saying something like, "Dear Rosemary, I'm delighted to be connected with your latest album." Then I persuaded him to add as a P.S. "I loved every word." That went on the album jacket.

On another occasion Ira was eating dinner with Warren Lyons, whose father was Leonard Lyons, the columnist who wrote "The Lyons Den" for many years and was a very close friend of Ira and Leonore's. During dinner, Ira spilled some beets and one of them got on his shirt. He started groaning vociferously, "Oh, that's just horrible! It's awful!"

"Ira," Warren said, "it's not so bad, really."

"Yes, it is," he insisted. "It's terrible when a songwriter drops a beet."

There was a dinner party at Ira's home one night with Jascha Heifetz, and Ira and some friends rigged Heifetz's fortune cookie. Everybody was in on the joke except Heifetz. After dinner, he opened the fortune cookie and read a fortune that said, "Another violinist is stealing your bowing technique." Everybody watched as Heifetz read the fortune with an expressionless face, then very quickly and carefully folded it up and put it in his pocket without a single comment.

One time, Ira and I were discussing Irving Berlin's song "I Love a Piano," with the famous line "I know a fine way / To treat a Steinway." We started tossing ideas back and forth for rhyming other brands of pianos. Ira came up with "I'm never bickering / When at a Chickering." We devised a couple more but we were stumped over Yamaha. "What kind of rhyme could you come up with for Yamaha?" I asked rhetorically. Ira began by pointing out that the proper Japanese pronunciation is "Ya-*ma*-ha," with the emphasis on the second syllable. How he knew that I have no idea, but he was always coming up with odd information like that. Then he said, "Let me think a minute." Half a minute later, his eyes twinkled. "I don't know about 'I Love a Piano,' " he said, "but how about, 'Oh, your daddy's rich and ya ma-ha's good looking'?"

One day I was waiting downstairs for Ira with Deena Rosenberg, who was in the process of researching her book *Fascinating Rhythm*. As Ira descended the steps, Deena asked him, "How do you feel, Ira?" He said, "I'm a rhapsody in bruise." Ira presumably had plenty of time to cook up a pun like that, but he had always possessed a quick wit. In *A Smat-*

tering of Ignorance, Oscar Levant tells the story of throwing his coat down to the ground and saying, "Ira, kiss my cassock." Levant did thoroughly peculiar things like that all the time. Ira's immediate response was, "Oscar is a masochist because he wants his cassock kissed!" (Ira's facility for instant wordplay was reminiscent of Noël Coward's. After Coward had seen Leonard Gershe's Broadway play *Butterflies Are Free,* someone asked him what he thought of Keir Dullea, who had played the lead. Sir Noël replied, "Keir Dullea, gone tomorrow.")

Ira's favorite joke was based on one of his own songs. It's the one about the lady who goes to an audition and sings:

> You say eether and I say eether,
> You say neether and I say neether;
> Eether, eether, neether, neether—
> Let's call the whole thing off!

The director says, "Thank you, Miss LeVEEN." And she says, "The name's LeVINE!"

I once asked Ira if he felt that an artist had to suffer in order to create a good piece of work. At the end of *Lyrics on Several Occasions,* Ira wrote that even with talent it takes years and years of practice to become a good lyric writer. But he didn't believe that one had to suffer and he insisted that he didn't suffer in writing his lyrics. I wanted to know about a song like "The Man That Got Away," his last big song, written with Harold Arlen for Judy Garland to sing in *A Star Is Born.* He denied that he had suffered or felt any sadness in writing that song or that it reflected any suffering in his own life. But I maintained that the song had moved so many people very deeply and had a great impact on their emotions.

"Good," he said. "I did my job well."

That's as much as he would say about it. He refused to acknowledge that a part of him was in that song. He did admit to me that he wrote "Someone to Watch Over Me" around the time he married Leonore and that the line "Although he may not be the man some / Girls think of as handsome" was about himself. That was certainly appropriate, given that

Lee was a real live wire and Ira not only was chubby and wore glasses from early childhood but was also very shy and tended to stay in the corner at social gatherings. He felt damn lucky to win Lee, even though *she* proposed to *him*. They had been going together so long that she finally said, "Well, how about it, kid? Can we get married?"

"Okay," he said. "All right, sure." The dichotomy between personality and work is endemic to most creative artists, and songwriters are no exception. Richard Rodgers was a very tough man who wrote extraordinarily romantic, lyrical melodies. Jerome Kern was considered quite cold at times and yet produced remarkably beautiful songs. But Ira expressed the essence of his soul in his lyrics, and maybe he was more like his lyrics when he was younger. There's a story about Ira talking to a friend about the song "Clap Yo' Hands," which has a line in it that goes, "On the sands of time / You are only a pebble." His friend said, "What do you mean by that?"

"Come over here," Ira said. They were on the boardwalk in Atlantic City and he went onto the beach and found a pebble. "See," Ira said, waving his arm at the expanse of shoreline.

I caught only glimpses of that kind of youthful enthusiasm in Ira, although he was always most animated when listening to songs and "reliving" his lyrics. He had a very romantic side, even if he required a plot situation to bring it out in a lyric. He said that no matter how creaky or thin or simple the plot was, he had to have that premise for inspiration. Even writing a generic love song like "Love Walked In" for what turned out to be a terrible movie, *The Goldwyn Follies,* he needed a plot. After that, he could draw on his imagination and feelings about romance. For example, "They Can't Take That Away from Me" is a lyric of deceptive brilliance:

The way you wear your hat,
The way you sip your tea,
The mem'ry of all that—
No, no! They can't take that away from me!

It requires some insight to understand that when you're in love, little things become immensely important and endearing. In most conventional love songs, the singer is usually praising the beloved, enumerating his or her finest qualities. But it took much more insight to observe that the object of your love can do unattractive things—"The way you sing off key"—and you still find it charming and delightful. And the lyric only gets better at the end:

> The way you hold your knife,
> The way we danced till three,
> The way you've changed my life—
> No, no! They can't take that away from me!

The genius to jump suddenly from the very mundane to the transcendental—"The way you've changed my life"—came from years of experience and perspiration and craft. But Ira also had to have the heart to be able to create something like that. He was an extremely sensitive man who was afraid to express his feelings in "real life," so he put them all into his lyrics. What other outlet did he have? I believe that he was always afraid of showing too much of himself in the lyrics, but he could get away with it when it was for a character. He was also capable of expressing opposing points of view in different songs in the same show. *Lady in the Dark* was about psychoanalysis and dreams. The verse of one song has this lyric:

> With you I used to roam
> Through the Pleasure Dome
> Of Kubla Khan.
>
> . . .
>
> I lost you through the centuries.
> I find you once again,

Yet in another song, a ditty called "One Life to Live," he wrote the lyric

> I say to me ev'ry morning:
> You've only one life to live,
> So why be done in?
> Let's let the sun in,
> And gloom can jump in the riv'!

He went from an almost Eastern sense of reincarnation and cyclical lives to a more existential, live-for-today attitude in the same show.

And just for sheer humor, Ira had a knack for making fun of precisely

the kind of introvert intellectual that he himself epitomized. His paean to
the hard-luck loser, "But Not for Me," begins by referring to such cultural
icons of his day as prototypical advice-to-the-lovelorn columnist Beatrice
Fairfax, the Eleanor Porter heroine Pollyanna, and the sports colum-
nist/cartoonist Thomas A. Dorgan, before it goes on to twit the fashion
for melancholic drama of the Chekhovian kind that was enjoying popularity in 1930:

> With Love to Lead the Way,
> I've found more Clouds of Gray
> Than any Russian play
> Could guarantee.

(As a song lyric for use in the show *Girl Crazy,* however, the humor
served to show that the character singing the song, played by Ginger
Rogers, enjoyed a certain detachment from her lovelorn situation.)

When I say that Ira was an intellectual, I realize that he might not be
recognized as such by modern academic standards. He certainly wasn't
a scholar per se. But he was highly intelligent and that, coupled with
his ability to hear and see the world through the vernacular of both the
working class and high society, gave him the extra charge he needed to
write the kinds of witty and sometimes sardonic lyrics he did. He was
able to converse on many subjects brilliantly. He was well versed in art,
for instance, and shared his brother's enthusiasm for the great emerging artists of the early twentieth century. George's collection, much of
which still hung in Ira's home, seems obvious and well chosen by current standards, not to mention extremely valuable today. But at the
time—he admired Picasso, Utrillo, André Derain, Henri Rousseau, and
particularly Georges Rouault—many of these artists were still somewhat
controversial. Ira could speak knowledgeably of these and other painters
and was always talking about things of which I knew very little,
although much of that was on account of my age at the time. However,
he read omnivorously, and he continued to read during the time I was
working with him, until it became difficult for him to concentrate. That's
when Leonore said that Ira had lost the ability of self-amusement. And
that's when he had his most unpleasant times, when he no longer kept
himself entertained and would get dizzy when he tried to read.

I don't know how much Ira was aware of the extent to which he was compensating through his lyrics. He didn't have other avenues for expressing himself, such as writing poetry or fiction. And he was very slow at writing words; he labored over them. They seem so simple to us now, but that's because he worked to craft them in a simple, natural, inevitable way. He was a night owl who worked best when other people were asleep, often all through the night. There's one story from the early days when he had been up all night and the maid arrived early in the morning. There was Ira, unshaven, with a tie still hanging around his neck, wandering the room talking to himself and looking like a derelict. The maid took one look at him, went to Leonore, and said, "Don't Mr. Gershwin never go to work?" She had seen him in this state before and couldn't figure out what this man was doing.

Probably as part of his general campaign of self-effacement, Ira liked to tell stories about dumb or embarrassing things he had done. One night he was at a party with a man who kept talking to him about music and asking him all kinds of questions. Ira finally turned to the person next to him and asked in a whisper, "Who *is* this guy?" The person said, "It's Walt Disney." Ira whispered, "Okay," and turned back and gave Disney a lot more attention after that. Ira also loved to recount stories about how people mistook him for George. He told me a story about J. Fred Coots, who wrote "You Go to My Head" and a few other hit songs. When Ira met Coots in the 1920s, Coots said, "Ira, you need to get more recognition. You need to have more people aware of who you are, because you're such a talented man. I'm going to help you. I'll introduce you to some important people."

Shortly after that, Ira was at a concert with Coots, who introduced him to a friend by saying, "This is the great George Gershwin." Coots went on and on about George until finally Ira took him aside and said, "What were you doing? Why were you introducing me as George Gershwin?"

"Well," Coots said, "do you want to be famous or not?"

Ira didn't *always* think of himself in such self-effacing terms. During the McCarthy witch-hunts, he was called before the California Fact-Finding Committee on Un-American Activities, chaired by Jack Tenney, a former Communist and musician manqué. The Gershwin home had once been used for a meeting of the Committee for the First Amendment, a group created by film directors John Huston and Billy Wilder to counteract Tenney's red-baiting. Ira was asked all the usual questions about Communist infiltration in the movie industry. At the end of the testimony, his inquisitor said, "Thank you very much for being here, Mr. Gershwin. I'm a great admirer of your brother George, who wrote all those wonderful tunes." Ira politely thanked the man and left, but later he told Leonore of his anger at the man's remark. "Scared as I was," Ira said, "I was thinking to myself, 'What about me, you son of a bitch? I wrote the lyrics!' "

*A*FTER Lee gave me a free hand to do whatever I wanted, I began going through the memorabilia in the basement and in Ira's closet upstairs. It was an exciting time because I never knew what I was going to come across. The things that were of greatest interest to me were the most personal items that Ira had saved, like George's little black book with his girlfriends' names and phone numbers, or a notebook of music paper that George kept in his pocket at the end of his life with ideas for tunes he had come up with. I never went into Ira's dressing area, so apart from his records and correspondence files, I didn't come across many personal items of his. He did keep a locked filing cabinet in an upstairs closet, which contained his most treasured items of George's, but it was another year or so before I was granted access to that. The memorabilia also included Ira's lyric sheets and other papers relating to Ira's career, George's musical manuscripts, and, of course, the scrapbooks. There must have been about fifty scrapbooks that had been assembled in George's lifetime by one person or another, including Ira. Lawrence Stewart had very carefully reassembled and updated them before I came on the scene, and I did my best to continue his work. After I'd been there for several years, I hired Mark Goldberg to come in and work exclusively on the scrapbooks because I no longer had the time. For example, I found a huge box of clippings relating to the infamous Hollywood blacklist that had never been put into a scrapbook, perhaps because they didn't directly relate to Ira. He had gone to Washington with Lauren Bacall and Bogart and several other people in the '50s to try to say, in essence, "Look, this whole thing is ridiculous." Their naiveté seems almost quaint in retrospect, and they were effectively laughed out of Washington. When I brought that box of clippings out, Leonore became particularly angry and would not talk about it, in fact became furious that I even brought it up. Ira was willing to talk about it, but it was obviously something that festered and was still very painful to them more than thirty years later.

But I could open practically any drawer in the house and find some piece of history. In a hallway I came across a bar area with bottles of booze, and when I opened a drawer I found a number of handkerchiefs with George's initials on them. By the record closet where I worked, there was a cigar box that had no cigars in it, only a single pipe. I recognized the pipe from a photograph I'd seen of George taken in 1937. As I said, the house often felt like a shrine or at least a museum dedicated to George's memory. Walter Reilly had a drinking problem and didn't get much done in the way of sorting memorabilia. On the other hand, he was quite wonderful to me. He early on recognized Lee's foibles and at one point he counseled me, "You've been confiding in Lee and telling her about intimate things, haven't you?"

"Yes," I said.

"Don't."

Lily Carter later talked about how Moss Hart had confided in Lee about his personal problems, and the first thing Lee did was tell everybody about it. She loved to gossip about people, and I should have known that. Yet there was something almost hypnotic about her—and, as I've said, I had begun to feel like family. I had been there only a short time when I began to feel as if I had known these people all my life. In fact, I had actually spoken to Ira once, some time before I met him. The story of that experience was recalled to me in a surprising way while I was working for Ira.

When I was about nineteen years old, I met Ed Jablonski, the author of a number of Gershwin books as well as several books on aviation and one book with Lowell Thomas. A friend of mine from Columbus who happened to be enrolled at NYU had looked up Jablonski's name in the Manhattan directory and just called him. Jablonski is the type of man who will invite you over to sit and talk about music if he senses an enthusiastic, youthful soul. (These days, Ed is so overburdened by worshipers at the Gershwin shrine that he is understandably less available for visitations. I was lucky to have happened along when I did.) My friend Mark became acquainted with Jablonski in this fashion and when I was in New York, he took me over to meet him. I was thrilled because I knew Ed's books, particularly *The Gershwin Years*. Ed decided to give his two young friends a treat that day by calling up Ira Gershwin. Ira had just been awarded some sort of medal of achievement, and Ed talked to him for a while about it. Then he allowed us both to say a brief hello. I got on the phone and said, "Congratulations!"

I was so nervous that I blurted out, "I just love your music, Mr. Gershwin—I mean your *lyrics!*"

I put in a few more words, then gave the phone back to Ed rather quickly. I didn't get over that experience for days. Now, going through Ira's correspondence, I came across a letter from Ed Jablonski to Ira talking about that day. He told Ira our names and mentioned that we were both devoted to musical theater, especially to Gershwin, adding, in typically witty fashion, "They were rather stunned to be able to speak with you—and rather speechless, which at least kept it short. . . . When they left they were still rather glassy-eyed." That about summed it up, and I was tickled to find an unexpected reference to myself in Ira's file. In retrospect, I am struck by the irony that I myself was soon to become one of Ira's protectors, helping to insulate him from the outside world of adoring fans—like me and my friend.

Walter tended to keep correspondence away from Ira, and had become rather lax about responding to letters that were not high priority. So when I opened a couple of drawers in the basement, I found them full of fan mail that had never been answered. Ira was very meticulous and wanted every letter answered, and he was aghast when I told him what I had found. Leonore screamed at me for having revealed it to Ira, giving him more worries. It made little difference, since Ira didn't have the energy to write or dictate responses, and the letters never were answered. In the past, however, Ira had been famous for answering all his correspondence, including a letter he received in the late '50s from a man who addressed him as "Miss Ira Gershwin." The man was a composer, recently arrived from Europe, and probably not very familiar with English names. Maybe he assumed that George and Ira were a brother and sister team like the Astaires. In any case, he wanted to collaborate with "Miss Gershwin," explaining that he would be at work until early in the evening and asking Ira to meet him at his apartment after nine P.M. Ira's reply was simple: "I'm very sorry, but I couldn't possibly meet you after 9 P.M. because I'm engaged to a very jealous young man who wouldn't allow it. Sincerely, (Miss) Ira Gershwin." The most famous unintentional quip in this vein—which happens to be absolutely true—

was made by a BBC radio announcer who said, "And now here is a medley of songs by George Gershwin and his lovely wife, Ira."

All the medals and awards that Ira had accumulated throughout the years were kept mainly in drawers, as they meant very little to him. But he did display the certificate for the Pulitzer Prize, of which he was very proud because he was the first songwriter ever to win the award. He won it for the musical play *Of Thee I Sing,* but at that time the Pulitzer was awarded only for words, not music. George S. Kaufman and Morrie Ryskind, who wrote the book, won along with Ira, but George didn't get a prize because he was "just" the composer. Ira was so embarrassed that he told George he would not accept the Pulitzer unless they included George. "This was the only time George ever got angry at me," Ira later said. "He insisted that I *had* to take the Pulitzer." Nonetheless, Ira continued to feel so bad about it that he hung the certificate in his bathroom for years. (The policy was soon changed, leaving *Of Thee I Sing* as the only musical to win a Pulitzer for which the composer did not receive an award.)

On one wall was a certificate from the mayor of Los Angeles proclaiming Ira Gershwin Day. And on the floor sat a little stool for Tinkerbelle the cat. At night, Ira would sit in one of the chairs, Lee in the other, and Tinkerbelle on the third; that was Ira's happy little family. Downstairs, Ira kept his collection of drawings and paintings, two of himself. George's own paintings were there along with the remnants of his once rather large collection of African art. There was also a portrait of George Gershwin in "an Imaginary Concert Hall," by the Mexican artist David Alfaro Siqueiros. (George was very friendly with both Siqueiros and Diego Rivera, and Ira had home movies that George took in 1935 of a trip to Mexico.) Siqueiros had painted the faces of all the Gershwin family and friends, including himself, in the first row: Morris and Rose Gershwin, Arthur Gershwin, Emily and Lou Paley, William Daly, the conductor, Leo Godowsky, and Mabel Schirmer. At that time in 1935, Oscar Levant had had a fight with George, so Siqueiros put Oscar in the second row.

Rows of volumes custom-bound in blue with all the Gershwins' published songs lined the shelves of Ira's music room. The rest of the books were about art, although I never saw him look at a single one of the art books. Lee was very interested in art and George had had a huge art collection, some of which Ira inherited, including a Chagall, a Picasso, a

Rouault, a Vlaminck, a Soutine, a Pascin, and a famous Modigliani of Dr. Dévaraigne painted in 1917, which was on an easel by the piano. As Lee became more and more paranoid with time, she had them all electronically armed. Then she began taking a lot of prescription drugs and, in her stupor, she sometimes triggered one of the alarms—and then had to call the security agency and say the code word, "rhapsody," to abort the alarm. "Rhapsody" was spoken a lot more than it was played in that house.

All this electronic arming seemed ludicrous to me because the greatest threat of thievery came from *inside* the house. Lee was aware of the staff's penchant for removing valuable memorabilia but repeated, mantralike, every time something disappeared, "You can't get good help these days."

*L*EONORE Gershwin was every bit as odd as I'd been led to believe, and then some. She was highly intelligent and could be very generous when she wanted to be, but I finally came to the conclusion that she was unbalanced in a number of significant ways. Leonore felt that she was entitled to act selfishly because she had sacrificed a great deal to protect Ira and the Gershwin name. And insofar as she did not appear to enjoy a healthy relationship with her husband, she had sacrificed quite a bit. Leonore and Ira had a peculiar kind of love-hate relationship; if she went out of town, he inevitably had some sort of accident or illness, forcing her to cut short her trip and come back to take care of him. To be sure, Ira was a serious hypochondriac and Lee seemed to be on to him. Once when I called and mentioned to Lee that I thought Ira sounded weak on the phone, she replied, "That, darling, is not true. You know Ira puts on little acts for people."

"Oh?"

"He doesn't want anybody to be as ill as he is."

Ira worried about everything imaginable, often staying awake all night. The situation became so extreme that Lee eventually stopped traveling altogether because of Ira's illnesses—or so she said. As a form of compensation, she subscribed to a newsletter called *Passport.* One day she was reading it at the breakfast table when Ira said, "I didn't know you still get *Passport.*"

"Even if I can't travel anymore," she said, "I can still read about it!"

That was the tone of a good deal of their relationship. One time, Leonore was out very, very late, and Ira became worried. When she finally came home, I remember him saying, "Oh, thank God! Thank God you're here."

I often wondered why Ira stayed married to Lee, but I had a feeling that he didn't believe he could find anybody else who would actually love and care for him. And after they had been together for so long, there was probably no point in making a change. Of course, Ira put up with more than Lee had to put up with. A great deal more.

Lee had the most brilliant perceptions of people and of events going on around her. If she was a supporter, her praise and her bolstering of one's ego could be endless, a trait which prompted Vincente Minnelli to say, "She cheers you up when you're feeling good." But her extraordinary eye for detail was so colored by her anger and frustrations about her life that it inevitably yielded a negative comment about one thing or another. One time, for instance, Leonore told me that when Jerome Kern worked with Ira on *Cover Girl* in 1943, Kern called Ira and said, "I want to work with you on a project, and we'll split the royalties fifty-fifty." Ira agreed, but, according to Lee, when the contract came Kern got sixty percent and Ira forty. Lee went on and on about what a terrible person Jerome Kern was to have done this. The story even appeared later in a book about Kern, having come from Lee. But I had long since learned that whenever Lee told me something, I should go upstairs to check it with Ira. When I relayed this story to Ira, he started laughing and said, "Where did you hear that?"

When I told him the source, he shook his head. "The truth is," he said, "that Jerry asked me to work with him and I was so thrilled to be collaborating with Jerome Kern that I insisted he take sixty percent and I get forty. He did offer me fifty-fifty, but I insisted on sixty-forty."

On another occasion, Lee and I went to visit Vincente Minnelli, whom Lee had known in the early days in New York. There was even a rumor that they had had an affair, long before Minnelli married Judy Garland. There may have been something to that, because although Lee never liked to have her picture taken, when Vincente came over to the house she asked me to take their photograph. Vincente was now living with a woman named Lee Anderson, who had been with him for a long time and eventually married him. We arrived at Vincente's house without having made any sort of appointment and the housekeeper let us in, but while we were waiting for him, Lee asked me to play the piano. I said, "I can't just sit down and start playing his piano!"

"Oh, come on," she said. "Vincente and I are old friends. I want to hear you play."

I obliged her, but a minute later Lee Anderson entered the room like Gloria Swanson in *Sunset Boulevard* and said, *"What* is going on? Who *are* you!" She was aghast at finding strangers in her living room. Lee got up and said, "Hello, I'm Lee Gershwin." Anderson then recalled having met Leonore and mentioned very specifically where and when they had met. "Oh yes, of course," Leonore said, "I remember."

Then Vincente came down, and they had a visit. But when we went back to the house, Lee said to Ira, "I met Lee Anderson and she made up some stupid story about meeting me at such and such a place." Yet it was obvious that Lee Anderson *had* met her at that place and that Leonore used that as an opportunity to say something bad about the woman because she didn't like her. Ira's only comment to Leonore was, "I wonder why she would have said that." Did he know the truth? Ultimately, Leonore may have been so filled with rage and frustration about how her life had diminished to essentially taking care of Ira that she took it out in this petty fashion.

Things weren't always that way, of course. In the early years in Hollywood, if Ira's porch light was illuminated, it meant that he was awake and you could stop by, no matter how late. He loved throwing parties and had lots of great ones in the '40s. Lee's place in society then was to be the perfect Beverly Hills hostess. She was, by all accounts, witty and funny and delightful to be around, and their home quickly became a place where careers started. William Holden stayed at their house when he came to California to make his first movie. Irving "Swifty" Lazar, the famous Hollywood agent, became a good friend of theirs and actually cultivated his clientele out of the Gershwin house. The Gershwins were largely responsible for his success in the sense that they introduced him to many major figures in Hollywood—producer Arthur Freed, director Richard Brooks, the song-writing team of Betty Comden and Adolph Green, Angie Dickinson, and others—some of whom also started their careers in the Gershwin home.

This notion of the Gershwins' cultivating so many careers was humorously remarked on by Harold Arlen, another frequent visitor, who referred to Lee and Ira's household as the Gershwin Plantation, although I'm not at all sure he originated the expression. In his song "For Art, ASCAP, and the Gershwin Plantation," which was never published but exists on a home recording made early in the 1940s, he urges Ira to get to work—the war is on and the royalties aren't rolling in as they once were. (ASCAP, the American Society of Composers, Authors and Publishers, is responsible for collecting and distributing songwriters' royalties.) Arlen couched the song as a dialogue between a reluctant Ira and the voice of his creative conscience:

> Through the night, the dismal night,
> My zest for rhyme keeps waning,
> And soon a voice within me cries,
> "Ira, my boy, the public needs entertaining."
>
> Then I question the little man who isn't there,
> For one good reason for my despair,
> One good reason why the likes of me
> Should be so burdened with ennui,
>
> Should not be able to sleep a wink,
> Even with the aid of a capsule pink,
> To turn and toss and nightly grapple
> For a song to be okayed by Sam and Chappell.
> . . .
> Ah, little man who isn't there,
> Why this burden do I bear?
> With a tear in his eye and with resignation
> He said, "Ira, my boy, 'tis for art, ASCAP, and the Gershwin Plantation."

The Gershwin house was originally decorated by Fanny Brice, who was Lee's best friend. Brice died in 1951 and a couple of years later they hired an architect and expanded the house, adding the music room in which I now worked with Ira. The architect, who had also done Harry Warren's house, was later arrested for some sort of shady business dealings, and it came out that he had been adding thousands of dollars to his construction bills and had bilked the Gershwins and the Warrens and everyone else. Still, they all seemed to love his work.

I doubt that Lee and Ira ever had much of a physical relationship. They apparently always had separate bedrooms—Lee used to make a point of saying that their house was built for Catholics. Harry Warren said that in the '40s, they used to tease Ira tirelessly that he had a woman on the side in Pasadena. It was a big running joke. Whether Ira actually had an affair, I don't know, but for his sake I hope he did. Leonore said that he was a voyeur, although she didn't elaborate. She once said to me, "There isn't anything I've never done, and there isn't anything that I regret." That's a great line, but I don't know that it was true. She was supposed to have had an affair with the director Lewis Milestone (who won an Oscar for *All Quiet on the Western Front*), probably during the time Milestone directed *The North Star,* a 1943 movie that Ira worked on with Aaron Copland. But the deeper truth is that Lee had been in love with George. He did not share her feelings at all, and at some point she realized that if she wanted to be part of the Gershwin circle, she would have to latch on to Ira because she wasn't about to get George. Ira was impressed with Lee because she was a real flapper in those days. Lee liked to talk about how, when she first heard *Rhapsody in Blue,* she said, "I don't get it. You can't dance to it."

On a table near the small library leading into Ira's bedroom was a copy of a wonderful 1973 coffee table book called *The Gershwins* that had a photo of George on the front cover and one of Ira on the back. Whenever the maid dusted, she always left the book with George's face up. Anytime Lee came into the room, she was careful to turn the book over so that Ira's face was up. The day Ira died, Lee turned George's face up. At the time, I thought she was doing this because she was now able to express openly her repressed feelings about George. But in retrospect I realize that Lee, being so afraid of death, just may not have been able to look at the picture of Ira so soon after his passing—a man she truly loved and to whom she had been married for over fifty years.

Maybe my opinion of Lee is colored by the number of blowups we had over the years, the result of what I can only call her rampant irrationality. It was always necessary to agree with Lee, for instance, because she would consider you an enemy if you didn't. As I grew older in the years I spent with the Gershwins, I inevitably started developing my own opinions on a number of subjects. I began to disagree with Lee on occasion, and then the sparks would fly. By the end of her life, we had made peace and were on friendly terms again, yet while I still retain a certain fondness for Lee, I have to say that she acted outside the bounds of rationality with startling frequency. To confuse matters further, her generosity and irrationality often overlapped, sending the most infuriating kinds of mixed messages. One such incident concerned a gold charm bracelet made from a watch fob that had once belonged to George Gershwin.

George never wore a wristwatch when he played concerts. Instead, he wore a pocket watch for which Kay Swift had given him a gold fob. On the chain, as a good luck charm, she had placed a small gold dove that she'd had specially made with a diamond in one eye and a sapphire in the other—their birthstones. She knew that it would be concealed under his jacket and would be a secret token of their love. George later acquired other charms for his chain. Alma Hearst, with whom he had a fling, gave him a small gold *A*. When *Porgy and Bess* opened, George gave Ira a gold charm of a whale; when you opened its mouth you saw the face of Jonah, commemorating a line from "It Ain't Necessarily So" ("Oh Jonah, he lived in the whale"). But Ira didn't have any place to put it, so he gave it back to George to wear on his fob.

When George died, Leonore inherited the chain and had it made into a charm bracelet, which she wore. She added a number of other charms, including one given her by Kurt Weill when *Lady in the Dark* opened, and one from Arthur Schwartz that was actually the Liberty Bell but which he gave to Lee as a wedding bell because the 1946 show that Arthur and Ira wrote, *Park Avenue,* was about divorce. To my great surprise, one day Lee unexpectedly made me a present of the charm bracelet. As I've said, she could be extremely generous at times, and I was thrilled to receive a gift of such enormous emotional weight—something that had once belonged to George Gershwin with tokens connected to other great songwriters as well. I was overwhelmed, especially since I suspected Lee's feelings about George and realized the bracelet must have had great sentimental value for her. But I wasn't sure I could actually wear it because it was a charm bracelet and it didn't look particularly good on me. After thanking Lee profusely, I told her of my reservation. "You have to use it," Lee said, "because if you don't wear it, what's the point?"

However, the clasp had been broken, and so she gave it to a cousin of hers who designed jewelry and who said he would fix it and send it back to me. This was in 1983, only two or three months before Ira died. About a month later, I had an emergency appendectomy and was in the hospital for some time. Her cousin told me that he had sent the bracelet back to the house but that it hadn't turned up, even though he had sent it by certified mail. The whole time I was in the hospital I was very worried about what might have happened to the bracelet. Leonore came to visit me every day with Emily Paley, and each time she managed to find some new thing to say to upset me. One of her best was, "Ira is doing very poorly because you're not there." But there was no mention of the bracelet.

After I returned to the house, I expressed my concern to Ira about the disappearance of the bracelet. Suddenly Lee piped up. "Oh, I have it," she said very casually.

"You have it?" I said, incredulous.

"Yes," she said, "but I'm not sure I want to give it back to you."

"Why not?"

"I don't know," she said. "I think I want to keep it."

This enraged me. Despite my initial trepidation over receiving such a gift, I had long since come to enjoy the idea of having it. "Thanks a lot, Lee!" I blurted out. "I'll always remember your generosity."

Lee went into the bedroom and returned with the little box, which she threw at me. "Here's your bracelet!" she said.

It was madness. I did get to keep the bracelet, however, and some years after Ira's death I had a rather eerie experience with it. The casting director Terry Liebling, who was Marvin Hamlisch's sister, was giving a party at which the psychic Peter Hurkos would be present. I brought the bracelet and privately gave it to Terry to hand to Peter during his demonstration of psychometry, or the psychic reading of objects, without letting him know anything about it. No sooner was the charm bracelet in his hand than he began to screw up his face in an expression of excruciating pain. "They operated in the wrong place!" Hurkos blurted out with some anguish. "He died too young. Too young!"

On a prior occasion, Lee announced that she was going to give me a gold tie clip that had belonged to George. But I had learned my lesson. "Lee," I said, "I couldn't take that."

"Fine," she said, annoyed. "Then I won't give it to you." And she never did. Ira observed all this very quietly, never saying anything to me about her except once when I told him that Lee had given me a withering look. "My wife has given many people withering looks," Ira said. He never seemed to be disturbed or surprised in any way by her behavior. I always wondered what he was really thinking. Did he hate her? Did he totally block her out? The only time I heard him raise his voice and yell at her after she said something unkind to him, he said in a voice dripping with irony, "Thank you! Thank you very much! Thank you!" It was far from being a total release for him, but it was as close as he came.

Lee and Ira were married for almost fifty-seven years, and part of his illness had to do with controlling her freedom to travel and spend money so lavishly, since he couldn't control her in any other way. He hated the fact that she spent outrageous amounts of money. Of course, he hated the idea of spending *any* money on things he considered unessential. Even essentials sometimes seemed pretty steep to him. Once when Lee was in New York, I called her from Ira's bedroom. The minute I said hello to her, Ira said, "Give me the phone! Give me the phone!" I had to ask her a few things so we chatted awhile and then I gave the phone to Ira. He talked to her for a minute and when he hung up he glared at me, irate. "Do you always talk that long when you make a long-distance call?" he asked.

"Well, yeah, I do." I'd only been on a few minutes, but he was steaming. As I've said, Lee could be extremely generous, except when she went a little nuts, and then she would hold it against you. When I wanted to buy a new car in 1982, I was going to have to finance it, but Lee said she'd lend me the money so I wouldn't have to pay interest.

I resisted her offer at first until I talked it over with my dad, who said I should take it. "Why?" I said. "She'll make my life miserable."

He said, "She'll make your life miserable anyway." And he was right. I took the loan from Lee and every time I tried to pay her back, she said, "No, no, no, no. You need the money. Don't worry about it, you can pay me later." Then after Ira's death, when she fired me, the first thing that happened was that her lawyer called me. "Lee says that you've been refusing to pay back the loan on the car," he said, "and she wants the money." Only now she wanted it with interest.

But then there was the other side of Lee, so inexplicably gracious, genuinely concerned for others in general and for my personal growth in particular. I would not have been able to go to New York as many times as I did on behalf of Ira if it hadn't been for Lee, because Ira wouldn't have spent the money. But Lee knew how exciting it would be for me and knew that I was at an age when it was important to discover new places. She also recognized talent and ability in me before I recognized it myself. I've never forgotten that. Lee was interested in meeting all of my friends. When they came over and sat down in the music room, she drilled them about their lives and made suggestions. She nurtured them and gave them gifts of incense or some little *chatchke,* and I think she was pleased with the influx of youth into the house.

Lee had a curious attitude toward money: she was constantly concerned about being *under*charged. If she took her car to be repaired and they said it would cost eight hundred dollars, she was sure to say, "Oh, it must cost more than that!" She would talk them into charging her another five or six hundred dollars and doing something in addition. That's just the way she was. Whenever she went to the airport, she would go inside the terminal and take out a twenty-dollar bill. She would then stand there holding the bill up in the air, watching as the porters raced toward her to see who could get there first. "Darling," she always said to me, "if you ever have any trouble, just hold up a twenty-dollar bill." That was her philosophy: Need help? Hold up money.

Lee also could be very funny, intentionally and unintentionally. She always wore a big, floppy, wide-brimmed white hat when she went out for a walk. One day I said, "Lee, why do you always wear that hat when you go out walking?" She put her hand on her head, pushed the hat down, and said, "Birds."

Among other things, Lee took great pains to teach me proper manners and all the social graces. Whenever we went out walking, she always had me walk on the outside because the gentleman is supposed to walk on the outside. When we turned a corner, I would inevitably end up on the inside and she would say, patiently, "Outside, darling." Then I had to run around quickly and get back on the outside. But I appreciated that. (Lee did this sort of thing for others, too. The songwriter and *New York Times* reporter Irving Drutman came to Lee and Ira's hotel suite in New York to interview Ira when the film *Rhapsody in Blue* was about to open, and as Lee opened the door, Irving rushed past her and ran down the hall to find Ira. "Young man," she called after him, "you go right out and ring the bell again and come in properly!")

Lee took me to meet Harry Warren because Ira was too infirm to go and she knew how much I wanted to meet Harry. I think she perceived herself as a patron who nurtured and propelled the careers of those in need. She seemed to accept and appreciate people who were "below her station," like René the cook, and me, for that matter. I didn't much

*S*inging at a family gathering in Detroit, probably a cousin's Bar Mitzvah celebration. I usually brought down the house by doing an impression of Louis Armstrong singing "Hello Dolly."

*K*athy Becker and I were voted best actor and actress in our high school graduating class of 1974. This was our yearbook photo.

Minnie's Boys, Players Theatre, Columbus, Ohio, 1975. I played Chico in our local production of the story of the Marx Brothers' rise to fame as seen through the eyes of their mother.

An early publicity photo taken late in 1977. Seated at George Gershwin's favorite piano (according to Ira). George wrote much of *Porgy and Bess* on the piano. Ira moved the piano to California after George's death.

*W*ith Ira Gershwin on his eighty-first birthday, December 6, 1977. Ira was a chocoholic so I gave him his initials in chocolate. Leonore didn't approve.

*W*ith Harry Warren, 1981. This photo makes me laugh hysterically because of Harry's expression. That was the way he looked a good deal of the time; but he was adorable.

*H*arry Warren holding my customized version of the *42nd Street* Broadway Cast album with David Merrick's name replaced by Harry Warren's.

$\mathcal{T}$he last photo ever taken of Ira, January 1983. We moved a piano up to his bedroom and I gave him a private concert almost every day.

$\mathcal{A}$SCAP magazine cover—ASCAP devoted an entire issue of their magazine to Irving Berlin's centennial and hosted an all-star tribute on his birthday (May 11, 1988) at Carnegie Hall. I sang early in the show and then rushed over to do my own show at the Lyceum Theatre twelve blocks away.

A youthful photo of Cole Porter (and one of my favorites).

*C*ole Porter at work (circa 1939).

George Gershwin in a mid-1920s
sitting; taken around the time he
composed *Concerto in F.*

My favorite photo of George
Gershwin, one of the last ever taken.
A publicity shot from RKO Studios.

$\mathcal{A}$ self-caricature by George Gershwin. He mindlessly doodled on a pad when he talked on the phone and threw the drawings away after hanging up. His houseman saved all the drawings and presented them to Ira after George's death.

$\mathcal{F}$our photos of a young Oscar Levant taken by George Gershwin, 1936.

like René, who was always drunk and even smashed up one of the nurses' cars one night. But Lee recognized his artistic abilities, complimented him on them, and supported them, ignoring all of his flaws. Yet if a friend of hers had exhibited any of those flaws, especially drinking, she never would have spoken to that person again.

Unfortunately, with Lee, you never knew what you were going to get, empathy or rage, compassion or spite. Early in my relationship with Ira, I was concerned about his isolation from the world and about how Lee was preventing him from seeing people. Even though there were times when Ira clearly didn't want to see anyone, and he often expressed embarrassment at the thought of anyone seeing him in his weak state, he could be persuaded to have people over and was usually happy with the visits afterward. If a visitor came to the door, Ira would generally agree to see whoever it was just because he was so starved for company. Lee, however, strictly prevented him from seeing people. I went to a gerontologist named Dr. David Rubinfine to discuss what I could do to help Ira's situation. Dr. Rubinfine said that Ira needed company more than anything else. When I mentioned this to Lee, she was absolutely furious, as if seeing a doctor constituted a betrayal of some sort.

In my naiveté in those early days, I once let drop that I had heard that George didn't like Lee. "George not like me?" she retorted. "What a ridiculous thing to say!" Then she told me that toward the end of George's life, when he was ill, she had given him a box of chocolates and he had said to her, "You're a sweet woman."

"Would he have said that to somebody he didn't like?" she said. The fact that such a paltry example of affection was all she could summon in her defense shows how desperate she was to believe her own fantasy, but even that was misinformed. In the last three weeks of his life, George had been starting to lose it himself. What actually happened was that when Lee left after giving him the box of chocolates, he took them and kneaded them up into a viscous mass and started crying and spreading them all over his body in a rage. He was quite ill by that time. This incident is mentioned in *The Gershwin Years* without identifying Lee, but it was clearly a reference to her. So who knows what emotional baggage Lee was carrying in connection with George? After she started to go senile, about a year before her death, she blurted out in the middle of a card game, "You know, George was really the one. George was the one I truly loved."

Lee gave many signs of resenting Ira for not being George, like sending him upstairs if he was having too good a time. And although she expressed concern about my keeping Ira occupied and making him happy, if I paid *too* much attention to Ira, she got angry. In retrospect, I realize that some of our carryings on must have irritated Lee more than I could know at the time. For instance, after I got comfortable enough with Ira to be genuinely playful, I learned how to make him laugh uncontrollably at times. I would sit down at the piano and suddenly announce, "Okay, Ira, here's a medley of your least favorite songs." Then I would roll through a string of his earliest published songs, written before he had begun his major collaboration with George, like "The Sunshine Trail," "Hot Hindoo," "Singing in the Rain," and "Fascination" (the last two not to be confused with their more famous namesakes). Ira would begin groaning with a mock agony that rose in intensity as each new dreaded song made its appearance, until by the end of the medley he was convulsed by streams of laughter. By then I would be laughing just as hard, and we must have sounded like a couple of schoolboys sharing an uproarious private joke. It always warmed my heart to see Ira in such a state. The sound of our laughter as it echoed through the rest of the house, however, probably had a very different effect on Lee. She may have felt left out of the fun, reduced to running the house so Ira could play.

Toward the end of the time I worked there, after Ira went upstairs each day, it was obligatory that I then sit and talk to Lee. If I didn't, she invariably became upset. There were days when I couldn't stay for one reason or another, but I usually did anyway just to prevent a scene.

$\mathcal{A}$s long as I was working for Ira, though, I tried not to let Lee's crazy machinations get in my way—and there was plenty to take my mind off her. As Ira's health continued to diminish, he started giving me more responsibilities. He sent me out as his representative whenever somebody wanted to do a Gershwin show or concert. I became his eyes and ears to the outside world. Ira also had all kinds of interesting visitors in his living room: Andre Kostelanetz, Comden and Green, Vincente Minnelli, Groucho Marx, Angie Dickinson, character actor Paul Stewart, and Lawrence and Lee. (Jerome Lawrence and Robert E. Lee were a famous and successful team who wrote *The Night Thoreau Spent in Jail* and *Inherit the Wind* and quite a few radio plays.) And then there was Irving Lazar. After Lazar accelerated his career in the Gershwins' living room, he represented Ira for a number of major deals through the years, and later came to resent Ira's attorney, Ron Blanc, who had usurped his position and was starting to make deals for Ira instead. Lazar worked on Leonore to try to turn her against Ron and get rid of him so that Lazar could resume his place and continue to get his commissions on deals. I was largely responsible for preserving Ron's place in the Gershwin world, saving his job by subtly working on Lee myself—no easy feat. (My intercession came back to haunt me later, however, when Ron fired me on Lee's behalf. I realized that he was just doing his job and saving his own skin, but the irony of it stung a bit. Playing his lawyer role, he got pretty tough with me and I resented him for a while, feeling he at least could have been gentler about it. He made me sign a paper saying that I had no further claim to any money from the Gershwins; that was upsetting to me, although it wasn't money I wanted but involvement in looking after Ira's works. I later patched things up with Ron, who eventually was relieved of his duties.)

When Ira sold Warner Brothers his interest in the publishing rights to many of his songs for a very large amount of money, he gave Swifty a huge bonus just as a show of goodwill, even though Lazar had nothing to do with that deal. Lazar had a germ phobia and used to wear gloves at one time because he was afraid of picking up any sort of disease. Or maybe he just didn't want mere mortals to touch him and take away his power. He was always an imperious sort of man, full of self-importance, and when he came to the Gershwin home he never acknowledged anyone who didn't seem useful or powerful. On those occasions when I happened to answer the door, he invariably walked past me without saying anything. One day Leonore said, "Irving, Michael is a very important part of our house and you must be kind to him and acknowledge him when you come over here."

"Oh, I'm sorry, Lee," he said. The next time he came over and I answered the door, I said, "Hello, Irving."

Painfully and deliberately, before he came in, he said, "Nice to see you, Mark. Where's Ira?" Lee was standing in the living room. Pointing to me, she said, "Did you say hello to Michael?"

"Yes!" Lazar said, turning to me. "Didn't I just say, 'Nice to see you, Mike'?" Not adhering to a small requirement like that from Lee could have destroyed a long-term relationship.

When Alan Jay Lerner was represented by Lazar, he always had the sneaking suspicion that Swifty never read anything he wrote—for that matter, never read anything that anyone wrote. After Alan finished the screenplay of *Paint Your Wagon,* he glued all the pages together and sent the script to Lazar. About a week later, Lazar sent the script back with a note saying, "It's the greatest script I've ever read." The pages, needless to say, were still glued together.

Ira was always faithful to his longtime friends. He knew that Lazar was trying to make money off him, but he didn't really care. He just liked Irving. Ira also had a long friendship with Norman Granz, the legendary jazz promoter and producer and the founder of Verve Records. His records of numerous jazz greats from the 1940s and '50s are among the greatest jazz recordings of that era, known for their artistic integrity and high quality. Ira loved to tell stories about Granz because Norman was a very colorful man who was very principled and did and said exactly what he wanted. Ira told me that Granz once had an argument with somebody in London and then got on a plane and flew home to New York. On the way, Granz kept turning over the argument in his mind, thinking he should have said this and he should have said that. As soon as he landed in New York, he bought a ticket back to London, immediately returned, and said all the other things he wanted to say to this person, and then once again flew back to New York. Granz's adoration of Ira is evidenced by all the Gershwin recordings he made on the Verve label, including *Ella Fitzgerald Sings the George and Ira Gershwin Songbook* and Ella and Louis Armstrong doing songs from *Porgy and Bess.*

Ira's friendship with Granz always intrigued me, though, because Ira never liked jazz all that much. He said that jazz was too "egotistical." He even gave me all of the Art Tatum records that Norman had given to him because he just didn't "get" Art Tatum. He thought Tatum was a show-off and played too many notes! (George Gershwin *loved* Tatum, however, and once, after hearing him play variations on "Liza" for the better part of an hour, pleaded for more when Tatum finally let up.) One day, Ira and I were listening to another pianist playing Gershwin songs at a furious pace. "That man ought to be given a ticket for speeding," Ira said. When Ella Fitzgerald recorded "The Lorelei" for her *Gersh-*

win Songbook, she sang the German phonetically so that it sounded like "ja ja," the way it is spelled, rather than "ya ya." When Granz played the recording for Ira, he gently pointed this out to Granz, who went back into the studio and, according to the take sheets, did quite a few more takes before he got a performance he was happy with. That was a rather expensive retake. Ira told Norman that he didn't have to bother doing it over, but Granz, ever the perfectionist himself, insisted on rerecording it.

Perhaps because of episodes like that, Ira adored Norman. Besides, Granz had great taste and cultivated friendships with artists like Picasso (for whom he named his later label, Pablo), and his album covers were among the most elegant of any that had ever been produced at that time. Picasso made drawings of Ella for Verve, and Ella's original five-record Gershwin set contained drawings by Bernard Buffet, the originals of which hung in the entranceway to Leonore's bedroom. Toward the end of Ira's life, Norman came to see him and played him the tapes of a new Gershwin album that Ella had done with the André Previn Trio, a record that wasn't finally released until a couple of years after Ira's death. Sadly, Ella was not in her best voice at that point. As much as I admired Ella then, I could hear that she was already a bit past her prime. Norman was extremely anxious for Ira to enjoy it, and watched him carefully as he listened. Ira occasionally nodded and smiled. When it was finished, Norman said, "You like the record, Ira?"

"Oh, it's absolutely wonderful, Norman," he said. They exchanged a few more pleasantries and Norman left. Ira turned to me and said with a sigh, "I don't think I've been so exhausted in my life. There was Norman looking at me with those puppy dog eyes, wanting me to like it so much. It made me a nervous wreck." Ira confided that he didn't especially like the record, since Ella's voice had begun to decline, and he found the jazz piano backing less to his liking than previous LPs with Nelson Riddle's orchestrations.

I don't believe that Ira had a malevolent bone in his body, and I can't think of a better story to prove that than the one about Mel Tormé. As part of his act, Tormé did an endless Gershwin medley that tore some of the songs apart in ways that Ira could not stand. I had once met Tormé while working for Ira and he had asked me what Ira thought of his Gershwin medley. I was very gentle and said that in a couple of spots Ira felt that a few too many liberties were taken. Mel got red in the face and launched into a long soliloquy about how, despite his having single-handedly made "Blue Moon" a hit, Richard Rodgers did not like his version of it. Then he added, "I wrote one of the greatest Christmas songs of all time, called 'The Christmas Song.' Do you know it?" I told him I did.

"One day in the mail," he continued, "I got a recording by Hugo Winterhalter and His Orchestra entitled 'The Christmas Song Cha-Cha-Cha,' and how do you think I felt about it?"

"I don't know."

"I loved it! I loved it because I know that different interpretations of the same songs are what keep them alive. Richard Rodgers has no right to complain about my version of 'Blue Moon,' because I revived it and made it a big hit for him."

Maybe Mel had a point. Peggy Lee talked about how Rodgers was dissatisfied with her recording of "Lover" because it wasn't in waltz time and was sort of way out. But Ira would accept things that were a little different, unless they were completely off the mark and made him nuts. When I heard Tormé do his *Porgy and Bess* medley at the Hollywood Bowl some years later, he turned the end of it into a swing thing, as he usually does: "Bess, you is my woman now, you is you is you is be-ba-ba-be-ba." He went all over the place, and at the end of it he sang, "I'm talkin' 'bout Por-GEEEEE!" with "Porgy" sung in a very high pitch followed by a long, jazzy "Yeeeaaahhhhh!" It was pretty tasteless. When I saw Mel backstage after that concert, he said, "Somebody told me once that Ira Gershwin didn't like the way I sang his songs."

That was me, I thought to myself, but Mel had forgotten.

"Oh, man," he went on, "I would be so upset if I knew that Ira didn't like what I did."

The next day, I told Ira about the conversation with Tormé. "Do me a favor," Ira said. "Write him a letter and tell him that I love his work."

"But you *don't* love his work," I said.

"I don't care," he said. "Write him a letter and tell him I think he's terrific."

So I did.

Ira's kindness to Mel Tormé was not atypical. Certainly I was the recipient of his compassion on numerous occasions. Less than a couple of weeks after I started to work for him, the authors Lawrence and Lee and Billy Goldenberg came to play the score of a show they had written. I was in the other room listening and then I sort of crept over by the doorway. Ira stopped the proceedings and said, "Mike, for God's sake, come and sit down and listen. You're a part of this house now." He was always so concerned about others' thoughts and feelings—to his own disadvantage at times.

In September 1977, shortly after my twenty-first birthday, I was laid up in bed with mononucleosis. I had been working for Ira for only a couple of months, but he began calling me every day to see how I was, and each time he sang a line of a Gershwin song. The first day, I picked up the phone and said hello, and I heard Ira's voice singing, "They all laughed at Christopher Columbus / When he said the world was round." Each day he sang me the next couple of lines of that song. He would say, "Well, let's see, where did I leave off yesterday? Okay. 'They laughed at me wanting you. . . .' " When he had run through the lyric of "They All Laughed" in this fashion, he went into "My Ship." He sang a whole sequence of songs to me until I got better, and I can't tell you how loved that made me feel during a time when I was physically very low.

The great harmonica master Larry Adler told Max Wilk about the time he was preparing to embark on his first concert tour with the dancer Paul Draper. Larry was nervous about the prospect and as he was getting ready to leave for his first engagement in Denver, the doorbell rang. Ira, who lived nearby, had brought him a going-away present of some formal dresswear: shirts, collars, studs, vests, and bow ties. "Larry," Ira said, "these belonged to George. You and he wore the same sizes, so I thought they might bring you some luck tonight." Adler concluded that Ira must be some sort of angel, an idea I'd have to agree with.

$\mathcal{E}$ VEN before I went to work for Ira, he had begun to be out of touch with the modern world and with the recent developments in the entertainment business. He couldn't bear to listen to any of the popular music that was on the radio (of course, neither could I), although he did not share the anger that most other songwriters of his generation carried. Yip Harburg, the great lyricist who had written the words for "April in Paris," "Over the Rainbow," and the classic Depression song "Brother, Can You Spare a Dime?," and who was a childhood friend of Ira's, once gave a lecture at UCLA on the craft of lyric writing. His audience was a group of aspiring songwriters, eager to hear tips from one of the great masters, but by the end of the evening Yip had alienated every single one of them. When he started to talk about contemporary lyrics, he suddenly became filled with venom and a mean sort of resentment. Everything he had said that was charming and sweet was destroyed by the rancor he produced in the last forty minutes of his talk. Although the year was 1978, Yip was still ranting until he became red in the face about the Beatles and the damage they had done with their "bad" lyrics. He was being filmed for a segment that *60 Minutes* was doing on him, but they used very little of that lecture in the finished piece. Yip concluded his remarks and walked to the side of the room where a bunch of us were standing watching him. "I got so worked up," he said with a puzzled look. "What did I say? Was it good?"

I think we were all too embarrassed for him to tell him how destructive he had been. Later that night, we went to dinner and Yip allowed as how "I've Got You Under My Skin" was the kind of lyric that could only have been written by a homosexual, referring to Cole Porter. I could never figure out what it was about that lyric that made Yip say that. Maybe he was still in a bad mood after his talk. Most if not all of the great popular songwriters felt threatened by the new sounds of rock 'n' roll and the new openness about sex, gay and straight, that went with it in the 1960s. The overwhelming success of rock had pushed them out of the picture, and they were angry and bitter about it. Harry Warren essentially stopped working in the late 1950s, writing only a title song for a film in 1962 and one more in '68, and then it was all over. The melodies still flowed and he worked faithfully in his studio writing them down. But who cared? Three Oscars or no, he was a has-been. The arranger and composer George Bassman is another example. Bassman started in the music business at an early age and went on to orchestrate and compose for hundreds of films. But he literally quit the business after a score he had written in the early '70s was thrown out and replaced by a score created by a rock band.

Ira wasn't like that. He looked at a song objectively and although he might say he didn't think it was particularly well crafted, he didn't get upset about it or feel personally displaced by its presence. After *My One and Only* opened in Boston, I took an audiocassette I had made of it for Ira to hear. He listened to the sustained applause on the cassette—wild cheers at the end of a show still needing work but satisfying an audience starved for "good" music—and started laughing. I asked him what he was laughing about.

"Don't those people know that I wrote those songs over forty years ago?" he blurted out with a big grin, as if he were putting one over on them. He felt it was just luck that in his old age he was making a comfortable living from songs he had written for the moment for mindless stage shows with creaky plots and with no thought about longevity. He never got over the fact that he was so handsomely supported by his earlier work. He was delighted about it, but also amazed.

Lauren Bacall was a huge fan of Stephen Sondheim, and she came over to the house one day and asked Ira if he had heard *Sweeney Todd*. He hadn't, and he asked me to get the record. Ira listened to it and recognized the brilliance of Sondheim's craft. However, he felt that the general subject matter was unsavory and he didn't like the idea of creating a work based on that source material. To me, that reaction was one sign of his unsurprising, old school thinking. Perhaps because Bacall had said that *Sweeney Todd* in her estimation resembled an opera more than a Broadway musical, Ira compared it to *Porgy and Bess* and asked me if Sondheim had done his own orchestrations. I told him he hadn't. "Then it's not really an opera," he said. "George worked for eight months on just the orchestration of *Porgy*. Unless a composer orchestrates it himself, it's not a true opera."

I've been told by other people that Ira was not Sondheim's favorite lyricist and that Ira knew this, so that may have colored Ira's feelings about Sondheim, even though he had great admiration for his craft. I thought Ira would appreciate the score from Sondheim's *Follies* because it was a pastiche of '20s and '30s musical comedy numbers. I played him "The God Why Don't You Love Me Blues," the lyric of which goes, "I've got the God why don't you love me? Oh, you do? I'll see you later blues." It's a very wordy song, sung at a furious tempo, and you have to listen very carefully, as you do with many Sondheim lyrics, to get every joke and nuance. Ira listened to it with great attention. "Sondheim is undeniably brilliant," he said, "but he goes too far. You're not going to hear all of that in the theater. Take my song 'I've Got the You-Don't-Know-the-Half-of-It-Dearie Blues.' That song works better because you get all the jokes, and you can understand all the lyrics."

J could never figure out exactly what was wrong with Ira, why he always seemed so sickly. (Remember that old joke? "He's got Gok's disease." "What's Gok's disease?" "God only knows.") I had heard that Ira had heart trouble and had previously had Bell's palsy, along with a succession of medical problems, some of which sounded like sheer hypochondria to me. From what I could see, the extremely sedentary life he led had simply caught up with him. He didn't like to exercise. In fact, he didn't like to do much of anything, and his body eventually gave out. His nurse had to fight with him to go outside and take a ten-minute walk, which never lasted ten minutes.

The Gershwins had a very famous Beverly Hills doctor—let's just call him Dr. Feelrich—who was as big a quack as I've ever met. An MCA executive who had died a number of years before had been a patient of his, giving rise to talk about negligence and misprescribing drugs. This doctor would come to the house, pat Lee's hand, and say, "Ira's going to be fine." He told her that everything was all right and just to give Ira the various pills he prescribed, including, at one point, placebos. Ira became furious when he found out he'd been taking sugar pills, feeling foolish and duped. He was constantly saying, and with good reason, "My doctor doesn't understand me." But Lee always said, "Oh, Ira, you have the best doctor in the world. How can you say he doesn't understand you?"

One day I asked Lee if she didn't think it would be worthwhile to get a second opinion. "Why should I get a second opinion," she said, "when we have the world's greatest doctor?" That was the end of it. Dr. Feelrich kept Ira so doped up that Ira started to lose it altogether. His mental acuity was going and he was bent over all the time. Just when I thought Ira was finally losing his senses, Lee put him in the hospital. When they changed his medication, his condition reversed and he came out of it fine; Ira's decline had essentially been a reaction to overmedication. We have to remember that Ira came from a generation, which never worried about exercise or diet, and for whom taking pills was the answer to every malady. Lee said that at one time in the '50s, they had all kinds of pills on the coffee table, and any time you felt bad you just took a pill. We're not talking about vitamins here; they were what are now considered dangerous drugs—amphetamines and barbiturates. They were readily available then, and still were in the '70s, when I observed that Lee could call up Schwab's Pharmacy and order anything she wanted—one hundred Valium, two hundred Inderol—and they would make a quick call to Dr. Feelrich's office and then deliver the drugs.

Certain of Ira's medications were known as "triplicate form" drugs.

To get them in California you have to present a form made out with two carbons, one of which goes to an office in Sacramento where they monitor not only the patients using the drugs but also the physicians prescribing them. Toward the end, Ira was on some triplicate form drugs, and one day Lee tried to order more over the phone. There was a new person in the pharmacy who told her they couldn't deliver them without a new triplicate form. With the British accent she sometimes liked to affect, Lee said, "This is Mrs. *Gehrsh-win.*" She asked for the person who used to send her pills from the pharmacy. The new person said he didn't work there anymore. "Well, this is Mrs. *Gehrsh-win,*" she said again, "and I insist that you call my doctor." The pharmacist explained that by law he couldn't do that.

"Well," she screamed into the receiver, "you can sit on my face!" And she slammed it down in a rage.

I had never heard Lee speak that way. I realized later that she was in a rage because she was stealing Ira's pills and must have become totally dependent on them. In the course of a month, three bottles of a triplicate form drug had been sent over to Ira's house. She was calling Schwab's and they were sending them over, no questions asked. Dr. Feelrich would presign the forms with instructions to his assistant to fill in the pertinent information and send the form on its way when a call came in from the pharmacy. Then someone in Sacramento, where the forms were filed, must have said, "Hey, why are three bottles of this drug going to this man's home in one month?" The doctor called up Lee and started screaming at her that she was going to get him in a lot of trouble. He threatened to cut her off. Lee was terrified and babbled, "We're going to lose our wonderful doctor!" The maid routinely found pills on Leonore's pillow because she took them in the middle of the night and her hands shook so badly that the pills went all over.

The whole matter was resolved in typical Lee Gershwin fashion, which is to say that she fired two of the three nurses. At that time Ira had round-the-clock nursing, and Lee concocted some story that the nurses had been stealing pills, when in fact she was taking them. But the cover story appeased everybody. The nurses were fired and things went on as they always had, with Lee now calling the doctor's office to get whatever she wanted. I thought it was foolish on the doctor's part, but Lee was very important to him and had said that she was leaving a third of her estate to his heart institute when she died. He ended up getting a lot less than that, but he profited nicely nonetheless. In any event, he was well aware of her intention and knew how to handle his clientele.

Toward the end, Ira was in terrible shape. He had stopped coming downstairs and wouldn't even get out of bed. When he behaved like this for over a week, Lee called the doctor, who came over and looked at Ira. To my great surprise, he came downstairs and announced, "Ira's fine. He'll be coming down in a couple more days."

"How?" I asked. "What's going to change?"

He looked shocked and insulted that I had questioned him. After all, he was just saying what Lee wanted to hear. As soon as he left, she turned to me with a smile. "Isn't he wonderful? He says Ira's going to be fine in a couple of days." She accepted that obvious fiction because she wanted to believe it. And this time, Ira never did get better and never came downstairs again. But he didn't *want* to come downstairs anymore. He wanted to stay in bed. Ira frequently asked to have the drapes drawn because he didn't want to see the sunlight, so Lee brought in flowers to brighten up his room. Angie Dickinson, one of the few people he was always happy to see, brought beautiful silk flowers for his room, although her shining presence was even more of a boon. But nothing could rouse Ira from his torpor for long. He lay in bed, looked at the ceiling, and said, "Why did you do this to me, God? Why me?" It was as if he had no idea why he was in bed like that—and perhaps he *had* no idea.

Lee found little ways to torment him. Ira loved chocolates, but the doctor said that chocolate wasn't good for him, and so Lee saw to it that he couldn't have chocolate. I thought, The guy's in bed, dying—what's the difference? June Levant used to give me chocolates, whispering, "Here, this is for Ira. Slip him a Hershey bar." So I smuggled chocolate into his bedroom when Lee wasn't around. He got chocolate stains all over the pillow, but luckily Lee never noticed.

Ira had gone into the hospital a couple of times with heart problems. He had one heart attack that I recall, after which his doctor went to see him. Ira was asleep so the doctor went away and when Ira woke up later, he came in again. "Ira, I was in to see you earlier," he said, "but I didn't have the heart to wake you."

"Imagine," Ira said. "The world's greatest heart specialist didn't have the heart to wake me!" The doc just gave him a blank stare. His manner was more graveside than bedside.

At one point Ira said to me, "I've had a very bad life."

"How can you say that?" I said. "You've had a wonderful life. The last couple of years haven't been good, but all in all you've had a *great* life."

And he said, "I'd trade it all for your youth." That was exactly what I didn't want to hear.

*B*ECAUSE of a peculiar brilliance that gave Leonore the ability to look at people and assess what made them tick, she knew how to push people's buttons. She was a specialist at manipulation who could immediately discover your weakness and never hesitated to go for it. One day, she launched into a long recitative about how her life used to be filled with music and how she never got to hear it anymore, ending by asking me to play the piano for her. I was not feeling great that day and I said, "Would you mind if I played for you tomorrow?" She took it as another betrayal and was on the verge of firing me for refusing to play the piano for her. I never heard the end of that. It became a virtual nightmare that continued for the rest of the time Ira was alive. At least once or twice a week, she said, "Oh, you won't play the piano for me. You won't do *anything* for me! All you care about is Ira."

She had genuine fits of anger about it and there was nothing I could do. One day when she made her usual complaint, I pointed out that I had played the piano for her two days ago.

"You only did that out of obligation, because you *really* didn't want to," she said.

"Okay," I said, "I'll play the piano for you now. I want to."

"No," she said, "I don't want you to play the piano now."

"All right," I said, "then I won't play the piano now."

"You see? You only care about Ira."

"First you want me to play the piano, and then you *don't* want me to play the piano," I said angrily. "Which is it?"

"I don't know!"

It was that kind of infuriating behavior that was so hard to endure. How did Ira manage it? I was always walking on eggshells, except that Ira needed me and she knew that she needed me for Ira's sake. Things were never the same after the piano incident. My growing independence coupled with my waning desire to fight with Lee turned what had been a smooth and joyful routine into an emotional roller coaster. I stopped coming by on a daily basis because I couldn't stand the confrontations with Lee. She would try to coax me back by leaving messages on my answering machine—guilt-inducing calls about how much Ira needed me, how he didn't get out of bed that day. Why couldn't I think of Ira and swallow my pride? That was a good question and, of course, I always returned as long as Ira was alive. Leonore's game-playing aside, it was not always easy to be with Ira toward the end, either. Once when I was trying—a bit too idealistically, no doubt—to help him change his attitude to a positive one, he turned to me and said, "You die your way and I'll die mine."

I did start to think seriously about leaving the Gershwins during this prolonged conflict with Lee, but I knew that when Ira passed on, it was inevitable that I would leave anyway, so I chose to hang on. I couldn't bear the thought of abandoning Ira, and Lee knew it. Toward the end of Ira's life, I asked him if he was concerned about what was going to happen to his work after he was gone. He was taken aback that I had brought it up, because he didn't like to think about death. He didn't believe in God or an afterlife and he never wanted to face that inevitability. But he did acknowledge that he was concerned about what was going to happen, that there wasn't anybody in the family he felt was capable of taking care of his estate. He altered his will to name Bob Kimball and me as Literary Consultants, responsible for overseeing and approving any presentation of Ira's works.

I was flattered because at that point in my life, my major concern was tending to Ira and his work. By the time he died, I had spent six years and one month not only as a companion but also as an archivist and historian of his material and I saw my future in that role rather than as a performer. I was very happy to do that for Ira because I felt that I owed it to him for the great joy and fulfillment he had given me just by allowing me to spend so much time with him. Those six years had only strengthened my love for him and his work. In spite of all the distractions, I still found it thrilling to be there with him.

Although none of what I am about to say was clear to me at the time, I have no doubt about it now. In many ways, Ira gave me my career. Through Ira, my whole world opened up and immutably changed. He not only crystallized my sense of who I was trying to become, but he also provided me with the connections, the advice, and the wherewithal to develop into that person. It's always hard to imagine what any part of our lives would be like if certain events had never happened or certain people had never crossed our paths. But without Ira, I wonder how I would have met all the other songwriters I've been so fortunate to come to know. One songwriter led to another, but the lineage can always be traced back to Ira, starting with Comden and Green, Harry Warren, Burton Lane, and Arthur Schwartz. So many people that I have encountered through the years were open to me simply because of my association with Ira—either friends of his or fans of the Gershwins who became interested in me and pursued me because of that association. My early acknowledgment as an interpreter of popular song came from Ira, then from his contemporaries and friends who spread the word. When I came to New York to make my debut at the Algonquin, Comden and Green immediately came to see me perform. Then Burton Lane came by, and then all of their friends started coming—Charles Strouse, Leonard Bernstein, Stephen Sondheim. So it all goes back to Ira. I carry so much of him with me all the time that inevitably I think about him every day in some way or another. It seems rather peculiar to me that my life is so centered around someone who is so far away from me now in some ways, yet ever present in another.

Long after I saw him for the last time, I continue to see so much of myself in Ira. His values, his appreciation of the finer things of life—of food, music, art, humor—are all expressed in his songs, which have become part of my daily awareness. Sometimes, in fact, his sensitivity and literacy make me feel rather inadequate, as though I've missed out by not knowing all that he knows. As I once wrote in my diary: What does he know? He knows the secrets of the universe. He has knowledge of the ages. He's an old soul and yet in this life, he has been "put to sleep like Rip Van Winkle," to quote "Bidin' My Time."

Carol Dryer, the psychic, had told me in a session shortly before Ira died to be prepared for hard times with Leonore. She had also warned me to expect many experiences that I would not be certain were real because my reality would be changing drastically during this period. In fact, I began to feel my reality changing almost immediately. I had rented a new apartment the day before Ira died. And the next day, when his death was announced, my new landlord called me on the phone.

"I heard your boss died," he said matter-of-factly. "You gonna be able to pay your rent now?"

chapter 4

FOR ME, FOR YOU, FOR EVERMORE

$\mathcal{I}$ had been preparing myself for the eventuality, the inevitability, of Ira's death for some time before the end. Through the deaths of some of my own relatives, I had already learned to be prepared for it, but I still felt a deep sense of loss. After you've watched someone you care about wasting away in a hospital or in their own bed for weeks and months, it may seem like a relief in some ways when they die, but it is still devastating. Rosemary Clooney, who lived next door to the Gershwins, woke me up with a phone call about seven in the morning and said, "Honey, there's an ambulance outside their house." Occasionally, ambulances would go over to Ira's because he had had a pain in his chest, so I was concerned but not overly. "What should I do?" I asked.

"I'll call you back," she said. About twenty minutes later, Rosemary called me back. "Honey," she said, "Ira's dead."

"How do you know?"

She said that Dante, her live-in mate, had gone next door when she saw two men leaving the house, and they told him that Ira had died. I called Ron Blanc to tell him and then I went over to the house. Leonore was sitting there. "Hello, darling," she said. "What are you doing here?"

"I heard," I said.

"Yes?" she said. "How did you know?"

"Rosemary heard the ambulance and called me." I hugged her and everybody started crying.

"Lee," I said, "I'm so sorry for all the problems we've had with each other." It had been a particularly bad couple of weeks between us. Then she said, "Come up and see Ira. I want you to say goodbye to him." I felt it would be very upsetting for me to look at Ira's dead body, and I had no desire to. But she insisted, so I went upstairs. Ira was still sitting in a chair with his head off to the side. He had gotten up early in the morning, was watching TV, and had literally just closed his eyes and drifted away, which was a blessing considering how scared he was of death. When the nurse checked on him a half hour later, he had already passed on. Oscar Levant, who spent his whole life terrified of death, had a similar passing; he closed his eyes and went to sleep. He probably expended more energy over his fear of death than over anything else. Think of what he could have done with all that energy!

"Kiss Ira," Lee said. I looked at her. "Go give Ira a kiss." She was holding her emotions in check, just as she had refused to display any feelings when George died. I gave Ira a kiss on the forehead. In my mind I could hear Lee's voice saying, "He had a very full life—a wonderful life. We mustn't be sad for him."

Then we went back downstairs and called the Groman Mortuary to come and pick up Ira's body. The Gromans lived on the same block, a couple of houses down, but after several hours the undertakers still hadn't come. I joked that we should have just gone across the street, knocked on the door and said, "Hey, are you going to come and get him or what?" How many bodies did they have to pick up that morning, anyway? Ron Blanc had arrived by that time and so had Paul Stewart, a character actor who was a close friend of Ira's, along with his wife, Peg.

"What did Ira say was his favorite piece of music written by George?" Lee asked.

"One of the themes from the Concerto in F," I said.

"I want you to play that on the piano as they carry his body out, dear," she said.

I couldn't *believe* that Lee and I were going to go into this particular dance again. "I'm really not in any condition to," I said. "I just don't feel like doing that."

In my grief for Ira, I did not feel up to performing, and, besides, she made it all seem like just an empty ritual.

"Are you going to deny a grieving widow her request?" Lee said. Okay, I thought, just shut up and do it. Then Lee said, "Nobody is to look at Ira's body when they take it away."

By the time the undertakers arrived, they found it was easier to carry him downstairs in the chair he had died in. As they were doing so, Lee had me ready at the piano. "Okay," she said. As they carried his body, I played that theme from the concerto. At one point, I looked up from the keyboard and Lee snapped, "Don't look!"

Ira's death was a huge blow to Lee, even though on some level she felt relieved that she could travel again. We all flew east to inter Ira's body in the Gershwin family mausoleum at Westchester Hills Cemetery in Hastings-on-Hudson, New York, where Billy Rose and Judy Holliday are also buried. It was the first time I had seen the mausoleum, a lovely granite structure with bronze doors, stained glass window, and marble interior and the name GEORGE GERSHWIN on the outside. (Lee later spoke of obliterating George's first name so that only the GERSHWIN would remain, reflecting the fact that it was a family plot, but fortunately this was never done.) This sad occasion prompted an argument between Leonore and Ira's sister, Frankie, over who was going to occupy the last spot in the crypt. There were only six places, which meant that after Morris and Rose Gershwin, George, Ira, and Arthur, there was one spot left. Leonore was quite adamant about being buried in the family crypt. "But Lee," Frankie said with understandable exasperation, "that was *my* spot." They had quite a to-do about it, until finally Frankie gave in. "You know, Lee," she said, "if it's that important to you, it's yours." To paraphrase Ira's lyric, it was a case of "Ha, ha, ha—who's got the last plot now?" As it turned out, when Lee died her remains were cremated and so there's still room for Frankie after all.

When we returned to Los Angeles, Lee proceeded to throw away Ira's things, either because she didn't want other people to see them or just because she felt like doing it. Many of his sketches and drawings went into the wastebasket. I was able to retrieve one sketch that I couldn't bear to see thrown away. Before giving his clothes away to the local charity thrift shop, she insisted on cutting out all the labels that said "Made for Ira Gershwin." Fortunately, not all of them were cut out and Rosemary Clooney was able to buy back many of his things, making me a present of a tailcoat with Ira's name still sewn on. Ira still had a couple of boxes of his book, *Lyrics on Several Occasions,* remaindered copies of the first edition that he had bought from the publisher. He had refused to do a book tour or promote it in any way, so it hadn't been especially successful. Lee wanted to have those destroyed. Ira had also bought all the remaindered copies of the English edition of the book, which had been published in 1981 and had been remaindered a short time later. Boxes of them had recently arrived at customs and were waiting somewhere to be picked up, and Lee ordered them destroyed, too.

"Why are you destroying all these books?" I asked.

"Because I want it to be a rare book," she said. "We can't have all these copies floating around." She did save some of the copies, but most of them were trashed. I didn't quite follow her logic. The point of having a rare book is that you hold back some extra copies to sell, but Lee was never concerned about money. She just wanted it to be rare.

I kept coming over to the house because there were plenty of materials to continue to organize and collate. I was also preparing for publication the very first *Ira* Gershwin songbook. Lee's usual routine was to leave the house about a quarter to one. She would go to Nate & Al's for lunch, as she did every day of her life. Then she would go shopping and come back with shrimp for the cats. She would sit in the music room in one of the swivel chairs and say, "What have you got for me today?" I realized that she now expected me to fulfill for *her* the role I had been playing with Ira. Particularly in the last couple of years of Ira's life, it had become my job to find something every day to occupy Ira and keep him happy, whether it was playing an unusual song on the piano upstairs or finding a weird lyric or recording or book or *something.* Now that Ira was gone, Lee apparently expected me to start doing the same for her.

At the time, I was finishing up the editing of Ira's songbook for

Warner Brothers Music. "Lee," I said, "I have to finish this book. I have a deadline to meet."

She was very angry about that, and I began to get the sense that I might not be staying on there indefinitely. But the event that actually precipitated my leaving Lee's employ derived from a tribute to Ira that had been planned at Cal State L.A. some months before Ira died. Cal State wanted to create an Ira Gershwin Scholarship and although Ira was reluctant about having anything established in his name, he had acquiesced because it was for college music students and he recognized the good it would do. Leonore made a sizable donation to the organization. The tribute was slated for November 1983 and by the time Ira died in August, I had already gotten John Bubbles of the famous black vaudeville team of Buck and Bubbles to agree to appear and sing "It Ain't Necessarily So." John was the original Sportin' Life in *Porgy and Bess* and I had come to know him fairly well in the last few years of his life. Even though he was confined to a wheelchair after several strokes, he wanted to sing that song for Ira. Gogi Grant was going to sing "The Man I Love" as she had done for the soundtrack of *The Helen Morgan Story*. The tribute was to be held in a huge banquet room upstairs in the Dorothy Chandler Pavilion in downtown L.A.

The trouble arose from an unexpected quarter. Warren Lyons had been a friend of Leonore and Ira's for many years. His father was Leonard Lyons, the columnist, and his brother is Jeffrey Lyons, the movie critic. Since Ira's death, Warren had wanted to produce a memorial tribute for him and became very upset about the fact that this other event had now become a memorial instead of just a concert. He told Leonore that it was going to be terrible and that she should not permit it to happen. So three days before the concert, Lee announced that it had to be stopped. She simply said, "This must not go on."

"It's too late to stop it," I said, "because it's sold out, and everyone is slated to appear."

"Well, I don't want it to happen, dear," she said. "This is wrong."

"If it's wrong," I said, "why did you make a donation to the charity? And why did you wait until three days before the event to make this decision?"

"Because it's my prerogative," she said, "and I don't want it to go on. Besides, I'll give everybody their money back."

"Lee, they can't do that," I said. "It would look terrible for the university and all the people who have committed to appear."

"Then *you* can't participate in it," she said.

"If I pull out," I reasoned, "John Bubbles will pull out and so will Gogi. Nobody will appear if I pull out because I got them all to agree in the first place."

"Well," she said in a huff, "what's more important, that stupid dinner or me?"

"That's not a fair choice."

"You're going to have to make a decision, Michael. If you insist on continuing with this tribute, you're fired."

She never directly acknowledged that Warren had said that the memorial was going to be a failure or that it conflicted with his own plans. In fact, prior to that time, she had been saying that she didn't want Warren to do a memorial. He may have been upset that she was stalling him and used the other concert as a way to galvanize her support for him.

It was one of her typical flip-flops, like the time we went to see the movie version of Sondheim's *A Little Night Music*. After we saw it, someone asked her what she thought of the movie. "I loved it," she said. Two minutes later, another person she was talking to said that he hated the film. Without blinking, Lee said, "So did I."

The day after our blow-up about the tribute to Ira, I got a call from Ron Blanc. "I hate to do this," he said, "but Lee says if you continue with this tribute, you're fired."

And that was it. I was fired. The next call from Ron was the one asking me to repay the car loan with interest.

The tribute did go on, though. I'm happy to say that today there is a scholarship in the name of Ira Gershwin at Cal State L.A.—the scholarship that cost me my job! In my more ironic moments I like to think of it as the Michael Feinstein Memorial Scholarship. The kicker is that Warren Lyons never did a memorial tribute to Ira. I ran into him several times and he always acted mystified at my cool behavior toward him, although I'm certain he knew exactly what had happened. In any event, I tried to reestablish contact with Lee after the concert. I thought maybe her anger would pass as it had before, but it didn't. A day before Thanksgiving, she dropped the ax. My world had turned upside down just as precipitously as it had seemed to soar when I was introduced to Lee and started working for Ira. I didn't know what to do. I kept hoping that things would change, but it turned out to be wishful thinking.

In a codicil to his will dated January 21, 1983, Ira appointed Lee executrix of his will; in the event of her death, his attorney Ron Blanc was named executor. Bob Kimball and I were named Literary Consultants, with the responsibility to approve all decisions regarding the presentation of Ira's musical and literary work. Ira expressly stated that his Executor or Trustee "shall not proceed to authorize a presentation unless each such consultant has determined, in his sole discretion, that the presentation will protect the artistic integrity of my work." But there was also a clause in Ira's will, as in Leonore's, that, for tax purposes, if Leonore survived Ira by six months, she would inherit everything in his estate. There was no question that Ron Blanc, Bob Kimball, and I would still be involved because that was also in Lee's will. However, six months after Ira's death, I learned that Lee had changed her will and I was out of it. Nobody, least of all Ira, dreamed that she would blatantly go against his wishes, but by the time Ira was gone, Lee was ruled by her own sort of skewed logic and no longer cared about what his wishes had been. She used to say, "Ira would have wanted it this way." But that frequently had no bearing on reality. She had her own agenda which no one could ever quite figure out. Poor Lee. In a way, I think she just wanted to be loved; yet she couldn't love herself and that made it hard for others to love her. By the end of her life, she had succeeded in pushing away many of the people who had been close to her. Her pessimism had caught up with her like a self-fulfilling prophecy. For Leonore, everything in the world was always awful—at least, everything other than people and places *she* frequented. According to Lee, there was only one good Chinese restaurant, the Mandarin; Nate & Al's was the *only* delicatessen. You couldn't get a good cook. The quality of merchandise was terrible. Everything was bad—bad, bad, bad. That's why she insisted on spending more money for things—it was the only way she believed she could get the best quality. Ironically, as her mental faculties began to deteriorate, she appeared to be more at peace, probably because many of those demons disappeared along with the synapses in her brain.

When my first album came out in 1985, consisting entirely of Gershwin songs, I sent a copy to Lee, but I never heard from her. I finally just gave up. By that time I had started performing and was beginning to develop a following. I realized that if I had not left Lee's employ, none of that would have happened. I would probably still be burying my head in musty boxes of papers and old transcription discs.

After I played on Broadway in 1988, I was approached to appear on a pilot for an ABC television show called *Omnibus,* which was to be a new edition of the old Alistair Cooke series. The producer was a wonderfully bright woman named Susan Lester. The show consisted of four segments featuring spokespersons for different aspects of the arts. In one segment, Peter Sellars talked about theater; in another, David Hockney discussed painting; Dudley Moore discussed Gilbert and Sullivan; and for the final segment, Susan Lester asked me to talk about Ira Gershwin. It was a wonderful concept for a program, but it was a little too erudite—or so thought the network execs; as a result, the show didn't make it. However, Leonore happened to be watching that program and saw my tribute to Ira and his lyrics. To my surprise she sent me a telegram saying, "I can't thank you enough for what you've done, and I long to see you."

A couple days later I got an invitation to attend a tribute to George and Ira at the Library of Congress. They had minted a Congressional gold medal for the Gershwins, a copy of which I still have. (This was not the Congressional Medal of Honor, for which regulations are established by the armed services. Although earlier recipients of the gold medal, which is administered solely by Congress, were mainly military and naval heroes from George Washington to Admiral Rickover, it had been awarded in recent years to entertainment and cultural figures such as George M. Cohan, Irving Berlin, Walt Disney, Marian Anderson, Roy Wilkins, and Elie Wiesel. Nonetheless, only 111 such medals had been approved in more than 200 years prior to the Gershwins'.)

At the dinner, the first thing I noticed about Lee was that she had become considerably more fragile and forgetful and she occasionally talked as though Ira were still with us. But she also went on about how much Ira loved me, reminding me that he used to refer to me when speaking to Lee as "our darling boy." A very tearful reunion ensued because of all that had gone on between us. Underlying my frustration and anger was a feeling of real devotion to Lee, which now came to the surface. Even though I was still out of the picture legally, from that point until the end of her life, she was always saying to Bob Kimball and Ron Blanc, "Ask Michael. Michael knows about everything. You must involve him."

The Librarian of Congress was there and people were getting up and saying appropriate things about the Gershwins and the extraordinary honor being paid to them. Then Ron Blanc asked me to say something, so I stood up. "A lot has happened for all of us in the last several years," I began, "but for me the only thing that matters is the present moment. It's wonderful to be here, and I'd like to make a toast to Leonore."

She hugged me and our relationship improved markedly from that time on. I can't say for certain whether her apparent change of heart stemmed from guilt about the way she had treated me or whether she had simply begun to lose her memory. Yet although I was out of touch with Lee for several years, I've been told by those who were still close to her then that she had perceived, just as I had, that the separation was a great blessing in disguise, and that she was pleased I had been more or less forced to develop another set of talents in the outside world. I'm told that she kept track of my fledgling career and was aware of my efforts to preserve the legacy of George and Ira even before my appearance on *Omnibus* and had been moved by what I was doing. On the most positive level, it's possible that she both forgave and forgot.

Still, it was disturbing when I or somebody else asked Lee a question and she would say, "Ask Ira, dear." Out of courtesy, everybody around her pretended that she wasn't becoming senile, and much of the time she acted perfectly normal and rational, so it was easy to forget if you chose to. Some of Lee's mental lapses could also have been caused by all the pills she had taken. When Ira died, she almost overdosed on barbiturates; on the day of his funeral, she was completely out of it, talking but not making much sense. I began going to visit her after our reunion at the dinner in Washington, and one day soon afterwards, she came downstairs and said, "I saw Jeanette MacDonald on television last night and she was singing a Gershwin song." Jeanette MacDonald never sang a Gershwin song in a movie. She was in a 1925 Broadway show called *Tip-Toes,* but never in a movie with Gershwin songs. What Lee was saying simply was not possible. I attributed that vision to the pills.

Some time after our reconciliation, Lee approached me about doing an album of unpublished Gershwin songs. Leonore and Bob Kimball had decided to start a recording company to cover the Ira Gershwin side of the fence, since the George Gershwin Estate and the Ira Gershwin Estate are two very separate camps. Lee's company was called Roxbury Recordings and was established by Lee with Bob Kimball and the Library of Congress for the purpose of recording Gershwin shows. It was to be bankrolled, for the most part, by Lee herself. The only non-show record planned for their original series of six recordings was to be an album of me singing unpublished Gershwin songs.

I was thrilled to do it because I had spent so much of my time with Ira going over his unpublished material. I knew it intimately, could separate the wheat from the chaff, and had a pretty good idea of how to present the songs in their best light. Lee stressed to me that money was no object and that she just wanted the album done right. She became very generous with her money in the last years. She had always loved to spend it, but now she began to break previous records for purchasing Gershwin manuscripts. (To her credit, Lee was among the first to realize that the value of George Gershwin manuscripts was rising dramatically. She actively pursued them at auction to capture as many as she could for donation to the Library of Congress. If in the process she helped push up the market value of all autographed Gershwin materials, she also salvaged some priceless items for the Library.) Needless to say, with Lee's full backing, recording the unpublished songs was a dream project for me—a chance to repay Lee and Ira for all their kindness as well as to put to use all that I had learned at Ira's feet.

Tommy Krasker, who served as an assistant to Bob Kimball, started working with me on the selection of songs and how the material would be orchestrated. I was given carte blanche; all the Roxbury recordings were to be released by Nonesuch Records, where I had helped steer the project. But by the time I was ready to start recording some months later, Leonore had become very fragile, both emotionally and physically.

Unfortunately, Leonore died just before I started recording. By then her nephew, Mike Strunsky, was on the scene. Mike had always been Lee's favorite nephew, and she had named him trustee of her estate. Initially I was delighted when I heard that Mike was named executor, because I had seen him often at Lee and Ira's home and had always found him to be a warm and kind individual and had gotten on very well with him. However, as we worked together on the recording project, conflicts arose regarding our conceptions of how the album should be created. What subsequently transpired is something that, in retrospect, both Mike and I deeply regret. We have since resolved the differences that came to the fore during the recording of the unpublished songs. But although I've come to terms with the events that ensued, at the time they were deeply disturbing to me.

Many of the problems that came up probably could have been resolved at the outset if I'd had a contract, but it hadn't occurred to me to ask for one. Nobody at the time could have imagined we would end up at loggerheads. The producer of the recording was John McClure, who has a legendary reputation, having produced 300 recordings with the likes of Leonard Bernstein and Igor Stravinsky. I met McClure two days before the recording and found him to be a rather pleasant fellow. I knew his reputation—he had also produced the first recording in the Roxbury series—and I wasn't at all concerned about working with him. But when we got into the studio, the first thing I noticed was that McClure didn't seem completely focused on the sessions. We had set aside six days of recording with the last day, Saturday, left optional if we needed it. McClure was inordinately concerned about not having to work on Saturday. He constantly asked me if I was going to be done recording by Friday so that he could arrange his flight back East for the weekend.

After every take I did, McClure used a different superlative to describe the greatness of my performance. But the performances were not intended as final takes, because these sessions were primarily for the purpose of capturing the orchestra. Once we got their best take down on tape, the musicians could go home and I could work on the vocals alone. I didn't know whether McClure couldn't tell the difference between a good take and a bad take or was just humoring me. My friend David Ross had done two orchestrations, and after one of them was recorded he asked if we could play it back because he hadn't heard one of the instruments and he wanted to make sure that we'd gotten it. McClure refused to play the tapes back and went on to another chart. He wasn't the slightest bit concerned.

Because of all this, the sessions didn't go smoothly for me. Our interaction was amiable enough on the surface as McClure joked repeatedly with the orchestra. In those days, I tended to sit on my anger more readily than I do now, and the idea of taking McClure aside and expressing my feelings was not an inviting one for me. Although I had already recorded half a dozen albums of my own, I didn't feel comfortable confronting a man who had produced hundreds of records. Yet I also knew that it was quite common (and still is), when an artist doesn't get on well with a producer, for another producer to be called in to complete the job. I expected that if things came to a head between McClure and me, I could count on Mike Strunsky to give me what I needed; after all, it's a lot easier to change producers than to find a new vocalist with the same intimate familiarity with the material. But Mike had been pleased with McClure's previous work for Roxbury and very much wanted to keep him in place. And Bob Hurwitz—president of Nonesuch Records, which would be releasing and distributing the album—also felt strongly about McClure; in fact, he had brought the two of them together on a previous Roxbury project.

The net result was that, when I found that I could no longer work with John McClure, I could not convince Strunsky to replace him as producer. Mike and I had different perspectives about the recording. I felt it was a Michael Feinstein album because my name was going to be on it; he felt that it was a Gershwin album featuring Michael Feinstein. Seen from our separate vantage points, this may have been a legitimate difference of attitude, but it made it extremely difficult to try to resolve our disagreement over McClure. In the end, taping was stopped. I couldn't imagine that we wouldn't be able to work something out, but as time went by we actually grew further apart in our feelings about the project.

Tommy Krasker had played a vital role as intermediary between Mike Strunsky and me during the whole process, but in retrospect I think he merely exacerbated the problems. Without his presence, the recording probably would have continued. In relaying information between Mike and me, Tommy often interjected his own version of what he wanted to see happen, so in the end neither one of us was hearing what the other had actually said. To make matters worse, Tommy frequently changed his opinion about what he liked or didn't like about the recording.

Between Krasker and McClure, I was completely off balance. In addition to all the other problems, I began to realize that they had a different musical vision of the album. Along with Mike Strunsky, they had decided that it would be a small album, mainly piano and voice. I envisioned a different kind of album that would involve piano and voice, two-piano accompaniment, rhythm section accompaniment, vintage orchestrations of some things and new orchestrations of others—a range of presentations tailored to the strengths and weaknesses of each tune. I had carefully chosen the songs to be recorded from a mass of quite variable offerings and was determined to protect George and Ira, as well as myself. Some of the songs were not great, but they could be shown to better advantage by creating a new arrangement in a particular style, sometimes quite different from the original. Tommy, being far more of a purist than I could ever be, was particularly concerned about artistic choices like that. However, I had learned from my years of poring over the unpublished songs with Ira, sometimes on an almost daily basis, that the only way this album would work was to make individual decisions about how to interpret each song based on its own merits and its vintage. That was to be one of the strong points of the album.

Since the project was never completed, many people have asked me what the original album of unpublished Gershwin songs was going to be like. To begin with, I knew the dangers inherent in releasing an album of previously unpublished songs that would be as high profile as this one. Many came from plot situations that were long since forgotten; some had been replaced by other songs early in the life of a show and so had not gone through a complete gestation. I approached all of these challenges and constraints with great excitement because I knew this would give me the opportunity to show the scope with which Gershwin material could be interpreted and would reflect my personal growth in the six years since the release of my first record, an album of all Gershwin songs.

For the earliest song on the Roxbury album, "Kitchenette," I was able to use the original orchestrations and sing it as a duet with Rebecca Luker, who has since starred in such diverse Broadway fare as *Phantom of the Opera* and *Show Boat*. For some tracks, I asked Stan Freeman to recreate the duo-piano style that he had perfected in the '40s with Cy Walter and that had served as the classic accompaniment for songs by Lee Wiley and Mabel Mercer. Stan did two dazzling arrangements, for "Love Is in the Air" (a 1925 second act curtain-raiser for *Tell Me More*), and a reject from *Lady, Be Good!* called "The Bad, Bad Men." ("Love Is

in the Air" is also the title for an entirely different song by Stephen Sondheim, coincidentally written in the same schottische tempo, which he
cut from *A Funny Thing Happened on the Way to the Forum.*) I asked
Eddie Karam to orchestrate a 1937 Fred Astaire reject, "Pay Some Attention to Me," in the style of Astaire's classic mid-1930s Johnny Green
recordings. I wanted "Wake Up Brother and Dance," to be a salute to
the RKO musical sound of the '30s. In the case of "Anything for You," a
1921 song written for *A Dangerous Maid,* the brilliant Russell Warner
orchestrated the song in the style of Frank Saddler, who did the other
orchestrations for that show. "Somebody Stole My Heart Away" is an up-
tempo cowboy song that was more or less written as a throwaway. But
I discovered one day when playing it as a ballad that at that slower
tempo the hidden beauty of the melody emerged and Ira's lyrics seemed
to take on greater weight as well. Mort Lindsay created a masterful
arrangement for it, rescuing a song that otherwise would have deserved
obscurity. I was proudest of that achievement.

Unfortunately, I was never able to finish the vocals at that time. In
the ensuing years, some of those songs have found their way, in different form, into other Roxbury projects. I have sung a number of them in
my concerts, and was finally able to come to an agreement with Mike
Strunsky that allowed me to rerecord some of them for an album to be
released in connection with this book. Many of the previously unpublished songs will gradually work their way into the public's consciousness, although I doubt that they will ever supplant the more familiar
Gershwin songs, whose history and associations are richly embedded
in memory.

I can't leave this chapter without saying a few words about copyright
as it relates to the works of George and Ira, from the classic to the unfamiliar. My feelings about copyright extensions have evolved over the
years. I do believe the copyright to a song should be protected at least
throughout the songwriters' lifetimes, and so I have no trouble supporting a law that extends copyright fifty years after the death of the last
surviving collaborator. But at some point the song should go into the
public domain, because many of these works are pieces of art that
belong to everybody in the same way that Shakespeare and Beethoven
do. Because of the division of songwriters' estates, control of the songs
sometimes devolves to people who have no particular interest in their

artistic value. Song royalties that are left to the songwriters' heirs cannot be expected to be lifetime endowments. If your parents die and leave you an inheritance, that's fine; but at a certain point you're expected to make your own way. Even the heirs of great fortunes have to manage the estate and reinvest their dividends to keep the money flowing in. But some of the people who control songwriters' estates feel they deserve to maintain control over their parents' royalties indefinitely. I don't agree.

Unfortunately, the fact that there is currently no fair and universal copyright law tempts many of the heirs, and their lawyers, to go through contortions and in some cases to falsify history to insure continued income. At one point, Ron Blanc suggested to Ira that he write a lyric for *Rhapsody in Blue* so that the George Gershwin Estate could extend the copyright on that composition, but Ira couldn't bring himself to do it. (He did recall that, as a joke, Fred Astaire had written a lyric for the slow theme of the *Rhapsody* many years before. It went something like, "Play me that *Rhapsody in Blue,* written by Gershwin, played by Paul Whiteman." Ira suggested they use Astaire's lyric, but fortunately it was never done. If it had been, the Fred Astaire Estate would now control the rights to *Rhapsody in Blue!*) George died childless in 1937. How long should his nieces and nephews be entitled to collect his royalties?

For similar reasons, both Gershwin estates have tried to make the case that there is no separation between music and lyrics in George and Ira's works. As much as I may sympathize with the heirs' intentions, I find it hard to support misrepresenting the historical facts of authorship. In the case of *Porgy and Bess,* the recently published sheet music selections credit "By George Gershwin, DuBose and Dorothy Heyward and Ira Gershwin" without differentiating who wrote what. The story itself was written by DuBose and Dorothy Heyward; DuBose wrote some lyrics alone, Ira wrote some lyrics alone, and they collaborated on some lyrics. The specific authorship of the lyrics for individual songs published from the opera has always been carefully delineated on the respective copies of the sheet music. For instance, "It Ain't Necessarily So" has lyrics solely by Ira, "Summertime" is solely by Heyward, and "My Man's Gone Now" is a collaboration. Ira was always meticulous about giving proper author's credit, to the point where he added Yip Harburg's name to a song written for *Cover Girl* because he contributed one line. Imagine my surprise when I recently picked up a copy of "Summertime" to find the song credit: "By George Gershwin, DuBose and Dorothy Heyward, and Ira Gershwin," with no distinction as to music and lyrics and with Ira's name attached to a song for which he did not write a single lyric. (Which reminds me of the story my friend Renee Sousa told me about teaching a voice class, when one of her students stood up and said, "I'd like to sing 'Summertime' by Porgy and Bess.") The Estate feels that if they can prove legally that both the music and lyrics were collaborative efforts, the songs that are now out of copyright in Europe can be kept in copyright. Once again, although I don't approve of their methods, I agree that copyright laws are something of a nightmare for all concerned.

In the course of writing this book, I've discovered firsthand how difficult it can be to get the rights to reprint a particular lyric when the estates, in some cases, have been divided among three or more publishing companies, each controlled by different interests. In certain instances, the estates would even like to censor history. I was refused permission to reprint the full lyrics to "That's Why Darkies Were Born" by Ray Henderson and Lew Brown, and although no reason was given, I'm almost certain that the heirs of the authors did not want the public to see those racist lyrics. I understand their motives, but it's a little like trying to pretend the Holocaust never happened.

I feel certain that if Ira himself had been presented with the choice either of extending the copyright on his and George's works by fudging the authorship credits or of giving up his royalties, as much as Ira loved money, his sense of honor would never have allowed him to change the credits for a single song. Finally, in trying to balance the legitimate interests of the heirs with the desires of performers and archivists to have access to this treasury of great art, I have to bring my focus back to the legacy of the work itself—something that can never die no matter what the copyright laws decree. In the end, those of us who love and are nourished by the music of the Gershwins and all the other classic songwriters are the ones who are left with the real riches. And, to quote Ira (by permission of the copyright holder), "Who could ask for anything more?"

chapter 5

MY ONE AND ONLY

TOMMY TUNE FLING

*N*ext to meeting Ira Gershwin and some of the other great songwriters from the Golden Age, my biggest dream was to perform on Broadway. "Gotta Sing, Gotta Dance!" I had always imagined Broadway to be the pinnacle of artistic achievement in the world of show music that I loved so much and hoped to be a part of in some way. I finally did get to have my own show on Broadway in 1988, but some years before that I had an experience behind the scenes during the creation of a Broadway show that so thoroughly disillusioned me about the glorious world of the Great White Way that I could never take my old fantasies quite so seriously anymore. Even now I have to laugh at my naiveté in not realizing what a rat's nest I was getting myself into when I eagerly agreed to represent Ira's interests during the creation of a Gershwin revival. What fun, I thought. I believe it was George S. Kaufman who said that the greatest punishment for Hitler would have been to banish him to working on the out-of-town tryout of a Broadway show. The *Nifty Nazi Follies,* maybe? (That was Fred Ebb's behind-the-scenes title for *Cabaret,* and I think it might apply to any number of shows.)

Several different people had been trying to get the rights to mount a Gershwin show on Broadway for some time, but Ira wasn't all that keen on the idea because a number of previous shows had died aborning. A late 1970s production of *Oh, Kay!* had closed in Washington. The producers still owed Ira money, and he was upset about that. He was also concerned that the original books of these shows were so creaky that they would require major rewriting. Fitting specific plot songs into a new story was a bit like forcing a square peg into a round hole, and often resulted in violence being done to the poor old peg.

In late 1981, I was contacted by a man named Bernie Carragher, who used to write for the *New York Times.* Carragher was trying to figure out a way that he and his consortium of backers could proceed in getting a Gershwin musical off the ground, specifically a revival of *Funny Face.* My initial impression from talking to Bernie on the phone was that these backers might be a good group of people. Bernie was an extremely genial and intelligent man with great ideas and the patience of Job. I talked to Ira and he was still pretty much against it, but Leonore seemed interested, and at that point Leonore was the one who really had control. All Ira wanted to do was keep the peace. With Leonore's tentative OK, Bernie got first Tommy Tune involved and then Peter Sellars, the choreographer and director.

Eventually, a meeting was arranged between Sellars and Leonore. Peter is very flamboyant, in the best sense of the word, an intriguing character and a genuine intellectual who immediately charmed Leonore. The idea he had for *Funny Face*—which the following year was retitled *My One and Only*—was tied in with other musical works that had also been written in 1927, including Stravinsky's *Oedipus Rex.* Sellars had been involved in the staging of the Stravinsky work, too, and found surprising parallels between the two apparently very different works. As I sat in on the conversation and listened, Peter went on and on about how significant the year 1927 was, how he wanted to use the idea of Russian constructivism in *Funny Face* and use airplanes as metaphors because the original story had references to aviation. All during this fascinating exposition, Leonore sat in rapt attention, nodding and hanging on every word.

After Sellars left, she said, "I didn't understand a goddamn word he said. But I know he's brilliant and we must proceed."

Negotiations started right away, and because Bernie was a first-time producer, a number of other investors came on board to round out the picture. Thank God Bernie was a first-timer. He was by far the sanest of the bunch; he put up with a lot of nonsense in making the show happen and didn't get nearly as much recognition as he deserved in return. The Gershwins required that other people be involved, which ultimately was unfortunate, because I think the final product would have been tastier if there had been fewer cooks. Peter and Tommy Tune seemed to get along quite well. I had met Tommy a few years earlier and found him to be unbelievably polite. I liked him. He is able to come off as a kind of flower child with a sweet Texas drawl and a blissful image—holding hands with the cast at the end of rehearsal and saying a prayer for the success of the piece they're working on—and yet he has a consortium of assistants who handle all the unpleasantness and allow him to remain above the fray. Tommy had already had great success on Broadway and was treated like a Golden Boy by everyone around him. The show Carragher wanted to put on probably wouldn't have happened without Tommy and he knew it. Tommy probably loved it that way, because he seemed to enjoy being worshiped and kowtowed to. Come to think of it, who wouldn't enjoy that?

I never fully bought the image, yet I didn't understand the full complexity of his character until later, when the situation began to deteriorate badly. At the time, Phil Oesterman, who had produced the classic musical *Let My People Come,* was Tommy's primary assistant, and Thommie Walsh was involved as assistant choreographer. Phil and Thommie took care of whatever Tommy Tune wanted.

Peter Sellars had a slew of challenging ideas in mind for *My One and Only*. He didn't want to use any miking, which he justified by pointing out that many of the theaters that exist today on Broadway existed fifty years ago, and shows were successful without amplification then.

Because it was a 1927 musical, he wanted it authentic down to the sound. Everyone was wildly enthusiastic about that idea and couldn't understand why anybody hadn't thought of it earlier. Peter insisted on using his musical director, Craig Smith, who was a Bach specialist and to my knowledge didn't have much experience with Gershwin, but who turned out to be a very nice guy. His orchestrator, the clarinetist Bob Wilber, is well respected in traditional jazz. Peter also wanted to use the original 1927 orchestrations, but the few that existed were not very good and the charts were incomplete. That's why Craig Smith was brought on. Tommy Tune insisted on bringing in Wally Harper, who had been closely associated with him on other Broadway shows but who had no interest in remaining authentic to the spirit of 1927.

I saw immediately that there was going to be a conflict. At one of the early rehearsals, I heard Wally play some dance music that couldn't have been further from 1927 and I watched a piece that Tommy had choreographed for himself and his costar, Twiggy. I went up to Sellars during a break and said, "What's going on here, Peter? I'm curious about the dichotomy of what you said the show was going to be and what it's turning out to be."

"Don't worry," he said, with a warm and comforting smile. "Everything about this show is going to be in the style of 1927. There's going to come a point when Tommy is going to have to adapt to the style because the only thing that will be incongruous about it are these dance arrangements and his dances. So it's only a matter of time until he conforms to my concept."

Of course, by the time the show opened for tryouts in Boston, Peter Sellars had already fallen into disfavor. It had indeed been only a matter of time. There is still debate as to whether Peter's concept would have worked. Among other things, he planned to use the entire Gershwin "Cuban Overture," which runs eight or nine minutes, and to stage it as a ballet sequence to represent Tommy Tune's character making a historic flight. I think they should have given Sellars a chance, because it certainly would have been a more interesting production. Unfortunately, problems continued to mount because of the personality conflict between Peter and Tommy until Peter was fired after opening night in Boston.

One of the frustrating things for Peter was that, as the previews in

Boston loomed closer and closer, there was no question that they were going to use amplification. Everybody got cold feet and wouldn't dare go without it. They kept changing ideas that he had proposed because they became convinced that Sellars's conception wasn't going to work and besides, Tommy had already formulated another concept.

The opening preview in Boston was a peculiar affair. Twiggy's marriage was in a precarious state; her husband, the actor Michael Witney, had a drinking problem and frequently menaced her. She cared deeply about him but couldn't deal with his drinking; she resorted to hiring a bodyguard because her husband kept attempting to see her. A few minutes into that first performance, a big commotion erupted in the second balcony—security guards ejected a belligerent heckler who turned out to be Twiggy's husband. The other startling development during the previews was that Twiggy began a romance with Tommy Tune which was a subject of a great deal of conversation at the time.

The show was clearly in a lot of trouble and the producers were asking everybody to come to Boston and look at it. One day, Maury Yeston, who had previously worked with Tommy on *Nine,* arrived with an "I'm here to fix the show" attitude. Tommy felt the show needed a new opening number, and if we couldn't find one by Gershwin, then Maury would write one. The producers had to explain to him that it would not work to interpolate Maury Yeston songs into a Gershwin musical. "Yeah," he said, "but you need this kind of song here and you don't have it."

My role as Ira's representative was to make sure that things were being done the way he wanted them done. I was also to make suggestions if they needed a particular number for a plot situation. However, I was becoming more and more disenchanted with what was happening with the show because Wally Harper had done a number of arrangements that were totally out of character. For example, the dance music he had created for " 'S Wonderful" was actually a Scott Joplin–style ragtime arrangement. He wrote a Joplinesque countermelody to " 'S Wonderful" that could not actually be played against the original melody without altering its structure. A countermelody should *complement* the familiar melody, not force it to be changed. When I heard this strange pastiche, I went up to Wally and said, "This is the wrong era."

"Oh, no, no, no," Wally interrupted me. "Scott Joplin's ragtime is quite appropriate." What could I say? There were songs that should have been performed authentically and were not. It was hard to accept the show as taking place in the 1920s; some songs sounded like the '30s and '40s, others like ragtime, but very few echoed the decade in which the original was written. In most instances, I didn't open my mouth about things because they weren't significant. But a couple of matters were extremely important. One was the song "Strike Up the Band," which was used as a first-act finale. Ira was against having "Strike Up the Band" in the show because he wanted them to use only songs that were either originally written for *Funny Face* or at least were not connected with another musical show that might be viable. And he was dead set against their using "Strike Up the Band" because it came from a show that could possibly be revived and he didn't want to start cannibalizing different scores. However, they started threatening that if they didn't have "Strike Up the Band," they wouldn't have an appropriate first-act finale and then the show could possibly fail. What it came down to was that if they were denied anything at all, and if the show failed, they could say, "Ira Gershwin tied our hands and that's why the show flopped."

So Ira relented, but not before I'd had a conversation with Sam Cohn, who represented not only Tommy Tune but also Mike Nichols, who was secretly brought in to fix the show. Mike's name does not appear in the credits, but he received a substantial amount of money. Cohn looked at me condescendingly and said, "Gee, you're younger than I expected. Well, of course you'll give us 'Strike Up the Band,' won't you?" I can't tell you how depressing it was to be involved in a show for the first time and to see the power plays that went on behind the scenes. They got their song, but "Strike Up the Band" still had a lyric that didn't make sense. It is a martial song; in the second eight, it goes, "Hear the cymbals ring! / Calling one and all / To the martial swing."

Tommy decided to remove the reference to "martial swing," and instead he just repeated the second line, "Calling one and all," which ruined the rhyme scheme. Ira was very upset about that because he didn't want people to think that he couldn't rhyme. So he wrote a new line: "Now's the time to swing." But Tommy never interpolated that line, and that really nettled Ira. In Ira's obituary in the *New York Times,* the producers of *My One and Only* were quoted as saying how valuable Ira's contribution was to the show and how helpful he was. What bull.

He could have actually been very helpful but was never given the opportunity.

I wonder what would have happened if Ira had been healthy enough to attend rehearsals and see firsthand what they were doing. As his representative, I felt an obligation to voice objections to the things I knew he didn't want done. And so one day during rehearsal, I spoke to Harper about incongruous elements such as the counter-melody to " 'S Wonderful." Wally became very offended. "If there's going to be somebody standing over me dictating what I have to do every moment of the way," he said, "I'm going to leave this show. I'm not going to put up with this."

As a coda, he added, "And I'm going to talk to Tommy about this right away."

I asked him not to do that, assuring him that I would talk to Tommy directly. But he was sufficiently pissed off at me that he stormed backstage in the middle of the rehearsal and said something to Tommy. Whatever it was, Tommy walked out onstage ten minutes later, pointed to me and said, in the foulest tone of voice I'd ever heard, "You! Backstage!"

When I went backstage, Tommy launched a tirade about how I was a traitor and a detriment to the show and I should get out of Boston because I was single-handedly keeping them from making the show a success. Who did I think I was, anyway? He never gave me the opportunity to respond or to ask him exactly what it was that Wally had said to him or to address the specific points. I called Ira and said, "I think I'd better come home because I'm not doing any good here." I explained what had happened and Ira was very sympathetic. "Maybe that's the best thing," he said. Leonore, on the other hand, immediately turned against me. "What have you done?" she demanded. "You've upset the star and the show's going to be a failure and it's going to be your fault! You're a fool to have behaved that way and you should be ashamed of yourself." All she said to me for the next two weeks was, "We're going to lose our star!"

That was pretty devastating, yet it shouldn't have been unexpected. I felt torn, because I knew that I wasn't wanted there but I also knew that by leaving at that point I was allowing the show to go even further afield. What upset me the most was that the show was being advertised as a Gershwin musical. Since it was capitalizing on the songs, why shouldn't the songs be presented in a way that showed them off to their best advantage? I wasn't being a purist; I was trying to find a way to accommodate Tommy's needs for dance music in a more authentic style. I didn't understand why they were ignoring Ira's requests for things that were very important to him. In the final number, George and Ira's "Kickin' the Clouds Away," they interpolated musical phrases from Gershwin concert works, little bits of *Rhapsody in Blue* and the Concerto in F. Ira asked them to take those phrases out. They did temporarily but then they put them back in again. Legally and contractually, Ira had the power to stop them but he didn't want to be called the bad guy, the one who caused the show to flop. So the brunt of everyone's anger fell on me. Phil Oesterman pulled me aside at one point for a personal dressing-down. "You know, you have a really bad attitude problem," he said, "and I don't think that you should be involved in this business. Tune is very upset at you and he said he rarely gets that upset at people. If I were you, I would just steer clear."

When the producers engaged Michael Gibson to replace Bob Wilber as orchestrator, they didn't bother to tell me. In the meantime, I brought Hans Spialek to Boston to see if he could become involved with the show. Hans had done the original orchestrations for " 'S Wonderful" and some of the other tunes in *Funny Face* in 1927. After he sat through a performance of " 'S Wonderful," he said, "I listened to the whole thing— and I didn't know what the song was!" Gibson thought I was trying to have Hans replace him and screamed at me one night in the bar of the Copley Plaza that I should get the fuck out of Boston. It seemed to be the going opinion.

So I returned to California and Leonore's constant upbraiding. But within a matter of weeks, the producers decided that they needed other songs to fill certain spots in the show and they didn't know who else could help them with the catalogue. Lo and behold, one of the producers requested that I come back to Boston, which I did. They held a meeting of the production staff—Tommy Tune, Thommie Walsh, Mike Nichols, Phil Oesterman, Bernie Carragher, and a couple of other producers—at which I was at the piano to play songs for them. I had done this before to help them find an opening number; early on Tommy had also called me in California and asked if it would be possible for him to hear every song the Gershwins wrote. I tried to explain that there were hundreds and that most of them were not available for this show, but he didn't want to hear that. Now they were looking specifically for a song for Twiggy to sing early in the show in which she would describe the kind of man she was hoping to meet. I came up with a song written in the early '20s that fit the situation, called "Boy Wanted." That meeting was pretty wacky because Tommy refused to talk to me, as he had since he first turned against me. So he either whispered something into some- one's ear and that person addressed the question to me, or he spoke out into the room without looking at me or acknowledging me in any way. "I think that's a very good song," he would say to the room. Then someone else would say to me, "Tommy thinks it's a very good song." If I wanted to say something to Tommy, I had to direct the conversation to someone else.

The whole time, I kept thinking to myself, *This* is show business? This is how a Broadway show is created? It was unfathomable to me that this kind of childish behavior went on, but I later discovered that it goes on routinely.

Peter Stone, who came in to work on the book, is a marvelous Broad- way veteran who has worked with difficult egos for many years and knows how to get along with people. At one point, he wanted to inter- polate a couple of other Gershwin songs that Ira had said were not available for one reason or another. "I'm sorry," I said, "but these songs are not available." Peter just snapped. "Michael, you're killing us!" he said. "What are you doing to us? Don't you understand we need the songs, god damn it?"

That evening, I called Ira. "I don't know what to do," I said.

"There's only one thing to do," he said. "Give them what they want. Forget it. Don't go there anymore. Leave them alone."

And for all of Leonore's antagonism toward me, she still came up with the best assessment of Tommy Tune I heard during the whole affair. "He's a barracuda," she once warned me. "I know, because I'm a barracuda, too."

That was the end of my involvement until I saw the show on opening night. I did get billing as musical consultant, although when *My One and Only* played in Japan, they printed a big glossy program with pic- tures of everybody except me. Where there should have been a picture of me there was a blank spot.

I was certain that the show was going to die a quick death because it was, at best, mediocre and had gotten poor reviews in Boston. Peter Stone had fixed up the book in a major way, but it was still a mishmash of musical styles, with some of the charts sounding like they came out of the '40s rather than the '20s, and, of course, that ragtime dance number. To my ears, the whole thing didn't gel. Nonetheless, when it finally came to Broadway, it opened to largely favorable reviews, with a few raves and only some dissenting voices. The most important notice came from Frank Rich of the *New York Times*, who gave it a money review. Speculation was rife about why he had done that, because it seemed to be the kind of show that Frank Rich would hate. The rumor went around that Rich's job was in jeopardy because he had given too many scathingly bad reviews to shows that were generally liked and accepted by all the other critics. This is sheer conjecture, but it was widely circulated at the time, given credence because *My One and Only* was precisely the kind of inauthentic pastiche that Rich had made it his job to expose.

But if I was surprised, Ira at least was happy that the show was a success. I had played Ira a cassette of the show's opening night in Boston and although he didn't think it was a great show, he loved the idea that it was successful. Listening to the applause at the end of the show was a thrilling experience for him, knowing that people were applauding his work. It made him extremely happy, and that offset much of the frustration I had experienced in trying to work with the show's creators.

Tommy and Twiggy remained romantically involved after the show opened until one night when Twiggy's emotions got the better of her. Not long into the run of the show in the fall of 1983, Twiggy's husband had a heart attack at a McDonald's and died. Despite all their problems, she was devastated. One day soon afterwards, she saw a movie on TV that she and her husband had made together, called *W* (in which, ironically, she and Michael, who also played her husband in the film, are menaced by her sadistic ex-husband). That night, during " 'S Wonderful," she broke down onstage and burst into tears. During intermission, Tommy asked her what was wrong and when she explained about the movie, he became absolutely furious. He believed that no matter what is going on in your life, you don't take it into your work; he told her that he had never worked with anyone so unprofessional and that he was never going to talk to her again. And for a long time, he didn't. They separated and though they both continued to do the show, he refused to speak to her. Twiggy called Mike Nichols and Bernie Carragher to explain the situation and ask for their help. Finally she called Sam Cohn, who simply told her, "Honey, your contract is going to be up soon and you'll be out of this thing, and then you can go into something better." Sam was interested in protecting his star client, Tommy.

After this had gone on for some time, Twiggy finally went backstage to Tommy's dressing room and confronted him. "I'm sick of this and I don't need it anymore," she said. "If you don't talk to me, I'm taking the next plane back to London." From that point on, he was civil to her, and when her contract was up she immediately left the show. In the last few years, they have reconciled their differences. The last time Tommy's name came up in my conversations with Twiggy, she spoke of him very warmly.

Because of my connection with Ira, I had considerable emotion invested in trying to keep the production faithful to his vision. And ultimately maybe my own ego became too heavily involved because I wanted to be able to show that I knew and understood the Gershwins' work. Regardless of my personal feelings about Tommy, audiences for the most part seemed to love the show. Maybe it was the mixture of Tommy's and Twiggy's personalities that gave the show a very distinctive flavor, even though I was bothered by the show's lack of musical identity. At that time, I probably wasn't able to look at the show in terms of how it worked simply as an evening's entertainment and to divorce myself from my opinions about the authenticity of the musical presentation. I still encounter people who speak unkindly to me because of my role in that show, either because they sided with Tommy Tune, which I can't do anything about, or because they think of me disparagingly as a purist. There I have to disagree. I don't necessarily feel that everything has to be performed as written, like some of the clinical recreations of recent years, which are too dry and don't have enough theatricality. In the case of *My One and Only,* I was not trying to make them adhere to what had transpired in 1927 but merely to respect certain essential elements of the Gershwin works that I felt shouldn't be tampered with. Any number of changes did have to be made for the sake of the show, and I had no objection to them, nor did Ira. But because it was called a Gershwin musical, I felt that certain elements of songs that people know and love, like "Strike Up the Band" and " 'S Wonderful," should have been respected. And they weren't.

My instinct that it's possible to combine authenticity and commercial success has been borne out by the Goodspeed Opera House in East Haddam, Connecticut, which has done a number of revivals of Gershwin shows, including *Tip-Toes, Funny Face,* and *Lady, Be Good!* For the most part, these little revivals have been very successful on their own, more modest terms. One of the things that struck me about Goodspeed's revival of *Tip-Toes,* for instance, was that they used orchestrations taken from vintage dance recordings of the mid-'20s that were authentically reconstructed and yet were filled with energy and joy and life. Goodspeed may not get the national exposure or the million-dollar salaries, but they are doing things right. Whether their approach would regularly work as well in the hot-house atmosphere of Broadway's multimillion-dollar productions is another question. Their production of *Annie* was moved to Broadway with great success, but a couple of their revivals fared less well there.

From my present perspective, it's a little easier for me to see that at the time of my conflict with Tommy Tune, I was beginning to feel my own voice and develop my own musical identity. It might have gone easier for me if I had simply hidden behind Ira's authority and insisted that I was just conveying his wishes and protecting his interests—which, to an extent, I was. But I had also internalized much of what Ira had taught me and had begun to fight on my own terms for the way I believed the music ought to be performed. It was probably inevitable that I would end up going head to head with Tommy and his own vision of what it took to make a show like *My One and Only* a commercial success. My standards were considerably more idealistic, and from their point of view I must have seemed like an insufferable nuisance most of the time.

Since then I've come to understand far better the elements at play in the creation of a Broadway show, the extreme pressures that cause tempers to flare and erratic behavior to be the norm (and I include myself in that description, having watched my own occasional outbursts of righteous anger and wondered at times who was doing all that yelling). I was so full of youthful bravado back then that if I ran into myself at that age today, I might find myself a little hard to take. After the big flare-up with Tommy, for instance, I sent a note to the entire staff of the show stating that I needed to meet with them all the following day to discuss necessary changes for the show—changes that I was determined to institute single-handedly. I was nervous about taking such a bold step, but I was certain that it was absolutely necessary to preserve the integrity of the show. Bernie Carragher came to me with good grace and very gently explained that this was not an appropriate way to handle the situation. Through my anger, I could see that he was right, and dropped the whole idea. I was clutching at straws because I wasn't being listened to. It never occurred to me that I was in my mid-twenties, an unknown, completely inexperienced in the world of Broadway, pitting myself against people with years of experience and huge reputations.

I had long forgotten about that incident by the time I made my debut at the Algonquin Hotel in 1986. Among my opening night cards and flowers was a photocopy of that very note, which was sent to me anonymously and without further explanation. Obviously, somebody had not forgotten. I wasn't sure what the message was supposed to be, but I got a real chuckle out of it. And in that moment, I realized that the Sturm und Drang of that whole episode in my life had lost its negative charge for me.

In any event, *My One and Only* is now largely forgotten in the wake of *Crazy for You,* which will undoubtedly be forgotten after the success of the next Gershwin pastiche to come along. Not long ago, I was in Cleveland and saw Tommy in a pre-Broadway performance of a musical called *Stage Door Charlie.* Afterwards, its composer Richard Sherman took me to Tommy's dressing room and we both had a chance to visit. I apologized for my behavior during *My One And Only,* and we ended our reunion with a warm embrace. I got the clear feeling that we had both grown a lot and that too much sadness and joy had come our way in the intervening years for us to dwell on a clash of egos.

chapter

6

RETURN OF THE SECAUCUS 87

*E*arly in 1982, while working at Ira's, I took a phone call from Don Rose, a gifted arranger living on the East Coast, who said that he had found the score of a lost Gershwin show from 1933 called *Pardon My English*. Don had spent years searching for this score, among others, and had even sent me a letter several years before that he had received from famed British psychic Sybil Leek, whom he had consulted about the missing score. Leek had written, "I feel that this music still exists and is in a warehouse somewhere near a river." Now Don was telling me that he had found the score in the Warner Brothers Music warehouse in Secaucus, New Jersey—not far from the shore of the Hudson River. Sybil had been right, after all. "I think you'd better come east," Don said, "because it looks like there are some original manuscripts here, along with a whole lot of other material."

I told Ira about it, but he was dismissive. "I don't think you're going to find much," he said in what turned out to be one of the great understatements of all time. The reason for Ira's pessimism was that when a show was unsuccessful in the '20s and '30s, as soon as it closed the musicians literally tore up the music and threw it out. It was not perceived as having any value, since new shows were constantly being turned out. As impossible as it may sound by modern standards, good songwriting teams might produce as many as three or four shows a year and they often had the sense that there was plenty more where that came from. If songs from a successful show became popular, of course, the publishers printed thousands of copies of the sheet music to sell, although even those editions were often rearranged and simplified for easy home consumption. A hit show always stood a chance of revival, but when an unsuccessful show closed, that was it; the complex orchestrations and instrumental parts were usually not kept since there was no use for them. Or so everyone thought.

Much as Ira was constantly amazed that so many of the songs he had written in the busy decades of the '20s and '30s later became famous standards that supported him handsomely in his old age, he was certain that all of the unsuccessful show scores had been discarded. Any original George or Ira Gershwin manuscripts connected with them, other than the ones he had personally retained or gathered, ought to have long since disappeared. Consequently, he didn't think they would find anything, and he had his doubts about the artistic value of material from flop shows, anyway.

At about that same time, Ira received a call from Bob Kimball, who filled Ira in on the find and added that the original score to *Pardon My English* was indeed among the papers. "I hope you didn't find the lyric to the title song," Ira replied with a laugh, "because it is the worst lyric I ever wrote." Ira wasn't thrilled but Bob convinced him and Lee that it would be worthwhile for me to go to New Jersey and help examine the cache. With Ira's OK, Warners brought a couple of boxes of materials from *Pardon My English* and Cole Porter's *Gay Divorce* (Fred Astaire's last Broadway musical, filmed in 1934 as *The Gay Divorcée*) to their New

York offices to be examined; they contained original scores and parts, and their significance was clear. Don Rose, Bob, and Henry Cohen, the rental manager, went out to Secaucus to have a further look and I flew out to join them shortly after.

To understand the significance of the find, you have to know how all that music got to be in the Warners warehouse in the first place. In the late 1920s, as silent films began to give way to talkies (after the immense success of Warners' hit film *The Jazz Singer*), the studio realized that it would need a music publishing firm to handle all the music it was beginning to generate. Warner Brothers Studios bought out three prominent New York music publishers in 1929—Harms Inc., Witmark, and Remick— and created Warner Brothers Music (now Warner-Chappell) to control the copyrights for music in their talking pictures. Harms, Inc. was the publisher of Richard Rodgers, the Gershwins, and Cole Porter. T. B. Harms had been set up largely to accommodate Jerome Kern, although it was sold off in the late '30s. The three houses among them also accounted for the music of Sigmund Romberg, Victor Herbert, and Vincent Youmans. Over the years, Warner Music used various storage facilities all around the metropolitan area to house original manuscripts and scores and eventually moved them to the Meadowlands area of New Jersey. In the '70s, they moved again to a warehouse on Secaucus Road, just off the New Jersey Turnpike, where the material was being kept along with considerably larger amounts of more modern scores.

Two employees at Warner Music played a key role in preserving and bringing to light what became known as the "Secaucus cache." Henry Cohen was the real hero of Secaucus. He had become aware that a large number of cartons containing old scores and original manuscripts were stored there. Although Henry didn't know the exact contents, he had seen the names of enough important composers and show titles among the material to realize that it had to be preserved. He also knew that it was in danger of being ignored or, worse yet, discarded by Warners executives always eager to make room for new material. Along with Bob Alexander, Cohen sent a memo to company executives listing the names of the composers whose scores were there and hinting at the depth of the riches. Nobody else at Warners apparently had seen the material or had any suspicion as to how valuable it might be. Once Henry brought it to their attention, however, the company let it be known that they would allow the material to be examined on their premises only with permission from at least one estate and one of the living writers. Kimball was asked to contact the Cole Porter estate and to call Ira Gershwin to see if he could obtain their permission.

It's not clear whether Warners actually would have gotten rid of the boxes if Henry Cohen hadn't intervened, but from what I know of how other studios have behaved, it is more than likely. I later heard through Bob Kimball that some low-level employees who worked at the warehouse and who, ironically, happened to be rock musicians learned that there was a possibility that the Warners brass were going to dump the material and they moved the boxes around so that they would be hard to find. (Whether they cared specifically about the scores or just seized the chance to thwart authority is hard to say. But they did play a role in saving the treasure.)

Bob Kimball was serving as artistic consultant for the Porter estate and initially he focused mainly on the Porter material while I spent most of my time identifying Gershwin papers. But we also overlapped; Bob had an interest in Gershwin and I was only too happy to examine the Oscar Levant material and some Harry Warren songs from *The Laugh Parade* that were among the discoveries. Al Simon, a Kern and Gershwin scholar (he had been the rehearsal pianist for *Of Thee I Sing*) was later retained by Warners along with Bob to look through the Jerome Kern scores; Bob Lissauer was later brought in to look for music by Vincent Youmans, and Richard Lewine examined the Rodgers and Hart material.

When I first arrived, I met Bob Kimball, Al Simon, and Henry Cohen at the Warners offices in Rockefeller Center and from there we drove to the warehouse. I had never been to Secaucus and I had no idea where we were going except that it was surprisingly close to Manhattan. As we drove into a sprawling industrial area, we approached a huge warehouse that looked like it had been built in the '60s with absolutely nothing distinctive about it. We entered through a small hallway that opened suddenly into a cavernous area filled with piles of sheet music, folios, boxes, and a number of old filing cabinets off in one corner. The warehouse appeared to be as big as a football field and as tall as an airplane hangar. There were rows of metal shelves twelve to fifteen feet high, most of which contained boxes of music currently published by Warner Brothers.

Shortly after arriving, it became clear to us that two distinct sets of rare and valuable treasures were to be examined. Near the entrance where we had just come in, a pile of eighty boxes of musical theater material containing mostly original unpublished manuscripts and orchestrations had been brought down from the metal shelves where they had been stored and were stacked on the floor. In another part of the room, stacks of printed sheet music were piled helter-skelter on industrial shelving. On closer inspection, we saw that the sheet music dated back to the turn of the century, including some old, oversized pieces of sheet music from before the First World War. I was struck by the fact that all of them were in perfect condition. Although the real gold lay in those eighty boxes of unpublished manuscripts, these published sheets were extremely exciting in their own way. Pristine copies of music from that era are very hard to come by—and this was a mother lode. I can't describe the sensations that went through me at finding sheets in such good condition from the 1895 Victor Herbert musical *The Wizard of the Nile* (his first success) or the 1903 Broadway production of *The Wizard of Oz*.

But the task at hand was to separate and evaluate the priceless manuscripts in the eighty boxes of unpublished material. Kimball, Simon, and I spent the next few weeks going through all the musical theater papers, pulling out envelopes and individual copies of material that related to the composers we were each focusing on. I filled four complete boxes until they were spilling over with Gershwin materials. Extraordinary discoveries and details were coming to light every day, but the biggest prize was clearly the Gershwin material, which dated back to 1918 and even included songs George had written in London. In all, about seventy previously lost songs of George's, many with lyrics by Ira, and the missing scores and in some cases parts to *Primrose* (1924), *Tip-Toes* (1925), and *Pardon My English* turned up among the discoveries. In addition, over thirty Cole Porter manuscripts were found along with a number of Rodgers and Hart holographs including the lost piano score to *Peggy-Ann*, which Richard Rodgers felt was his and Hart's most significant effort from the '20s.

The Kern manuscripts were a real find. Perhaps because of their age,

Kern's manuscripts are among the rarest of any songwriter's, yet suddenly we were sitting on hundreds of original Kern pieces from the earliest periods of his creativity. The manuscripts ran from the teens to
1931, including complete scores for *Very Good Eddie, Leave It to Jane,
Dear Sir, Sweet Adeline,* and *The Cat and the Fiddle,* among others.
Thirty minutes' worth of music cut from the original score of *Show Boat*
just after its premiere and dozens of unpublished Kern songs also turned
up. And there was more: lost manuscripts of Sigmund Romberg, Victor
Herbert, and Rudolf Friml, all major figures in the earliest years of American musical theater. And even if the orchestrations for the Kern and
Gershwin shows weren't all created by the composers, they were just
as significant in a way. Orchestrators like Hans Spialek, Frank Saddler,
and Robert Russell Bennett, who had worked with the composers on
their shows, helped to create the Broadway sound of that era.

   As we worked at sorting the cache, we tried to figure out where this
material had come from and how it had gotten to Secaucus. The music's
actual provenance was never clearly determined and in some cases
didn't add up. For instance, Warners had sold off the catalogue of T. B.
Harms, Kern's publisher, many years before the discovery was made.
Yet numerous items from the T. B. Harms catalogue, many in Kern's
elegant hand, were still there. One theory was that the publisher Max
Dreyfus, a major figure at Harms, had kept this material privately at his
country place in Brewster, New York, and that after he died his family
had given it all to Warners or someone had simply taken it and stored it
in the warehouse.

   Sorting through the boxes, I counted eighty-seven original manuscripts in George's own hand, and I was correct in every case except
one, where what I thought was a George Gershwin manuscript turned
out to be by William Daly, a close friend who in some instances worked
on orchestrations for Gershwin shows. I had somehow missed another
manuscript in George's hand, though, so the final tally remained at
eighty-seven. It was an extraordinary experience to hold in my hands all
of these manuscripts that Ira considered to be long lost. When I called
and told him about the find, he still had trouble believing it.

   Somebody had gained access to the material a few years earlier and
had sent some of it to the Goodspeed Opera House in Connecticut,
which was mounting a production of Gershwin's *Funny Face.* By the

grace of God, the folks at Goodspeed used it and returned it, probably not knowing that they might have had original George Gershwin manuscripts in their hands. Unfortunately, some of the other material had been pilfered and later turned up for sale in an autograph shop in Manhattan, including a couple of songs that George had written for *George White's Scandals of 1921* and the complete pencil manuscript of his first attempt at writing a larger work. That piece, the half-hour operetta *Blue Monday*, written in 1922, had been performed only at the opening night of *George White's Scandals of 1922*. When I called the autograph shop asking them where they had gotten the material they were selling, they told me, "Oh, a guy who played in the orchestra of the original show sold it to us." The auction house refused to give me any more information. Happily, the Library of Congress had a budget that year to purchase manuscripts and was able to buy *Blue Monday* from the dealer. I often wonder what else may have disappeared.

But we could hardly feel dispirited by such minor losses as we eagerly sifted through our treasures. The four of us (Bob Lissauer had joined us by then) were fairly spellbound by the whole experience, although after a while we became rather blasé about it and began trying to one-up each other. Sitting at the table, I blurted out, "Look! Here's the original manuscript for 'I Got Rhythm.' "

A few minutes later, Bob Kimball countered, "Okay, here's the original of 'Let's Do It.' "

Bob Lissauer produced the original "Bambalina" and Al Simon held up a manuscript from *Show Boat*. It went on that way for several days. When we broke for lunch, we left the warehouse and went to eat at the closest place around, the Plaza Diner in Secaucus. I was on a special diet at the time and it was murder trying to get anything even vaguely low-fat. All the food at the diner was fried and the only thing that was fresh were the salty waitresses in their pink uniforms. We sat around talking about Gershwin, Porter, Kern, and Noël Coward while the truck drivers looked at us like we were from outer space.

I think we all appreciated the contrast between our spartan surroundings and the glorious trove we were unearthing. By any standard, it was a remarkable cache of material. Since that time, some of the unpublished works and scores have slowly been disseminated and once again made available to the public. However, not all of the songs are viable, because many of them were written for a plot in a show and don't make sense outside of that context. But just the fact that many of the songs came from flop shows did not necessarily mean that they were second-rate, either, any more than a painting by a great artist that never sold during his lifetime is necessarily a lesser work.

Ira already had lyric sheets for most of George's newly discovered manuscripts but in many cases did not possess the music, making the find all the more significant. He often could not remember how the music went for those of his lyrics for which he didn't have written music. Now we were able to marry the lyric sheets from his home in Beverly Hills with the music we found in New Jersey. It was a wonderful feeling, reuniting and revitalizing songs that might never again have seen the light of day.

We learned other things from the discovery of many of these original song copies. "Fascinating Rhythm" is one good example. Gershwin originally wrote the first eight bars as an instrumental in London in 1924, Ira coming up with a lyric later that year. On the manuscript I found a dummy title that George had suggested for the melody, "Syncopated City," which is so evocative of the era that you almost wish Ira had written a set of lyrics to fit that title. (He did write a lyric along those lines much later but it lacked the verve of his original inspiration.) On George's 1926 piano recording of "Fascinating Rhythm" (with Fred and Adele Astaire providing the vocals), he plays a little interlude between choruses that I always thought he had tossed off on the spur of the moment. The Secaucus manuscript reveals that he had originally notated it as an integral part of the song. It was probably performed that way in *Lady, Be Good!* yet was never published in the sheet music. A middle section for the song "Somebody Loves Me" also turned up in a vintage orchestration found in Secaucus (and later recorded by Maureen McGovern). And I discovered an earlier version of "The Man I Love" with an unknown verse. The famous chorus that we know from that song was originally an introduction and George decided he liked it so much he made it the chorus. Now we finally had the early version to compare with its well-known counterpart. We also found two songs that Jerome Kern had written with Noël Coward, which came as something of a surprise, since to my knowledge it had not been officially documented that Kern ever worked with Coward (although Howard

Dietz in his autobiography mentioned seeing a copy of a Kern/Coward song).

In one instance I found proof of something that the composer Vernon Duke had written about in his autobiography. Duke was an early protégé of George Gershwin's. Born in Russia in 1903 as Vladimir Dukelsky, he was trained at the Kiev Conservatory of Music but fled Russia with his family during the Revolution. In America, he had taken the name Vernon Duke at George's suggestion. Duke later wrote "April in Paris," "Autumn in New York," "I Can't Get Started," and the score of *Cabin in the Sky*, including "Taking a Chance on Love." In Duke's early days in New York, George hired him to help with *George White's Scandals of 1924*. In his autobiography, *Passport to Paris*, Duke says that he created the original piano copy of "Somebody Loves Me." There in the Secaucus cache was a copy of "Somebody Loves Me" in Vernon Duke's hand, which I recognized from a couple of examples I'd seen in Ira's file. Duke also claimed that he had ghosted one instrumental piece for George. Among the papers I found was a copyist's manuscript of this piece, called "Black and White March," that said "George Gershwin" on it—but the original manuscript was in Vernon Duke's hand and it confirmed that Duke had indeed ghosted it.

Among the most surprising finds were manuscripts of compositions that George had written for a show produced in London in 1924 called *Primrose*. It is rather mysterious that that material was in New Jersey rather than somewhere in London, since the complete score of *Primrose* with all the vocal selections was printed in England and the songs were never popular over here. Even more surprising in some ways were manuscripts of other songwriters that we never expected to find—a concert work by Victor Herbert, who died in 1924, a couple of Leonard Bernstein's song manuscripts from *On the Town*, and Harry Warren manuscripts from *The Laugh Parade*, which were all thought to be lost. We even found manuscripts of a number of songs that Oscar Levant had written for the movies in Hollywood in the late '20s that had no business being in New Jersey. They were written for RKO rather than Warners, but Levant was under contract to Harms at the time and RKO had no music publishing company then, so that must explain their presence.

There was some question as to who owned the manuscripts and what was going to happen to them, among other legal issues. The way the discovery was first made public didn't help matters any. In November 1982, Don Rose called a news conference in Miami with Ellis Rubin as his lawyer. Rubin had once represented some of the Watergate burglars and his name was sure to attract attention from the press—as if a discovery of this magnitude needed a celebrity lawyer. Don also claimed the right to arrange, conduct, and record the works and get a ten percent cut of any royalties accruing from the sale of the works as a kind of finder's fee. His claim was deemed baseless and the ensuing counterclaims of ownership by the various estates resulted in all the material being quickly locked in a vault at Warners' offices at 75 Rockefeller Center.

As far as the Gershwin material went, both sides agreed to hand it all over to the family to go to the Library of Congress in exchange for Warner Brothers' having the right to publish and disseminate it at Ira's discretion. (Similar arrangements were eventually reached with the estates of the other songwriters; the remaining material was recently placed on deposit with the Library of Congress, where it belongs.) The manuscripts in George's hand and the few in Ira's were separated from the other rare material—manuscripts done by a copyist of an unknown Gershwin song, say—and I hand-carried them on an airplane to the Library of Congress Music Division in Washington, D.C.

To do that, I had to be made an official courier for the Library of Congress so I could be properly insured and protected legally and financially. I felt like a CIA operative by the time the proper clearances were obtained. I was to take the shuttle from La Guardia to Washington National, but at that time construction was going on at La Guardia and things were very confused. You put your stuff on one conveyor belt to go through the X-ray machine and a different conveyor belt took your luggage into the airport luggage system and then onto the plane. However, someone had taken down the signs indicating which was which. I very carefully put the large envelope containing the priceless manuscripts on the belt to go through the X-ray machine, but when I walked through the metal detector and around to the other side, I discovered that the manuscripts weren't there. The belt I had put them on was taking them into the bowels of the airport, heading irretrievably toward the luggage hole. Panicked and furious, I started screaming at the top of my lungs. Security guards came over, no doubt thinking that I was some kind of crazy or, worse yet, a terrorist. "You've got to get that envelope!" I yelled at them. "You've got to save it!"

Who knows what would have happened to it. I had visions of the envelope falling off a baggage truck onto the runway and Gershwin's manuscripts being swept into the air like that suitcase full of money at the end of Stanley Kubrick's film *The Killing*. I was white in the face and the guards said, "Calm down and tell us what's wrong."

"I need that envelope," I said. "Right away! I thought it was the X-ray belt . . . and the Gershwin manuscripts . . . I will be murdered. My life is over!" I was babbling like a maniac. Somebody who was sympathetic ran back behind the wall where the conveyor belt had disappeared and retrieved the envelope for me. It was a very scary moment. After that, the rest of the trip to Washington was blissfully uneventful.

Some of those songs, incidentally, were among the ones I attempted to record for that ill-fated project of unpublished Gershwin songs. Ira and I had pieced them together by marrying George's music manuscripts with Ira's lyric sheets. In other instances, we found the original versions of material that Kay Swift had written down from memory, like "Thanks to You," which had previously existed only in Kay's version. What we found in Secaucus was actually a copy that had been prepared for publication and differed only slightly from Kay's version in the bridge. A number of specific plot songs that could not be extracted for public consumption also turned up.

Unfortunately, we still have very little of certain Gershwin shows, like *Treasure Girl*, a 1928 flop that ran for only a couple of months before closing. For some reason, eight selections from that score were published, an unusually high number from one score. Many more individual manuscripts from *Treasure Girl* turned up in Secaucus, but we found no orchestrations, so there's no way of reviving the show. What we have instead are weird, disembodied songs, like "A-Hunting We Will Go" (in which Ira rhymed "passionate" with "cash in it"), "Dead Men Tell No Tales" and "I Want to Marry a Marionette"—bizarre titles and songs that were obviously written for plot situations. Ira had a wonderful memory but it was selective and he couldn't recall all the specifics, especially in the instance of *Treasure Girl*, which was one of the first flops that George and Ira worked on and which I'm sure he wanted to forget.

Since scores from a flop were quickly destroyed after the last performance, it was surprising to find scores not only for *Treasure Girl* but also for *Pardon My English*, another flop. In that case, the complete show turned up—all the original parts that the musicians had played in the pit. Artie Shaw played in the orchestra of that show and actually was able to identify his part from some of the doodles that he had drawn on the music. Shaw said that during the run of the show, he used to anger the conductor and orchestrator, Adolph Deutsch, because after playing it a couple of times, he memorized his part and never opened the book. Deutsch, whom Johnny Green called "the single greatest orchestrator per se of our time," used to scream at him, "You've got to read the music!" But Artie never did, hence all the doodles on his folder.

Aside from the thrill of actually holding these historical artifacts in my hands, I was delighted to see the physical evidence that could be used to settle certain disputes and rumors that I had been hearing for years. In one instance, the published version of a Vincent Youmans song called "Bambalina," rather famous at the time it came out, lists music by Vincent Youmans and Herbert Stothart. The Youmans family always suspected that Stothart, who wrote some of the songs in the show in which "Bambalina" appeared (the 1923 *Wildflower*), later put his name on some of the Youmans songs that he actually had no hand in. And, indeed, the original manuscript of "Bambalina" revealed only Youmans's name. We were also able to discover in what keys certain songs had been sung on the stage. Sometimes notations told us where a certain song occurred in the context of the show, or we discovered duplicate orchestrations of the same song, reflecting certain changes in a show. Finding material that enabled the reconstruction of a complete *Show Boat* was monumental. In other cases, the cache of material did not complete the scores for the shows but did help narrow the gap. And yet I find it frustrating that a number of archival reconstructions of shows based on the discovered material have not been totally kosher or aboveboard. The new production teams haven't always indicated where certain segments had to be newly orchestrated or where editorial choices were made because not all the information was known about a specific aspect of a show.

For example, in the original stage version of *Strike Up the Band*, "I've Got a Crush on You" was performed as a fast-paced one-step. That song then became a slow, bluesy number when Lee Wiley recorded it in the late '30s for Liberty Music Shop. It was her idea to do it that way, although it was never sung in the show like that. But when that show was reconstructed in the '80s for an L.A. production, they first performed "I've Got a Crush on You" as it was originally written and then did another chorus of it as a slow, bluesy song. That certainly is not an authentic re-creation and yet there was no explanation of it in the program notes. Besides that, there had been two versions of *Strike Up the Band*—one in 1927 that closed out of town and one that made it to Broadway in 1930; the show they were re-creating was an amalgam of the 1927 and 1930 versions. Once again, there were choices that had to be made about which songs to use and it can get very convoluted, but an audience has the right to know. For the recording of *Let 'Em Eat Cake* made in 1987, Kay Swift actually composed the verse and final sixteen bars of a song called "First Lady and First Gent" but was not given credit. The only music that existed for the song was a lead sheet in Gershwin's hand of the first few bars. The rest of the song, including harmonies, was created by Kay. What would it have hurt to give her credit?

About nine months after the discovery, the *New York Times* ran a front-page article by Tim Page about the Secaucus find, listing the bare essentials. The story ran on a Saturday and garnered remarkably little attention, given the extent of the find. But in 1987, five years after the original discovery, the paper ran a second front-page story about the discovered material by the same reporter, this time on a Tuesday. The manuscripts had been stored in Warners' vault while the parties argued over possession and copyrights. I still cannot understand why it took the *Times* five years to decide that the Secaucus cache was a big deal after all. But suddenly the story was picked up by the international media and I received a flurry of calls from around the world. The *Times* had printed the lyric for "Freud and Jung and Adler" as an example of the kinds of songs that had been discovered in Secaucus. Yet that lyric came from Ira's lyric file and had existed all these years. And although we did find the original music in Secaucus, the identical music had already been written down from memory by Kay Swift. I wrote a letter to the editor asking, "Why did you print on the front page of the *Times* a lyric that was not found in Secaucus and that has existed all along?" Their response was that they didn't know everything that was there when it was first discovered in 1982 but now that the material had been properly organized and catalogued, they had an overview of what it was about—which was ridiculous. It taught me the power of the *New York Times* in that merely by their printing this story, years out of date and misleadingly presented, everybody jumped on the bandwagon and it became a major news story. The *McNeil-Lehrer News Hour* even did a piece. I kept telling people that this had happened five years ago, and they kept saying, "Yeah, yeah, but tell us about it anyway!"

People who read the *Times*'s brief story in 1982 no doubt thought that Secaucus must contain plenty of gems that had not been heard in sixty years and that were now going to be bestowed on the world. That was true, but I was always quick to point out that there are hundreds and hundreds of *published* songs by the same writers that are obscure and that in many cases are of better quality than the things that were discovered in Secaucus. They may have been cut from a show before it got to Broadway or they may have been in a flop show, but they are eminently worth recalling and singing and recording. It's also true that not every unpublished song by masters like Kern and Rodgers and the Gershwins is a masterpiece. Some of the Secaucus things were not published because they weren't considered commercially viable, and with good reason.

$\mathcal{W}$ELL before the cache of Gershwin manuscripts turned up in that Secaucus warehouse, Ira had showed me a number of unpublished George Gershwin songs that he could never bring himself to release to the public. Of about a hundred Gershwin melodies in varying states of completion that he possessed, some were mere fragments or sketches but others were full-blown songs of differing vintage and levels of quality. We spent a lot of time going over them and discussing the possibilities of publishing them, and we got very close at times, whittling down the selection to about twenty of the most viable. But Ira always ended up saying, "Look, let's wait." Or "We'll see." Or "Let's hold off awhile." Over the course of the six years I was there, we constantly talked about this songbook and sometimes spent two afternoons a week playing through the material with Al Kohn from Warner Brothers. Nevertheless, it became clear to me that it was highly unlikely that any of the songs would ever be released during Ira's lifetime. For one thing, he was concerned about how the songs would be perceived by the public. He wanted them to be popular and to be presented in a way that would garner some attention at a time when American classic pop was not as popular as it is now. But he couldn't conceive of a way that would properly present the songs. It was as if they were the last remnants of a gold mine, a few remaining gems from a once vast collection of jewels and, as a result, they took on more importance than they may have merited.

Ira recognized these songs as the last representations of his brother's work that had not been heard by the public and he knew that they would be carefully scrutinized and judged. The world would be saying, "Okay, here is some pristine Gershwin material without the accumulated baggage of nostalgia, without the association of having been performed by everybody from Fred Astaire to Ella Fitzgerald. Now we'll see if George really deserves his great reputation."

The problem with that thinking, of course, is that the familiarity and associations are a part of Gershwin's great appeal. An unpublished Gershwin song being released today doesn't have the advantage of having been heard over the last fifty years. When you think of "They Can't Take That Away from Me," you think of Fred Astaire. Many people have memories connected with that song and the movie he sang it in, not to mention all the great singers and instrumentalists who have performed it since, and a great deal of sentiment has built up through the years. I maintain that if "They Can't Take That Away from Me" were published for the first time today, it would go unnoticed.

Ira wanted to change certain lines to remove the songs from their more limited function within a plot situation in a show, but by that time he was no longer as facile at rewriting lyrics and didn't feel up to doing any heavy work. Once in a while he would have a spurt of inspiration and would start to work, but he got tired very quickly. "I can't think," he would always say. "I'm dizzy. I'll do it later." Other times, when we played through one of the unpublished melodies, he often said, "I remember George playing it this way." And he made little changes in the melody from the way George's manuscript showed it. Ira's memory was usually very accurate, so perhaps George had made changes through the years. Some of the melodies had never had lyrics written for them and they remain 32-bar melodies that are problematic. Unless

you get somebody either to write lyrics for them or to put them into
some larger form, they're essentially useless. Yip Harburg wrote Ira a
letter in 1978, asking if Ira would let him lyrically collaborate with his
idol, something he never got to do in life save for one bit of juvenilia.
Ira gently refused Yip. Privately, by behavior only, he revealed a jealousy toward Yip in this regard that would have clearly made it unbear-
able for him to endure such a collaboration. Yip was Ira's age and could
still knock off a clever lyric line with the best of 'em, whereas Ira had
trouble putting a sentence together some days. He just couldn't bring
himself to let Yip do a job that he still hoped he could do. Or maybe it
was simply that if Ira couldn't do it, then nobody else was going to,
either!

And so, most of the unpublished material was never released. When
Ira was queried as to why he hadn't done something with it earlier, he
became defensive. "But I have," he said. And it's true that he did dip
into that material on a couple of occasions. The first time he took a
posthumous melody of George's and made something out of it was for
the 1939 World's Fair. With the help of Kay Swift, he fashioned it into a
song titled "Dawn of a New Day" that became a theme of the New York
World's Fair. (One critic said that the song reminded him of a theme
written for Crown in *Porgy and Bess.*) The back of the sheet music
claimed that George and Ira had written the song earlier in anticipation
of the fair, but that was incorrect.

Then, in the mid-'40s, Ira was asked by the producers William Perlberg and George Seaton to write a musical film for 20th Century-Fox
that was to star Judy Garland and Dick Haymes. As it turned out, they
couldn't borrow Judy Garland from MGM, and Betty Grable eventually
went into the film, which was titled *The Shocking Miss Pilgrim.* Ira told
me that when Perlberg and Seaton approached him and asked him
whom he would like to collaborate with, he'd said, "I'd like to work
with my favorite collaborator, George." In spite of the fact that Ira had
worked with Jerome Kern and Kurt Weill and Harold Arlen and Vernon
Duke and Burton Lane and other greats, he still considered George the
greatest and best composer he knew. The producers approached two
other composers but each had already contracted for another project,
according to Ira. He then suggested that a score be fashioned from his
brother's unused material, and Perlberg and Seaton convinced the studio

to go along. Once again with guidance from Kay Swift, Ira crafted a complete score from George's unpublished melodies.

By 1945, when they were working on *The Shocking Miss Pilgrim* (which was released in 1947), Kay Swift had already salvaged a lot of the unpublished Gershwin melodies. A couple of years after George's death, Kay had come out to California and begun to go through George's tune notebooks. When she found a fragment that looked familiar to her, she wrote it down. If she remembered how he played it at the piano, she wrote out a full piano part for it. She and Ira very carefully went through almost every scrap of George's music that existed and organized and numbered the unpublished melodies. Kay had an astounding memory. At one time, she had memorized the complete vocal score of *Porgy and Bess*, all 559 pages of it—not out of any particular desire to do so but just by dint of her familiarity with it. Through the years, people have questioned the accuracy of Kay Swift's memory but, for the most part, without evidence. Here's one small example. In 1972, she notated from memory "Comes the Revolution," which was written for *Let 'Em Eat Cake*, a 1933 musical. In 1982, among the Secaucus material, we discovered an earlier version of that same music as written for *Pardon My English* in 1932 (George had recycled the melody in *Let 'Em Eat Cake*). It turned out that the harmonies of the song as Kay had written them down in 1972 were identical to George's 1932 manuscript. When Kay remembered, she *remembered*. But on the rare occasion when she didn't, she would say so and attempt to reconstruct harmony after having issued that caveat. When she tried to reconstruct the harmonies for "The Union League" (also from *Let 'Em Eat Cake*) she made the attempt on two different occasions several years apart and with wildly varying results. Yet *both* sounded like Gershwin.

One of the manuscripts Kay and Ira came across while they were working on *The Shocking Miss Pilgrim* was a melody that eventually became a song titled "For You, For Me, For Evermore." On the original lead sheet in George's hand, Ira had written the words "Gold Mine," which was Kay Swift's name for it. (In one instance for *Pilgrim*, Ira and Kay couldn't find anything among George's unpublished melodies that would suit a certain scene and so Kay actually created the music entirely on her own for one of the minor choruses in the film, the suffragettes' song called "Stand Up and Fight.")

The third occasion on which Ira worked with George's unpublished tunes was for his last professional work in 1964, a terrible movie called *Kiss Me, Stupid*, which starred Dean Martin, Ray Walston, and Kim Novak. (I sometimes sing the songs at parties attended by *Stupid*'s director, Billy Wilder, to nettle him lovingly—much to his consternation.) Ira fashioned three songs that, in the context of the film, were supposedly written by amateur songwriters. Unfortunately, he did his job too well, because the songs are in fact mediocre. One of his ways of writing an amateurish song was to use a cliché idea, like this one he had started in the '30s:

I'm a poached egg without a piece of toast,
George G. Nathan without a play to roast.
I'm a haunted house that hasn't got a ghost,
When I'm without you.

Consequently, Ira considered his last major work to be the score of *A Star Is Born*, which he wrote with Harold Arlen in 1954.

Through the 1960s, there was frequent talk of doing more with the unpublished material. George Balanchine planned a ballet based on the unpublished pieces but decided instead to use familiar tunes for what eventually became the 1970 ballet *Who Cares?* Andre Kostelanetz was also supposed to make a recording of the pieces with Dick Hyman on piano. Gene Kelly and Saul Chaplin went through that material with an eye to coming up with a filmic idea. Nothing ever materialized.

Ira was just as protective of George's published legacy, devoting many years to tending the Gershwin archives. In the early '70s, an album was issued called *Switched-on Gershwin* that was a Moog synthesizer version of *Rhapsody in Blue*. Gershon Kingsley put the orchestral part on the Moog, and the piano solo was played acoustically by a fine pianist named Leonid Hambro. The second side consisted of selections from *Porgy and Bess*. The cover drawing of George was a parody of a mid-1930s photograph taken by Nikolas Muray, depicting George with a big Afro. Ira was deeply offended by that. He thought it practically sacrilegious that somebody would alter his brother's image in any way. He couldn't do anything about that recording because it consisted of previously recorded material; he did write a letter of complaint about the cover and it was changed. I actually liked the Moog recording of *Porgy*, especially a very exciting rendition of the fugue sequence. In the '50s, Ira stopped a recording entitled *Jazz Impressions of Rhapsody in Blue,* an arrangement of variations for piano and orchestra by a man named Calvin Jackson. I also liked this recording, which I found in Ira's collection—it was notated rather than completely improvised—but Ira was offended by it when it came out and had it stopped. It was pretty interesting stuff, but Ira didn't want anyone monkeying with *Rhapsody in Blue.* I don't know if he would have been able to stop it legally, but through intimidation and the efforts of the music publishers he did stop it.

Although Ira was especially protective of George's concert works, he had fond memories of some offbeat interpretations he had heard over the years. He told me about two men visiting George in the late '20s and announcing that they had worked out an interpretation of his Concerto in F that they performed entirely a cappella. According to Ira, the pair proceeded to sing the whole thirty-minute work and their rendition was "pretty good." Somehow I find that hard to imagine.

For many years, *Rhapsody in Blue* was on a restricted play list, which meant it could not be played on the radio or performed without written permission from the publisher. It was not removed from that list until the late '70s, by which time the restricted list had become largely irrelevant. But at one time, the airing of pieces of music on radio was carefully protected. You can still find on some record albums from the '50s the notation to the effect that "these songs are not permitted for radio airplay and permission must be obtained from the publisher." I'm not at all sure how such a restriction was enforced.

Among the unpublished manuscripts was one song that Ira and George had written for *Lady, Be Good!* called "Leave It to Love." We had only the music for it and could never find the lyric. When I first asked Ira about it, he said, "I saw that lyric lying around here the other day." He said that for the six years I was there. I don't know how many years ago he had seen it, but we were never able to locate that lyric, which was one of the frustrations of my job—especially since Ira kept saying that it was among his favorite lyrics. My work there often resembled the ultimate treasure hunt as I took certain of Ira's lyrics for which he could not remember the melodies and went through a box of miscellaneous pieces of Gershwin music, trying to match a piece of music to the lyric. I actually succeeded in marrying the two on one occasion, with a song called "Gather Ye Rosebuds."

Unfortunately, many other songs existed only in Ira's memory of the melodies that George had played. For example, in 1913 or 1914, George gave a recital for the Finley Club and Ira still had the program in his files. George had played a piano solo called "Tango" that was never written down and didn't exist anywhere except in Ira's memory. He remembered it very clearly in his head and could hum it but, sadly, he couldn't hum it well enough to have it notated with harmonies. A brief fragment of "Tango" and another early song George wrote called "Since I Found You," which is believed by most to be the very first song he composed, with lyrics by a neighborhood friend named Leonard Praskins, exist on an air check of a 1936 radio show. Irene Wicker, who was known as the Story Lady, did radio biographies of famous personalities for children through the 1960s. In 1936, she did one on George Gershwin featuring a pianist named Milton Rettenberg (a classmate of Ira's), who played a bit of "Tango" and the first few bars of "Since I Found You." I tracked down Rettenberg in the late '70s and asked him where he had gotten the music for those two pieces. He said that when they were preparing the program, he went to see George with Irene, and George wrote out lead sheets of both those pieces.

"Do you have them?" I asked.

"No," he said. "There was a fire years ago in my house and I lost them along with many other things." So I came that close, but no cigar.

Andre Kostelanetz came to visit Ira while I was there and he talked about meeting George in 1926 when George was writing *Oh, Kay!* Kostelanetz said he was amazed at observing George play one melody, then another, writing them down in quick succession. That's when George told him that he wrote six songs a day to get the bad ones out of his system. Ira responded that one time when he was working with George on a show out of town in Boston or Philadelphia, they had checked out of his hotel and were driving back to New York. About an hour away, George remembered that he had left one of his tune notebooks containing all of his ideas in the hotel. They drove back to retrieve it, but it was gone and they couldn't find it. George was not the least bit distressed. "Oh well," he said calmly, "there's more where that came from."

Oscar Levant once said that there was no gap between George's desire and his ability to execute what he wanted to do. It all just flowed from him naturally, like water from a fountainhead, and so he didn't have the anxiety that some creators have expressed. What was normal for George happened only rarely for some of the best-known composers. Victor Herbert's most famous song was "Kiss Me Again." He woke up in the middle of the night with a melody playing insistently in his head, wrote it down on a piece of paper at his night table, and went back to sleep. When he woke up in the morning, he had no memory of the melody or even of having written it down, but there it was.

I found a letter in George's correspondence file from Anne Brown, the original Bess, asking if she could change a brief section of *Porgy and Bess* (after it had closed on Broadway) for a subsequent performance of some of the music from it that she was doing in concert. In George's reply to her, he said, "I don't mind if you make this particular change in the opera because you know that I am the first one to agree to make a change for something if it works theatrically. So go ahead and try it. But if it doesn't work, I expect you immediately to restore it to exactly the way I wrote it." That was a remarkably generous thing to do, compared with the way other composers were. Richard Rodgers and Jerome Kern would not have heard of letting a performer change something like that.

The other side of the coin is that George was unabashedly pleased with himself. I suppose you could call him egotistical, except that one can forgive him since he had the goods to back it up. Still, more than one funny story has become legend about George's unflagging admiration for himself and his work. Once in a taxicab, George was thrown about in the backseat by a sudden stop and yelled to the driver, "Careful, man, you've got Gershwin in the car!"

But my favorite story is the one Johnny Green told me some years ago. He was once listening to George go on and on about himself to a lady friend after one of his concerts. Finally George stopped and said to the woman, "Well, enough about me. What did *you* think of my performance?"

*M*y experience with both the Secaucus cache and working with Ira on the unpublished songs in his possession fed into my lifelong archival impulse, one that probably dates back to that collection of dusty old 78s that I discovered in the basement of our home in Columbus. These days, the impulse takes the form of fighting to preserve the diminishing treasury of sheet music, scores, and manuscripts from the classic era and of helping to disseminate as much of it as I can to other performers who might like to use it in some fashion. Sometimes, for instance, a performer trying to find a copy of a piece of music by a composer as well known as George Gershwin or Irving Berlin can have problems figuring out where to go. If you can't find it in the sheet music store, then where do you look? Now there is a network of people and archives that you can go to and I'm part of that network. I always have suggestions for anyone looking for a piece of sheet music, and the first thing I do is look in my basement to see what I have.

Unfortunately, so much classic material has disappeared, like the original conductor's book for the score of *The Wizard of Oz*. It was stolen some years ago and nobody knows where it is. I have copies of certain things that MGM doesn't have anymore because they got rid of much of their collection. I can also suggest any number of other sheet music collectors or, depending on the composer, individuals who specialize in the cultivation of certain composers' works. The Library of Congress, the UCLA Sheet Music Archive, and the archives of other colleges are all likely sources. Of course, it's sometimes hard to gain access to the material even when it's there. They may have it but they may not know they do, or they will not give you a copy of it. The bureaucracy can be very frustrating, as I know from experience. Maybe that's why I keep adding to my own collection. You never know.

The story that best conveys both the sense of pride I have about preserving archival materials connected with this music and some of the adventure involved in acquiring them concerns Todd Duncan, the original Porgy in the Gershwin musical. I own a limited edition, autographed score of *Porgy and Bess*, of which only 250 copies were made. It's a very handsome, leather-bound edition, published by Random House and signed by George and Ira Gershwin, DuBose Heyward, and the director, Rouben Mamoulian. For many years I had wanted to have a copy of that score, and while I was working for Ira he once offered to give me a copy—then I looked in the closet where he had kept them and discovered they were all gone. In time, I found a copy at a dealer's and purchased it on the lay-away plan. But I later came across another one that was unique in that it was not only signed by the original four but also had been signed by members of the original cast: Anne Brown, the original Bess; John Bubbles, the original Sportin' Life; Ford Buck, who was Bubbles's partner and played a small role; Edward Matthews, who sang "A Woman Is a Sometime Thing"—in all, a half dozen principal members of the original cast. Each cast member had written his or her name and then in parentheses the name of his or her character. The only major signature that was missing was Todd Duncan's.

The book cost me $7,500 (plus some of the canceled checks with George Gershwin's signature that Ira had given to me) and ever since I bought it, I'd wanted to add Todd Duncan's autograph to complete that page. I called Todd on a couple of occasions on my way to Washington, hoping to see him, but I'd been told that he was not in good health. He once told me himself that he was not up to company and yet, when I'd seen him on television in the last several years, he seemed to be rather robust. So when I went to Washington in connection with the fiftieth anniversary of D-Day in June 1994, I decided to take the *Porgy and Bess* score with me, on the off chance that I might have an opportunity to get Duncan to sign it. It had been some time since I'd last called him and I figured that his physical condition was probably not very good, but I thought I'd still give it a shot.

On the day before I left for Washington, I called and spoke to a very curt housekeeper whose name was Dolores. She snapped at me on the phone. "Mr. Duncan is not well—he's in bed," she said. "What do you want?"

"I want to know if there's a chance of seeing him," I said.

"No. Absolutely not."

I was very apologetic and said that I didn't in any way want to intrude but wondered if there might be a chance of his signing my *Porgy and Bess* score. "I don't know," she snapped. "Call tomorrow."

So I took the score with me on the flight to Washington and when I arrived, I called again. This time, Todd was awake, but Dolores informed me crisply, "He won't talk to you."

"If you could just tell him my name," I pleaded.

She did, and he got on the phone.

"I don't know if you remember me," I began.

"Yes, of course, I remember you," he said. "You worked with Ira Gershwin."

"Is there any chance of my saying hello to you and having you sign

this score?" I explained the nature of the score and the page of auto-
graphs. "If it's in any way an intrusion, I completely understand, but I
wanted to ask."

"I'm really not well," he said, "but if you can come right away, I'll
sign it."

I was thrilled and immediately went over to his home, a beautifully
kept house on Upshur Street. I knocked on the front door and a woman
other than Dolores came out and took me around to the side and then
into the kitchen. There in all her splendor sat Dolores, a big-boned
woman with signs of weariness on her face clearly announcing that she
was suspicious of the world. "Hello, Dolores," I said, giving her a big
smile. Deadpan, she said, "Hi. Now what you got there?"

I told her what it was. "Why do you want him to sign it?" she asked
suspiciously.

"Because he was the original Porgy and I'm a huge appreciator of his
work," I said. "And this is a very rare score."

"What's rare about it?"

"Well," I said, "it's a limited edition score."

"What do you mean? What do you mean by 'score'?"

I opened it up and I showed it to her. "It's the complete music for
Porgy and Bess," I explained. "See, in the back, it's signed by George
and Ira Gershwin and DuBose Heyward."

"So!" she said. "What's so big about that?"

"It's very rare," I repeated, not knowing what else to say. "As a matter
of fact, I paid seven thousand dollars for it."

Now she looked at me as if I were the most demented person she'd
ever encountered. "Seven thousand *dollars!*" The look on her face said,
"Look at this poor, crazy white boy. What I could do with seven thousand dollars!" She kept repeating the amount like a mantra. "Seven thousand dollars! Seven thousand dollars!"

Finally, in her most interrogational tone, she demanded, "Now that
you got it, what're you going to do with it?"

"Eventually I'm going to leave it to the Library of Congress."

That seemed to register. For the first time, she softened a bit. So I
opened it up to the page where I wanted Todd to sign.

"You got a pen?" she asked.

I suddenly felt ridiculous. I searched my pockets and all I had was a ballpoint pen. I couldn't believe that I hadn't thought to bring something a little more appropriate. I lamely handed it to her and showed her where I would like Todd to sign, if possible. "Okay," she said, "hold on."

"Please be very careful with the book," I said as she carried it off.

"Don't worry," she snapped. "I got it."

She went upstairs and I heard a little commotion. "He wants you to come up," she called. As I bolted up the stairs, I heard Todd's unmistakable, mellifluous voice saying to her, "Don't ever do that again."

Todd was sitting up in bed, a male nurse seated on one side and Dolores on the other. Todd looked much thinner and more gaunt than I'd seen him in recent interviews. He was dressed but was half-covered and spread out on the bed and looked very weak. I said hello and he replied, in a very courtly, dignified way, "Hello, Mr. Feinstein."

He extended his hand in the wrong direction. I stepped closer to the bed and said, "Hello, I'm here." He turned toward me and again extended his hand. "I'm very sorry, Mr. Feinstein," he said. "I'm blind." My heart sank, because I didn't know that he had gone blind. "I lost my sight about four months ago," he said very quietly.

I got pretty choked up. "I'm terribly sorry," I said. "I had no idea. I wouldn't have asked you to sign this if I'd had any inkling of your situation."

"I'd like to try," he said gamely. As much sympathy and admiration as I felt for Todd at that moment, I was also having second thoughts. Great, I said to myself. He's going to try on a seventy-five-hundred-dollar score. I could imagine pointing to the page in the future and saying to people, "See that blotch of ink over George's and Ira's signatures? That's Todd Duncan's handwriting!"

At the same time I felt pretty guilty for having that thought and I figured, Okay, Michael, you've come this far—just show a little trust. It was still a thrill to meet him, regardless of the outcome. Then he said, "I need you to guide my hand."

I tried the pen to make sure it was working and then I guided his hand to the top of the page, because there was more room at the top and only a little space at the bottom. He wrote "Best wishes" with a little upward curve but in beautiful handwriting.

"How's that?" he asked.

"It's great!" Then he signed his name and in parentheses he wrote "Porgy." Under that, he wrote "1935," left another space, and wrote "1994," perfectly spaced above the rest of the signatures.

"Is it okay?"

"It's a lot better than my handwriting," I said.

"I just felt my way."

"It's beautiful," I said. I stood there looking at him, thinking, My God, this score was signed by almost everyone responsible for this historic work of art in 1935, all of whom are dead except for Anne Brown, who now lives in Scandinavia, and Todd.

"I can't really articulate how much it means to me to meet you," I said. "The sound of your voice singing this music still resonates in my head." Which it does. Duncan had a glorious baritone; standing there, I was thinking about how moved George must have been the first time he heard Duncan's voice. The story goes that George heard him sing just eight bars before he stopped him and said, "Will you be my Porgy?" Duncan quietly thanked me.

"I know your other work, too," I said. "*Cabin in the Sky* and *Lost in the Stars*."

"*Lost in the Stars* is my favorite," he said.

I became conscious of taking up his time. Not wanting to impose any longer, I thanked him again and rather hesitantly told him I would like to send him one of my albums. "But it can't compare to your work," I said. "Don't expect too much." For years, Todd taught voice at Howard University, which is where he was working in the '30s when he met Gershwin, and he continued teaching there until illness overcame him.

The next day, before I went back to L.A., I had lunch at the Library of Congress and I took the score with me. I showed it to Dr. James W. Pruett, then head of the Music Division. "I'm really not sure if something like this interests you," I said, knowing that they have the original manuscript of *Porgy* along with all the worksheets and much more material. "I imagine that you already have, for copyright purposes, one of the copies of the limited edition." I told him the story of my visit to Todd Duncan and I opened the score to the page with the signatures on it. Very quietly he said, "We don't have anything like that and we would very much like to add it to the collection."

"Okay," I said, "but you'll have to wait until I die to get it."

"You know," Dr. Pruett said, "we can take it on deposit, which means that it's still yours and you can have it back any moment you want it. But we can keep it for you." So I left it there and it's now with the rest of the *Porgy* material. That morning, he also showed me a two-page manuscript of some of George's working out of an instrumental section of *Porgy* that had notations of some of his lessons from Joseph Schillinger. Because those two pages showed his working process and the influence of Schillinger, they had just paid $50,000 for them. I thought Dolores would be happy to hear that.

This may sound disingenuous, coming from someone who is an obsessive collector with a basement full of recordings, sheet music, photographs, and every conceivable form of music memorabilia, but I feel that that score of *Porgy and Bess* belongs to the world. Meeting Todd Duncan and having him complete a historical document by adding his signature to it, not to mention witnessing the great dignity with which he did so, gave me so much pleasure that merely possessing the score could hardly measure up.

As I left the Library of Congress that afternoon, I found myself almost unconsciously whistling a tune. Stopping for a moment, I identified it as "I Got Plenty o' Nuthin'."

interlude

A LITTLE THEATER HISTORY

American music was undistinguished until the turn of the century.
Stephen Foster had made an impression with his ballads, and people
enjoyed the music of the minstrel shows, but very little of this music
made an impact on the rest of the world. Slowly people in other coun-
tries became aware of spirituals and ragtime, and by the start of the
First World War, the sound of the blues began to insinuate itself.
Here was a strange new quality in musical form, the very basis of jazz,
a sound that quickly spread through the universe. The American the-
ater lagged badly, and not until Victor Herbert did anyone even think
in terms of an American musical. Herbert was well established at the
outbreak of war in 1914, but what happened in the United States after
the war shook the musical world—so much so that Victor Herbert
was left behind.

Suddenly a cluster of bright young men with names like George
Gershwin, Vincent Youmans, Richard Rodgers, Jerome Kern, Cole
Porter, Irving Berlin, Arthur Schwartz, Jimmy McHugh, and
Harry Warren swamped Tin Pan Alley and Broadway with vital,
tuneful songs that had a flavor and character recognizably American.
All the influences seemed to meld at this time—the blues, the Negro
themes, the ragtime, the folk music of multiple cultures brought by the
immigrants, and the classical traditions and training of Europe. . . .

*The result was a new chapter in musical history and a wave of song-
writing that was extraordinary in both quality and impact. The world
began to dance and sing American music. The time was right. Music
was about to become Big Business, abetted by a burgeoning recording
industry and a fledgling giant called radio.*

*Above all, it was the United States' good fortune to have an abun-
dance of eager young men ready with an incalculable quantity of words
and music. It was a condition that had never existed before and may
never exist again. The waves of European immigration in the late nineteenth and early twentieth centuries brought talent in copious amounts.
. . . Many of the young songwriters of the twenties were first-generation
Americans. Their roots were mainly German, Russian, Italian,
African, and Hebraic, all of which somehow blended with the American ethos to produce a new sound.*

—TONY THOMAS, *Harry Warren and
the Hollywood Musical*

*I*f all the talk in these pages about Broadway musical theater is a little
confusing, and if names like Victor Herbert and Sigmund Romberg seem
only vaguely familiar, you may find this interlude helpful. It's far from
scholarly—I'm an archivist, not a college professor—but it does trace
briefly the development of musical theater through the Golden Age I'm
most familiar with, and includes a few words about Tin Pan Alley. If
that's old hat to you, feel free to skip ahead to the next chapter.

To begin with, American popular music of the first half of this century
comprises several different but related forms that are sometimes confused because they overlapped during much of their prime. The three
major forms are roughly categorizable as jazz, Tin Pan Alley, and musical theater. Although jazz numbered some prominent white performers
and composers among its key players, it was predominantly the product

of the black experience, combining African rhythms, improvisation, call and response elements, and a pentatonic or "blues" scale with European instruments. Musical theater, although it appropriated some elements of ragtime and jazz, and although a number of black songwriters and performers scored successes on Broadway, was an essentially European import dominated by white, especially Jewish, composers and lyricists who in many cases were immigrants or the children of immigrants. Tin Pan Alley produced songs similar in form to much of musical theater except that they were not tied to plot and were often of lesser quality. Their main function was to sell sheet music (and, later, records).

The basis of musical theater was imported from Europe in the late nineteenth century. Until the turn of the century, the typical fare in most theaters consisted of Viennese and other European operettas in translation. Even the major American composers of operetta—Victor Herbert, Rudolf Friml, and Sigmund Romberg—had been born and educated in Europe and tended to write in the refined musical tradition of flowing melodic lines set to rhythms that lacked the syncopation shortly to become the trademark of American popular music. Story lines were often borrowed directly from Viennese and British operettas set in exotic foreign locales. As the name implies, operettas were lower-scaled spin-offs of European grand opera, capable of appealing to a wider and less refined audience. According to the venerable theater historian Miles Kreuger, from the American debut of Gilbert and Sullivan's *H.M.S. Pinafore* until the Broadway opening of Franz Lehár's Viennese operetta *The Merry Widow* in 1907, "the American Musical Theater was dominated by the prevailing styles of British shows: first the satiric comic operas and later the more romantic musical comedies as mounted in London primarily by George Edwardes. Almost every hit on the London boards was swiftly wafted across the Atlantic to be staged on Broadway." (Come to think of it, not that much has changed, has it?)

Alongside these European transplants, the more characteristically American form of the revue developed by blending, often haphazardly, elements of vaudeville comedy, burlesque, the black minstrel show, and the English music hall. Comedy and music were intermingled, the music itself leaning more heavily toward ragtime and other syncopated, black-influenced rhythms, although presented in anything but a pure jazz format. Revues usually consisted of a series of short sketches, often satirical, interspersed with songs that were the work of a number of different composers and lyricists. The songs were frequently expanded into dance routines that gave the producer an excuse to parade large numbers of skimpily dressed chorus girls before an avid audience.

In the hands of a master showman like Florenz (Flo) Ziegfeld, the Broadway revue of the first two decades of this century was essentially American in language, rhythm, and tone, but it was also all over the place. Plots were virtually nonexistent and individual songs were provided by a variety of songwriting teams, so a show's success depended on the unifying appeal of charismatic performers like W. C. Fields, Will Rogers, Al Jolson, Fanny Brice, and the black comic Bert Williams. As a show was perceived as sagging over time, new songs or comedy routines were constantly interpolated into the mix. This provided a golden opportunity for fledgling songwriters to have new compositions showcased to a wide audience, always holding out the hope of a smash hit and instant recognition—as happened with George Gershwin and "Swanee."

What we refer to now as American musical comedy grew out of a gradual blending of the more coherent dramatic plot line of the operetta with the comedy and syncopated rhythms of the revue. This combination of elements became enormously popular largely through the work of George M. Cohan. Literally born on the road to a family of touring vaudevillians, George joined their act as a baby, had speaking roles by age nine, and by the time he was eleven was serving as the family's business manager. Before Cohan, according to popular music historian David Jasen, musical comedy in America "consisted of vaudeville stars doing their turns in exotic costumes in front of colorful scenery with scripts that had little or no plot." Beginning in 1904 with *Little Johnny Jones,* Cohan changed all that through his glorification of Americana in song hits like "The Yankee Doodle Boy" and "Give My Regards to Broadway." Suddenly it was all right to create shows around American places and people and, for the first time on the legitimate stage, to use words like "hell" and "damn."

Cohan's daring was no doubt abetted by the patriotic fervor of shows like *George Washington, Jr.* and the songs "You're a Grand Old Flag" and "Over There." Cohan succeeded by replacing the exotic and somewhat high-flown sentiments of turn-of-the-century operettas with his own distinctively breezy, fast-paced productions marked by patriotism and an unmistakably American flavor. While musical revues like the Ziegfeld Follies and, later, George White's Scandals continued to run on Broadway year after year with ever new agglomerations of comedy sketches and songs by different authors, Cohan imprinted the idea that a single composer could create a coherent work utilizing many of those same elements. In 1918, he actually collaborated on a theatrical revue with his successor as master of the musical comedy song, Irving Berlin. (The story of Cohan's rise and his dazzling impact on American musical theater is told with great verve and relative accuracy in Michael Curtiz's 1942 film *Yankee Doodle Dandy*. James Cagney won an Oscar for his portrayal of the great song and dance man.)

The elements that are responsible for what we know as modern musical comedy, however, came from the unique collaboration of the English librettists and lyricists P. G. Wodehouse and Guy Bolton working with the New York–born composer Jerome Kern on a series of shows at the 299-seat Princess Theatre during the teens. Kern had begun by writing songs to be interpolated into the British and Viennese musical imports that had dominated Broadway to that time. His songs initially served to make the imports more palatable to American tastes, but by 1912 Kern was writing complete scores; when he introduced Guy Bolton to his old friend P. G. Wodehouse, the revolutionary theater trio was born. Inspired by Gilbert and Sullivan and using smaller, eleven-piece orchestras in the pit with two-piano accompaniment, as opposed to the classical orchestras of traditional musical comedies, the new team created the archetype of the modern musical comedy with its more popular sound. Theater historian Lee Davis, for example, contends that the American musical theater actually began on the night of April 20, 1915, at the Princess Theatre with the opening of *Nobody Home,* "the first musical to treat seriously music, book, and lyrics as equal creative partners." (Davis disputes the notion that *Oklahoma!* was the first musical to do that, as many people believe.) The Princess shows were more intimate and used fewer cast members than the big, sprawling revues that had preceded them. Along with the legacy of George M. Cohan, these were the shows that influenced Irving Berlin, the Gershwins, Richard Rodgers, and just about everybody else who followed.

The process of interpolating songs into a theatrical comedy along with dancing and comedy routines went through a significant transformation in the '20s and '30s. Songwriters developed the art of using song lyrics to advance the action in a show rather than merely stopping the action to entertain the audience and then returning to the plot. In his autobiography, Alan Jay Lerner talks in detail about where theater songs should occur, namely, at a spot where there is no other way to express what needs to be expressed at that moment *except* through a song. According to Lerner, that three or four minutes of song must advance the plot and give you an understanding and insight that moves you along so that by the end of the song, you're in a completely different emotional place. Lerner also says that you must be careful that what you say in the song does not duplicate anything that has preceded or will follow it, so that in a sense the song is a revelation.

Lerner and Loewe, of course, were masters at knowing precisely where to place a song in a show, as were the Gershwins. When Ira wrote a song, he sometimes wrote dialogue leading into it, conceiving a whole scene for presenting the song. When he wrote "I Can't Get Started" with Vernon Duke, for instance, he created the whole sketch that surrounded it. If you look it up in Bob Kimball's book of Ira's lyrics, you'll find his dramatic introduction for the song, with lines like "Gosh, I can't seem to get to first base with you. Never a smile, never a kind word. Good God, what would I have to give you for a kiss?" (Her answer is "Ronald Colman.") Ira put himself in the situation of the character and worked very hard to imagine the larger context, as most of the great lyricists and composers have done.

The same development later carried over into movie musicals. Saul Chaplin, who began by writing songs such as "Shoe-Shine Boy," "Until the Real Thing Comes Along," and "Bei Mir Bist Du Schon" with lyricist Sammy Cahn, went on to become an Academy Award–winning arranger, musical director, and film producer. He told Max Wilk that the days when songs were isolated events arbitrarily placed in a film left us with Nelson Eddy and Jeanette MacDonald in the 1930s. "At that time," Chaplin said, "the important thing was to rear back and sing; they used to scream in each other's faces." He cited the 1954 film *Seven Brides for Seven Brothers,* with a score by Gene DePaul and Johnny Mercer and musical direction by Chaplin and Adolph Deutsch, as the quintessential example of the integration of songs into the plot of a movie to the extent that it would not work as a film *without* the songs. For example, early in the movie the seven brothers are despondent because they don't have any women. "Howard Keel walks in," Chaplin continued, "and says, 'You're so depressed, why don't we go out and *get* the girls?' He sings a song called 'Sobbin' Women.' By the end of the thing, he's got them so roused up that they all ride off and kidnap the women! Now, if you remove that song, the scene won't make any sense."

Apart from a handful of composers, musical theater showed remarkably little *direct* black influence. Without question, the syncopated rhythms of ragtime, the spiritual, and early jazz had a radical impact on the sound and structure of popular songs. (African American forms like the blues and rhythm and blues also laid the groundwork for rock 'n' roll, which made up a kind of second wave of American popular music and which some music historians would argue was actually antithetical to the popular music of the '20s through the mid-'50s.) But the initial influence of black rhythms was strongly filtered through the experience of the (primarily Russian) Jewish immigrant stock directly responsible for reshaping the course of American musical comedy, especially Kern, Berlin, and the Gershwins.

A few black composers dabbled in Broadway, including Will Marion Cook, who in 1898 wrote the first black musical to reach Broadway, *Clorindy (or the Origin of the Cakewalk),* and followed with *In Dahomey* in 1903 with Bert Williams; and Eubie Blake, whose *Shuffle Along* was a success in 1921. Although Scott Joplin never had a Broadway show, his development of ragtime profoundly influenced theater music; his opera *Treemonisha* was performed posthumously. Racism played a part here as well; most of the country was still segregated, and between 1920 and 1932 black audiences in the South and Midwest were served by a separate theater circuit known as the Theatre Owners Booking Association, or TOBA (although black musicians who toured under its auspices interpreted its acronym as Tough on Black Asses). To be accepted, black composers had to be extraordinarily gifted—the Jackie Robinson syndrome—and so Broadway musical theater remained largely a white field.

Tin Pan Alley represents a lineage that goes back to the 1700s. In the 1800s, composers like Stephen Foster received very little money for the songs they wrote. Early editions of one of Foster's most famous songs do not even give him proper credit, as plagiarism and outright thievery were commonplace. E. P. Christie of the famous Christie's Minstrels tried to take credit for a number of Foster's songs. The cover of the sheet music for "Old Folks at Home" claims it to be an "Ethiopian melody" composed by E. P. Christie, not Stephen Foster. (Foster sold the song to Christie in the year of its publication, 1851.) It wasn't until 1914, with the formation of ASCAP, that songwriters started to get some kind of protection for their art. Operetta king Victor Herbert and his attorney Nathan Burkan were most instrumental in the creation of ASCAP to ensure that composers would get royalties for live performances of their works for profit. One would have to purchase an ASCAP license to have the right to perform publicly any of the songs registered with the organization. However, radio broadcasters became annoyed at having to pay royalties for broadcast performances of songs and records and in 1940 BMI (Broadcast Music, Inc.) began to provide serious competition for ASCAP.

The term Tin Pan Alley signifies both a kind of music and a locus of musical creation. The district that was home to most of the music publishing houses that printed sheet music for popular songs changed its physical location through the years, migrating from the Bowery in lower Manhattan in the 1890s as far north as the current theater district, where the "Alley" faded out in the mid-1950s. But according to tradition, the name originated shortly after the turn of the century when a composer, writing a series of articles for the *New York Herald* about the boom in popular music publishing, visited a publishing office in what was then the heart of the district on West 28th Street. He described the cacophony of songwriters and song pluggers pounding away at their pianos as sounding like a lot of tin pans clanging together in the kitchen. (Song plugging was as much a part of the Alley as songwriting. Pluggers, often aspiring young songwriters themselves, were hired by the music publishing houses to play and sing new songs for an endless stream of vaudevillians and other performers hungry for fresh material.) Early classics such as "The Sidewalks of New York" and "The Band Played On" got their start on Tin Pan Alley.

Even though Tin Pan Alley was dedicated to the creation and marketing of single songs to appeal to the masses, the name has sometimes been used in a broader context to include theater songs and film songs with popular appeal. In fact, there was plenty of overlap. Many of the people who wrote for Tin Pan Alley went on to write theater songs, and many of the publishers who published songs in Tin Pan Alley also published show music. One distinction between theatrical and popular songs was that a popular song might sell for a nickel while a piece of theater sheet music could fetch fifty cents or more and could not generally be found in Woolworth's or other places that stocked standard sheet music. Prices varied over the years and there were price wars and ensuing problems when some of the larger chain stores started carrying sheet music and lowered the price from fifty cents to a dime or so.

In general, the music publishers who ran Tin Pan Alley were out to make money by exploiting songs that would appeal to the masses. Cliché ideas were encouraged because they worked. Songs about "Mammy" and "Alabamy" and all those trite "June-moon-spoon" rhymes were exactly what these publishers wanted. For that very reason, the more sophisticated writers who worked in musical theater strove to avoid easy rhymes and obvious sentiments, in some cases making fun of them in songs like Ira Gershwin's "Blah, Blah, Blah" and his sarcastic "Popular Song Quiz." The literary devices that lyricists like Ira and Larry Hart put into their songs for the most part did not show up in Tin Pan Alley hits.

The full color artwork on the covers of Tin Pan Alley sheets had a great deal to do with the success of certain songs; some sheets were illustrated by the likes of Maxfield Parrish and Norman Rockwell while others were adorned by photographs of the famous performers who introduced the songs, including Al Jolson and Fanny Brice. Certain publishers were known for having lousy songs but beautiful covers, which was just the point (and one which carried over into the album cover art of the pop and rock era, when the most glamorous photos and most inventive cover designs often cloaked the worst records).

The lineage of American popular song, and of the musical theater that was once inextricably intertwined with it, is continuing to snake its way though our own era. Stephen Sondheim, after all, got started at an early age when his score for a musical was critiqued in depth by Oscar Hammerstein II, who then went on to teach Sondheim much of his craft. Where it will wind up, only heaven knows. There is plenty of current evidence to suggest that its best years are behind us, but when I hear new songs by the likes of Sondheim as well as John Bucchino and Michele Brourman, I have to question that assumption. The tremendous volume of high-quality material that once poured forth is certainly no longer being produced today. But as long as there is still somebody around to whistle, hum, sing, or merely appreciate a classic song, the tradition will live on.

And speaking of tradition, I'd like to devote the next few chapters to an appreciation of some classic songwriters I most admire and enjoy.

I GET A KICK OUT OF COLE

It's fun, it's fine,
It's too divine.
It's smooth, it's smart.
It's Rodgers, it's Hart!
What debs, what stags!
What gossip, what gags!
What feathers, what fuss!
Just between the two of us,
Have you heard that Mimsie Starr
Just got pinched in the Astor Bar?
Well, did you evah!
What a swell party this is!
—COLE PORTER, *"Well, Did You Evah?"*

*A*t every "swell" party I've ever played, there comes an inevitable question: "Do you know any Cole Porter?" After all, what is a swell party without the sophisticated sounds of Cole Porter? Sophisticated. That word is inseparably connected to the Porter name—an element that is just as important to the success of a Beverly Hills affair as champagne, black tie, and glittering diamonds. "We have Michael Feinstein playing Cole Porter," proclaims the hostess. Or better yet, "We have *Bobby Short* playing Cole Porter." Not Gershwin or Kern or even Noël

Coward. A party just isn't as important with these other guys. On one memorable occasion, my hostess (who made sure I entered her home by the service entrance) continually tested me throughout the night to make sure I was complying with her request. All through the evening, as I launched into the chorus of a new number, she would sidle up to the keyboard and ask me accusingly, "Is *that* Cole Porter?" I had the feeling that I could have played the Stephen Foster songbook and she wouldn't have known the difference. (It's too bad I didn't think of Foster that night. Imagine "Camptown Races" with a beguine beat—sounds catchy, no?)

Born a little over one hundred years ago, Cole Porter was one of the major contributors to the Golden Age of American popular song. The fact that he supplied both words and music puts him in an even more elite position (Irving Berlin and Noël Coward being the only other words-and-music men from that era who spring readily to mind). To answer the question of why Porter is worth knowing today, you need only listen to the words and music of any number of his most popular songs. Porter, like many of his contemporaries, was able to express basic human emotions—sometimes cliché ideas—in clever, subtle, and fresh ways. He always strove to find a way of saying "I love you" without being obvious. He deplored the obvious because he knew that the success of his work relied on the endless fount of fresh ideas generated by a tireless craftsman who wouldn't settle for the mundane.

The subtlety lacking in many of today's songs has moved a lot of the younger generation toward the world of Cole Porter, a world of revelation through concealment. A number of contemporary artists have started performing the songs of Porter, with varying results. A controversial album titled *Red, Hot and Blue* put out a few years ago features twenty-one artists performing twenty-two songs (all to benefit the American Foundation for AIDS Research). Most of the performances on the disc are largely unrecognizable in comparison to what Porter originally wrote; many of the tracks are ignorant interpretations missing the point of what Porter was trying to say. A few tracks are interesting and even enjoyable, but they are in the minority. At the glitzy publicity party in L.A. celebrating the release of *Red, Hot and Blue*, I was spotted by a nice man who was covering the event for *Rolling Stone* (a magazine that doesn't know I exist). He gave me a big Cheshire Cat grin and said,

"Michael, I bet I know what you think of the album." I laughed and said, "I'll bet you're right."

Then he said, "I suppose you think that Cole Porter is turning over in his grave?"

"He's not turning over in his grave," I replied. "He's on a rotisserie." If Porter was incensed by Frank Sinatra's interpolation of the line "You give me a boot" in "I Get a Kick Out of You," what could he possibly have thought about Tom Waits's unrecognizable rendition of "It's All Right with Me"? But maybe an album like that will lead people who hear it to seek out the more sublime interpretations and interpreters of Porter's art; I don't know. It still is significant that songs of Porter were selected for this venture. His lyrics contain innumerable references to High Society—a world he knew better than any other and loved to poke fun at:

> No rich Vanderbilt gives me gilt underwear
> But I've still got my health so what do I care!

or

> In spite of the vodka shortage at the Colony
> (I happen to know it's practically gone)
> And in spite of those daily cracks
> That we're headed to get the ax,
> Cafe Society still carries on.

Porter was from the Midwest—Peru, Indiana—and his socialite friend Elsa Maxwell was from Keokuk, Iowa, a fact that they both never forgot:

> I'm dining with Maxwell, with Maxwell, my dear.
> She's tired of princesses
> In their Coco Chanel dresses,
> And she's longing for sausages and beer.
> I've covered our tracks well,
> For I'm saving Miss Maxwell
> From her ninety-nine most intimate friends.

Porter created more sexy and sexual lyrics than any of his contemporaries (Lorenz Hart came closest to Cole in this area), and it seems to me that he was able to go a bit further than usual because of that aforementioned word—sophisticated. If the lyrics hadn't been written by "sophisticated" Cole, they might have otherwise been considered smutty and unsingable, but Cole had license. It is true, however, that a number of his lyrics were censored from the airwaves, in Hollywood and, inevitably, in Boston. (Censorship didn't start with rap music.) The original lyric of "Easy to Love" contained the couplet

> So sweet to waken with,
> So nice to sit down to eggs and bacon with.

That was unacceptable with the Hays office, Hollywood's self-censorship bureau, and it was changed to

> So worth the yearning for,
> So swell to keep every home fire burning for.

"Love for Sale" was completely unacceptable for the airwaves, as was the famous cocaine reference in "I Get a Kick Out of You." "Some get a kick from cocaine" was replaced by "Some like the perfumes of Spain"—not a Porter lyric. A Boston casualty from the 1950s show *Out of This World* was

> After quieting all my urgin's
> For several vestal virgins.

Cole Porter was certainly one of the greatest lyric writers of the twentieth century. His words read like poetry—even though it's dangerous to divorce a lyric from its music. The contemporary feeling of many of his words is uncanny. And his facility for humor, certainly the most difficult kind of lyric to write, is, to me, his most impressive achievement. In song after song, he knows how to take a joke and build it to a climax in one chorus, then he adds level after level of funny lines in each succeeding chorus. "Anything Goes" is a perfect example. Porter saves some of his best lines for the third chorus:

> If Sam Goldwyn can, with great conviction
> Instruct Anna Sten in diction,
> Then Anna shows
> Anything Goes.

Porter's love songs contain a unique combination of warmth, reserve, and passion. The masochistic passion expressed in "So in Love"—

> So taunt me and hurt me,
> Deceive me, desert me,
> I'm yours 'til I die,
> So in love with you, my love, am I

—is tempered by the reserve of

> What a rare night for romancing,
> Mind if I make love to you?

Many of his love songs contain a unique melancholy feeling:

> There's no love song finer
> But how strange
> The change
> From major to minor
> Ev'ry time we say goodbye,
> Ev'ry single time we say goodbye.

Versatility is the hallmark of a great lyricist. Leafing through *The Complete Lyrics of Cole Porter* by Bob Kimball, you encounter so many different kinds of exceptional lyrics that the mind goes numb after a while. I have a lot of favorite Porter songs—songs that I am passionate about, songs that frequently occupy the private soundtrack of my mind: "Why Shouldn't I?," "Just One of Those Things," "Dream Dancing," "Easy to Love," "All Through the Night," and a song that I have been singing obsessively of late, "So Near and Yet So Far" (I am equally obsessed with Fred Astaire's 1952 recording of it).

There are also, however, a lot of Porter songs that I find very difficult to sing and play and don't particularly like. I have discovered that I am not alone among performers in this feeling, including Barbara Cook and Rosemary Clooney. Some entertainers simply have more of an affinity for Porter than others. I do not feel that I am as well matched to Porter as I am to, say, Berlin or Arlen. My favorite singer is Rosemary Clooney, a woman with whom I share a wonderful friendship and who is considered to be one of the best vocalists alive today. She was the first female vocalist to be featured on the cover of *Time* magazine and she knew Porter personally as well as having recorded an album of his songs. Yet she also shies away from some of his works because she finds many of his vocal lines unsympathetic to the singer. They contain strange intervals that, while technically correct, are not well thought out for the vocalist.

And so says a former Broadway ingenue who has introduced the works of many Broadway greats, from Arthur Schwartz to Leonard Bernstein. This woman told me (on, as they say, condition of anonymity) that she doesn't particularly enjoy singing the Porter catalogue. When asked about specifics, such as "Easy to Love" ("Oh, yes, I love that one") or "So in Love" ("Oh, a great song"), she admits she likes some, but many others don't attract her. Whenever I hear Julie Wilson sing a Porter song, any Porter song, she makes me love it. Julie Wilson is one of the great interpreters of his catalogue. Bobby Short, too, turned me on to many Porter songs that I love hearing him sing but cannot sing myself. He relieves me of the desire to attempt many of them, because his renditions are quintessential: "Let's Fly Away," "You've Got That Thing," "You Don't Know Paree," and so many others.

Likewise, Steve Ross has enticed me with his renderings of "King" Cole. One of his greatest performances is of the title song "Can Can." I so flipped over his perfect rendition that I tried to sing the ditty in my Broadway debut in 1988. I sang it okay, but couldn't begin to approach Steve's organic performance. Why is it that these entertainers make Porter songs work that I can't? I'm frankly not sure. Perhaps they have an ability to create a reserve or an "arch" quality that certain of his songs require and that eludes me completely.

I have horrified friends by admitting that I don't like such venerable hits as "I've Got You Under My Skin," "Love for Sale," "In the Still of the Night," "Miss Otis Regrets," "Begin the Beguine," "I Love Paris," and, most notably, "Night and Day." "Night and Day"? you say with raised eyebrows. Porter's most popular song? A song that even prompted Irving Berlin to write Cole a fan letter saying he was "mad about it"? Yup. Having had such a severe emotional response to "Night and Day" and others, I set out to discover what it is about some of his songs that unsettle me. To begin with, I find a lot of Porter's melodies more perspirational than inspirational. They are contrived by the mind, not the heart. "Night and Day" is a stepwise melody, a device he uses frequently. I find it boring. After the first several bars, the melody descends to the basement on the words "I think of you" and then jumps an octave up to the fifth (on the repeat of "night and day"), leaving me hanging there feeling like I've just been taken on a bum cab ride and then dumped.

Many of Porter's songs have this effect on me. They don't get me in my *kishkes* in a positive way, because they don't travel melodically where I feel they should go. Mind you, I'm not saying I could do better. Many feel that "Night and Day" is the perfectly constructed song. I have sung it on occasion because the lyric carries me through and almost makes up for the deficiencies of the melody. Still, at bottom, I don't have a feeling of completeness or resolution when I hear it. (Not long ago I was hired to perform for a series of twelve industrial shows across the country, one of the requirements being that I sing "Night and Day." In spite of my dislike of the melody, I found that I was able to sing it by concentrating on the lyric and I have sung it frequently since then by request. This is the only instance when I have been able to transcend an unfavorable element in a song.) Many of the devices in Porter's music don't work for me, although when they do—it's magic! The harmonizations that Porter uses under the stepwise notes of "All Through the Night," for example, leave me breathless. But Porter's use of contrived or schematic melodic formulas often leaves me cold and makes me wonder if writing melody was as spontaneous a creative act for Porter as it was for Gershwin and so many other classic songwriters.

I had already begun to suspect Porter's difficulty with writing music when Ira Gershwin told me a revealing story. His brother George gave a party once and Cole attended. At one point George said, "Cole, let's write a song together—I'll write the music, and you write the lyrics." Porter immediately replied, "No, I don't want to do that. For me, the delicious torture of creating a new melody is the greatest challenge!" In 1982, at the Warner Brothers Music Warehouse in Secaucus, I found a piece of evidence to reinforce this story. Robert Kimball showed me a manuscript by Porter that was quite interesting. The notation started in Cole's hand (which was a deliberate and heavy holograph), but it soon diminished and eventually petered out to be replaced by the hand of Albert Sirmay, Cole's close friend and musical associate. It clearly showed the difficulties Porter experienced with music. I was accustomed to Gershwin's hand: his manuscript appearing as if he couldn't write it down fast enough, yet always perfectly legible.

Knowing that Porter worked so hard on his music makes me appreciate his achievements all the more. He was obsessed with work and even though he had more natural ability as a lyricist, his lyric worksheets show that he worked just as hard on them to achieve the final result. After he had a tragic horseback riding accident in 1937, he was almost always in pain, enduring three dozen operations on his legs and eventually losing his right leg to amputation in 1958. Never once did he reveal his intense pain in public—a remarkable feat. He used to have dinner parties at which he sat at the head of the table and just drank, not eating a thing. Somebody brought to the house a young fellow who had no idea who Porter was, saw him drinking all night, and finally said to him, "Jesus, you drink like you have a wooden leg!" There is no recorded witty retort from Porter. Even though he loved his wife, the socialite Linda Lee Thomas, he was gay, and while it was no secret in theatrical circles, he was very private about his personal life—Cole was ever the gentleman. There are those who find veiled references in Porter's lyrics to his sexuality. For example, in "A Picture of Me Without You" is the line "Picture Central Park without a sailor," supposedly alluding to the preferred cruising spot for gay men in uniform. But it is otherwise difficult to say what effect it had on his writing.

Ultimately, none of that is important. Porter was adored by his contemporaries, a generous man who was a big fan of other writers' music. He went to see *My Fair Lady* six times and proclaimed it the greatest musical he had ever seen. Once Porter and Ira Gershwin were standing offstage in Las Vegas, watching Frank Sinatra perform, and when Sinatra went into Ira's "A Foggy Day," Porter turned to Ira and said, "I just heard my favorite song." Every songwriter I have encountered who knew Porter loved him. Though he had plenty of money, friends, and diversions, his work—his songs, his music—was what sustained him. It was his unique expression. What a testament to his single-minded spirit and great courage that he was able to create sublime work while in constant pain, pain that would have tumbled any other mortal.

Thank you, Cole, for taking us with you on your trip to the moon on gossamer wings. So many are grateful, I among them. But it really is best to conclude with your words:

> Each time today's troubles confound you,
> Just for fun, little one,
> Look, look around you.
> It's a swell planet,
> If you take time to scan it,
> And it all belongs to you.

chapter 8

GOD BLESS IRVING BERLIN
(and Irving Caesar and Jerry Herman and Jule Styne and Sammy Cahn and All Those Guys)

*I*n 1938, Irving Berlin wrote, "Let me be a troubadour, / And I will ask for nothing more, / Than one short hour or so— / To sing my song and go." Berlin's hour spanned more than one hundred years, and he molded his "simple songs" for hundreds of millions of people, affecting the world in a glorious and transcendent way. It doesn't seem at all strange to speak of Irving Berlin in a way that others might reserve for a religious leader, because to my way of thinking, he changed the world. The vibrations of songs such as "White Christmas," "Easter Parade," and "God Bless America," among hundreds of others, have through the years brought many people together and created a special unity that only a gift of God, in the guise of a short, wiry man, could bestow. Berlin's prodigious talent is unparalleled in the annals of popular songwriting history. In contemplating his astonishing output of a little over one thousand songs—an even more staggering figure when one recognizes the consistent quality of his work—one has to keep in mind that he wrote both the music and lyrics for most of these numbers. There is no question in my mind that this man, with practically no formal education, was divinely inspired.

Berlin always felt that "if a song didn't write itself—then give it up" (a sentiment that was echoed by Harry Warren). This is not to say that it came easily to him or that he didn't work extremely hard on his creations. Of course he did. For example, he took a long time to come up with the lyric for "Always," and finding the last line of the song was particularly difficult. He had finished the melody, but the last few words wouldn't come. Berlin temporarily put the song aside until inspiration struck in the middle of the night and he gratefully completed the lyric. Sometimes the words and music flowed simultaneously, but it was different with each song and he never knew for certain how it would work.

Berlin began his songwriting career as a lyricist, though in the early days he didn't think of himself as one. He was simply a man who wrote special material and verse for the friends he worked with on the Bowery. He parodied all the songs of the day, especially those by his idol, George M. Cohan (with whom he later became great friends). Examining the lyrics of his first published song, "Marie from Sunny Italy" in 1907, hardly anyone would have predicted his impending success, especially with lines like "Please come out tonight, my queen. / Can't you hear my mandolin?" In later years Berlin discouraged people from singing the song; he was quite embarrassed by it. On a visit to his publishing offices in 1987, I had the temerity to ask for a copy of this epic. His longtime office administrator Hilda Schneider gave me a cold stare and said, "Next!" (Original copies of the sheet music at one time fetched thousands of dollars.) With his second published song in 1908 ("The Best of Friends Must Part"), Berlin started writing melodies, too. Even though Berlin began his career as a wordsmith, Ira Gershwin always felt that Berlin's ability with words was underestimated, overshadowed by his melodies. Ira believed that Berlin would still have been considered an immortal lyricist even if he had never written a single tune.

Because Berlin never acquired more than a rudimentary ability to read or write music, he always had to use a musical secretary who could properly notate his songs for him. In many cases his transcribers later became hit songwriters in their own right—Harry Akst ("Baby Face"), Arthur Johnston ("Pennies from Heaven"), Harry Ruby ("Nevertheless"), and Milton Ager ("Hard-Hearted Hannah") were among them. Once, a young George Gershwin transcribed a song ("That Revolutionary Rag") for his idol and begged Berlin for a job as his musical secretary. Berlin refused Gershwin, telling him that he shouldn't waste his time working for other people. "What the hell do you want to work for anybody else for," Berlin told him. "Work for yourself." Based on his exceptionally prolific and varied output, a rumor began to circulate that Berlin had ghostwriters working for him. In the teens, a story made the rounds (it continued for decades) that, in the jargon of the day, a "little colored boy" was writing hits for Berlin. Rodgers and Hart even wrote a song about it that goes

There's a boy in Harlem
And he writes all the songs.
Manhattan belongs to him.
Oh, he won't leave Harlem,
But his tunes get about.
He pounds them out
When the lights are dim.

Irving knew about the story and often jokingly acknowledged it. From 1929 until 1931, the songwriter experienced a dry spell and couldn't seem to produce a hit song. He turned out a few minor hits but nothing that ignited the public's fancy. During this fallow period, Berlin encountered songwriter Harry Warren, who asked him, "What happened to your colored boy? Has he been sick?"

Berlin smiled and snapped, "He died."

Although Berlin was very protective of his family and tried to keep his personal life out of the public spotlight, he remained accessible to his fans until late in his life. But as he moved into his eighties and nineties, he became increasingly reclusive, remaining in his Beekman Place home and communicating with the outside world mainly by telephone. Unfortunately, that image of an irascible old Berlin barking into the phone at unwelcome callers is the one that has remained for many people who didn't know him in more gregarious and easygoing times.

But even the younger Berlin was a complex soul made up of fascinating contradictions generated by his business acumen and personal eccentricities. Original Berlin sheet music sometimes featured his name in large print above the song titles, and some ten covers even featured his photograph (a highly unusual occurrence for a songwriter). Berlin himself presumably made these decisions, especially after he assumed control of his own publishing company in 1944; latter-day editions of his songs often still featured his name modestly above the title. Movies containing a Berlin score also regularly featured his name, as in "Irving Berlin's *Holiday Inn*" and "Irving Berlin's *Blue Skies.*" This was a singular and remarkable achievement not duplicated by any other songwriter.

Berlin was also an old-time song plugger who, in the early days, could belt out a song with great gusto and conviction. (In later years, when his vocal abilities had diminished, the comic Joe Frisco commented, "You have to hug him to hear him.") He was always promoting his songs through the newspapers, radio, and, later, television. He was also a very skillful businessman. A dispute over his desire to donate the royalties from "This Is the Army" and "God Bless America" led to a split with his music publishing partner, Saul Bornstein, in 1944. The upshot was that Berlin retained control of all his own songs free and clear. During the 1940s, he reprinted some of his songs without verses, in wartime editions and on thinner paper to abide by the requirements to conserve at that time. However, after the war was over, he never reprinted some of his most famous songs with the verses again. The standard Berlin editions of songs such as "How Deep Is the Ocean?" and "Say It Isn't So" became just the choruses, and it was often hard to obtain the verses. I always suspected he did that to save money, but his daughter Mary Ellin Barrett insists it was purely an artistic decision. Even after the practice of collecting songs into folios became widespread among music publishers, Berlin published fewer folios than most. Once again, it seemed clear to me that he felt he would make more money by publishing single songs, but Mary Ellin claims that he simply preferred keeping his songs as single sheets "because he liked to see the individual songs on the shelf."

Unfortunately, this practice eventually backfired on Berlin; although I have no access to ASCAP's figures, I'd be willing to wager that today his songs (with the possible exceptions of "White Christmas," "Easter Parade," and "God Bless America") are much less popular than George Gershwin's in terms of performances and royalties. Berlin held very tight reins over whom he would actually allow to perform his songs in a show or a movie. As he grew older, he became more possessive of his "children" and frequently denied others the right to perform his material. The 1950 MGM film version of *Annie Get Your Gun*, with Betty Hutton and Howard Keel, was not rereleased because Berlin reportedly didn't like it and refused to renew the studio's music license when it expired in 1978—perhaps sensing wisely that the film's depiction of American Indian culture was no longer acceptable to the public.

There's also a charming story, widely circulated, that reflects the aging Berlin's feistiness. For years, it goes, he denied Steven Spielberg the right to use his song "Always" as the title song of his motion picture, although Spielberg offered him exorbitant amounts of money. Unfortunately, the story is apocryphal. Berlin never spoke to Spielberg, but through his lawyer said that he would grant permission to use the song only if Spielberg would change the title of the movie from *Always*. The director wouldn't, and the song did not appear in the film. It is true, however, that when Beverly Sills asked permission to perform *Call Me Madam*, Berlin, then in his nineties, refused, saying, "I have future plans for that show."

In perhaps the most notorious instance of withholding rights, Berlin reportedly denied Jimmy Breslin permission to use *three words* of "A Pretty Girl Is like a Melody" in a novel. (Breslin's publishers, assuming that they would have no trouble obtaining clearance for such a brief quote, had already started printing the book, which then had to be reset. The irascible Breslin was so outraged that he devoted an entire newspaper column to Berlin's intractability.)

Yet at the same time Berlin was very generous and faithful to friends who made requests of him, and he allowed unrestricted use, for example, of "Puttin' on the Ritz" in Mel Brooks's *Young Frankenstein*. He would not allow anyone to print his lyrics in full in a book or periodical under any circumstance, but then suddenly allowed his friend, musicologist Ed Jablonski, the right to reprint his lyrics in an article he was preparing.

Through the years, Berlin donated the royalties for some of his songs to various organizations, the most famous being "God Bless America," the proceeds of which go to the Girl Scouts and Boy Scouts, and from the show "This Is the Army," royalties going to Army Emergency Relief. Yet he was considered by some to be very tight with his money. A few years ago, I took a trip up to the newly relocated Irving Berlin Music Corporation offices and noticed that the receptionist was using an old-fashioned plug-in style switchboard. The switchboard, which looked like it was ready for the Smithsonian, was worked by a sweet woman named Sue, who wore the old-style headset. "Sue," I said, "I can't believe that you've got this beautiful new office and you still have this antique switchboard." She informed me that it had been relocated from the old offices because (and she whispered) "Mr. Berlin is kind of cheap, you know." In 1988 when I performed at the 100th Birthday salute to Berlin at Carnegie Hall, I was looking forward to the usual dividend accorded performers appearing in such a show. I expected to receive the orchestration prepared for the one-shot appearance after it was used in the program. But I never got it. Nor did anyone else, for that matter. Even though thousands of dollars had been spent in preparing the music for the all-star cast assembled that evening, Berlin reportedly ordered all orchestrations destroyed at the conclusion of the performance! We were all flabbergasted at that news. Did this order come from Berlin or from somebody protecting him or carrying out old directives? Mary Ellin maintains that her father was quite infirm by this time and no longer involved in the everyday running of the company, and, given his age, that certainly makes sense.

Furthermore, my personal experience of Berlin has been marked by his generosity—and a touch of his strangeness. My album of Berlin songs, *Remember*, which was released in 1987, contains nineteen compositions; I would have had to pay a prohibitive royalty rate to include all the numbers on one disc. Standard fees for song performance licenses are set on a per song basis. But the Berlin office charged me a lower flat royalty rate that allowed me to include all of the songs—a demonstration of kindness that I will never forget. I was told that he liked my work, which gave me enormous satisfaction. I had been more excited in some ways recording Berlin than Gershwin because of the richness of his work and the abundant variety of choices inherent in the material. But it had been a strange feeling to know that Berlin was still alive at the time, and I'd often wished that I could call him up and ask him where the inspiration had come from for certain songs I was recording.

After the album came out, I was sitting with Liza Minnelli at the kitchen table celebrating my birthday when I suddenly said, "Gee, I wonder if Berlin really likes the album."

Normally my better sense would have prevailed and I would have shied away from approaching the Grand Old Man of Song. But I had been emboldened by a chain of events. I had been contacted through the Berlin office and asked to perform at a benefit for the Girl Scouts. I agreed to do it, partly because of the connection with Berlin and partly because, even though I wasn't being paid, I *would* get two cases of Girl Scout cookies of my choice. I love the mint cookies and the peanut butter cookies, so how could I resist? (That was probably one of the most unusual fees I ever got for performing. One time I got a Rolex watch, but I still prefer the cookies.) After I performed that night, Berlin's attorney came over and congratulated me on my work, mentioning that Berlin liked my record of his songs. And so I decided to call. I had gotten his phone number through Ed Jablonski and I thought, What the hell? It's my birthday and I'm going to call him. Liza egged me on, saying, "Go on, call him. What can you lose?"

You have to understand that hardly anybody ever called Irving Berlin. If you wanted to talk to him, you would call his office and he would call you back. Maybe. He did maintain regular phone contact with Jablonski, Harold Arlen, and a number of other friends. He occasionally called Ira, and Ira always became very jolly, thrilled that Irving had called him. One day, Berlin said, "Ira, you and I are the only ones left and the hell with everyone else." Ira loved to repeat that. In any event, I dialed his number. Berlin's phone rang twice and then I heard a high-pitched, raspy voice say, "Hello."

"Mr. Berlin?" I said.

"Hello?" The reply came as a question.

"Excuse me, Mr. Berlin?"

"Hello?" was again the response, each repetition growing louder. I thought, Oh God, he's really hard of hearing. This isn't going to be easy.

"I'd like to speak to Mr. Berlin," I said.

"Who's calling?"

"Michael Feinstein."

"Who?"

"Michael . . . Feinstein."

"What does he want with Mr. Berlin?"

"Well, I've just done an album of Berlin songs," I said.

"You what?"

"I've just done an album of Berlin songs and I understand that he likes it."

"*What?*"

"I did this album of Berlin songs and it's sold very well and I heard that Mr. Berlin likes it. I wanted to find out what he thought of it."

"Ah, forget about him!" he said with great aggravation as he slammed the phone down. It was one of the oddest phone conversations of my life to that point, but reflecting back on it now, I'm struck by my own brashness. Berlin was ninety-nine at the time and, according to Mary Ellin, hard of hearing, almost blind, and easily startled. The fact that he even answered his own phone is rather remarkable. At least I did get to speak with Irving Berlin, sort of. But I would give anything to have known him a bit earlier in his life. Of all the songwriters I have performed, Berlin is the one for whom I feel the most sympathy. The word that comes up for me in listening to his work is "energy." Songs like "Alexander's Ragtime Band" and "Let Me Sing and I'm Happy" are shot through with a kind of nervous enthusiasm, a vital force that reverberates in my own heart whenever I sing them. Berlin may have been eccentric toward the end, but I believe the part of him that will be remembered is the energy and lyricism that comes through his songs.

Berlin was very supportive of and helped to start the careers of many great songwriters, from George Gershwin to Ann Ronell, who wrote hits as disparate in tone as "Willow Weep for Me" and "Who's Afraid of the Big Bad Wolf?" He was a particularly ardent fan of Cole Porter, to whom he once wrote: "Anything I can do, you can do better." Bob Kimball, who knew Berlin by phone, insists "he was always generous about other songwriters, especially George and Ira Gershwin." And yet there are stories indicating that he was so jealous of some composers' achievements that he would snub them, even though nobody could have possibly displaced him as King of Tin Pan Alley. Burton Lane told me that Berlin was quite generous to him when they met early in Burton's career, but later he told a different kind of story about Irving Berlin on the opening night of *Finian's Rainbow* in 1947. Burton had written a couple of Broadway revues earlier and a show called *Hold on to Your Hats* in 1940 with Al Jolson, but *Finian's* was certainly the most important show in his career up to that time and it became a huge hit. During intermission of opening night, Berlin came running up the aisle and ran into Burton. "Hi, Irving," Burton said.

However enthusiastic the audience response might have been to that point, Burton was naturally quite nervous and was hoping for any word of praise from the master.

"Hi, Burton," Berlin said. "Where's Yip?"

He was looking for Yip Harburg, who had written the show's lyrics, and immediately ran on. Burton felt deflated that Berlin just couldn't bring himself to say one word of praise to him for *Finian's*. Leonore Gershwin said that Berlin turned green the first time he heard *Rhapsody in Blue*. (He had also been announced as writing a concert piece for Paul Whiteman for the same Aeolian Hall event that produced the *Rhapsody*, but never obliged, although three of his songs were performed that night.) I heard one story about how Berlin snubbed Frank Loesser at Lindy's after *Guys and Dolls* opened. Yet Mary Ellin Barrett remembers her father calling Richard Rodgers after the opening and asking ironically, "What are we going to do about the kid?"

How someone as phenomenally successful and universally respected as Irving Berlin could suffer from insecurity and jealousy is one of the great mysteries of human nature. I recall a story about a lyric writer named Grant Clarke who had a number of hits in the teens and later wrote the lyrics to "Am I Blue?" At one point, Grant, who had known Berlin from the early days, was really down and out. In desperation, he went to see Irving. "I'm in a terrible position," Grant said to him. "Can I please borrow some money?"

"Grant, I have a firm policy," Berlin said. "I never borrow or loan money."

"That's one thing about you, Irving," Grant said. "Success hasn't changed you a bit."

In fact, though, Berlin gave money to many friends and associates, including Arthur Johnston, the conductor Frank Tours, and Elsie Janis (a huge star from the early days of musical theater), and frequently forgave debts outright.

Then there's the story that so many people have told about Berlin on the set of *Holiday Inn*. He was talking to its musical director, Robert Emmett Dolan, about the background score for the movie, and Bobby was describing a dramatic scene in the film. "Then, they will kiss and there will be a chord," he said. And Berlin said, "My chord!" He may have said it tongue in cheek, but not according to Harry Warren, who used to love to tell that story. He'd call me and say, "Ever heard the 'my chord' story about Berlin?" Harry Warren actually had more songs on the Hit Parade than Irving Berlin, but he couldn't take much of Irving. During the Second World War, when the Allies were making air strikes against Germany, Harry turned to a friend and quipped, "They bombed the wrong Berlin."

It occurs to me that some of the stories of Berlin's eccentricities may have been generated by fellow songwriters jealous of his success, because some of the most persistent are frankly hard to believe. I had heard for years, without giving the story much credence, that Berlin was addicted to drugs. Then Ira Gershwin told me that in the teens and '20s, it was common knowledge that Irving Berlin used to smoke opium and spent a good deal of time in opium dens. "I don't know why he stopped," Ira said—not meaning to be humorous but just curious. The rumors of Berlin's drug use persisted until his death at the age of 101. If that's true, it's the best advertisement for taking drugs that I can think of. When I asked Mary Ellin about these stories, she told me that she once asked her father if he hadn't, in his Chinatown days, smoked opium. Berlin said yes, he had smoked opium once, had fallen asleep, and never tried it again.

There was a bawdy set of lyrics written as a parody of the Cole Porter perennial "You're the Top." It started out, "You're the top! / You're Miss Pinkham's tonic. / You're the top! / You're a high colonic," and continued with "You're the breasts of Venus, / You're King Kong's penis." Robert Kimball printed these lyrics in his book *The Complete Lyrics of Cole Porter*, stating that the lines were possibly by Porter but that there was no conclusive evidence. Shortly before his death, Berlin revealed to Kimball that he was in fact the author of the lyrics but asked Kimball not to reveal that information until after he was gone. Kimball respected his wishes, although legend has it that Berlin began his career singing bawdy parodies of innocent early popular songs like Victor Herbert's "I Want What I Want When I Want It." Berlin himself had been the target of a wickedly witty parody of "Always," written in the '20s and published in the *Dramatists Guild Quarterly* in 1967. Berlin believed it had been penned by Buddy DeSylva in the intricately clever rhyming style of Lorenz Hart. If so, it is one of DeSylva's sharpest lyrics:

I'll be loving you
Always
Both in very big, and
Small ways.
With a love as grand
As Paul Whiteman's band
And 'twill weigh as much as
Paul weighs,
Always.
In saloons and drab
Hallways
You are what I'll grab
Always.

See how I dispense
Rhymes that are immense,
But do they make sense?
Not always.

In his later years, Berlin became much more eccentric and reclusive, and those who had known him earlier could not reconcile this inaccessible High Lama of popular song with the joyful young creator with whom they had shared so many fun times. "He had been quite gregarious early on," Bob Kimball told me. "But he did become a different person late in life." Berlin suffered from bouts of depression that became worse as he grew older, and isolating himself in his townhouse probably didn't help, nor did living in a rapidly changing world that he must have sensed was passing him by. His telephone calls became increasingly mystifying to old friends and acquaintances. Miles Kreuger, the musical theater historian, said that he once answered the phone in the middle of the night to hear a voice screaming and shrieking about something. It took Miles several minutes to realize that the man who was having this crazy outburst on the phone was actually Irving Berlin.

Ira Gershwin told a story about a call from Berlin that obviously stuck in his craw because some thirty years after the incident occurred, Ira still got excited when he recalled it. While Ira was writing the film score for *Cover Girl* with Jerome Kern, he received a phone call from Berlin. The year would have been late 1942 or early 1943; Ira and Kern were working on a score that included a song later nominated for an Academy Award, "Long Ago (and Far Away)." However, Berlin was calling about another song that Ira and Kern were writing, entitled "That Girl on the Cover." Berlin had gotten wind of the song and was quite irate about it. He called Ira demanding that he change the title of the song to "Cover Girl." Ira asked why.

"You just can't use that title because I wrote a song called 'The Girl on the Magazine Cover,' " Berlin said, "and it's too close to my title."

Ira very calmly pointed out to Berlin that many songs through the years have had the same title, that in any case you can't copyright a title, and what did it matter, anyway? For *Strike Up the Band*, George and Ira had written a song called "Soon," and six years later Rodgers and Hart also wrote a song called "Soon." Ira wrote a song with George called "My Fair Lady" in 1925. And there was a turn-of-the-century song called "Strike Up the Band (Here Comes a Sailor)." It just happens to be one of the accepted conventions of songwriting (and other art forms), and could be considered a problem only if the title was so specific that it would be a clear violation of the original—for example, if someone were to write a new song and call it " 'S Wonderful."

In any event, Berlin lambasted Ira, saying he didn't care that you couldn't copyright a title or about any of the other facts Ira was citing; he did not want them to use that title, period. Being a rather gentle soul, Ira listened to Berlin's tirade and assured Irving that he would see what they could do. He hung up the phone and called Kern. Kern was not as forgiving as Ira. Despite the fact that Berlin and Kern were great friends and Berlin had been something of a mentor to Kern, he became very angry about the incident and, mainly because of Berlin's demanding, imperious attitude, refused to change the title. Ira agreed with Kern, by now voicing suspicions that "Irving must have something up his sleeve with his song, or he wouldn't be making such a big deal about ours."

Sure enough, Ira later discovered that Berlin had a movie deal brewing and that his song "The Girl on the Magazine Cover" was being sold as the title of the motion picture. Berlin continued to call Ira on a regular basis, demanding that he change the song, until Ira, who was a man of very few unkind words, in exasperation one day said to Kern, "Fuck Irving!" It was one of the few times I ever heard him use that word in retelling a story. He had apparently reached that point after his most recent conversation with Berlin, who told Ira that he had written an alternate lyric on which Ira could put his name without giving Berlin any credit—if he would simply change the title of the song. Berlin felt he was doing him a favor. Ira obediently wrote down the Berlin lyric, which I later found in his files penned at the bottom of a worksheet for "The Girl on the Cover." It was an average Berlin effort, but the existence of it corroborated Ira's story. Ira, of course, never adopted the Berlin lyric. He would have never considered putting his name on something he didn't write. As it turns out, the film that Ira and Kern were working on ended up being called *Cover Girl*, and the executives at Columbia studios decided to rename "That Girl on the Cover" accordingly. The crisis was solved, and Kern remained close with Berlin.

Ira wasn't the only recipient of hectoring phone calls from Berlin. Harry Warren told me several stories about receiving similar calls. In one case, Warren had given a sketch of a song he had just written called "Carnival" to Berlin's musical secretary Helmy Kresa to copy, but when he got it back, it had been reharmonized as well. Harry told Helmy he could do that sort of thing for Berlin but not for Harry. He soon received a return call from an irate Berlin demanding to know if Harry had implied that Berlin let his secretary reharmonize his songs. Harry sidestepped the question. On another occasion, Harry got a call out of the blue from Berlin, who said with great irritation, "You used part of my tune in your song!" He was referring to a song of Harry's that had recently appeared in a film. Harry racked his brain but couldn't think of any Berlin melody that might have crept into the song in question.

"Which song of yours would that be, Irving?" he asked.

"The one I'm working on!" Berlin shot back.

Berlin was always the highest paid songwriter in Hollywood, receiving percentages and reversionary rights that were unheard of for most other songwriters, even George and Ira Gershwin. He also received more money than any of his peers for the use of a single song in a motion picture. He knew how to take an older song from his catalogue and sell it as the title of a new motion picture, thereby receiving an enormous fee and, at the same time, repopularizing it with the cinema audiences. Until about a year before his death, he called his office frequently to get the latest sales figures for his songs and check up on all other aspects of the business. A founding member (in 1914) of ASCAP, he was an inspiration for the extension of the song copyright laws, as ASCAP lobbyists and lawyers worked to keep the elder statesman's songs in copyright throughout his life.

Another aspect of the genius of Berlin was his ability to create the perfect song for the right performer. He was perhaps the greatest writer of his era for special material. In 1909 he wrote the first piece of Yiddish dialect material that Fanny Brice ever sang. The song was called "Sadie Salome—Go Home!" and it laid the foundation for a characterization she performed for the rest of her career. (It was also the first ethnic Jewish hit on Tin Pan Alley, which termed it a "Yid Song" to go with their "Wop Songs" and "Coon Songs.") For Jolson, he wrote "Let Me Sing and I'm Happy"—a perfect anthem for the World's Greatest Entertainer. For Ethel Waters, he created "Suppertime," a genuinely moving account of a poor black woman attempting to set the dinner table for her children, knowing that her husband has been lynched by a mob of whites and won't be coming home. Belle Baker preferred to sing optimistic lyrics set to a minor-key melody. No problem for Berlin: he whipped up the bittersweet "Blue Skies," for Belle to sing in the Rodgers and Hart musical *Betsy* (much to their chagrin). And what about "Top Hat, White Tie and Tails" for Astaire, or "White Christmas" for Crosby, "I Got the Sun in the Morning" for Ethel Merman, or "Better Luck Next Time" for Judy Garland? All perfect combinations of singer and song.

Berlin also knew how to revive and adapt an older song of his and reintroduce it to the public. He wrote "God Bless America" in 1917 but waited until the eve of war in Europe in 1938 to present it to the world as sung by Kate Smith. He gave the 1933 "Heat Wave" to Marilyn Monroe, who in turn gave it a very sexy 1954 presentation in *There's No Business Like Show Business*. Berlin rewrote the lyric of 1930's "Puttin' on the Ritz" and turned it into an immortal classic for Fred Astaire sixteen years later in *Blue Skies*. Alice Faye reintroduced his 1911 smash hit "Alexander's Ragtime Band" as the title song of the 1938 film, which also featured Ethel Merman. Years later, when Merman of all people decided to join the disco craze by doing a dance album of songs connected with her career, Berlin revised one couplet for the more pacifist days of 1979, from "So natural / That you wanna go to war" to "So natural / That you wanna ask for more." (The borrowing, incidentally, was duly noted by Ira Gershwin, who had made a sort of cottage industry out of the phrase "Who could ask for anything more" by using variations of it in several of his own songs.)

Regardless of the era, Berlin created the perfect expression for the times. In every age, generations of people have been grateful for his ability to express their feelings in his deceptively simple way. As a performer, I find it a blessing to sing his songs. They are spontaneous expressions of joy. There simply is something special about a Berlin song. Berlin's personal eccentricities, his irritability, and his insecurity all fade into insignificance the minute I start to hear, or sing, one of his songs. In that moment, I can only be awed by the mixture of craftsmanship, unsentimental emotion, and, yes, divine inspiration in songs such as "Remember," "Cheek to Cheek," "How Deep Is the Ocean?" and "What'll I Do?"

*T*HERE'S another Irving who didn't have anything like the gift Berlin did but who probably epitomizes another kind of classic professional songwriter—mildly talented and vastly egotistical—and that is Irving Caesar. No one could have a higher opinion of Irving Caesar than Irving himself. Irving had a handful of standards among the numerous songs he turned out through the '20s and '30s. But as time progressed, Caesar's lyrics became creakier and creakier in comparison to those of Berlin and Ira Gershwin and Lorenz Hart and Cole Porter, and his career diminished. In his own way, Irving is a charming man for whom I have great affection. He is vastly intelligent and even at his advanced age (he was born in 1895), he is well aware of what is going on in the world. He's a wonderful humorist and an engaging storyteller (in fact, don't ever get Irving up to speak at a show or an honorary dinner—he'll never get off). He's old-fashioned enough to believe in the triumph of the human spirit over adversity and has written songs of social comment like "There's No Color Line Around the Rainbow." But that ego. . . .

Irving and George Gershwin rode to prominence together on the runaway success of "Swanee" in 1920. Through the years, Irving has taken more and more credit for the creation of many of his famous songs, while diminishing the amount of time it took to write "Swanee." When he told the story in the '50s, he said that he and George had created the verse and chorus of "Swanee" in about half an hour while George's father and his friends were playing cards in the next room. When Irving was interviewed by Max Wilk for his book *They're Playing Our Song* in 1973, he told Max, "What the hell, Gershwin and I wrote 'Swanee' in about eleven minutes flat!" The last time I heard Irving tell the story (to Joe Franklin), he said, "Wrote the song in two minutes." He got to the point where he was saying, "George played the vamp, then I sang the melody. Just as fast as he could play the melody, I came up with the lyric. I just sang it through, and that's how we wrote the song." At one point, I actually heard him say that he was responsible for the melody—that George had written it down but that it was his idea.

Irving's ego is so great that, even though he cannot read or write music, he once created a symphonic composition that he hummed to copyists. They wrote it down and orchestrated it for him, although it is now lost. He sent it out to some orchestra and it disappeared in transit. Irving never got over his resentment about George ceasing to collaborate with him so he could work with Ira instead. He still gets extremely angry at the mention of mild-mannered Ira's name, saying that Ira stole the idea for "Cheerful Little Earful" (a 1930 hit with Harry Warren) from a line in an unpublished 1917 Gershwin/Caesar collaboration titled "Good Little Tune." Irving met Leonard Bernstein early in his career when Bernstein was looking for work. Caesar had the young Bernstein write down "Good Little Tune" for him, let him sleep in his office, and helped him in other small ways. After Bernstein became famous, Caesar once remarked to him, "Leonard, I'm ashamed of you that you forgot about me!"

But in the '20s, Irving was still a very prominent and prolific lyric writer, supplying the lyrics to "Tea for Two" and "I Want to Be Happy" for Vincent Youmans's *No, No, Nanette* in 1925 and for "Crazy Rhythm" in 1928. In 1931, he wrote the lyrics for a German tune that, in its American version, became "Just a Gigolo," and he had another big hit in 1936 with "Is It True What They Say About Dixie?" Irving was also very close friends with Al Jolson and lived with him for a while. (They must have needed a mansion to house both of *those* egos.)

Until very recently, he lived in the Omni Park Central Hotel where he owned his own unit. That hotel had been refurbished and remodeled many times and made into an all chrome and glass wonder—until you went into Irving Caesar's apartment. It was mind blowing to enter that ultramodern building, go up to Irving's apartment, see the door swing open, and walk into a place that was a fully intact remnant of the 1930s, replete with dark wood paneling, separate faucets for hot and cold water, and old-style toilets. He never let the hotel remodel anything and I'm sure they couldn't wait for him to move out. Irving has not been in great health the last couple of years; he has failing eyesight and wears very thick glasses. Yet only a few years ago, he managed to walk to his office on Seventh Avenue almost every day. One day when he was crossing the street, he was grazed by a car; he was stunned and lay for a moment in the crosswalk. Seeing a frail old man lying there, people gathered around him, very concerned, asking, "Are you all right?"

Irving picked himself up from the ground, brushed himself off and said, "Get out of my way! I wrote 'Swanee'!" And he kept going on his way. That's a serious ego. Once I was in a taxi cab with Irving and, as usual, he was expounding on his songs, talking about "Tea for Two" and so on. As he was singing a phrase from "I Want to Be Happy," the cab driver, a woman, said jokingly, "Hey, hey! There's no singing in this cab." And I said, "Even if he wrote the song?"

"You wrote that?" she said to Irving, amazed.

"Yeah, I wrote that," he said without missing a beat. "Wrote that in 1924 with Vincent Youmans for *No, No, Nanette*." Anyway, when we got to our destination, Irving leaned over to the driver and, starting to sing a line from "Tea for Two," said, "Here, honey. 'Pic-ture you up-on my knee—' Now you've heard it from the horse's mouth." And with that he got out of the cab. Irving loves to sing his songs for anyone who will listen, but he never sings the last word or two. He always trails off with a little self-congratulatory comment at the end. For example, he'll sing, "The folks up north will see me no more, / When I get to that Swanee— Wrote the song in two minutes!" Or, "There will come a day, / Youth will pass away, / Then what will they say / About me? / When the end comes I know / they'll say just a gigolo, / as life goes on— One of the greatest songs I ever wrote!"

Irving is one of the elder statesmen of the Friars Club, but because his eyesight is poor, his table manners are not the best. He took me there for dinner once and ordered lamb chops; he still had a very hearty appetite. When the lamb chops arrived, he sort of felt around the plate and, much to my horror, picked up a chop with both hands and took a big bite out of it, almost devouring the whole thing in one go. Irving is very meticulous in the way he dresses, even though it must be quite a job for him to dress so well every day. The music publisher Frank Military told me that when he ate lunch with Irving at the Friars Club, by the time they had finished, Irving's solid tie had spots all over it. As they were leaving, one of the women working behind the desk said, "Oh, what a beautiful pattern on your tie, Mr. Caesar," not realizing that it was all grease and gravy spots.

The night I dined with Irving at the Friars Club, he had several drinks after dinner. He started talking about how he did not consider George Gershwin a major composer. "I can sum up George Gershwin in one sentence," he said. "You cannot please the muses *and* the masses." He then started to talk about how the music critic Abram Chasins claimed that Gershwin had stolen from Rachmaninoff and how Rachmaninoff was always polite about it and chose to ignore it. As Irving related the anecdote, his voice grew louder and louder and his long-suppressed anger rose to the surface. He started ticking off some of Gershwin's hits, like "Someone to Watch Over Me" and "I Got Rhythm."

"Those are nice songs," he said. "And I'm very proud of some of my songs, too." Irving went on and recited all of his own hits. "George Gershwin's songs will have a limited life," he said, "but my children's songs will live forever."

In the '30s, Irving wrote a number of children's songs (some with Gerald Marks) that became extremely popular and were sung and taught routinely in New York public schools—published as collections entitled *Sing a Song of Safety*, *Sing a Song of Friendship*, and *Sing a Song of Health*. When you meet people of a certain generation, they can always sing these songs, which were quite useful and innovative at the time but have since become very obscure, not to mention outdated. In some cases, Irving took the idea to absurd lengths, as in "Tommy Tax," which goes in part:

Who pays our Forest Rangers
Who sleep in lonely shacks?

Who-oo? You-oo,
And little Tommy Tax;
Who pays our Lighthouse Keepers
Who never can relax?
Who-oo? You-oo,
And little Tommy Tax!

. . . .

It's only fair to do our share,
For Tommy isn't wealthy,
And ev'ry cent is really spent
To keep us free and healthy;
Who paid our loyal soldiers,
Who paid our WAVES and WACS?
Who? You,
And little Tommy Tax!

Irving really believes that his children's songs are absolutely his most important work. In an attempt to keep up with the times, Irving's most recent lyric is "Who wants marijuana / When I wanna wanna / What you wanna wanna?" It goes on, "Hugs and drugs, / drugs and hugs, / We'll get our kicks / When our kisses mix." The whole idea of the song is, Don't do drugs, make love instead. Of course, these days, drugs may be safer than love in certain circumstances.

Irving's oversized regard for himself also tinges his opinion of other composers. I once asked him about Oscar Levant and the first words out of his mouth were, "Oscar couldn't write."

How's that?

"Oscar was a very talented pianist," Irving went on. "George loved him. I loved him. But he was crazy—very selfish."

"But you wrote a whole show with him," I replied, "and you say he couldn't write? What about 'Lady, Play Your Mandolin'?"

"Yes, we wrote that tune, and I'll tell you how. I wrote that song in five minutes!"

Irving then went on to relate how Oscar had only the first musical phrase and the beginning of the verse. "Then I developed the tune *and* the verse," he said, and proceeded to sing them for me. "I constructed that verse! I'd be a liar if I said I didn't. Oscar was talented, wonderful to have around if you were the host. Terribly clever, but a problem! Life is too short, for Christ's sake."

Irving may have had a point there. Yip Harburg told me about working on a song with Oscar. They'd start to work one day and when they got together again the next day, Yip would say, "Let's work on that song some more." And Oscar would say, "No, it's no good. I threw it out."

Not that Irving was a walk in the park himself. My favorite story about Irving Caesar may be one that Ira told me. In 1943, Irving wrote a show called *My Dear Public*, which he claimed was going to be one of the great Broadway successes. The show almost closed out of town, but finally limped into New York with Irving's name all over it. It was "Irving Caesar Presents: Music by Irving Caesar. Lyrics by Irving Caesar. Book by Irving Caesar. Produced by Irving Caesar." When the reviews came out, they really laid into Irving. "The piece is presented by Irving Caesar, who, even if you don't ask me," wrote Robert Garland in the *Journal-American*, "should be ashamed of himself. The book—which is incredible—is by Irving Caesar, too. . . . The songs also have a Caesarian flavor, heaven help them." The *Daily News'* review was headlined: "Caesar Is Buried, Not Praised," and Louis Kronenberger called it "one of the most terrific bores I have ever sat through."

Irving, quite upset with the reviews, all of which were pans, called up Ira and asked, with surprise and indignation, "Why is everybody blaming me?"

*I*RVING Caesar is one of the great characters of American popular song, but, in fact, the field is full of colorful characters with fascinating stories to tell. One of the great pleasures I've had in getting to work with songwriters when I record their songs, as I have done so far with Jerry Herman, Burton Lane, Jule Styne, and Hugh Martin, is hearing directly from them the stories of how they got started. Sometimes the stories are every bit as magical as Irving's stories are funny and exasperating.

Jerry Herman, who wrote both words and music for *Hello, Dolly!*, *Mame*, and *La Cage aux Folles*, told me that he began to fall in love with musical theater when his parents took him to see *Annie Get Your Gun* at the age of fourteen or fifteen. He had a great ear and when he got home, he was able to play four or five songs in the show from memory. From that day, he wanted to write simple, hummable songs, but he never dreamed that anything that was so much fun could be a career. So he made songwriting his hobby and enrolled in Parsons School of Design to become an architect and designer. He wrote songs and played them at home until one afternoon when Jerry was eighteen, his mother, Ruth, said to him, "I want you to take these songs that you're writing to a friend of a friend."

The friend of a friend happened to be Frank Loesser. Jerry was well versed in the theater because his parents took him to see everything, so when he heard the name Frank Loesser, he was quite intimidated. "You're my mother. Of course you think they're good," he said to Ruth about his songs. "I'm not going to go."

As far as Jerry was concerned, the issue was decided. But then Ruth said something that has stayed in his brain all these years. "I think it was the most wonderful thing a mother ever said to a son," he told me. "She said, 'Would you please waste a half hour of your life?' How do you say no to that? So I went with my little briefcase to Frank Loesser's office and found Mr. Loesser sitting behind his desk with a cigar. I was scared to death."

"Play me something, kid," Loesser said. He was clearly only doing this as a favor to the friend of the friend, whose name Jerry no longer even remembers. When Jerry played his first song, Loesser perked up. "I played him a second song and he perked up even more," Jerry said. "He got on his intercom and said, 'Hold all my calls.' He kept me there all afternoon, made me play everything I'd ever written. And finally he said, 'What are you doing in design school?' He literally changed the course of my life."

Loesser suggested that Jerry go to a university, get a good education majoring in music or drama, and keep on writing songs. Jerry left Parsons and enrolled in the University of Miami, where he wrote his first musical and had it performed before an audience. When he graduated, he was still writing songs, which he began playing in little revues in clubs because the era was past when a new writer could get his songs interpolated into a Broadway show. And, of course, nobody would hire a kid with no experience to write a whole Broadway show. Eventually Jerry was discovered by Gerald Oestreicher playing his songs in an off-

Broadway revue called *Parade*. Oestreicher wanted to produce a musical set in Israel, which was only thirteen years old at the time. It was like something out of a Mickey Rooney–Judy Garland movie. The guy came over to Jerry after the show and said, "I'm going to be doing a musical on Broadway next year. I'd like to have lunch with you." A year later, Jerry had a Broadway musical called *Milk and Honey*, which ran for two years.

That started his career, but the real boost came when David Merrick went to see the show and then, as Jerry puts it, "He summoned me to his office. David Merrick didn't invite you. He would summon you." After some preliminary discussion, Merrick handed Jerry a script that said on the cover, "Matchmaker, Draft Number One." It was Mike Stewart's first draft for what would become *Hello, Dolly!* Merrick just asked Jerry to look at the script and see if he came up with any ideas. It was a Friday, and Jerry went back to his apartment, locked himself in, and proceeded to write four songs in the next thirty-six hours. On Monday morning, Jerry returned to Merrick's office and, with the help of a friend, performed the four songs. "I think Merrick was more overwhelmed at the speed and the enthusiasm that I obviously had for the property than he even was with the material," Jerry recalls. "But he must have liked the songs, too, because when I finished the fourth song, he stood up behind his desk and said, 'Kid, the show is yours.' "

That's how Jerry Herman got *Dolly*. But it really started because of Ruth Herman saying to him one afternoon, "Waste a half hour of your life."

*S*o many great songwriters have died in recent years that I'm getting wary of turning to the obituary pages. When I do learn of the death of someone I've admired or known personally, I can almost hear Leonore Gershwin's voice saying, "Yes, dear, but he lived a very full life." In the past couple of years, we've lost two songwriters whose names will always be linked because of their longtime collaboration, and I need to pause and say a little something about each of them.

Jule Styne and Sammy Cahn had fifteen number one hits together, which by itself would be enough to make them memorable, yet they also had distinctive careers with a number of other collaborators. And each was unacknowledged in certain ways. Jule Styne was one of the most underestimated songwriters to have great success both on Broadway and in Hollywood. For most of his career, through the 1960s and even into the '70s, he was largely unknown and unacknowledged by the general public. It wasn't really until the revivals of *Gypsy* that he started to become a household name and to take his place in the firmament of Broadway composers. Jule referred to himself as a great "collaborator," choosing to shape his songwriting talents to fit the style of whomever he was working with at the time, and that may be the reason it took so long for him to be recognized in his own right.

A child prodigy, he studied piano at the Chicago College of Music when he was eight years old and soon was performing with symphony orchestras. An accident at the factory where Jule worked injured his right hand and impeded his progress; he was also told that he would never be a concert pianist because his hands were too small. In his teens, he began playing in jazz and dance bands and later played alongside Benny Goodman, Glenn Miller, Bix Beiderbecke, Wingy Manone, and Frankie Trumbauer. He wrote his first published song in 1926 to impress a girl who offered to date him if he would play the song for her at a club; it became his first hit, "Sunday." But because he didn't think highly of songwriting, he wrote very little over the next dozen years. So Jule was a late bloomer, not writing in earnest until he was well into his thirties. Once he began, he turned out a string of hits for B movies at Republic Pictures, even though he often had to write songs that Roy Rogers could sing to his horse.

Early in his career, Jule changed his named from Julius Stein because he was constantly being confused with the head of MCA, Dr. Jules Stein; despite the spelling, Styne's first name is pronounced "Julie." In his early forties, Jule decided he wanted to become a Broadway composer—an extraordinary feat to aspire to at that time in his life. Yet he knew that he had it in him, even though no one else could have had an inkling that Jule Styne was going to turn out to be one of the great Broadway songwriters—and his first Broadway collaborator was Sammy Cahn. After one abortive attempt in 1943 called *Glad to See Ya*, they wrote *High Button Shoes* in 1947, which was a surprise hit. Two years later with Leo Robin, Jule wrote *Gentlemen Prefer Blondes*, which he fashioned for Carol Channing. From that point on, Jule wrote regularly for Broadway and Hollywood. Through the '50s, he slowly earned respectability among his peers on Broadway, having to overcome the extreme snobbism of Broadway composers toward any newcomer. And he began to have an influence on his colleagues too. Jule liked to boast, with some justification, that he turned Betty Comden and Adolph Green into lyricists who could write hit songs that could be taken out of the context of a show, "songs that people sing in the streets," as he put it. He felt that the songs they wrote before that with Leonard Bernstein were "book" songs and that if any of them became popular it was a fluke.

Jule had a gift for simplicity, something that he said was instilled in him by Vincent Youmans, his favorite songwriter, who often constructed songs like "Tea for Two" from short, simple, repeated phrases. But Jule told me that he was also influenced by all his years of classical training. "I played Bach morning, noon, and night, and that's the greatest bass line," he said, referring to the inspiration for his bass line in "Time After Time."

As I've said, Jule was a great collaborator who shaped his music to the lyricists he worked with. He loved Sondheim because of his ability to write dramatically. He was amazed that Frank Loesser could write a whole lyric in his head. It took Frank five weeks to write "I Don't Want to Walk Without You, Baby," but when it was done and Loesser sang it to Jule at lunch one day, Jule was thrilled. He once went to visit Loesser when Frank was working on *Guys and Dolls* out of town. Loesser was stuck for rhymes when Jule happened to call from the lobby and said, "Can I come up?" Frank said, "Don't come up unless you have a lot of rhymes for *mink.*" He was working on "Take Back Your Mink" at the time. Frank was a great wordsmith and after he was divorced from his first wife, he referred to her as "the evil of two Loessers."

Jule also wrote for singers—most notably, of course, Frank Sinatra—and he had a singular ability to get inside the singer and hear his voice. He wrote a lot of hits for Frank, mainly with Sammy Cahn, but finally it became too much for Jule and he told Frank, "We have to split. I'm no good for you because I'm writing everything for you, and you have to sing other things." Of course, Jule had to *write* other things too, because at that time every song he wrote was a Sinatra song. Sinatra was angry because he thought Jule was blowing him off, although he wasn't. In fact, Frank wouldn't do "Just in Time" because he thought Jule had really written it for Fred Astaire.

By the time Jule passed away in 1994, he had finally been acknowledged as a grand old man of American musical theater, largely on the strength of *Gypsy* in 1959 and *Funny Girl* in 1964. That was very gratifying to him because he had worked very hard for that mantle and certainly deserved it.

Jule was a real character. A compulsive gambler who always needed money because he blew so much of it on the races, he was a dynamo who worked as fast as he talked. Comden and Green defined his way of speaking as "Stynes (or Styne-ese), *n.* language circa middle 20th century, spoken and understood by only one man. Noted for its incomprehensibility. Delivered in darting, unfinished, broken phrases." Stephen Sondheim, who wrote the lyrics for *Gypsy* and three of Jule's Tin Pan Alley efforts, said that the rhythms of Jule's speech told you all you needed to know about his character. "In the middle of every sentence he has another thought, and then another. You ask him a question and five minutes later he'll come out of the tunnel, and he's talking about Ethel Merman. A tumble of ideas." Jule was nothing if not prolific; he was the only composer I ever encountered who was very happy to throw out a song if somebody didn't like it—and immediately come up with another. His collaborators appreciated that quality but sometimes were vexed by it; if they made even the slightest comment about a tune, instead of changing it he would throw it away. Jule had such specific ideas about how a song should sound in a particular situation that if you told him that you needed a song that depicted England in 1910, he would come up with an appropriate tune. But if the producer then mentioned that the year had been changed to 1915, Jule would insist that the tune he had written was all wrong and come up with another.

Maybe the funny way Jule spoke was an expression of his astonishing energy. My friend Joel Silberman tells a story about being in a meeting with Jule when he was doing a hard sell on an idea he had. As Jule was rattling on in Styne-ese about his project, he quietly took a little bottle out of his pocket and slipped a tablet of nitroglycerin under his tongue and then continued with his hard sell. The fact that he was having an attack of angina did not deter him from arguing his case as forcibly as ever. A heart attack wasn't going to get in the way of Jule Styne selling a project. That's a perfect illustration of who he was. When I was working with Jule in the studio on an album of his songs, he was on dialysis three times a week and obviously had limited energy. Yet I constantly had to rein him in because he always wanted to present his songs in new ways. At one point he started yelling at the engineer because of something the guy did that Jule didn't like. The engineer said, very gently, "Take it easy, Mr. Styne. You're going to get an ulcer."

"I'll never get an ulcer," Jule screamed back, "but I'll give plenty of 'em!"

Although I never much cared for Jule's only Oscar-winning song, "Three Coins in a Fountain," I treasure "Time After Time," "Put 'Em in a Box, Tie 'Em with a Ribbon," "Make Someone Happy," "Just in Time," and almost anything from *Gypsy*. Like Irving Berlin and Harry Warren, he was a chameleonic composer. The songs he wrote in the early '40s were in the Tin Pan Alley mode, which is why everyone was surprised when he started writing dramatic songs for the theater. He understood character development and plot needs and was able to create tension and drama in his songs. It reminds me of the story of an early producer saying to George Gershwin, "Play me that tune that smells like an onion"—and George knew what tune he was talking about. Jule had that kind of sensitivity and could translate specific emotions into specific kinds of music.

Jule frequently peppered his conversation with phrases like "Rachmaninoff once told me" or "As Gershwin said to me. . . ." Because Jule was prone to exaggeration, you never knew how much of these quotations was true. Yet they were always illuminating. For example, he once told me, "Rachmaninoff said you should always compose away from the piano, because if you compose at the piano, you're limited by the notes on the keyboard." By that he meant that he wanted to hear the whole orchestra in his head when he was composing and not just the specific range and timbre of the piano.

Jule was very forthright in his comments about people. I once asked him something about working with Barbra Streisand in *Funny Girl* and he responded tersely, "Barbra Streisand— great singer, terrible person!"

I would have loved to be around in the glory days when Jule Styne and Sammy Cahn began their collaboration, because that must have been quite a team to see in action. In fact, they were the first notable words-and-music team I ever met together. Sammy Cahn was underestimated as a lyricist, partly because of his obvious egotism and chutzpah but also because of the rapidity with which he wrote lyrics. He actually said on one occasion, "I may not be the best, but I'm the fastest." Jule Styne told me that he thought Sammy could have been the best lyric writer of our time. "He could have been in Al Dubin's class," he said, referring to the great Harry Warren collaborator, "but Sammy wanted to perform." Indeed, Sammy's 1974 Broadway show *Words and Music*, which consisted entirely of Sammy performing his own songs with a few other singers and a pianist, was probably a first of its kind for Broadway.

Many of Sammy's lesser-known lyrics admittedly weren't top-drawer, but he could also turn out great lyrics with the best of them. He especially admired Cole Porter, and meeting Porter was one of the great thrills of his life. He may have been feeling the Porter influence when he wrote "I'll Walk Alone" in 1944, using a Porteresque rhyme in the lines

I'll walk alone
They'll ask me why and I'll tell them I'd rather;
There are dreams I must gather . . .

Those don't sound like the words of a man who came from Brooklyn.

Sammy's wife, Tita, loves to tell a story that she feels best illuminates Sammy's drive, so similar to Jule Styne's. When he drove to Hollywood from New York with his then collaborator Saul Chaplin, he saw a man standing at the train station in one of the towns they passed through, a young child by his side and another in his arms. Obviously, the family's big activity for the day was standing at the station watching the trains as they rumbled by. "I never would have been able to do that," Sammy later said, "because I would have been thinking, What is that thing and where is it going? But mostly, How do I get on it?" Sammy had a deep curiosity and an ability to become immediately absorbed in the human drama, which is what allowed him to write the kinds of lyrics he created.

In many ways, Sammy Cahn was a contradictory personality. When you met him, he could come off as borderline obnoxious in his constant self-aggrandizement, going on and on about all the hit songs he'd written. And yet when I played at his parties, he would come up to me and say, "Play anyone's songs you want except mine." Of course, later in the evening, we would always get around to Sammy's songs, but he genuinely loved the other guys' work as much as his own. I was intrigued watching Sammy perform his songs because he often overemphasized certain words in the lyrics, making sure that everyone got the rhymes.

Although he could write very tender love songs, they were overshadowed by more clever lyrics such as "Come Fly with Me" or "High Hopes." Sammy Cahn was the quintessential lyricist for Frank Sinatra, knowing exactly how to express Sinatra's persona in a lyric. Even after Jule stopped writing for Frank, Sammy went on to collaborate with Jimmy Van Heusen on another ton of songs crafted expressly for Sinatra. Frank knew he could always call on Sammy whenever he needed a parody—one of Sammy's legendary strengths. Those parodies irritated the hell out of Jule, though; whenever he was feted, he would ask warily, "Are they going to sing a Sammy Cahn parody about me?" He would explicitly ask not to have one written, but then Sammy would invariably stand up and improvise one anyway.

Nonetheless, Sammy wrote some of his best lyrics for Jule, including one of my favorites, "I Fall in Love Too Easily." I was once having lunch with Sammy and Larry King at the Carnegie Deli in Beverly Hills (it has since disappeared). Larry was proudly introducing his new wife to Sammy for the first time. Their wedding had been given plenty of press coverage, which had also been rife with speculation as to exactly how many times Larry had been previously married. At one point during lunch, Sammy whispered in my ear, "Now, *he's* a man who falls in love too easily!" Thinking about that lyric now, I realize that while Sammy was making a joke, he was also completely serious about the appropriateness of his lyric:

I fall in love too easily,
I fall in love too fast,
I fall in love too terribly hard,
For love to ever last.
My heart should be well schooled
'Cause I've been fooled in the past,
But still, I fall in love too easily,
I fall in love too fast.

Tita said that Sammy was without self-pity right up to the end. On the Wednesday before he died, the doctor came into the hospital room and said, "Mr. Cahn, we have a slight hitch."

Of course, there was more than a hitch. In doing some exploratory work, the doctor had nicked Sammy's lung and the lung had collapsed. "You'll have to go home on Monday instead of Friday," the doctor told him. Sammy knew what it meant. Tita, trying to cheer him up, said, "I know what a terrible blow this is, Sammy. But it's just one more obstacle and we'll get through it."

Sammy looked at her. "Tita," he said, "please don't get corny."

It's true that Sammy rarely exhibited sentimentality and that his blustery personality and the cleverness of many of his lyrics might make you doubt that he had the capacity to feel or express love. Yet when you read a lyric like "Look to Your Heart," you find something very different there. It's as simple and heartfelt as a lyric can be and it says, more eloquently than I could ever express it, much of what I feel about Sammy and Jule and the other great songwriters I've known who are no longer with us:

Look to your heart,
When there are words to say
And never leave your love unspoken.
Day by day,
We go our thoughtless way,
And only when we pray,
Do we remember those we love.
Too late we find,
A word that's warm and kind,
Is more than just a passing token,
Speak your love,
To those who seek your love,
Look to your heart,
Your heart will know what to say,
Look to your heart, today.

chapter 9

I'M JUST WILD
ABOUT HARRY WARREN

*H*arry Warren won three Academy Awards (and was nominated eight other times), had more songs on the radio program *Your Hit Parade* than Irving Berlin, and between 1932 and 1957 wrote the scores for more musical films than any other composer who ever lived. Yet few people know his name. Dogged by a lack of recognition throughout his career, Warren used to refer to himself as "Harry Who?" after years of hearing that response when people were told that Harry Warren had written the music for standards like "42nd Street," "Lullaby of Broadway," "I Only Have Eyes for You," "Chattanooga Choo Choo," "Jeepers Creepers," "You Must Have Been a Beautiful Baby," "There Will Never

Be Another You," "Nagasaki," "That's Amore," "I Found a Million Dollar Baby in a Five and Ten Cent Store," "Cheerful Little Earful," and "On the Atchison, Topeka and the Santa Fe"—to name just a few.

Harry used to tell story after story about how he was slighted in some way or not properly recognized. If it weren't so sad, it might have been comical, because it seemed that Harry just wasn't fated to get his due in spite of the fact that he had done more to deserve recognition than some of the most famous names in the business. George and Ira Gershwin always said that they were envious of Harry's mid-'30s stream of mega-hits and would have given anything to have written some of them. The odd thing about Harry is that it's usually the lyricists who are forgotten. Everybody knows that Hoagy Carmichael wrote "Stardust," for instance, but few remember that the lyric was written by Mitchell Parrish. (Mitchell Who? you say.)

Warren had come to Hollywood briefly in 1929 to work on one film and quickly retreated to New York. But he returned three years later to write the score for a picture with lyrics by Al Dubin called *42nd Street*. That film spawned four big hits, including the title song, "You're Getting to Be a Habit with Me," "Shuffle Off to Buffalo," and "Young and Healthy." Harry was so successful, he stayed on in Hollywood and wrote the songs for the great Busby Berkeley movies for Warner Brothers that followed *42nd Street*, including "We're in the Money," "I'll String Along with You," "September in the Rain," "She's a Latin from Manhattan," and "About a Quarter to Nine." After Warner Brothers, he worked for 20th Century-Fox, MGM, and Paramount. In the '40s at Fox, Warren started writing songs for the Alice Faye/Betty Grable/Carmen Miranda movies, including "Down Argentina Way," "I, Yi, Yi, Yi, Yi, I Like You Very Much," "No Love No Nothin'," "The More I See You," and "I Had the Craziest Dream," which was a big hit for Harry James and Helen Forrest. He also wrote the scores for two Glenn Miller films, producing a number of tunes that Miller made into hits, like "I Got a Gal in Kalamazoo," "Serenade in Blue," and "At Last." (Miller's 1941 recording of Warren's "Chattanooga Choo Choo" was the first ever to be awarded a gold record.) But Miller wasn't the only jazzman to appreciate Harry's craftsmanship. His first hit, the 1922 "Rose of the Rio Grande," was connected with Duke Ellington throughout Ellington's career. "Clementine," written in 1927, was popularized by legendary trumpeter Bix Beiderbecke. And

Harry's 1935 hit "Lulu's Back in Town" decades later became a favorite of the great bebop pianist Thelonious Monk. Warren also wrote "You'll Never Know," "Remember Me," "Shadow Waltz," "This Heart of Mine," and I'm leaving out a ton of hits. In all, he wrote songs for an astonishing eighty-one movies, including the theme songs from *Marty*, *An Affair to Remember*, and *Separate Tables*. By 1975, more than fifty million copies of his sheet music had been sold. But for all that, he remained Harry Who?

Like Irving Berlin and many other great songwriters, Harry was never formally educated in music, although he did learn to play the drums and piano from a local barber who also ran a music store. As a kid growing up in Brooklyn Heights, Harry held all kinds of jobs, most of them related to the theater: he played drums in a dance hall band in Canarsie, sold fruit at a Yiddish theater in Brownsville, and later worked as a stagehand in a vaudeville theater. He worked as assistant director for the Vitagraph Movie Company in Brooklyn, a silent film studio where he also played the piano on the sets, especially for Corinne Griffith, a huge star of the day. He provided mood music for the actors and dance music when they needed to follow the beat in a dance scene. He went on to play piano in silent movie theaters (including an early open-air theater), where his knowledge of opera and a fertile imagination allowed him to improvise melodies freely. After a stint in the navy, he worked as a song plugger and began writing songs himself.

At a rough estimate, Harry probably wrote the full scores for at least sixty of the eighty-one films he worked on. And he wrote for virtually every major performer: Fanny Brice, Dick Powell, Ruby Keeler, Dick Haymes, Jolson, Cagney, Astaire, Crosby, Garland, and Gene Kelly. The only person he may not have worked with directly was Frank Sinatra but, of course, Sinatra sang and recorded many of his songs.

I was introduced to Warren in 1979 through Leonore and Ira. I had told them that I wanted to meet Harry, and one day Lee took me over to his home. Ira and Harry had worked together initially in 1930 for a stage revue called *Crazy Quilt* and in 1948 on the score for *The Barkleys of Broadway*, which was Fred and Ginger's last movie together. (It was originally supposed to star Judy Garland, but she became ill and was replaced by Ginger.) The songs that Harry supplied for Ira's lyrics were quite different from his other melodies and I asked him about that. "I had to write more sophisticated tunes," Harry said, "because I knew that

Ira had worked with George and he needed a different kind of melody." (Unfortunately, some of their best songs together were written with Garland in mind and never made it into the show after Ginger came on board. They held back the songs they had written for Garland because they knew that Ginger, with her limited vocal range, couldn't do them full justice.)

For all of Harry's musical and personal sensitivity, he was also a street-smart guy. Far from having the air of a genius, which he was, he looked like your average fast-talking, New York–bred regular Joe. He was proud of his Brooklyn Italian background—his real name was Salvatore Guaragna—and he said that he got his love for Italian opera, especially Puccini, from his family. (One of Harry's most treasured possessions was a framed manuscript page from *La Bohème* that had been given to him by Ralph Edwards when he was honored on *This Is Your Life*. I later saw it hanging on the wall of his studio.) The last of eleven children born to Italian immigrants, this gentle soul had such a rough exterior that anyone who met him for the first time was invariably surprised to discover that he had written so many hauntingly beautiful melodies. Perhaps as a defense, he kept his sensitivity well hidden. When I once mentioned in front of his daughter, Cookie, that I thought Harry was sweet, she looked at me as if I were suffering from a severe delusion.

The day Lee introduced me to Harry, I played a song that he had written with Ira in 1945 that was never published. At first, he said he didn't remember the song. Then he asked me to play it through a second time and when I did, he pointed out two chords I had played that were incorrect—so it came back to him pretty quickly.

I was thrilled to hang out with Harry. I started going to visit him and helped catalogue some of his sheet music because his health was beginning to fail and I was aware that the clock was ticking. I loved his company and he, like Ira, loved the fact that someone my age was so enthusiastic about his work. For a period from 1979 until his death in 1981 at the age of eighty-seven, I spent my mornings working with Harry before going over to Ira's house in the afternoon. I felt as if my good fortune had just doubled, to be able to divide my days between two great geniuses of American popular music. When I arrived at Ira's each day, he invariably began by asking, "Well, what happened with Mr. Warren today?" Harry was such a colorful character and always had such great stories to tell that Ira was eager to hear the latest from his old friend.

Harry was also given to sudden outbursts of temper, in which he came off sounding like he hated everybody. But that was part of his defensive pose; he didn't hate people so much as he loved playing the role of the curmudgeon. Bing Crosby called him a "genial curmudgeon" as well as a "practicing self-deprecator," and the two roles went hand in hand. Likewise, although Harry was not anti-Semitic, he often referred to Jews as "kikes," just as he talked about "spics" and "wops." It was his vernacular—the residue, I suppose, of growing up in a tough part of Brooklyn. Because he spoke Yiddish, he was frequently mistaken for being Jewish himself. One of Harry's early jobs was selling insurance. They hired him because he could speak Italian and they sent him to the docks to interview workers who claimed compensation, but he discovered that he couldn't understand their Sicilian dialects and had to give up the job. He had also begun to realize that the company wasn't working within the law and he didn't like taking advantage of people who were, for the most part, immigrants like his parents.

Harry worked steadily in Hollywood from the time he arrived there in 1932 until the late '50s. Then everything dried up. After *An Affair to Remember*, he wrote title songs for only a few more movies, the last for a 1968 film called *Rosie*. Yet he continued to write and had stacks of manuscripts in his studio, all composed in the later years when few producers wanted his songs. It was all the sadder because Harry was one of those people from whom the melodies seemed to flow endlessly. I once asked him what advice he would give to an aspiring songwriter and he very simply said, "If a song doesn't write itself, leave it alone"—a line that has also been attributed to Irving Berlin. That was how it always happened for Harry, and what's more astonishing is that he seemed to be able to write any kind of musical piece that was needed—ballads, blues, dance tunes, waltzes, polkas, or novelty numbers (although he once admitted, "I love to write waltzes more than any other kind of melody"). In 1955, he even wrote the theme song for the hugely successful television series *The Life and Legend of Wyatt Earp*, starring Hugh O'Brian—one of Harry's few TV jobs. Yet he had no trouble with larger conceptions; if you listen closely to the score of *The Harvey Girls*, for instance, you can hear the main theme threaded throughout the movie like an operatic leitmotif.

As his eyesight started to fail, Harry stopped writing down his melodies and began turning on the tape recorder instead; he left behind several hours of fresh melodies, most of which are extraordinarily good. His friend Nick Perito had bought him some manuscript paper with wide staff lines but Harry couldn't read that either; after one attempt to use the paper, he gave up in disgust. He also wrote a great variety of rather free-form piano pieces. One was a waltz reminiscent of Debussy, another a somber Irish-tinged opus. Some were collected in a book Harry himself published as *Piano Vignettes*. In 1962, he wrote a complete Mass, but with characteristic bad fortune, he wrote it in Latin at the very time when the Catholic Church stopped celebrating Mass in Latin. Then one day in the '70s, he received a phone call from a man who identified himself as a Catholic priest. "Ah, for Christ's sake," Harry said, "who is this really?" But the caller was in fact a priest from the music department at Loyola Marymount College who wanted to perform Harry's Mass. After Harry realized that it was not a joke, he sent the priest a copy of the music. His Mass was performed and Harry was always proud to play a tape of it for friends. And rightly so. It may not have the polyphonic complexity of some classical Masses, but as you might imagine from Harry, its sense of melody is unmatched, just one gorgeous line after another. When I play themes from his Mass on the piano, people say, "My God, is this the same Harry Warren who wrote 'Jeepers Creepers'?"

But it is. As I said, Harry could write almost anything. When the film *The Sting* came out using Scott Joplin's "The Entertainer" for theme music, Eubie Blake suddenly started appearing on television talk shows playing ragtime. Harry was incredulous. "What's the big deal about ragtime?" he said. "I can write rags." He was from that school: What's the big deal? But that doesn't mean Harry didn't have very strong ideas about exactly how his music should be performed. For his birthday one year, one of his friends hired a woman to deliver a singing and dancing telegram, a birthday song with new words written to the melody of "42nd Street": "Happy birthday, dear Harry Who." Harry was appalled by the poor woman's performance.

"No, no, that was terrible," he told her. "The tempo was too fast. I want you to do it again, but slower." He went on to give her notes on her singing telegram and she was quite bewildered until he said, "Hey, I wrote the song." Then she got red in the face, not realizing that she was singing and tap dancing a parody of "42nd Street" for its author. Properly chastened, she gave a much better performance the second time and Harry thanked her generously.

When I started hanging out with Harry in 1979, he played me his recent piano pieces and a pile of songs for which he had supplied his own lyrics, not having a collaborator. "Would you mind if I tried to do something with these?" I asked. "I'd love to try to get you a job."

He laughed. "Yeah, right," he said. "Good luck."

I was twenty-three but I was determined to help him, because it seemed so unfair; the man was filled with talent. I called up June Levant and told her about Harry and all his songs. Many of his new themes sounded as though they could easily be adapted for a ballet. June put me in touch with Jack Larson, the former actor who once portrayed Jimmy Olsen on the television series *Superman*. Jack had since written the librettos for a number of ballets and the text for several operas with music by, among others, Virgil Thomson. He was also the longtime companion of the writer and director Jim Bridges, who had recently made *Urban Cowboy* and was very hot at the moment. When I mentioned Harry's name, Jack and Jim asked to meet him the next day. Apparently Jack had once wanted to meet Alice B. Toklas but she had died just before he went to see her, so now he wasn't taking any chances.

Of course, they were completely taken with Harry. He played them his melodies, and Jim decided on the spot that he wanted to develop an idea for a movie musical for John Travolta based on Harry's music. Paramount was looking for a follow-up project for Travolta after the success of *Urban Cowboy*. Jim wrote a script called *Manhattan Melody* and Harry started writing songs for it, combining new pieces with trunk songs of his that had never been heard. Jim also wanted to interpolate a couple of Harry's standards. The script was about an aspiring contemporary songwriter who has no success and no particular talent but who walks into an old pawnshop in New York and finds a briefcase that belonged to the previous owner, recently deceased. The briefcase, of course, contains wonderful old songs—it had originally belonged to a songwriter who was murdered. The aspiring young songwriter starts passing off the songs as his own until the real composer's granddaughter turns up and exposes him as a fake. Jim worked diligently on the story, doing research that involved seeing as many of Harry's old films as he could in private screenings at Paramount. I joined him and it was wonderful to see on a large screen original prints of many of these films, which I had seen only on television, if at all. Harry never attended, in spite of the fact that he made a hobby of collecting his films on video-cassette.

Jim's script was wonderful but after he turned it in to Paramount, the studio decided it wanted Travolta to make *Grease 2* instead, and the whole thing fell apart. Paramount paid Bridges a large sum for his screenplay but he never cashed the check, returning it so that he could retain ownership of the story. The project then moved to 20th Century-Fox, where Danny Melnick, a Hollywood veteran married to Richard Rodgers's daughter Linda, was head of production. One day I had to audition some of Harry's songs for Melnick, who was going to be producing the movie. I played through the songs and when I finished, Danny said, "Now play them in a contemporary style." He wanted to hear the songs the way they were going to sell, the way the kids would like them. I knew at that moment that the project was doomed.

Fox wanted Jim to direct *The Verdict* with Paul Newman. As a rule, Jim always wrote and directed his own movies, but he agreed to direct *The Verdict* if Fox would promise that the moment it was wrapped, they would go into production on *Manhattan Melody*. Unfortunately, that deal fell apart too and in the middle of the whole process, Harry became ill and died. So the last attempt to resuscitate Harry's career was a failure. The curse of Harry Who? had come full circle.

I later discovered that Bridges had based aspects of his screenplay on my relationships with Harry and Ira. He got part of the idea from seeing me in action with Harry, watching how intrigued I was and how overwhelmed I felt at times by all of this classic material. He talked about doing something even more specifically related to my relationship with the two of them, something about a young composer or performer becoming obsessed with the legacy of an older composer, but that never came about.

The one event that did bring Harry a modicum of attention before his death was the stage version of *42nd Street*. When that production made it to Broadway, a number of articles were written about Harry, garnering him more recognition than he had received in many years.

He even made a television appearance to accept an award presented to him by Dean Martin. Still, after the initial flurry of attention over the show died down, his phone didn't ring any more frequently. Another factor working against him was the producer David Merrick, a man legendary for his shady exploits.

Merrick had approached Harry a number of years earlier about making a Broadway musical based on the movie *42nd Street*. They arranged to have lunch at the Polo Lounge (which Judy Garland always referred to as the Polio Lounge). One of Merrick's ploys was to keep people waiting, and on this occasion he kept Harry waiting thirty minutes. Harry got up to leave and Merrick arrived just as Harry was going out. At lunch, Harry informed Merrick that he didn't own the rights to the songs, which were written for hire and so belonged to Warner Brothers. In the early days, Harry hadn't paid much attention to the legalese in his contracts. That was the last time David Merrick ever had any contact with Harry Warren. He never again acknowledged Harry's existence throughout the entire creation of *42nd Street*. He went to Warner Brothers Music Publishers and made a deal in which he was given the rights to use the songs that Warren and Al Dubin had written for the movie of *42nd Street* and any other Warner Brothers movie musical that Harry had worked on.

A very shrewd man, Merrick reaped an extraordinary amount of money from that deal. He got the rights to all the songs in exchange for two percent of the gross: Warner Brothers Music got one percent, Harry Warren got one-half percent, and Al Dubin's estate got one-half percent. Harry was making one-half percent from this show even though the Dramatists Guild minimum for a composer is normally two percent. Harry tried in vain to have the guild intercede, but because the songs had been written while Harry was under contract to Warners, the guild couldn't help him. Harry then claimed that the songs weren't written for hire and spent the rest of his days trying to get a copy of his original Warners contract—to no avail.

During tryouts, Gower Champion or his assistant called Harry frequently to tell him how the show was going. But Merrick, who was the sole investor in *42nd Street*, did not acknowledge his presence. Warner Brothers soon realized what a lousy deal they had made with Merrick; they subsequently discovered that Merrick was using one song of

Harry's that Merrick did not have the right to use because it had been written for a stage show, not for a film. Warners used that as leverage in an attempt to renegotiate their contract with Merrick. But Merrick simply said, "If you wish to renegotiate the contract, I will close the show." He very well might have done that and Warners was loath to call his bluff, so they left it alone and the contract stood.

The producer seemed purposely to keep Harry's name off the show, which was always billed as "David Merrick's Song and Dance Extravaganza *42nd Street.*" The souvenir program contained photographs of everybody connected with the show except Harry Warren, and offered a bio of Harry that had been written in 1962 and never updated. When Harry died, there was no acknowledgment of his death from the stage. By contrast, in performances of *Crazy for You,* when George's and Ira's birthdays come around, they always make an announcement at the end of the show and sing "Happy Birthday" to them. But I feel that Merrick kept Harry's name out of *42nd Street* because he wanted it to be known as his show. When the cast album came out, Merrick actually autographed copies of the album in a record store as if he had written the music himself.

Harry was devastated by this. He didn't travel east for the opening of the show, even though he was physically able. In my opinion, Harry's anger about David Merrick contributed to his illness and death. I witnessed how furious the whole thing made him. For instance, shortly after the opening, Harry was sent a copy of the cast album. It was signed by the entire cast (but not, of course, by Merrick) and set in a frame. "This is great, Harry," I said when he showed it to me. "Do you want to put it up?"

"No!" he barked.

"Why not?"

"Well, look at it. My name's not on it." Sure enough, it said "David Merrick's Song and Dance Extravaganza *42nd Street"* and "Directed and Choreographed by Gower Champion." At the bottom it said "Produced for Records by Thomas Z. Shepard." Then I got an idea. "You mind if I take this out of the frame?" I said.

"I don't care what you do with it," Harry said. I took it out of the frame and with a black marker I covered David Merrick's name and in white ink wrote "Harry Warren."

"Now do you want to put it up?" I asked.

"No! That Gower Champion, he just stole everything from Buzz," he said, referring to Busby Berkeley. "Take his name off."

"But I thought you liked him," I said.

"Not anymore!"

So I blacked out Gower Champion's name and put in "Busby Berkeley." Then I said, "*Now* can I put it up?"

"No, get rid of *him!*" he said, pointing to Thomas Z. Shepard.

"What do you want to do?" I asked.

"Poor Al," he said. "Al never got any credit either." So I put "Lyrics by Al Dubin." Before we put it back in the frame, I took two Polaroids of Harry holding the album cover. He dictated a letter to David Merrick that said, "Mr. Merrick, I've made a few alterations on the cover of the cast album of *my* show. Hope you like it. Love and kisses, Harry Warren. P.S. I'm submitting your name for inclusion in the Dictionary of Infamous People." We sent the letter, along with one of the Polaroids. Needless to say, Harry never received a reply. (At Harry's funeral in 1981, a large floral wreath was prominently displayed with a banner that read "42nd Street." Everybody thought it had come from David Merrick, that he had decided to recognize Harry at least in death. But then we discovered it was from Pat Dubin, Al Dubin's daughter.)

42nd Street ran for eight years and Harry never got proper credit during all that time. The night I went to the show, shortly after it opened, I stood in the lobby and asked people at random if they knew who had written all those great songs. Not one person could tell me. Some thought it was David Merrick. Most flatly said they didn't know. Was it Busby Berkeley? Ruby Keeler? They had no idea. How extraordinary that at a major Broadway show nobody gave even a moment's thought to who had written the songs!

Then again, that was precisely the kind of thing that dogged Harry throughout his career. Early editions of his first published song omitted his name. In 1924, one of his songs was performed at the famous Aeolian Hall Concert in which Paul Whiteman introduced *Rhapsody in Blue,* but Harry's name wasn't listed in the program. (In the copy of the program that I found in Ira's file, Harry Warren's song title is listed, but not his name.) When he won the Academy Award for "Lullaby of Broadway"—beating out both Irving Berlin ("Cheek to Cheek") and Jerome Kern ("Lovely to Look At")—Harry had to fight his way into the Biltmore Bowl where the awards ceremony was held because the guards thought he was a gate crasher. Even in a tuxedo, he just didn't look like he belonged there. At five feet six and stockily built, Harry looked like what he was—a guy who had come up on the streets of Brooklyn. In those days, they announced the winners beforehand, so Harry already knew he had won the Oscar, adding another layer of irony to his rejection by the gatekeepers. At the Academy dinner, the photographers took every winner's picture except his. "They thought I was a waiter," Harry recalled. At a gathering, he once heard the popular composer and conductor Victor Young, who had his own radio show for many years, say something derogatory about his songs. Harry went up to him and said, in that direct way of his, "Who are you, you son of a bitch, to talk about me that way?"

"I'm really sorry," Victor said. "I was saying that out of jealousy. Actually, I think you're wonderful and I'm going to play a medley of your songs on the air next week on my radio program." Harry tuned in the following week and heard his works being introduced as "a medley of songs from Busby Berkeley's movies." He was supposed to tape an appearance on Dinah Shore's television show in the '70s, but when he arrived at the studio they wouldn't let him in because his name wasn't on the list. So Harry went home. The producers called up frantically from the show, saying, "Why aren't you here?"

"Those bastards wouldn't let me in," Harry said.

"Would you please come back again?" they pleaded.

"Ah, the hell with it," he said. "I'm not going."

When he worked at Warner Brothers, there was a grip who also had the name Harry Warren. Harry sometimes opened his pay envelope to discover that he had been given the grip's check. Then he had to argue with the paymaster, insisting he was Harry Warren the songwriter. When another guy named Harry Warren died about a year before Harry passed on, they played Harry's songs at his funeral. As incredible as it sounds, Harry swore to me that the story was true, and why not?

Harry's third Oscar winner, "On the Atchison, Topeka and the Santa Fe," achieved prominence through a recording by the song's lyricist, Johnny Mercer. Harry told me that as he strolled down Broadway at the height of the song's popularity, he could hear it blasting out of one music store after another. Everywhere he looked, there were big signs in the windows touting "Johnny Mercer's newest song success!"

Ironically, Harry was one of Mercer's early supporters. When Johnny first came to Hollywood, Harry helped connect him to Richard Whiting, with whom Johnny wrote a number of great songs, including "Hooray for Hollywood" and "Too Marvelous for Words." At the time, Johnny was working on "I'm an Old Cowhand" and was having trouble getting through it. Harry wrote part of the melody and helped Johnny finish the song. Not thinking it was a particularly notable song, Harry refused the credit that Mercer offered him. But after it went into a Bing Crosby movie and became a big hit, Harry always lamented that he had written part of that melody and never got credit. I have no other corroboration for it, but Harry would never have fabricated a story like that, not only because he was very honest but also because he didn't need to—he had enough hits to his credit. And one of his most enduring standards, perhaps one of the greatest ballads of the whole era, "There Will Never Be Another You," was lost in a ridiculous 1942 Sonja Henie movie called *Iceland.* Fortunately it was picked up by singers like Shirley Bassey and by countless jazz instrumentalists and it entered the literature in that way.

All of this strange bad fortune probably helped Harry develop his great sense of humor. He was driving to the golf course with Harold Arlen one day when it came over the radio that Harry had won his third Academy Award. Neither of them said a word to each other. They got out of the car and started to walk toward the club, whereupon Harry turned to Arlen, who had won an Oscar of his own for "Over the Rainbow," and said, "Walk two Oscars behind me."

For all his commercial success, Harry hated Hollywood almost from the beginning. He came to Hollywood to write one score, planning to go back east right after. But the contracts were so lucrative—$1,500 a week to start, during the depths of the Depression—that he couldn't resist staying. He made more money working on one picture than he would have made in a year writing for Broadway. But for a guy from Brooklyn, living in Burbank in the summer of 1932 was like being "at an Indian outpost" or some town in South Dakota. He often talked about how impossible it was to work for all of the "idiots" at the movie studios. He quickly learned to pit one producer's ego against another's in order to get a song into the movies. If Hal Wallis didn't like a particular number, he would take it to Jack Warner and say, "Hal hates this song."

Warner would say, "Let's hear it." When Harry played it for him, Warner would say, "What the hell does *Wallis* know about music? I like it. I'm going to use it." (He probably learned this trick on the job. When Warner and Busby Berkeley both expressed displeasure with "Lullaby of Broadway," Harry played it for Al Jolson, who was starring in another Warren/Dubin film at the studio. Before Harry was halfway through the song, Jolson raced back to Warner to ask to sing it in his film. The minute Berkeley heard of Jolson's enthusiasm, he decided to use it after all.)

Harry's continuing obscurity is all the more lamentable when you consider that *42nd Street* played a seminal role in the history of movie musicals. When talking pictures burst on the scene in the late '20s, stage musicals were very popular; Hollywood soon started luring away Broadway's best composers, choreographers, writers, and directors for the talkies. The studios bought stage vehicles that frequently ended up on celluloid with a new score written for the screen. Producers cavalierly threw out scores written by Porter, Rodgers, and Gershwin, occasionally retaining the "hits" from their shows. Realizing they would need new companies to handle their sound rights, Warner Brothers bought up the New York music publishing houses of Harms, Remick, and Witmark, so they made money on both fronts. Merrie Melodies and Looney Tunes both originated as cartoons built around songs in the Warner Brothers Music catalogue—another promotion gimmick. Warners didn't care *what* songs were in their movies as long as *their* company published them. With the advent of the Depression, the need for escape grew and the movie industry began to create original musicals for the screen.

But by 1930, movie musicals had become box office poison because the novelty had worn off, revealing the fact that filmmakers had not developed effective ways of translating stage musicals to the screen. Their approach was too static. Long shots of the stage and a scarcity of close-ups and interesting camera angles made the audience feel like they were watching a grainy stage show from the second balcony. The public soon tired of movie musicals; the songs were tuneful but the plots were paper thin. In fact, movie musicals were so dead in 1931 that the score Irving Berlin wrote for a movie called *Reaching for the Moon* was actually discarded. The movie starred Douglas Fairbanks and Bebe Daniels, and was made for the then monumental cost of $1.1 million (equivalent to over $40 million today). By the time it was finished, however, musicals were anathema and they cut all the musical numbers out of the film (with the exception of one Bing Crosby number) and made it into a straight comedy. Berlin reportedly nursed a grudge over this humiliation for the rest of his life and anyone mentioning the film to him would be cut off immediately.

When George and Ira Gershwin came to Hollywood in 1930 to write a movie called *Delicious*, their first film, movie musicals had been effectively interred. Before *Delicious*, which came out in 1931, there had been a 1930 film version of the 1925 Broadway show *Song of the Flame*, on which George collaborated with Herbert Stothart and lyricists Otto Harbach and Oscar Hammerstein II, but George had nothing to do with the film. There was even a *silent* version of the 1926 musical *Oh, Kay!*, with predictable results. Ira talked about how they sold the rights to *Funny Face* in 1927 for practically nothing because films were still silent then and film rights to stage musicals were meaningless. That changed dramatically in just a few years, but until *42nd Street*, musicals were highly problematic. So when Darryl F. Zanuck wanted to buy the novel *42nd Street* and make it into a film for Warner Brothers in 1932, it was a tremendous gamble. Warners allowed him to go ahead and he brought out Harry Warren, already under contract to one of Warners' music publishers, and paired him with Al Dubin, who had been in Hollywood for two years and had written, among other songs, "Tiptoe Through the Tulips" (revived many years later by Tiny Tim). Although they had written a couple of songs together back east, Warren and Dubin weren't a team yet, but that would soon change. Busby Berkeley had made a strong impression on Broadway as a choreographer with bright new ideas and he had recently directed the musical sequences in the 1930 Eddie Cantor film *Whoopee!*, including an aerial shot of chorus girls that reportedly had movie audiences applauding. The combination of his revolutionary camera angles and close-ups, Lloyd Bacon's rapid-fire direction, Warren and Dubin's songs, and Ruby Keeler's freshness made *42nd Street* a breakthrough film. Something about Keeler's charm was most appealing to audiences of that day, even though in retrospect, as she herself admitted, she had rather limited talents (a fact frequently trumpeted to his friends by her then husband, Al Jolson).

42nd Street became the most successful film musical until that time and started the revival of film musicals. Harry was considered one of the hit makers and became an indispensable part of the studio system. Hollywood studios could afford bigger and better orchestras than the pit orchestras in most theaters, and prior to *42nd Street* Harry had never heard any of his songs played by such a lush and beautiful orchestra. The first piece of music he actually heard played by a Hollywood orchestra was a three-minute instrumental number that he supplied as background music for one scene. When you see the movie, you immediately recognize it as a Harry Warren melody, yet it is never credited or identified in any way. Harry said that when Leo Forbstein gave the downbeat to the orchestra and they started to play this melody, a melody he had previously heard only on his own piano, he burst into tears. That was one of the great thrills of his life.

Chief among the ironies in Harry's career is that what kept him in Hollywood was his expression in song of his nostalgic love for New York. When he first came out to Hollywood, there were no good restaurants and no night life; it was dead compared to New York and he loathed it. He had very few friends or contacts in those early years and he was always trying to go back, hoping that his contract would lapse, but it was always renewed. Busby Berkeley was frequently stuck for ideas and, according to Harry, "he'd sit on the sound stage with his chin in his hand with eighty to a hundred chorus girls running around, waiting for us to write a number." Al Dubin came up with many of the situations that spurred Berkeley's creative frenzy. Titles like "Shuffle Off to Buffalo" or "Young and Healthy" were the real germ of many of Busby's most imaginative sequences. Dubin's philosophy for writing a love song was to say in the lyric the things you would whisper into the ear of a woman while you were dancing with her.

Al Dubin was a colorful character who was six feet three, weighed over three hundred pounds, and loved to eat. Not only would he have six steaks at one sitting and stuff himself until he was sick, but he also drank and did drugs and disappeared for days at a time, making the rounds of the whorehouses. That was a real problem for Harry, because he never knew where Al was and neither did anyone else. When they were loaned to Sam Goldwyn for the 1933 Eddie Cantor picture *Roman Scandals*, Goldwyn was always asking, "Where's Dugan?" Harry told one story about a melody that he had written for Dubin to set, only to have

Dubin disappear without writing the lyric. Several days later, Harry got a phone call from Dubin and shouted at him, "Where the hell are you?"

"I'm in a whorehouse," Dubin answered.

"Where?"

"In Mexico."

"Great! Is that what you called to tell me?"

"No," Dubin said. "I've got the lyric for the song."

The song was called "Where Am I?" and Dubin dictated the lyric over the phone:

> Where am I?
> Am I in Heaven,
> Or am I really with you?
> Who are you?
> Are you an angel,
> Or just a dream
> That's too good to be true?

The song was a mild hit but it was always a great source of humor to Harry that those lyrics were written in a brothel. Dubin wrote anywhere and everywhere, often scribbling lyrics on scraps of paper, napkins, or whatever else was handy. Harry told me that Al wrote "Shuffle Off to Buffalo" on the back of a greasy menu from a restaurant in San Francisco.

Dubin died tragically at a young age in a New York hotel room in 1945, addicted to drugs and alcohol. Burton Lane was supposed to collaborate with him in 1944 on an Olsen and Johnson revue called *Laffing Room Only*. Dubin disappeared without producing a single lyric and Burton had to write the lyrics himself. Out of respect, though, he did put Al's name on all the songs. Three years later, he had a hit with a song from that revue called "Feudin' and Fightin'," for which Dubin had supplied the title and nothing more. It's a very good lyric, raising the question of why Burton never wrote lyrics other than on that one occasion.

After Harry and Al Dubin wrote the score to the 1935 film *Go into Your Dance* for Jolson, they all drove to Palm Springs, where Jolson was to appear at a benefit. It was before the release of the movie and Jolson publicly introduced two of the songs, "She's a Latin from Manhattan" and "About a Quarter to Nine." The songs went over very well and they were driving back to Los Angeles, Jolson and the driver in the front seat, Warren and Dubin in back. The driver turned to Jolson and said, "Gee, Al, those are great songs. Who wrote 'em?" Jolson stretched out his arms and said emphatically, "Who *wrote* 'em?"—implying that he was the author! Jolie was so egocentric that he couldn't give due credit for authorship even in the presence of the creators.

Harry's aspirations to return to the theater never died out altogether. His contract with Warner Brothers expired at the end of the 1930s and he was packed and ready to return to New York to have another go at Broadway when he got a call from lyricist Mack Gordon. Like Al Dubin, Gordon was European by birth (Warsaw rather than Zurich), had an impressive string of movie hits ("Did You Ever See a Dream Walking?," "Stay as Sweet as You Are," "You Can't Have Everything," "There's a Lull in My Life"), and loved to eat. A 1938 photo of Gordon and Dubin standing side by side puffing on matching stogies looks like an ad for a Big and Tall Men's Shop. Sadly, like Dubin, Mack Gordon died relatively early at fifty-five.

Gordon talked Harry into staying to work on one more film, *Young People*, which proved to be Shirley Temple's last picture for 20th Century-Fox—and the first of many for Warren and Gordon. It was quickly followed by *Down Argentine Way*, with Betty Grable and Carmen Miranda; another hit-laden team was born and lasted through fourteen films over four years. (Yes, you heard me right. They could really crank 'em out back then.) In 1946, Harry worked with lyricist Ralph Blane on a film called *Summer Holiday*, which, because it was based on O'Neill's *Ah, Wilderness!*, gave him a chance to write the more theatrical songs he was so eager to create. With Harry's luck, of course, the studio ended up butchering the movie and cutting four of Harry's songs out of it by the time it was released in 1948. The film was considered a radical departure for its time, with much of the dialogue set to music, and MGM didn't quite know what to do with it. Harry was very proud of the work he did on it and always considered *Summer Holiday* his favorite film, but it ended up one of the big disappointments of his career. It's one of my favorite scores, too.

In 1956, Harry finally did return to Broadway to write the score for a show called *Shangri-La*, based on James Hilton's *Lost Horizon* with lyrics by Lawrence and Lee (who later wrote the books for *Mame* and

Dear World). The show was one of the legendary flops of the time, readily abetted by the kinds of catastrophes that could only happen to a Harry Warren show. To begin with, it opened during a June heat wave and a newspaper strike. As Carol Lawrence, who was in the show, tells the story, the night before the show opened, a huge mountain set made of Lucite collapsed. Whenever they had to refer to the mountain or to the High Lama, they were forced to gesture toward a dinky little hill that had originally been intended for use only in scenes when the mountain was seen in the distance. This caused the audience to go into convulsions. The other problem with the show was that the star, Dennis King, who had been a major star of operettas on Broadway in the '20s, had since become senile. He replaced Lew Ayers before the show opened and had terrible trouble remembering his lines and couldn't get through the rehearsals. Everybody was certain that King wasn't going to get any of the key lines right for the song cues and they were prepared to help him when it was needed. One of the cues leading into the title song was a line spoken by King, who had to ascend to the top of a wall made of rope webbing from which several of the dancers in the cast were hanging. King was then supposed to say, "My God, I've never seen a place like this! What do you call it?"

Another cast member, Martyn Green, who was famous for his interpretations of Gilbert and Sullivan, was to answer "Shangri-La!"—the cue for a huge production number. To everyone's great concern, King never got the line right in rehearsal. Incredibly, on opening night, he scrambled to the top of the netting, looked around, and said his line perfectly, ending with, "What do you call it?" Martyn Green was so shocked that King got the line off correctly that he replied by saying, "Shaggila . . . Shuggaga . . . Shugalagigga . . . Guggaga!" He couldn't say it right; several of the dancers on the ropes started laughing and a couple of them fell off from hysterics. The brass section were sputtering into their horns.

Carol Lawrence played opposite an actress named Shirley Yamaguchi. Shirley was a good actress but she had a little trouble remembering her lines from time to time, too. When she forgot a line, she improvised, which might have been all right except that her improvisations were always in Japanese. In the middle of a scene, she might all of a sudden lapse into another language. Needless to say, the show became a joke on Broadway and quickly closed. According to Carol Lawrence, "It was the typical scenario of a Broadway show gone askew. We didn't have a Jerome Robbins to come in and fix it. Someone like that is one in six trillion." Harry was greatly depressed because he felt that it contained some of his best work. He went back to Hollywood and shortly after wrote the score for *An Affair to Remember,* the title song of which was his last hit.

I still hope that someday *Shangri-La* will be recorded so that the music is preserved. It was done on network television as a one-shot special decades ago. Although only two of the songs were published, Harry had the whole piano score in his possession. Some of the songs are average, but a few are real standouts.

There are several theories that seek to explain why a songwriter as phenomenally successful as Harry Warren wasn't better known. The most obvious theory says that songwriters who work for the movies do not become as closely identified with their songs as do Broadway composers. Already in the '30s and '40s, films were associated more with their directors and their stars, unlike Broadway musicals, where the songwriters' names were prominently featured. We know movie songs but we don't know their authors.

That may be true, but Harry lacked one other essential ingredient for Hollywood recognition: he wasn't a schmoozer. He didn't rub elbows with the producers or go to all the big Hollywood parties and hang out with the men who could have made him a bigger name. Nor could Harry play the piano or sing to speak of. If he had been a decent performer of his own songs, like Hoagy Carmichael or Johnny Mercer, he would have been much more popular. But for all his dreams of recognition, he shied away from the public eye. He never took out those big ads in the trade papers that other songwriters did, touting all their hits. When he was asked about his relative anonymity, Harry simply explained that he wasn't an extrovert. "They asked Michelangelo why he didn't sign his paintings," he once added. "And he said, 'If they don't know that I did that painting, then the hell with 'em.' " (And I'm sure Mike talked just like that.) At the urging of his friends, Harry once hired a publicist, but fired him a few weeks later, embarrassed at seeing his name in the gossip columns.

Harry told me that one day he went to a Sunday brunch at a restaurant in the San Fernando Valley that had a patio in back featuring a strolling violinist. The violinist began to play "The Boulevard of Broken

Dreams," a song that Harry had written for the 1934 movie musical *Moulin Rouge* and that later became Tony Bennett's first hit record. The woman sitting at the table next to Harry asked her husband, "What's the name of that song?" Her husband didn't know.

"I *know* that song," she said. "Oh, what is the name of it?" Then she turned to the people at another table and asked them but they didn't know either. Finally she turned to Harry and said, "What's the name of that song?"

" 'The Boulevard of Broken Dreams,' " Harry said.

"Thank you."

"You're welcome." And that was it. He never told her that he wrote the thing.

As much as I loved Harry, I have to admit that, to a certain extent, he seemed to revel in his lack of recognition and loved to play the curmudgeon. After so many years, he'd gotten awfully good at it. One day we went to Paramount Studios to have a meeting about the *Manhattan Melody* project and as we were leaving, the guard started looking around in my car. Harry screamed at the guard, "We've got your whole film library in the trunk, you goddamn son of a bitch!"

Another time, we went out to dinner to an Italian restaurant on Pico Boulevard and he ordered a very specific pasta but when it came, he denied having ordered it and said he wanted something else that was simpler. The waiter quietly took it back and brought the second pasta and when we finished Harry asked for the check, which came to about $18. Harry couldn't see very well, so he asked me how much it was. When I told him, he said, "Hah! Not worth it!" That's when I realized that so many of the old guys could never get over what they paid for things in the teens and '20s. What to me seemed cheap for such a good restaurant sounded like an exorbitant amount of money to Harry.

Harry's own explanation for his lack of fame, which he gave to Max Wilk in *They're Playing Our Song*, reflects a curious mixture of curmudgeonliness and self-pity. "I'm a Capricorn," he said. "They call the Capricorn the hard-way guy, you know; you always have to go the hard way. If there's a hot-dog stand and there's a lot of people standing around and I keep saying, 'Give me a hot dog,' he probably waits on everybody but me, and when finally it gets to me, he says, 'Wait your turn.' " Harry was not a bitter man by any means, but he was often vitriolic about Hollywood lawyers, and with good reason. He complained that the legal language in his contracts confused him and he didn't realize that he had signed over to both Warners and Fox the legal authorship of his music. When several songs from the first Glenn Miller movie at Fox became big hits, Harry was stunned to receive a small royalty check. Harry and Mack Gordon went to see the studio lawyer, who all but laughed in their faces as he informed them that their contract gave half the royalties to the music publisher (owned by the studio), another quarter directly to Fox, and left the songwriters to split twenty-five percent between them. It wasn't just the money that galled Harry; it was his feeling that the lawyers were putting one over on him and enjoying the game—which I'm sure they were.

When I think about things like this that happened to Harry, I have to agree with his self-assessment. It was almost as if he were surrounded by some kind of karmic force field that caused anything related to his fame and recognition to go strangely askew. Steve Allen tells a bizarrely funny story that illustrates the Harry Warren force field at work. It seems that the Italian-American organization UNICO decided to honor Harry with a banquet in Los Angeles. As a composer and sometime pianist himself, Allen was a logical choice to emcee the event, which also featured clarinetist Gus Bivona leading his orchestra. When Steve arrived at the ballroom of the Beverly Hilton Hotel where the affair was being held, he overheard some attendees expressing confusion about why Warren was being honored by UNICO, since they assumed he was Jewish. All during the dinner, Bivona's orchestra played the music of—Steve Allen. Bivona had just recorded an album of Allen's tunes orchestrated by Henry Mancini and he thought it would be fun to air them out. When Steve realized what was happening and mentioned to Gus that they ought to be playing Harry's music, Bivona assured him that Harry would be well represented during the presentation ceremonies following the dinner.

When the ceremonies began, two representatives of the county and city of Los Angeles delivered brief speeches of praise for the guest of honor, each addressing him repeatedly as Harry *Warner*. An unknown Italian singer named Joe Vina lip-synched to a record of a song not written by Harry. Another singer who was supposed to sing a medley of Warren songs came unprepared and without any arrangements. She asked the pianist and drummer to *fake* something, then proceeded to sing the wonderfully up-tempo "Lullaby of Broadway" as a dreamy ballad. Fortunately, after creeping through the first two lines, she forgot the rest of the lyric. Allen speculates that she was either drunk or stoned. The audience roared with laughter through most of these mishaps; their hilarity was not directed at Harry, certainly, but it was hardly designed to make him feel honored.

Steve had hired a couple of then little-known comedians, Pat Harrington and Bill Dana, to perform a routine of theirs, and he used the unexpected outburst of laughter to bring them on. They immediately went into a comedy bit about the sinking of the Italian ocean liner *Andrea Doria*, a tragic event during which several members of the crew had sought to save themselves before helping passengers into the lifeboats. In retrospect, as Steve himself acknowledges, this may have been the politically incorrect gaffe of all time. The routine might have worked on the comedy album that Dana and Harrington had recently recorded, but at an all-Italian banquet it caused havoc. An attaché of the Italian embassy stormed out after loudly castigating the comics; the one remaining singer was drowned out by the audience. One Harry Warren song had been performed the entire evening, and that had been butchered. All in all, it was another day in the life of Harry Who?

*A*s I said, Harry was a rough and tumble guy; besides his other vices, he loved pornography. His favorite movie was *Debbie Does Dallas*. He had a small studio a hundred feet away from his home and he had rigged an alarm system on the sliding glass doors of his house located nearest the studio. Whenever his wife, Jo, left the house to walk over to the studio, she triggered the alarm, giving him time to turn off the porno movies and put on an old tape of one of his musicals. They had stopped sleeping together many years before. Their teenage son, whose name was Harry Jr., but whom they always called Sonny, was a student musician when he died from pneumonia in 1938 at age nineteen. Sonny was sick for only twenty-four hours and then he died very swiftly. Harry and Jo were devastated; they closed their home in Beverly Hills and moved to an apartment. For some reason, Jo always blamed Harry for Sonny's death and from that time on, she never slept with him again. Harry used to say, "I don't even have to have sex with her. I just want to have her close to me, have her sleeping next to me." But she never would.

By the '70s, Jo was growing more senile and Harry tried to leave her several times but could never bring himself to do it. Once they had a big fight and they both went to their bedrooms and slammed the doors. Harry was sitting on his bed saying to himself, "That's it. I've had it. I'm going to leave her. I'm not going to put up with this any longer."

He packed his suitcase, drove to a hotel in Beverly Hills, checked in, went across the street to the market and bought some cold cuts, turned on a ball game, and was sitting in his room in his shorts watching the game and having a great time. Then he got to thinking about Jo, growing angrier by the minute. "Damn it, it's my house," he said to himself. "*I'm* the breadwinner. Why should I have to leave? *She* should go." He checked out of the hotel about three in the morning and came home, unpacked his suitcase, and went to bed. They got up the next morning and had breakfast and continued as if nothing had happened. She never even knew that he had gone. Sometimes I wonder why Harry stayed married to Jo. But he had a strong sense of family and he was Catholic and I don't think that he could have lived with himself if he had divorced her. He had affairs and he enjoyed a drink when he wasn't working, but he couldn't leave Jo. He told me about one affair with a schoolteacher in the San Fernando Valley, apparently a rather plain woman. "She's nothing special," he said to me once, "but she adores me." Harry was a very romantic man and he needed someone in his life he could have that kind of connection with.

I have no idea why Jo blamed Harry for Sonny's death, and Harry didn't especially like to talk about it. He mentioned Sonny very rarely, although one of the songs that he wrote for *Manhattan Melody* was titled "Just Call Me Sunny." And then one day he said, "I got a really weird phone call last night." I asked him what kind of phone call he meant.

"Well, it was about ten o'clock and I answered the phone," he said. "Somebody asked to speak to Sonny. I got all scared and started breathing heavy and I just said, 'There's nobody here by that name.' And I hung up the phone. You know what? This is the first time anybody's ever called for Sonny in all the years since he died." He assumed that it was somebody who had known Sonny thirty years before, instead of just taking it as a wrong number.

Harry flirted with death himself at times. He frequently drove to a golf club in the Valley to hang out with the guys, even though he didn't golf. He arrived there rather early and drove home late in the day, often after he had gotten a bit *ferschnockered*, a Yiddish term for plastered that Harry was fond of using. Ascending the hill toward Mulholland Drive one time to go back to the Beverly Hills side of the city, he passed out and the car kind of drifted to the side of the road and stopped. Luckily, he didn't get in any sort of accident and was gently awakened by the police several hours later and taken to the drunk tank where he had to sleep it off. He came home the next day and continued with that routine for quite some time until his eyesight became so bad that he couldn't drive at all. Of course, he wasn't supposed to drink in the first place since he suffered from gout.

After Harry became ill and during the time he was writing songs for *Manhattan Melody*, he kept saying, "I don't really feel up to writing. I'll start writing when I feel better." He had gone to the doctor because he was having problems with his equilibrium and the doctor had said, "You know, I might not be able to help you with this condition."

Harry started screaming. "You mean I'm going to be this way for the rest of my life!?"

Even though he was eighty-seven years old, he was very youthful. But despite his protestations, he continued to write songs; he overcame the dizziness and physical discomfort he was experiencing and kept writing. It was second nature. When I arrived at his house during those years, he often had a new song to show me that he had written the previous night. His last song was a piece called "Ungrateful Heart," which he wrote less than two months before he died. I arrived one Monday, not knowing whether he would still be alive, and there it was sitting on the piano, half-notated because he could hardly write at that time. But he remembered the song and sat down and played it for me, singing his own lyric with a faltering voice. I learned it immediately.

You say you're leaving, ungrateful heart.
No more deceiving, ungrateful heart.
You always knew that you'd go away.
Was it a game that you had to play?
You said you loved me, just what went wrong?
Have I been blinded by love's sweet song?
If you must leave me and we must part,
I'll always love you, ungrateful heart.

It isn't the greatest lyric in the world but it is certainly poignant in the context of that time in his life and his relationship with Jo. Harry was a romantic from start to finish.

Bedridden toward the end, Harry retreated to his childhood in Brooklyn. He would drift off and be back on the streets as a kid, playing with his friends. If you talked to him, he would come back to the present for a while. One day while I was visiting, he lay there mumbling and began to cry. Tears were rolling down his face. "Why are you crying?" I asked.

"Because I'm going to go to hell," he said.

"Why do you think you're going to go to hell?"

"Because I've been very bad. I've done very bad things."

"Harry," I said, "you've created so much wonderful music. You've made so many people happy. Think of all the beautiful things you've done for the world. You've done much more good than you've done bad. I bet you're going to go to heaven." He seemed to be at peace with that, settled down and drifted off again.

I used to play songs for him on the little cassette recorder by his bed. When I first did that, I put in a tape of an earlier song he had written called "Too Many Tears." Harry opened his eyes wide and said, "That's my song!"—thrilled like a little child to hear something he had written.

One day before Harry became too ill, the nurse helped move him over to the piano. As he sat by the piano, I asked him if he wanted to hear a song. He said, "Play 'My Heart Tells Me.'" I've always been intrigued that that was the last song he asked to hear because it is a song of indecision that he wrote in 1943:

My heart tells me this is just a fling,
Yet you say our love means ev'rything.
Do you mean what you are saying,
Or is this a little game you're playing?
My heart tells me I will cry again.
Lips that kiss like yours could lie again.
If I'm fool enough to see this through,
Will I be sorry if I do?
Should I believe my heart or you?

It seemed symbolic of Harry's relationship with Jo, which was always tenuous and unhappy. For a man who wrote so many wonderful love songs with heartfelt melodies, Harry had a very downbeat life. He had plenty of money but not the happiness he wanted, nor the recognition, and the death of his son and Jo's reaction to it was probably far more traumatic than he would ever admit. I think we were so close because, according to a mutual friend, Harry had said that I reminded him of his beloved Sonny. Or maybe he just liked having someone take such an interest in his work, someone who accepted his irascible nature. One day, for instance, I pointed out in passing that the bridges of two of his songs were identical. He looked at the sheet music and said, very angrily, "I only wrote five songs. Got it? Five songs. Every one of the songs I wrote is a variation of one of those five. Okay?"

Another time, he was talking about what lousy pianists songwriters are. "Berlin plays with one finger," he said. "Kern plays with two, and I play with three."

Yet even his angry outbursts and caustic comments were so undercut by his essential gentility that they were never upsetting. He had a dear friend named Alice whose husband, Irving Kahal, had written some songs with Harry in the '30s. Alice had been a Broadway chorus girl but she had a terrible voice and Harry hated the way she sang. Unfortunately, she remembered lots of obscure songs that Harry and her husband had written and loved to sing them. But even the famous songs sounded obscure when Alice interpreted them. Whenever she sang, Harry would bellow in his curmudgeonly way, "Alice, shut up, for Christ's sake!" Toward the very end, when Harry wasn't often conscious, Alice said to me, with a twinkle in her eyes, "Would you like to hear Harry say something?"

"Yeah, sure," I said. And she leaned over to Harry and started to sing in his ear. He came out of his comatose state and said, in a full, booming voice, "Alice, shut up, for Christ's sake!" Then he closed his eyes and went back to his coma.

I was with Harry and his family the night he died at Cedars Sinai Hospital. I had never been with anybody who was dying and I wanted very much to be there for Harry. I used to sit with him often and hold his hand and sing into his ear; it just felt good to be with him. At one point, he started to have very labored breathing and it looked as if he was going to leave us. The nurses rushed in but then, as quickly as it started, it stopped—as though he made a decision not to check out at that moment. He started breathing normally again. It was quite late at that point. One of the nurses said, "He's not going to die tonight."

"How do you know?" I asked.

"I've been doing this for over twenty years," she said, "and I know. Why don't you go home and get a good night's sleep?"

"I really don't want to take the chance."

"I know," she said. "Please believe me. He's not going to die tonight." So I went home and got a call at six in the morning that Harry had died. I was very depressed about not having been there. But I had had rather vivid dreams that night and Carol Dryer, the psychic I knew at that time, suggested that maybe it was important for me to be in my dream state to help him make the transition from that vantage point. I believe that's possible since we had such love for each other; at least, I took comfort in the idea. The fact is that I adored Harry; he was truly adorable and I would do anything for him. One day, he called me up and said, "I need you to find a song of mine, 'Let's Bring New Glory to Old Glory.' "

"You don't have a copy of it?" I said with some surprise.

"No," he said, "but you can find anything. Can you get it for me?" Whatever he wanted, he'd call me because he believed that I could do it for him, even though in that particular instance I couldn't locate a copy of the song and I felt terrible about it.

I was fortunate enough to know a number of songwriters like Harry who were "old and forgotten" and they were delighted to be able to talk to somebody about what they'd done. One of the things I'm most proud of is that I've taken the initiative to contact these songwriters rather than saying, "Aw, they're not interested in me and they don't want to be bothered." That's just not true. In most cases, the songwriters did appreciate the attention and did want to be bothered and I'm grateful for what they've given me in return. But nobody affected me as deeply as Harry—not even Ira—because Harry was so *alive*. Totally apart from his genius as a composer, he was irresistible and one of the most accessible men I've ever encountered.

I'm not the only one who had a high opinion of Harry as more than just a great songwriter, either. He seems to have been almost universally admired by the people who worked with him on all those films. In Tony Thomas's book *Harry Warren and the Hollywood Musical*, Tony quotes Herbert Spencer, one of the best orchestrators in the business and the man responsible for arranging many of Harry's songs while he was at Fox. Spencer said that, like many orchestrators, he had developed a sixth sense about how much strain was involved in a particular composer's creation of his final product. "The strain is sometimes very apparent—the music comes to you almost smelling of perspiration," he said. "It was never this way with Harry's melodies. I'm sure he had to dig to get them, but they were so logical in their lines and developments they sounded as if they had written themselves. There's no explanation for this. It smacks of the divine, and I have often wondered if Harry himself realized it. Working with him was a pleasure because, aside from his being a very warm and humorous man, he was always there to discuss his music with the arrangers. This was not the case with men like Irving Berlin and Cole Porter, who turned in their sketches and left. Harry seemed to write with orchestration in mind and if we did well by his music it was because we had him on hand to work with—and he was *simpatico*. That's the word that best fits Harry Warren in my mind—*simpatico*—musically and personally."

I still have vivid dreams about Harry. He is present in the dream state more than any of the other songwriters I've known. I feel a great sense of his presence and I believe that that may have to do at least in part with his lack of recognition. Along with a very deep connection with Harry, I continue to feel a responsibility to make his name more familiar and to get out some of his less well known music. With Harry, I had the feeling of touching the very source of musical inspiration in the form of a short, stocky, bespectacled, shy, and frequently sour-faced genius. Just thinking of him brings back a feeling of love that resonates in my chest. It's the same feeling I get when I listen to one of his songs, because they contain his energy, too. And in that form, he is still available to anyone who has the good fortune to hear a Harry Warren song or listen to one of his many film scores.

A few years ago, I finally found a copy of "Let's Bring New Glory to Old Glory" and when I did, a wonderful feeling of Harry's presence suddenly surrounded me. I felt excited holding the sheet music in my hands. I just wish I could have called Harry up and dropped it by his house.

BLAH, BLAH, BLAH:
THE ART OF WRITING SONG LYRICS

It may be said that the music of songs is continually being played without the accompanying words; played on the radio and records or whistled in the street. This is not a fact. The words are inherently present in every performance of the tune, amateur or professional, if only in the title, for never does a song achieve any sort of public unless the words have at some point made a joint impact with the music on the individual and public ear. Once heard, the words, when they are good words, may be superficially forgotten but they are emotionally remembered. The old defensive and competitive cry of the composer, "Nobody whistles the words," is simply not true.

—RICHARD RODGERS, from the Preface to
Oscar Hammerstein II, *Lyrics*

One of the classic arguments in songwriting is whether the words or the music is more important. The most common question songwriting teams are asked in this regard is which comes first, words or music? To which Irving Berlin's famous answer was, "The contract comes first!" (Sammy Cahn's reply was, "The phone call.") There are a few exceptions in the classic era, composers who wrote their own lyrics most or all of the time: Porter, Berlin, Coward, and later Harold Rome, Frank Loesser, Hugh Martin, Jerry Herman, Stephen Sondheim. But as Oscar

Hammerstein II explains in his book, *Lyrics*, "There is, as a matter of fact, no invariable or inevitable method for writing songs. Sometimes the words are written first, sometimes the music. Sometimes two or more collaborators lock themselves in a room and write words and music at the same time. The kinds of songs, the individuals involved, and the conditions under which they work dictate the process." He goes on to point out that in the case of both grand operas and Gilbert and Sullivan operettas, the libretto was generally written first and then set to music—apparently the most logical way to proceed, given the more flexible nature of music. Hammerstein postulates several reasons for the fact that just the opposite procedure has traditionally been followed in the creation of American musical comedy. Transplanted European composers in the first decade of the century had a tendency to place musical accents on all the wrong syllables of their adopted English language, and even American-born composers had difficulty setting unorthodox, syncopated rhythms to preexisting lyrics.

Hammerstein, who for the first twenty-five years of his career worked with such composers as Jerome Kern, Herbert Stothart, Sigmund Romberg, Rudolf Friml, George Gershwin, and Vincent Youmans before going on to collaborate exclusively with Richard Rodgers until his death in 1960, acknowledges that once he started working with Rodgers, he mostly wrote his lyrics first. His collaborator then set them to music—the way it used to be. In either case, however, he is careful to emphasize the closeness of the collaboration and the equal importance of both functions. "It must be understood," he wrote in 1949, "that the musician is just as much an author as the man who writes the words. He expresses the story in his medium just as the librettist expresses the story in his. Or, more accurately, they weld their two crafts and two kinds of talent into a single expression. This is the great secret of the well-integrated musical play."

I couldn't agree more with the great lyricist of "Some Enchanted Evening," "The Song Is You," and "When I Grow Too Old to Dream," especially since I believe that a song is more than the sum of its parts. Extremely witty or moving lyrics can occasionally stand on their own on the printed page, but they hardly have the same kind of impact without the music behind them. The melody and harmonies alone can be an effective vehicle for orchestral arrangements or jazz improvisations, but those exist on a different level of emotional involvement—and if you know the lyrics, you're probably singing along subvocally or are aware of the sentiments on some level, as Dick Rodgers so eloquently put it.

This is not such an obvious statement for the uninitiated, though, and it took me some time before I began to realize its truth. Lyricists are greatly underrated; for one thing, it's easier to come up with yet another pretty melody for a ballad than it is to invent a new way of expressing love in 32 bars. How do you say it again when there are so few rhymes for "love." In French there are twenty-one rhymes for *l'amour*, but in English there are less than half a dozen: shove, above, glove, dove. (Marshall Barer wrote a charming song on the advantage that French lyricists enjoy.) Ragtime composer Eubie Blake said he wrote "I'm Just Wild About Harry" by opening the phone book. He picked out a phone number and translated the digits into notes on the piano. But because the process of writing music seems so mysterious to most nonmusicians, they assume that it's harder than expressing an original sentiment in very few words.

In fact, until I started working for Ira, I was much more consciously absorbed by the music of all the great songs than by the lyrics. I wasn't even aware of lyrics until almost the end of high school, when I found the paperback edition of *Lyrics on Several Occasions* that had been republished in 1973 with an introduction by Comden and Green. My awareness of the craft of lyric writing in general and of Ira's lyrics in particular didn't fully blossom, however, until I met Ira at an age when the ideas expressed in his lyrics started to make more emotional sense to me. It was Ira who awakened me to the importance and beauty of a good lyric, and because he was the first lyricist whose work I became aware of and studied seriously, I still tend to view other lyricists through the filter of his writing; my assessment of those lyricists is of necessity a biased one.

Rereading *Lyrics on Several Occasions* when I was working for Ira and being able to ask the author about minor details of interpretation was a once-in-a-lifetime opportunity. In some cases I did not even know the music that the lyrics were set to until I found the appropriate record in Ira's collection and played it. That was a different kind of education— to read the lyric and then to hear the music later and discover how the words scanned. Ira not only instilled in me an appreciation for the nuances of lyric writing, his own and others'; he also taught me a great deal about interpreting songs. Occasionally I sang for Ira and he quizzed me about why I was treating the lyric a certain way. He taught me about phrasing. "No, try it this way," he might say. "I think you're pushing too hard. See, this is a joke line here and you don't need to push the joke."

Because I see and feel so much of Ira in his lyrics, because they trigger personal memories of our years together, the meaning of his lyrics resonate more deeply for me than they might for other listeners. Having said that, I do believe that there are certain very clear values to his approach to writing that ought to be fairly apparent even to a casual observer. As I see it, Ira's great contribution to the art of lyric writing lies in his ability to express deep emotions with a very light touch. I would even say a whimsical touch, although that word has slightly different overtones. I am continually struck by the clarity and the succinct quality of his use of words, but, of course, any lyricist has to be succinct when working in a 32-bar form. That was and remains the great challenge.

But the key to Ira's writing is the warmth underneath the whimsicality. Although I can think of a couple of lyricists who in some ways were more clever, Ira had a certain kind of warmth that is uniquely his and that, combined with his wit, raises him to the first rank of lyricists, even if the precise nature of that warmth is hard to put into words. The great thing about Ira, though, was that he *could* put it into words. For all his whimsicality, he had an astonishing command of language, from the most mundane vernacular to extremely sophisticated turns of phrase and wordplays. Part of that no doubt derived from the years he spent with George, roaming the city's streets, absorbing verbal and linguistic nuances the way George picked up musical ones. Both men had the capacity to ingest and transform all kinds of raw material from their environment. And Ira clearly had a brilliant mind for language, capable of great moments of inspiration and flights of fancy. But a large part of Ira's unique capability also came from good, old-fashioned perspiration, from reading and research into the past uses of language and the study of what it was possible to do with words.

One of the salient features of Ira's area of the house was a section of bookshelves containing what amounted to a vast reference library for a lyricist. It was not well rounded in any other way, but it served Ira's purposes. His library contained a wealth of unusual books—rhyming dictionaries and all sorts of peculiar volumes relating to the history of language and words, along with many books of poetry. Ira loved Gilbert and Sullivan and especially prized his collection of the first editions of W. S. Gilbert. He shared this passion with Groucho Marx, who had a complete set of the first editions of Gilbert and Sullivan scores. Although Groucho's literary output was limited to several books of memoirs and letters and coauthorship of a play, he was clearly a brilliant wordsmith with improvisational gifts. When he came to visit Ira, they often sang their favorite W. S. Gilbert lines back and forth to each other.

Most of the reference books in Ira's library were quite old, dating back to the '20s and '30s. On a big wooden stand, Ira kept a dictionary marked "Property of Cole Porter," which he had inherited from Porter. It wasn't actually left to him but somehow, fittingly, wound up in his home. I wonder who has it now. I found two copies of Clement Wood's *Rhyming Dictionary,* published in 1931, which was for many years the bible of lyricists. One was inscribed by Ira, and in the other one E. Y. Harburg had written his own name in ink. Yip Harburg and Ira had attended Townsend Harris Hall high school together, sat next to each other at City College of New York (which Ira never finished), and shared a love of light verse, both having an occasional item published in Franklin P. Adams's "Conning Tower" column in the old New York World. And like Ira, Yip was an admirer of the lyrics of W. S. Gilbert, which he had never heard set to Sullivan's music until Ira played him a record of *H. M. S. Pinafore* on the Gershwin family Victrola. When he heard that record, Harburg later told Max Wilk, "I had my eyes opened. I was starry-eyed for days. I couldn't sleep at night. It was that music— and the satire that came out with all the emotion that I never dreamed of before when I read the thing cold in print!" The influence of Gilbert and Sullivan on Yip and Ira and countless other creators of the new American popular songs cannot be overestimated. Operettas like *Pinafore* and *The Mikado* and *The Pirates of Penzance* had everything that turn-of-the-century American songs and operettas lacked: complex rhythms, intricate rhymes, and social and political satire packed into clever, witty lyrics.

Unlike Ira, Harburg went on to earn a B.S. degree and went into the electrical supply business with another classmate. But after building up a quarter-of-a-million-dollar business by 1929, Yip went bankrupt during the Depression. At that point, Ira sent Yip a rhyming dictionary and said, "It's time to go to work." Many years ago, Yip left his copy in Ira's home, never bothering to reclaim it, and Ira later gave it to me. (Although Oscar Hammerstein II admitted to using a rhyming dictionary, he was wary of them, explaining that they were of little or no use and could in fact be a handicap when trying for the clever double and triple rhymes so effortlessly and gracefully spun out by W. S. Gilbert or Lorenz Hart. In that case, he once wrote, "My advice would be never to open a rhyming dictionary. Don't even own one.")

In the margins, Ira had written some additional rhymes for certain words. Under "eeny," for instance, he had written in "wienie" and "blini," the sorts of things that might not have occurred to Clement Wood. After "wienie," he had written in parenthesis "hot dog," in case someone might look at it and get the wrong idea. I don't recall seeing any Yiddishisms in the margins, although Ira loved Yiddishisms. In the score to *Of Thee I Sing*, the scene in which the French ambassadors make an entrance is full of silly pseudo-French like:

Garçon, s'il-vous-plaît;
Encore Chevrolet coupé;
Papah, pooh, pooh, pooh!
À vous tout dir vay à vous?

The last line sounds French but is actually Yiddish and means, "Where does it hurt you, where?" That was Ira's little inside joke; *Of Thee I Sing* was a riotous satire and Ira hid all kinds of things like that in the score. He loved to say, "I know French: À vous tout dir vay à vous!" It's a tribute both to Ira's peculiar wit and to his fine ear that he could make that rather unexpected connection between Yiddish and French.

Rhyming is probably the sine qua non of all lyric writing, and Ira prided himself on being able to come up with perfect rhymes in all sorts of tricky situations. Many of his rhymes are witty and surprising, as in "Isn't It a Pity?" where he rhymes "sour" with "Schopenhauer" and "China" with "Heine." Or in "These Charming People," where he rhymes "born yet" with "lorgnette" and "blokes pass" with the intentionally mispronounced "faux pas." When he wrote triple rhymes as clever as Larry Hart's ("climate is" and "time it is") or double rhymes as subtle as "me a" and "idea," they were always sonically perfect. In Ira's heyday, "perfect" or "proper" rhymes were part of the form, unlike many modern songs where half rhymes are quite acceptable. Oddly enough, the era just preceding Ira's also tended to settle for less than perfect rhymes. The popular songs of the 1890s through the turn of the century had used a lot of improper or approximate rhymes and the new generation of lyricists made up of Ira, Larry Hart, Yip Harburg, Howard Dietz, Dorothy Fields, and many others all prided themselves on their ability to juxtapose perfectly rhymed lines intelligently in some sort of clever but heartfelt sentiment. These lyricists expressed a certain snobbism about anybody who didn't use proper rhymes, because that meant that they were taking shortcuts.

W. S. Gilbert and later P. G. Wodehouse in England probably paved the way for this development with their ingenious use of perfect rhymes, although it took some time for their influence to filter into American songwriting. Irving Berlin's first published song has off rhymes in it, like "beauty" and "suit me." Ira told me that the original version of the Otto Harbach/Louis Hirsch song "The Love Nest," which was one of the biggest hits of the '20s, rhymed "warm" and "farm," although the published version later mysteriously changed it to rhyme "charm" and "farm." I don't know how somebody as highly regarded as Harbach could have had the nerve to rhyme like that, but there it was. Early in the 1920s, lyricists still got away with more than they did by the end of the '20s, when musical theater started to come into its own with Kern and Hammerstein's *Show Boat* and the shows of Rodgers and Hart and the Gershwins. Not only were the rhymes better, but they displayed far more variety, more inventiveness, and much less reliance on formula. More to the point, the classier rhymes were increasingly used to convey a wittier and more profound sense of emotion. That's why Irving Caesar began to work less; even though he had a lot of proper rhymes, he didn't dig as deep emotionally as some of the other writers did.

As rhymes became more proper, lyricists grew ever more resourceful. By 1956, for "On the Street Where You Live," Alan Jay Lerner was writing:

People stop and stare,
They don't bother me.
But there is nowhere else on earth
That I would rather be.

That's a very clever rhyme because it was sung by an English character, and with British pronunciation, "bother me" and "rather be" are perfect double rhymes. It wasn't enough just to create polysyllabic rhymes; they also had to fit into the context of the song. That's why Lorenz Hart was so brilliant; he came up with intricate triple rhymes that made perfect sense, but he also used interior rhymes and rhymes based on hyphenated words, as in "Mountain Greenery:"

Beans could get no keener re-
Ception in a beanery

Or, in "Thou Swell":

Hear me holler
I choose a
Sweet Lolla-
Paloosa
In thee.

Hart insisted that he never did it just for the sake of showing off his ability to rhyme (although that last example sure seems like it). Arthur Schwartz used to tell a story about how Hart got angry at people for saying that he was rhyming for the sake of being clever. "For God's sake," Hart said, "I wrote, 'I took one look at you, / That's all I meant to do.' I could have written, 'I took one look at you, / I threw a book at you.' "

Subtle points of technique and originality became increasingly important for these writers. In the lyric of "You Started It," written for *Delicious* but never used, Ira wrote:

I know just how I got this way;
You started it.
Can't sleep at night and dream all day;
You started it.

But after the bridge, it goes, "Who is it keeps on raising Cain / And started it?"

Ira was proud that he had used the word "and" instead of "you" again. He mentioned that Stephen Sondheim had written an article for the *Dramatists Guild Quarterly* in which he praised DuBose Heyward for a seemingly minor lyric detail. Heyward wrote most of the lyrics to *Porgy and Bess* based on his original story, including "Summertime," in which his lyric goes: "Summertime and the livin' is easy," rather than "Summertime *when* the livin' is easy," as might be expected. Sondheim had written that the "and" as used there was "worth its weight in gold" because it "sets up a tone, a whole poetic tone, not to mention a whole kind of diction that is going to be used in the play; an informal, uneducated diction and a stream of consciousness." I asked Ira how he felt about Sondheim's comment. "Frankly," he said, "I find very little difference between 'and' and 'when' in that situation." He thought it was a silly thing for Sondheim to say, especially since Heyward didn't write lyrics as such. He wrote the libretto of *Porgy* and George set most of his words to music with minor adjustments.

Sondheim's comments nettled Ira because he had heard or perhaps just had a feeling that Sondheim was not a fan of his work. But Sondheim is hypercritical of many lyricists, including masters like Lorenz Hart and Cole Porter. In "Let's Do It," for instance, Porter wrote, "Electric eels, I might add, do it, / Though it shocks 'em, I know."

Sondheim questioned that. "How do you know?" he asked, going on to answer his own question: "Porter needs to rhyme with 'Waiter, bring me shad roe.' " He said the line was unnecessary otherwise. So you can see that some of Sondheim's critiques are microscopic judgements. Then again, who is as good as Sondheim is today when it comes to sticking to the tradition of proper rhymes while coming up with *new* rhymes and ideas?

While I was working for Ira, he received a request from David Wallechinsky, the author of the *Book of Lists*, to create a list of his ten favorite lyric writers. Ira agonized over it. Finally he was not able to make the list because he didn't want to show favoritism. But in the course of the discussion, he said, "How do you compare the genius of Cole Porter to the genius of Lorenz Hart, or to the genius of Irving Berlin, who if he had written only lyrics would still belong in the pantheon of great wordsmiths?"

My personal estimation of Ira is that he belongs in the top five. I hesitate to name the five, but if backed up against a wall I would say they are, in no particular order: Ira, Cole Porter, Lorenz Hart, Oscar Hammerstein, and Yip Harburg. Noël Coward is one of the great lyric writers, but he was British, so maybe he's in a separate category. Hart was certainly the cleverest, given his ability to create fiendishly difficult triple rhymes that were always connected to an intelligent text. Ira worked much harder than most on his lyrics. They did not come easily to him as they did to Hart or to Buddy DeSylva. Ira once observed DeSylva take a legal pad and write a lyric to one of George's early melodies, writing down first one line and then another. He left several blank lines and wrote another, supplied one a little farther down, and then went back and put in the second line and then the fourth line and in an hour, he had a finished, polished lyric. By contrast, it took Ira weeks to write "I Got Rhythm." He went through the conventional process of rhyming before he hit upon the revolutionary idea of not rhyming:

I got rhythm,
I got music,
I got my man—
Who could ask for anything more?

Obviously, those lines don't rhyme—a device which, at the time, was unheard of. But because of the short musical phrases, Ira felt that if every line rhymed, the melody would have sounded too singsong and would have had what he referred to as a "jingly Mother Goose quality."

Ira was much more romantic than Porter, more romantic even than Hart. He was whimsically clever, whereas Yip Harburg was more cerebrally clever and liked to put a lot of social commentary into his work. You certainly find that in songs from *Finian's Rainbow* like "The Begat," which first talks about all the begetting that went on in biblical times before bringing it up to the present day with lines like

When the Begat got to gettin' under par,
They Begat the daughters of the D.A.R.

And

Though the movie censors tried the facts to hide,
The movie goers up and multiplied.

But the greatest example is his "Brother, Can You Spare a Dime?" During the McCarthy era, Yip was blacklisted and his lyrics were searched for subversive subtexts. According to Yip, the search reached ludicrous depths when his song "Happiness Is a Thing Called Joe," written for Ethel Waters to sing in the 1943 film *Cabin in the Sky*, was later deemed to have been written in praise of Joe Stalin. They needn't have looked so hard; few lyrics can be more straightforwardly subversive than "Brother, Can You Spare a Dime?" Used in a sketch for a 1932 show called *Americana*, that song became the virtual theme song of the Depression, was sung by both Bing Crosby and Al Jolson, and is probably a good example of a song whose lyrics are more memorable than its melody— although Jay Gorney's moody theme suits the words perfectly. The genius of Yip's lyric was not to make it an obvious, sentimental plea for a handout in the depths of the Depression but rather a reminder that the guy on the breadline was the same guy who had helped build the country and fight to defend it:

> Once in khaki suits,
> Gee, we looked swell,
> Full of that Yankee Doodle-de-dum.
> Half a million boots
> Went sloggin' through Hell,
> I was the kid with the drum.
> Say, don't you remember, they called me Al—
> It was Al all the time.
> Say, don't you remember I'm your pal—
> Buddy, can you spare a dime?

Late in life, Yip explained the genesis of the song to Studs Terkel for his oral history of the Depression, *Hard Times*: "And how do you do a song that isn't maudlin? Not to say: my wife is sick, I've got six children, the Crash put me out of business, hand me a dime. I hate songs of that kind. I hate songs that are on the nose. I don't like songs that describe a historic moment pitifully. The prevailing greeting at that time, on every block you passed, by some poor guy coming up, was, 'Can you spare a dime?' Or: 'Can you spare something for a cup of coffee?' " But Yip realized that a phrase like that would work only if he could make it into a song that wasn't just about a man asking for a handout.

Once I built a tower to the sun,
Brick and rivet and lime.
Once I built a tower to the sun,
Brother, can you spare a dime?

As Yip put it, "This is the man who says: I built the railroads. I built that tower. I fought your wars. I was the kid with the drum. Why the hell should I be standing in line now? What happened to all this wealth I created? . . . It's more than just a bit of pathos. It doesn't reduce him to a beggar. It makes him a dignified human, asking questions—and a bit outraged, too, as he should be." (The royalties for that song have since been directed by the Harburg Estate to the National Coalition for the Homeless, something I have no doubt would have pleased Yip.)

Oscar Hammerstein was the most romantic lyricist of them all, of course, with songs like "I Have Dreamed," "No Other Love," and "I'll Take Romance." And when I say romantic, I mean that he knew the difference between genuine romance and sentimentality. Max Wilk tells the story about the time Hammerstein, whose friends all called him "Ockie," put one over on Jerome Kern. Kern liked to write a melody and then give it to his collaborator to write up. Collaborating on the score of *Show Boat*, he gave Hammerstein a ballad and the next day Ockie handed him back a lyric that began:

Cupid knows the way,
He's the naked boy
Who can make you sway
To love's own joy;
When he shoots his little ar-row,
He can thrill you to the mar-row

As Kern began doing a slow burn, Ockie handed over the real lyric:

Why do I love you?
Why do you love me?
Why should there be two
Happy as we?
Can you see the why or wherefore
I should be the one you care for?

Comparing those two sets of lyrics may help give you an appreciation for the craft of lyric writing, the value of compression and understatement.

Ira often said that most lyrics should sound like rhymed conversation and his strong suit was his ability to take the vernacular of the time and turn it into lyrics, as in "Of thee I sing, baby!" or " 'S Wonderful" or "Sunny Disposish," which has the lines:

> It's absolutely most ridic',
> Positively sil'.
> The rain may pitter-patter—
> It really doesn't matter—
> For life can be delish
> With a sunny disposish.

There's more to a song like that than mere colloquialism, of course. On superficial examination, many of the lyrics in "Sunny Disposish" can be perceived as perfunctory or not very deep, but they can also be seen from today's perspective as quite metaphysical. We read in all kinds of books on natural healing, from Norman Cousins to Deepak Chopra, what an important role a positive attitude plays in well-being. That's precisely what those lyrics express. If you want to dismiss them as sappy or silly, you certainly have the right to, yet those songs have altered moods and influenced a generation. And perhaps sensing that they could appear sentimental if taken the wrong way, Ira used vernacular and humor to undercut any sense of mawkishness.

Ira went beyond colloquialism in several ways. He had a knack for turning clichés on their ear and using them against themselves in ways that few other lyricists with the exception of Porter would have dared. In perhaps his most Dada use of the vernacular, Ira created what he called "a mild spoof on the theme-song theme" for the 1931 film *Delicious*, which he titled "Blah, Blah, Blah." As I've already said, it was more than mild; for its time, the song was downright revolutionary and stands as one of the most surrealistic parodies of love songs ever conceived. Let's begin with the last two lines of the verse:

> I studied all the rhymes that all the lovers sing;
> Then just for you I wrote this little thing:
> CHORUS
> Blah, blah, blah, blah, moon,

Blah, blah, blah, above;
Blah, blah, blah, blah, croon,
Blah, blah, blah, blah, love.
Tra la la la, tra la la la la, merry month of May;
Tra la la la, tra la la la la, 'neath the clouds of gray.
Blah, blah, blah, your hair,
Blah, blah, blah, your eyes;
Blah, blah, blah, blah, care,
Blah, blah, blah, blah, skies.
Tra la la, tra la la la la, cottage for two—
Blah, blah, blah, blah, blah, darling, with you!

Eat your heart out, Eugène Ionesco! As the years progressed, Ira's lyrics became much darker and deeper, exemplified by his last great song, "The Man That Got Away," which he certainly couldn't have written in the '20s. Crafted for Garland's character of Esther Blodgett, a singer down on her luck, the song clearly has resonances with Garland's personal life at the time. From its opening lines—"The night is bitter, / The stars have lost their glitter"—building to couplets like "The road gets rougher, / It's lonelier and tougher," a side of Ira emerges that is very different from his whimsical, vernacular wit. By 1954, when he wrote that song for the Judy Garland version of *A Star Is Born*, Ira was nearing sixty and may have been reflecting on his own life with its narrowing options and his problematic marriage from which, by that point, there was no thought of escaping.

Even then, of course, his tendency was to *want* to write wittily. Lawrence Stewart, Ira's onetime secretary and coauthor of *The Gershwin Years*, asked Ira to save the manuscript drafts of his lyrics for *A Star Is Born*. They are among the very few rough drafts of lyrics Ira ever saved and they are revealing. In the margins of the manuscript, according to Stewart, Ira had left discarded humorous rhymes ("groovey, movie, and hotter than Vesuvi") and couplets ("I rate a razzing, Perhaps he's Alcatrazing"). Compared with the lines that made it into the final version ("The winds grow colder / And suddenly you're older"), the discarded lyrics, though utterly Gershwinesque, are way too "smart" for this song. Ira knew it and had the craft to leave them out; but as Stewart notes, it was almost as if Ira "was compelled to be ingeniously inventive, even when the material would not permit it."

Ira's work bears a definitely recognizable style, as does that of Hammerstein and Porter. I would love to count the number of times Porter's lyrics, for example, mention "the gods,": "Why the gods above me, / Who should be in the know, / Think so little of me, / They allow you to go." Or, "The gods that nurse / This universe / Know little of earthly cares," or "The high gods above, / Look down and laugh at our love." When people parody Porter, they always put in something about "the gods."

And yet, although Ira is definitely in the pantheon, because of the transcendent brilliance of his brother he has too often been discounted as the lesser of two Gershwins, or left to bask only in George's reflected glow. That has begun to change in the last several years, especially with the arrival of Bob Kimball's book *The Complete Lyrics of Ira Gershwin* and through the efforts of many people, including me, to bring Ira's work more to the forefront. Lyricists in general are more widely acknowledged these days than they were in the past. Because in recent years so much of Top 40 music is dissonant and filled with a kind of verbal violence, some listeners are turning to other musical choices, whether jazz or classic American pop.

"Classic American pop" is a rather clumsy way of describing the music that flourished from the '20s to the '50s, but I don't know what else to call it. We feel a need for what these lyrics have to say, even though some people think that they are old-fashioned. In *Lyrics on Several Occasions*, Ira discusses a 1955 treatise on popular song written by S. I. Hayakawa, in which the famed semanticist expressed concern about the dangers of believing the idealized statements expressed in popular songs. Hayakawa argued that classic song lyrics could create emotional problems for people who are raised believing in unrequited love or in sentiments that are not necessarily true, like the notion that "Some day he'll come along, the man I love."

Nonetheless, I believe those lyrics when I sing them. Occasionally listeners will say that those lyrics sound dated or silly. In response I might urge them to look at the wit, the intelligence, the cleverness, and the eloquent, elliptical ways those lyrics use to state the obvious. One of the lyrics of which Ira was proudest was "They All Laughed," because it's a love song that never uses the word "love." He took it from an old print ad from the '20s that went, "They all laughed when I sat down to play the piano." The ad detailed how a man learned the piano by taking a correspondence course. At a party he announces that he is going to play the piano, and everybody laughs—until he sits down and plays. Ira took that idea and turned it into a very clever lyric, another example of how he plugged into the vernacular.

Ira was in a good position to refute the point Hayakawa was trying to make because he so disliked the cloying expressions of love that he generally strove for humor and lightness in his lyrics. He tried to find light and whimsical ways of expressing what he had to say—to some ears, perhaps too light and too whimsical at times. Yet all the great lyricists had humor in different measure, although Oscar Hammerstein for example, didn't write as many funny songs as Ira. "I Can't Say No" is a brilliant comedy song (seeing Celeste Holm perform it fifty years after its creation is one of my treasured memories), but for me it doesn't evoke the same kind of out-and-out belly-laugh response that some of Ira's songs do. Ira wrote a song with Burton Lane around 1952 called "Ach, Du Lieber Oom-Pah-Pah" that was a German takeoff based on an earlier piece he'd written with George in the '30s called "The Little German Band." Part of the chorus goes:

> Ve don't finger *Meistersinger*
> But our Straussian valtzes
> Makes the people longer linger—
> Und the traffic halts-es!

In an earlier song he wrote with George in 1936, "By Strauss," they were clearly kidding songwriters in general and themselves in particular:

> Away with the music of Broadway!
> Be off with your Irving Berlin!
> Oh, I'd give no quarter
> To Kern or Cole Porter,
> And Gershwin keeps pounding on tin.
> How can I be civil
> When hearing this drivel?
> It's only for nightclubbing souses.
> Oh, give me the free and easy
> Waltz that is Viennesey—
> And, go tell the band

If they want a hand,
The waltz must be Strauss's.
Ya ya ya—
Give me Oom-pah-pah!

In addition to everything else, as a writer of lyrics for Broadway and
movie musicals, Ira had to think in terms of character—exactly who was
singing and to whom the singer was directing the song. Even if there
wasn't a specific show with characters already limned out in a script or
screenplay, Ira got his inspiration by visualizing the character—for
instance, in "Now That We Are One," a sort of companion song to
"Once There Were Two of Us," both written with Jerome Kern in 1938.
In an attempt to pull Ira out of his deep depression following George's
death, Kern sent Ira some melodies and asked him to put lyrics to them.
Although there was talk about a show with Kern, I am not aware of a
libretto or a book for it. Yet Ira was clearly imagining two very different
people, two specific New York types, albeit with his accustomed wry
humor:

Now that we are one,
Which one shall we be?
Shall we be you?
Shall we be me?

F'rinstance, where'll we live?
What's to be home base?
I'm all for the West Side;
You're for Sutton Place.

Shall we have our hamburgers rare or medium?
You like double features—I call them tedium.

_H_AVING said earlier that the perfect song requires the perfect combination of music and lyrics, so that one element cannot be more important than the other, I have to admit that in certain types of songs, one *is*
more important than the other. "The Babbitt and the Bromide" is more
about the lyrics than the music, and the lyrics could almost be spoken as

effectively as sung (in the original stage version, these lines were split in half by Fred and Adele Astaire):

Hello! How are you?
Howza folks? What's new?
I'm great! That's good!
Ha! Ha! Knock wood!
Well! Well! What say?
Howya been? Nice day!

Like "Blah, Blah, Blah," this song is close to theater of the absurd. But even though the music is subservient to the lyric, it still has to be appropriately subservient. If it isn't written with an understanding of its context, it can undercut what the lyric needs to say. It still has to express an emotion—even if what it expresses happens to be the absence of genuine emotion. The genius of all the great songwriters resides in their ability to understand when a particular melody or lyric is right and when it isn't. George worked on six different melodies for "Strike Up the Band" before he felt that he had what would be an appropriate title song for that show. Only then did he give it to Ira, even though each time he played the tune for Ira, Ira said it was fine. George was digging for something deeper, and he worked until he was finally satisfied. Then it was up to Ira to match it, to make it work. In some ways the job is easier for a composer because he only has to write one 32-bar melody and then it's up to the lyricist to write the different expressions of emotion when the song is reprised later in the act or used in part in another section of the show. But the tune has to be a damn good tune to start with so it can serve all of those functions.

The equal importance of words and music as a general rule, however, is attested to in a very pragmatic way by the fact that royalties are almost always divided equally between composer and lyricist. That goes for all recordings, so that the lyricist collects his or her equal share even for instrumental versions of a song. Ira was always extremely careful and gracious about giving credit on his songs. Once Yip Harburg suggested the title "Make Way for Tomorrow," for which Ira wrote up appropriate lyrics. When the song was published, Ira made sure that the credits said "Lyric by Ira Gershwin and E. Y. Harburg," even though Yip had merely supplied the title. Conversely, Ira never asked for credit when he supplied the last line of "Over the Rainbow." Yip and Harold Arlen were working in his living room on the score of *The Wizard of Oz*, struggling for a last line. Ira said, "How about, 'If happy little bluebirds fly beyond the rainbow, why, oh why, can't I?' "

I asked Ira why he chimed in uncharacteristically that way. "They'd been working at the piano for a long, long time," he said, "and I wanted to make it a short evening." Then he added quickly, "But don't tell anyone." Yip, incidentally, did credit Ira for coming up with the idea of making "Over the Rainbow" into more of a pop song. When Arlen originally played the melody for him, it was ponderous and operatic-sounding. "My God, Harold," Yip said, "this is a twelve-year-old girl singing a song of yearning. It isn't Nelson Eddy."

Arlen was crestfallen. Yip called Ira in and Ira suggested to Harold, "Can you play it in more of a popular style with rhythm?" Arlen played the melody again with a kind of stride accompaniment and that's when Yip was able to start to work on the lyrics, beginning with the title. Faced with getting Dorothy to the other side of the rainbow, Harburg was daunted by the plaintive quality of the third note of the theme. It had to be an expansive sound, an open vowel, and he went from "o" to "over" to "Over the Rainbow."

Unfortunately, once the songwriter has struggled to craft the perfect lyric, there's no guarantee that performers will interpret it the way the writer intended. Interpretation, as the performer's artistic license is often euphemistically known, is largely a matter of taste, although some fairly solid rules do apply. Ira was very specific about how he liked to hear his lyrics sung. When Frank Sinatra made changes in the songs, it used to drive Ira crazy because he felt that what Sinatra did weakened the lyric. "I don't mind if someone makes a change and it actually is an intelligent one that strengthens the lyric," he said. But when Sinatra sang "A Foggy Day," for instance, he inserted words for no reason: "I view the morning with *much* alarm." Adding the word "much" weakened the line to Ira's way of thinking. Ira had good reason for concern. Ever since Sinatra added that word, almost everybody sings it that way. I even heard a recording by a Scandinavian singer who, having learned it phonetically, sings the Sinatra "much." So Frank Sinatra has now effectively rewritten Ira's lyric.

The primary requirement for Ira was to have the lyrics interpreted intelligently. He could usually tell if somebody understood his lyric or not. I have always said that I could tell if a jazz instrumentalist understands the lyric. That awareness probably came from Ira, simply because I never paid as much attention to lyrics before I met him. Ira was never egotistical but he was very proud of some of his lyrics, and with good reason. He would say to me, "Listen to this phrase in the verse of 'Sunny Disposish,' " referring to the rhyme of "platitudinous" and "attitude in us." If his sister-in-law Emily Paley were sitting with us listening and pointed out something like that, Ira would just beam. There were so many ways I learned things just by being around Ira that I could hardly imagine a better teacher.

I once played a recording of Ray Charles singing "How Long Has This Been Going On?" that I loved but that Ira did not like at all. I loved Ray's deeply soulful approach but Ira found it a little wide of the mark. Sarah Vaughan made a recording of the same song for Norman Granz's Pablo Records in the late '70s that went even further afield than Ray's version. It began with a Latin feel and then went into a jazz-fusion section that kept repeating the chords over and over again as Sarah sang, "How long, how long, how long, how long. . . ." When I played that, Ira started yelling at the record player, "*Too* long! Take that off!"

Lena Horne's pronunciation of certain words is, to put it mildly, very stylized. Lena had done a recording of "Someone to Watch Over Me" in the mid-'70s, and when she went into the chorus, she sang what sounded like, "They-ull's a someone. . . ." Ira yelled, "*They-ull's?* What does *that* mean?"

By comparison, every songwriter I ever met loved Fred Astaire. This may surprise most people because Astaire is not particularly known for his singing ability, but the songwriters all insisted that he was the best interpreter of their songs. Astaire had a way of interpreting lyrics that always very clearly expressed the meaning of the song with an inherent rhythm and understanding that was very pleasing to the authors of those songs. Yet Astaire loathed his own voice. At his home he kept reels of film containing all of his favorite dance sequences from all of his movies, but he had excised every single vocal preceding those dance sections. I hate to disagree with the master, but Astaire is one of my favorite singers, too. The first commercial recordings of Astaire singing the songs that were written for the Astaire and Rogers movies by Berlin and Gershwin and Kern—songs like "Pick Yourself Up" and "The Way You Look Tonight" and "Isn't This a Lovely Day?" and "Cheek to Cheek" and "A Fine Romance" and "They All Laughed"—are the definitive recordings of those pieces as far as I'm concerned. I don't think they have ever been surpassed as clear documents of how those songs were meant to be performed. I certainly like other versions of those songs, but Astaire's are the most pleasing to me.

Perhaps because of my predilection for Astaire over more stylized interpretations of those songs by later vocalists, some people accuse me of being a purist. And yet I make all kinds of musical changes in my interpretations of songs. I don't, however, change lyrics, because I don't feel that I can say it any better than those guys did. I share Ira's dislike for the way Sinatra improvises new lyrics in an attempt to sound "hip." His approach has nothing to do with the song and everything to do with his machismo persona, as when he sings, "That's why that *chick* is a *champ*" instead of "That's why the lady is a tramp." A friend has suggested that maybe my dislike for Sinatra's hip persona has colored my feelings about his singing. But the persona is an integral part of the singing, especially if he has to make everything macho and hip and swingin' to the detriment of the songs. At a tribute to Ira in 1975, Sinatra sang "A Foggy Day." When he finished, he said, "It wasn't as good as Fred Astaire, but it was louder." I had to agree.

Sinatra's habit of adding extra words often destroys the scansion and even the whole music form in some cases. At Sinatra's request, Ira wrote an opposite-sex version of "The Man That Got Away," but Sinatra has taken it on himself to change a lot of the lyrics that have nothing to do with gender: "And suddenly you're older" becomes "And suddenly you're a lot older." "For you've been through the mill" becomes "Because you have been put through the mill." And Sinatra even changed the title line to "The gal *who* got away," although Ira purposely wrote "that" as a paraphrase of the fisherman's expression "You should have seen the one that got away." Crosby took a lot of liberties, too, but there was something essentially organic and musical about what Crosby did. I find his interpolations charming, even though he made his share of inappropriate changes.

Jonathan Schwartz is considered the ultimate Sinatra fanatic in spite of the fact that Sinatra once had him taken off the air for criticizing the third record of his *Triology* set. One time when Jonathan was interviewing me, I said I didn't like the way Sinatra takes liberties. Jonathan wouldn't hear of it. "In some sixteen hundred commercially released tracks," he said, "he's taken lyrical liberties with only forty-one of them."

"Are you sure?" I asked.

"Absolutely," he said.

"I don't believe it," I said. And I still find it hard to believe, although I realize now that some of my memories of Sinatra altering a lyric are actually cases of his using vocal swoops and stylizations—changing the pitch of a particular note, going down and up and down again, for instance. Even though I'm aware that he is a great singer and that millions of people adore him, mannerisms like that just drive me up the wall. What is the process that goes through his head when he comes up with something like "You stick around, Jack," which he interjected in the middle of George Harrison's "Something"? Is it premeditated or does it come out spontaneously? I suppose I'm prejudiced because his interpretations of songs are so different from the way I approach them, and Sinatra's many fans may well find my style foreign by comparison.

Songwriters themselves have very mixed opinions about Sinatra, even though most of them were thrilled to have him sing their songs. Ira disliked any number of liberties that Sinatra took yet was delighted that he sang Gershwin so often. He loved to point out that on *Trilogy*, the newly recorded three-LP compilation/retrospective of Sinatra's career, the only songwriters represented with *two* songs were the Gershwin Brothers. Jule Styne felt that Sinatra was the single greatest American popular singer, as did Sammy Cahn. Both, of course, owed a large number of their hits to Ol' Blue Eyes. One day, Johnny Green (author of "Body and Soul") launched a diatribe about Sinatra's way of taking liberties with songs; then several months later he told me how much he loved Frank. I suppose both feelings were true for John—but not for me (pun intended). I spent several hours recently listening to Sinatra recordings back to back with Crosby recordings. Bing is the master for me, for sheer delight in tone and warmth of interpretation. As I listened to Sinatra, he got more and more on my nerves. Mind you, I am well aware that this is a minority opinion and I freely acknowledge Sinatra's *vocal* talent—a great natural instrument—but his message continues to elude me.

As I've said, I don't feel the same way about taking musical liberties.

It's fine to take a liberty if it's in good taste—or if it's part of an interpretation that is so far away from the original that it is clearly a different entity. Lee Wiley's recording of "I've Got a Crush on You" is a case in point. The original version of the song was a one-step, a fast-paced dance number first sung by Clifton Webb and Mary Hay in the 1928 flop show *Treasure Girl* and then interpolated into the revised version of *Strike Up the Band* in 1930. It remained a fast-paced number until the late '30s, when Lee Wiley recorded it as a ballad. When Ira first heard her version, he was surprised and, although he didn't dislike it, he certainly found it disconcerting. But after playing it several times, he decided that he did like it that way. His only comment was that he might have written the lyric differently if he had realized that it was going to turn into a ballad, even though the alliteration of some of the lyrics sounds quite nice in a slow tempo: "Could you coo, / Could you care / For a cunning cottage we could share?" And so I learned from Ira that you don't have to interpret everything exactly as it was written.

Richard Rodgers is the best-known stickler for having a song sung exactly as he wrote it, placing very heavy requirements on those who use his orchestrations and admonishing them not to change a note. This holds true today, a decade and a half after his death, as his heirs still require strict adherence to his wishes. Having been born out of the jazz world, Gershwin was more malleable, as was Harold Arlen. On Arlen's own recordings of his songs, he takes a lot of liberties and does all kinds of vocal tricks that I wouldn't have dared to do in his songs if I hadn't heard him do them first. I don't always like the things he does, such as adding a countermelody to "Ac-cent-tchu-ate the Positive" that wasn't very interesting. Arlen, whose father was a cantor, had a wonderfully soulful sound to his voice. After he became famous, his father used to interpolate melodies from his songs into the synagogue services, so that portions of his songs were suddenly being sung with liturgical Hebrew lyrics. I wonder what that sounded like. I can't quite imagine "Over the Pesach" or "Ac-cent-tchu-ate the Hanukkah."

I do research into the songs I perform because I like to know where the lyric came from and what led to the creation of the song. That may give me a little insight or a clue as to how to interpret it. Knowing the plot situation for which the song was created is sometimes helpful, although it can get in the way if it's a ridiculous plot.

"Alexander's Ragtime Band" by Irving Berlin is an example of a song that has been performed so many times that it is dismissed by the public, who no longer pay attention to what the lyric says. This frequently happens to songs that are so popular, almost *too* good, that they are overplayed and eventually tuned out. But although that song has lost its impact, it was revolutionary when it first burst on the scene in 1911. "Alexander's" isn't truly a ragtime song, yet it incorporated ragtime elements in the melody in a day when ragtime was widely considered trashy music. Berlin himself said, "It is not a rag; it is a song about ragtime." But by creating this particular song, Berlin made ragtime respectable. He introduced it himself at the Friars Club at a show called *Friars Club Frolic* and it was nicely, if not rapturously, received. Still, he knew that he had something special. He touched a public nerve, and in those days before widespread sales of phonograph records and radio, when success was still measured in sheet music and piano roll sales and vaudeville performances, the song caught on in a way that was previously unheard of. I don't think any song had ever been as popular, and part of its success had to do with the irreverence of the lyric:

Play a bugle call   .
Like you've never heard before,
So natural
That you wanna go to war.

It was clever and charming and it started a craze for ragtime songs. Berlin wrote a multitude of them after that—"Ragtime Jockey Man," "The Ragtime Nightingale," "That Mysterious Rag," and "The Ragtime Soldier Man," which is only a slight variation on the melody of "Alexander's Ragtime Band."

Perhaps inevitably, the freshness of "Alexander's" diminished through the years until, by the time we get to the '80s and '90s, it's just another song that has been around forever. Nobody has any idea of the impact it had all those years ago. That's why, when I recorded it, I decided to sing it very slowly at first to make the lyrics suddenly stand out again. My interpretation is far from purist; for one thing, an interpretation also has to have theatricality to show off the best strengths of the performer.

Most of these songs were written for movies or for stage shows that had great production value behind them, and once you extract a song from that context, it takes on a completely different quality.

Conversely, sometimes the fun lies in performing a song in its original form because we have gotten so far away from it that the original now sounds fresh. "Thanks for the Memory" is a great song but it has been used for so long as play-on music for Bob Hope that it has lost much of its initial charm. When I sang and recorded that song, I tried to recapture that initial charm with the result that it became one of my most requested numbers. One day while browsing through the sheet music of different songs at the piano, I came across "Thanks for the Memory" and started playing through it. It had such a great sense of yearning that I was bowled over by its power and freshness, realizing that it was a rather poignant gem that had been neglected. Then I dug out the original Decca recording by Bob Hope and Shirley Ross and listened—and cried. From then on, I began performing it only to discover that it was a favorite song of many others, including lyricist Alan Bergman, who offered me *all* the original lyrics that Leo Robin had written for the number. I had unfortunately already recorded it; that's why my recorded version contains only the two published choruses and none of the extras. When Rosemary Clooney told me that she intended to put the song on her next record, I sent the extra choruses over to her and she included some of them. (Incidentally, Leo Robin was one of the most talented and self-effacing people I ever knew. He retired from lyric writing in the '50s and never again put pen to paper until Frank Sinatra, more than twenty years later, asked Robin to write him one more chorus of "Thanks for the Memory" for his new recording. Leo did and they were the last lyrics he ever wrote. Bob Hope always credited that song with helping to start his career in Hollywood. At Leo's funeral, he told how Leo wrote the song especially for Hope to sing in *The Big Broadcast of 1938*, his first feature film, and how it gave his career a tremendous boost when it became a hit.)

Another song that became a cliché through overexposure is "Melancholy Baby." You always hear some comic imitating a drunk saying, "Play 'Melancholy Baby.'" It's a beautiful song, but it has just been sung too often. Occasionally when someone sings it straight, it becomes evident why the song was such a hit.

One of the advantages of the archival approach to performing songs is that I often turn up lyrics that most vocalists aren't aware of. A large percentage of sheet music is published in only the simplest form, so when I'm working on a song I will check other sources to see if other editions of the sheet music, or vintage recordings, exist. If the song came from a movie, I'll try to get a copy of the film. "Too Marvelous for Words," which was written for the 1937 movie *Ready, Willing and Able* starring Ruby Keeler, has been recorded a multitude of times through the years with the one verse and chorus printed in the sheet music. Yet when I obtained a copy of the original movie, I heard extra lyrics being sung in different sections of the film—lyrics that were also written by Johnny Mercer. I collated them and created three choruses that I sang on my *Forever* album.

When you start digging, you never know what you're going to encounter and it can be an exciting process if you love this music. When I recorded "A Fine Romance," I sang a verse that Jerome Kern had written but never had published and that I found on an unreleased Fred Astaire recording from 1936. For " 'S Wonderful," I added extra lyrics that I found in Ira's file, such as "My dear, I feel so tingle-ish, I'll even overlook your Engle-ish." I also came across some extra couplets for the male version of "Someone to Watch Over Me" and I used them in my performance of it. One of them was accidentally left out of Robert Kimball's *Complete Lyrics of Ira Gershwin*:

> Although she may not be the miss some
> Men think of as lissome

Yet vocalists frequently don't look any further than the piece of music that's in front of them; they will do a chorus or two followed by an instrumental break and then come back and sing the same lyric they just sang.

Discovering lost lyrics is fun but it also requires knowing how to integrate them into an effective performance. "I'll Get By" was written in 1928 and became a hit all over again in the '40s after it was used in the Spencer Tracy movie *A Guy Named Joe*. Fred Ahlert, who composed the song, wrote a new verse for the 1943 publication and changed one of the lines in the chorus. When I recorded "I'll Get By," I started with the 1928 verse, sang the 1928 chorus, then used the new verse Fred had written in '43 as a kind of interlude, sang the new lyric, and as a result created what I would consider a complete version of that number.

I get great joy from using the historical/archaeological aspects of my being and combining them into a performance. And yet a number of people have come up to me after hearing "Too Marvelous for Words" and asked suspiciously if I wrote those new lyrics. With an accusatory tone, they probe, "Where did those lyrics come from? What are you *doing* with these great songs?" Well, folks, it's in my blood, and I've got to do it.

One night I was in a club watching Harry Connick Jr. perform, when he suddenly said, "I'm going to introduce the next song like Michael Feinstein: This number was written in 1926 by so and so and revised fifteen years later with additional lyrics—" He made a joke out of it because he doesn't have any idea who wrote many of the songs he sings and he doesn't seem to care. I think it's criminal not to know. Certain jazz instrumentalists even make a point of knowing the lyrics of a song when they play it, using them as inspiration for improvising, as the great saxophonist Lester Young said he did. I think you can tell whether instrumentalists know the lyric by the way they phrase the melody.

Although it is exciting to find alternate lyrics, I'm not adding anything that the lyricist didn't intend to be sung. Sometimes, though, a singer will change a lyric to update it. In "But Not for Me," the verse goes, "Beatrice Fairfax don't you dare / Ever tell me he will care." Beatrice Fairfax was the Ann Landers of her day. I heard one singer clumsily sing "D-e-a-rrr Abby," trying to stretch the one-syllable word to fit over two notes. I recently sang "But Not for Me" at a party in Chicago attended by my friend Ann Landers, who humorously chided me for not substituting *her* name for the forgotten Beatrice Fairfax. In this one instance, I may have to make the change to appease my friend. Perhaps Ira wouldn't mind if I make sure it's the correct *four*-syllable substitution: "Dear Ann Landers." And it would relieve me of the necessity of explaining who Beatrice Fairfax was every time I sing it.

Ira was nettled hearing a Kate Smith recording of "Love Is Here to Stay," for which the original lyric is "The radio and the telephone / And the movies that we know." Kate sang, "The radio and the TV" because she wanted to be hip. But television wasn't even part of American life when Ira wrote that lyric in 1937 and, besides, it's one syllable short. If she had sung "television," it would have been one syllable long. What a tangled web we weave. . . .

Ira always said he labored just as diligently on the verses as he did on the choruses of the songs. Every songwriter I've ever encountered has talked about how important the verses are to them. Many years ago, the singer Molly Lyons made a record called *Verses Only* in which she sang only the verses of the songs without the choruses. I asked Ira what he thought about that and he said, "I feel thwarted!" When Frank Sinatra rerecorded "Stardust" for his *Trilogy* album, he sang only the verse and not the chorus. Maybe he was inspired by Molly Lyons.

Most people may not be familiar with the distinction between a verse and a chorus in traditional popular music. If you were weaned on rock 'n' roll, you may think of the introductory part of the song as the verse and the repeated hook as the chorus. Maybe this is a good place to clear up the confusion. Classic American popular song form consists of 32 bars, divided into four 8-bar sections. I do not know how songs developed into that form, but at least since the early part of this century, it has been the standard of an American popular song. That 32-bar form that I'm referring to is generally called the chorus or refrain, the familiar part that most people know and sing. However, there is also an introductory part created for many popular songs, especially show tunes, called the verse or, less frequently, the introduction. Jerome Kern referred to his choruses by the old English term (derived from the German), "burthen," a variant of "burden." (Stephen Sondheim named his first publishing company Burthen Music.) Shakespeare used that word to refer to the chorus or refrain of a song, but why Kern chose to use "burthen" instead of "chorus" is unknown. Kern was an inveterate rare-book collector and may have come across the term in those old volumes—or maybe he was just a traditionalist. Of course, in Shakespeare's day, the refrain was usually a set of words repeated at the end of each verse, so the meanings have shifted somewhat over time.

The verse usually runs about 16 bars and is considered by many to be an incidental part of the song; the chorus is invariably the part that makes a song famous. Most verses are not as highly melodic as the choruses, maybe because they serve as a transition from dialogue to song. Yet Ira always pointed out that he and George worked just as hard on the verses because musically and lyrically the verses were carefully constructed to set up and amplify what came in the chorus. In the case of a song like Rodgers and Hart's "Bewitched (Bothered and Bewildered)" from *Pal Joey*, the verse is essential to the enjoyment of the song because it says so much about the character in the show and foreshadows what's to come later in the plot. OK, so maybe the verse isn't absolutely essential, but I guarantee that once you've heard the verse sung before the chorus, you'll always miss it if it isn't sung the next time you hear "Bewitched." However, in many Tin Pan Alley songs the verses are often uninteresting and quite dispensable because the songwriters knew that the verses were not going to be given much attention and consequently didn't expend much energy in creating them. On popular dance records of the '20s and '30s, the verses were exploited much more, and you will usually hear the verse played at least two times in the body of the record: a chorus and then a verse, a chorus, another verse, and another chorus.

The chorus usually follows an AABA structure, in which each section is 8 bars long and the B section is often referred to as the bridge or release because it generally involves some form of modulation or key change. The bridge creates a diversion from the first two 8-bar segments, yet is short enough that the listener quickly returns to the familiar part of the melody for the purpose of memory and singability. The best bridges are the ones that seamlessly connect the more familiar parts of the chorus in a natural way; George Gershwin was very skilled at conceiving bridges that go pretty far afield but come back to the inevitable and necessary spot.

Classic song form is hardly inflexible; George Gershwin's first published song is 20 bars in length and Jerome Kern frequently experimented with the form. Gershwin told Kay Swift that it was very important to him to have some kind of lift or change at the end of the song, some kind of musical trick that nonetheless seems natural or inevitable—like his quotation of a snatch of Stephen Foster's "Swanee River" near the very end of "Swanee." Assuming that the first 8 bars of a song is identical in melody to the next 8-bar section, then the last 8-bar section, the one that follows the bridge, usually takes a melodic turn in another direction to give the song a little bit of a lift. Ira often tried to match this lift with his lyrics, as in "They Can't Take That Away from Me," in which he lists all the mundane things about the beloved's personality that are endearing before inserting the penultimate line, "The way you've changed my life." It's the same sort of idea.

One night at a gathering with the composer Milton Ager and his daughter Shana Alexander, Leonard Bernstein was playing through a bunch of popular songs at the piano. As the evening wore on and Lenny had had a few drinks, he began to forget the bridges of a number of the songs he was playing and every time he forgot a bridge, he simply substituted the bridge of "The Man I Love." It worked perfectly in most cases and he later developed it into a fairly funny parlor trick. It's true that one can interchange many bridges with other similar-sounding bridges. Kay Swift told me that she was upset hearing the singer Ruth Etting sing one of her songs fairly straight in the first chorus but in the second chorus toss in vocal variations that rendered the melody unrecognizable. She complained to George about this, to which George responded, "Just be grateful that she sang it straight in the first chorus."

RACE has played a less than admirable role in the revision of certain lyrics, although the trend in recent years has been to remove any racial references that could be construed as offensive, even if they were not intended that way by the lyricist. Most white lyricists have been very obliging when it comes to adapting lyrics for black vocalists. Oscar Hammerstein wrote an alternate set of lyrics to "Soliloquy" from *Carousel* for Sammy Davis Jr., replacing the section of the song that goes, "My little girl pink and white." Harry Warren's song "Lulu's Back in Town" was sung in the 1935 movie *Broadway Gondolier* by both Dick Powell and the Mills Brothers. The published music has this lyric by Al Dubin in the bridge:

> You can tell all my pets,
> All my Harlem coquettes,
> Mr. Otis regrets
> That he won't be around.

That version was written for the Mills Brothers, because Dick Powell sang, "You can tell all my pets, / All my blondes and brunettes." They weren't about to let the Mills Brothers sing *that*, so Dubin created two different versions.

When Irving Berlin rewrote the lyric of "Puttin' on the Ritz," he completely changed the idea of the song. The 1930 version was originally about the folks up in Harlem and can only be viewed today as racial stereotyping:

VERSE

Have you seen the well-to-do
Up on Lenox Avenue?
On that famous thoroughfare,
With their noses in the air,
High hats and colored collars,
White spats and fifteen dollars.
Spending ev'ry dime
For a wonderful time.

CHORUS

If you're blue and you
Don't know where to go to,
Why don't you go where Harlem sits,
Puttin' on the Ritz.
Spangled gowns upon a bevy
Of high browns from down the levee,
All misfits,
Puttin' on the Ritz.
That's where each and ev'ry Lulu Bell goes,
Ev'ry Thursday ev'ning with her swell beaus,
Rubbing elbows,
Come with me
And we'll attend their jubilee
And see them spend their last two bits,
Puttin' on the Ritz.

Berlin rewrote that as an elegant song for Fred Astaire in the 1946 movie musical *Blue Skies*, giving it very different lyrics and a whole different meaning. Suddenly it was an ode to enviable elegance and the (white) swell life that Astaire epitomized for moviegoers of that era. That's the only example I can think of where a composer made a major change in the lyric of a popular standard and it not only was accepted but perhaps even went unnoticed by the general public.

A more intensive controversy has shrouded *Show Boat*, particularly the song "Ol' Man River." The original 1927 lyric began, "Niggers all work on de Mississippi." By 1936, it had become "Darkies all work on de Mississippi." Later there was a third: "Colored folks work on de Mississippi." Now, of course, we have the politically correct version, "Here we all work on the Mississippi" ("African Americans" just wouldn't scan). Miles Kreuger's joke was that by the 1966 revival, *nobody* worked on the Mississippi, because the opening black chorus was dropped entirely. Hammerstein, who wrote insightfully about prejudice in "Carefully Taught," from *South Pacific*, was a highly principled man; the whole point of "Niggers all work on the Mississippi"—and of *Show Boat*—is that it was intended as social protest and was not ever meant to be derogatory. Based on Edna Ferber's 1926 novel about miscegenation, *Show Boat* was a revolutionary theater statement for its time in several ways. For one thing, it resolved the conflict between free-form vaudeville fun and serious, logical narrative as the dominant form of musical theater. For another, it was the first fully integrated Broadway musical and the first to embody a plea for racial tolerance. When you listen to more of the lyric to "Ol' Man River," you get a better picture of what Hammerstein was after:

Niggers all work while the white boss play
. . .
Don't look up
And don't look down.
You don't dare make
The white boss frown.

However, Hammerstein himself insisted that he didn't write the number as a protest song but "because we needed it for a spot in the first act."

When John McGlinn was preparing to record the original, complete score in 1988, Willard White, playing the role of Joe, refused to sing the word "niggers" even when the context was explained to him by the musical director and producers of the recording, and he and the black chorus members walked out. Even before Harold Prince's revival of *Show Boat* opened in October 1993 in North York, a suburb of Toronto with a large black population, it was picketed by folks who insisted that it was *still* racist. Maybe "Ol' Man River" doesn't have the sharp racial irony of Andy Razaf's "Black and Blue" with its pointed refrain "What'd I do to be so black and blue?" But even Razaf's 1929 lyrics might not pass muster by today's politically correct standards, even though they were electrifyingly radical at the time:

> I'm white inside, it don't help my case.
> 'Cause I can't hide what is on my face.

In mounting his new production of *Show Boat*, which came to Broadway in 1994, Hal Prince was very careful to address issues of race in the context of the staging, along with certain other theatrical devices including the use of dance (showing, for instance, how the Charleston was invented by blacks and only later appropriated by whites). Lyrically, he steered a middle course; the opening chorus sang "Colored folks work on de Mississippi."

Porgy and Bess also suffered from a growing backlash among the black community, receiving mixed reactions from Negroes in 1935—including Duke Ellington, who called the score "grand music" but condemned it as not truly written in the "Negro musical idiom." By the '50s and '60s, the black community was generally more outspoken about *Porgy and Bess*, or perhaps was simply paid more heed by the mainstream media. When first approached about performing in *Porgy and Bess*, Todd Duncan, the original Porgy, was offended at the idea of a white man trying to express the music of black people. As George played the score for Duncan, beginning with the overture on the piano, Duncan said it sounded like "Chopsticks" to him. He turned to his wife and whispered, "This stinks." But by the end of the performance, he was so carried away that he was in tears, and realized that Gershwin had created a true masterpiece. Leontyne Price, after touring in *Porgy* for many years, said, "I'll be very happy to go back to Egypt and *Aïda*. I'll go down the Nile but I will not return to Catfish Row."

As the years progressed, Ira remained very sensitive about the relationship of *Porgy and Bess* to the black community. There was increasing controversy over the uses of the word "nigger" in *Porgy* because it appeared dozens of times in the original score. DuBose Heyward, the author of the libretto and descendant of an aristocratic white South Carolina family, was opposed to removing the "nigger" references from the opera, yet Ira felt very strongly that they should be changed. As soon as Heyward died, the first thing Ira did was to remove all uses of "nigger" from the score and replace them with other words. The 1951 recording of *Porgy and Bess* was the first virtually complete one but was also the first sanitized version, lyrically speaking. The original published scores of *Porgy* have "nigger," but sometime in the '50s the score was reprinted with all of those references deleted. By the time I was involved with Ira, he lamented that he had removed the references because even though "nigger" was still a derogatory term, he felt that it didn't carry quite the same onus that it had at one point. He came to believe that the references were appropriate in the context of the opera and that if he had realized what was going to happen to the use of the word, he never would have changed it.

I think that was a bit of a misperception on his part because the word still has a more derogatory charge to it than Ira realized. There was a brief period beginning in the '60s when black performers like Richard Pryor and Dick Gregory purposely used the term "nigger" in public as a way of defusing its negative power. But Pryor publicly recanted that attitude in one of his concert films and the public perception has changed back again.

When the 1973 Houston Grand Opera production of *Porgy* was put on record, three uses of the word "nigger" slipped through. I say "slipped through" because Ira didn't want the word on the album and had requested that they remove it. Yet the producers and director of the show felt that, for dramatic impact, it was important to use the word and it was reinstated. This is clearly a sensitive issue with many nuances to it. Quite a few of the so-called coon songs from around the turn of the century written by black songwriters were just as derogatory as the ones written by whites. In the same vein, Irving Berlin wrote a song about a cheap Jewish businessman, called "Cohen Owes Me Ninety-Seven Dollars." The fact that it came from a Jewish songwriter makes it only marginally less objectionable and it's not a song you're likely to hear played these days.

Playing a less provocative role in the controversy over *Porgy and Bess* are the uses of vernacular and dialect, as in "I Got Plenty o' Nuthin'." At the request of a singer I knew who was working on the role of Porgy, I asked Ira specifically about that. Ira stressed that those were merely suggestions for style and that he had no desire or expectation for anyone to adhere phonetically to the dialect. If someone sang "I got plenty of nothing" instead, it didn't bother Ira at all, and the same went for the use of dialect throughout the score.

George Gershwin wrote an obscure song with Irving Caesar called "Nashville Nightingale," the original lyric of which included a reference to "darktown Tetrazzini," meaning a black counterpart of the famous Italian soprano Luisa Tetrazzini—a line which Irving later changed. In the verse of her song "Bojangles of Harlem," Dorothy Fields wrote a lyric that always makes me cringe: "Ask anyone / Up Harlem way / Who that man Bojangles is. / They may not know / Who's president, / But they know who Bojangles is." The Ray Henderson/Lew Brown song "That's Why Darkies Were Born" from *George White's Scandals of 1931* may be one of the most outrageously bigoted lyrics of all time. It is stunningly bad, representing the worst sentiments of the era. The basic theme of the song is that someone had to do the world's manual labor, namely, "the colored man," who should accept his "destiny" because that's just the way things are. Along with picking cotton and planting corn, "Someone had to slave and be able to sing . . . Had to be contented with any old thing." And in their spare time, they got to teach white folks to sing. These stereotypes continued all through the '30s and beyond, only underlining the Gershwins' and Heyward's achievement in writing *Porgy and Bess*. In 1937, for instance, Lorenz Hart wrote a song titled "All Dark People" that included the lines "Play that music for me and my sweet. / All dark people is light on their feet." Later the same year, Gus Kahn concurred by saying "All God's Chillun Got Rhythm," which was sung in *A Day at the Races* by Ivie Anderson and an all-black chorus.

Race, however, was a relatively minor area of contention in popular song lyrics compared to sex. To begin with, many of the love songs that we know and enjoy from the Golden Era were written with sexual subtexts that the lyricists were careful to conceal. Irving Caesar made this clear in talking to me about a song he wrote in 1936 called "Holiday Sweetheart." It is not a well-known song because it was sung in a British revue, *Transatlantic Rhythm*. Irving tailored "Holiday Sweetheart" for Ruth Etting, who was famous for torch songs like "Ten Cents a Dance," "Mean to Me," and "Love Me or Leave Me." The song exudes the kind of self-pity that characterized the unrequited-love song which Etting had made her specialty.

I'm just a holiday sweetheart,
Just for two weeks in September,
Then all the year to remember
Someone who wants to forget.
A holiday sweetheart,
Tennis and swimming and dances,
Thinking I've learned what romance is,
Glad being somebody's pet.
When he left he said he would write,
But I'm quite sure he won't.
Once I used to think that they might,
Now I know they don't.
Not to a Holiday Sweetheart,
Happy enough when I start out,
Coming home crying my heart out,
Lying to friends when I say,
"Yes, I've had a wonderful holiday."

After he sang it for me, Irving smiled. "Look how delicately I tell the story that she was screwed," he said. The idea from Irving's point of view was to make the audience feel sorry for the singer/narrator who had been seduced and abandoned. (The English author Ian Whitcomb interviewed Irving Caesar on videotape some twenty years ago and said that when he played back the tape he noticed that as Irving was reciting and talking about all the tender love songs he'd written, there behind him in his hotel room was a pile of *Screw* magazines.)

Many songs were obviously about sex and its ramifications, but lyricists could never say so directly because of the censors. When Leo Robin wrote "Thanks for the Memory," the censors made him change the line "That weekend in Niagara when we never saw the Falls" to "That weekend in Niagara when we *hardly* saw the Falls." But Leo thought that "hardly" was much dirtier. He felt as if he'd pulled one over on the censors. Johnny Mercer was quite shocked when he got by the censors in 1941 with "The Fleet's In": "Hey there, Mister, / Better get your sister, / 'Cause the fleet's in."

Cole Porter probably wrote the most risqué theater lyrics of all, clearly putting sexual double entendre into many of his songs, which in turn were either censored, banned, or not even considered for airplay. "Katie Went to Haiti," which Ethel Merman introduced in 1939, is the story of a wealthy matron's pleasure trip to the tropics. With each successive chorus, the song becomes more risqué in revealing her exploits; the first chorus ends,

> 'Cause Katie knew her Haiti
> And practically all Haiti knew Katie.

The second,

> 'Cause Katie still had Haiti
> And practically all Haiti had Katie.

And finally,

> For Katie made her Haiti
> And practically all Haiti made Katie.

In "Kate the Great," also written for but never sung by Merman, Porter tells how Catherine of Russia "never would mix in affairs of state, / But in affairs of the heart, how Kate was great." Later he asks us to

> Think of the history she made.
> Why, she made the Congress,
> She made the Premier,
> She made the clergy,
> And she made 'em cheer.
> She made the butler,
> She made the groom,
> She made the maid who made the room.

It goes on, but you get the idea. Oh, by the way, Porter's mother's name was—you guessed it—Kate.

The point of these songs is quite similar to the 1955 Noël Coward song "A Bar on the Piccolo Marina," which begins,

In a bar on the Piccolo Marina
Life called to Missus Wentworth Brewster
Fate beckoned her and introduced her
Into a rather queer
Unfamiliar atmosphere.

As she continued to drink,

Hot flushes of delight suffused her.
Right around the bend she went.
. . .
Night out, night in, knocking back the gin
She'd cry "Hurrah, Funicula, Funiculi, Funic yourself!"
Just for fun three young sailors from Messina
Bowed low to Missus Wentworth Brewster,
Said "Scusi" and politely goosed her.
Then there was quite a scena.
Her family in floods of tears, cried
"Leave these men Mama."
She said "They're just high spirited like all Italians are,
And most of them have a great deal more to offer than Papa."

When Ira Gershwin wrote "The Saga of Jenny," which Gertrude
Lawrence turned into a hilarious bump and grind number in *Lady in the
Dark*, he had several lines implying none too subtly that Jenny was
promiscuous:

Jenny made her mind up when she was twelve
That into foreign languages she would delve;
But at seventeen to Vassar it was quite a blow
That in twenty-seven languages she couldn't say no.

and

Jenny made her mind up at thirty-nine
She would take a trip to the Argentine.
She was only on vacation but the Latins agree
Jenny was the one who started the Good Neighbor Policy.

When *Lady in the Dark* was made into a television special in 1954, he had to rewrite that section because television's censors would never allow it. In Ira's Christopher Columbus sequence ("The *Nina*, the *Pinta*, the *Santa Maria*") from the 1945 film *Where Do We Go from Here?* with music by Kurt Weill, a character stops the mutinying crew that is about to seize Columbus by letting them know the wonders that await them in the New World if only they stay the course. But one of those was a little too wonderful for the censors, and Ira was forced to change this couplet: "The girls are delightful, / Their sweaters are quite full."

The original lyric of Howard Dietz's "I Guess I'll Have to Change My Plan" was about a man pursuing an affair with a married woman. The verse says,

> I beheld her and was conquered at the start,
> And placed her on a pedestal apart.
> I planned a little hideaway
> We two would share one day.

But when the song was published, Dietz rewrote and softened his own lyric, which is not hard to understand when you read the rest of it and remember that the year was 1929:

> But on second thought this resignation's wrong,
> Most women want the man who comes along
> With love more secret and more true
> Than they're accustomed to.
> And besides, it gives a most romantic edge,
> When one is barely hanging on the ledge
> Of abysses,
> So I find
> I do not mind
> If she's a Mrs.

Then the chorus goes,

> I guess I'll have to change my plan.
> Supposing after all there *is* another man.
> I'm glad I bought those blue pajamas

Before the big affair began.
For all is fair in love and war,
And love's a war that makes it fairer all the more.
Forbidden fruit I've heard is better to taste.
Why should I let this go to waste?
My conscience to the wind is tossed.
I found the one girl I lost.

Although it was sung that way onstage, none of those lyrics ever went into the published sheet music. I found them on a recording of the songs of Dietz and Schwartz that was made in the late '60s. Obviously, Howard Dietz supplied the lyric for that recording and it's the only place that it exists other than in Dietz's personal archive.

Peggy Lee always said that it was her provocative interpretation that caused her recording of the Gershwins' "Aren't You Kind of Glad We Did?" to be banned from the airwaves. But Peggy had a habit of making herself the focus of things; in this case, the lyric itself was cause enough. Ira wrote "Aren't You Kind of Glad We Did?" for a plot situation in *The Shocking Miss Pilgrim* in which two people find themselves without a chaperon in Victorian Boston and share a kiss. Anticipating that without the innocuous visual setting of the movie, the song as it appeared on the printed sheet music "would be considered improper by those who didn't listen too well," Ira rewrote the last couple of lines of the verse, changing

What's done, is done,
But wasn't—and isn't—it fun?

to

With just one kiss,
What heaven, what rapture, what bliss!

Unfortunately, the literal-minded censors still perceived the song as being about the sexual act. A few recordings were made but they were banned by the radio networks and never aired. Sarah Vaughan did record that song in the mid-1950s, however, but she misread the bridge of the lyric, which goes,

Socially, I'll be an outcast:
Obviously we dined alone.
On my good name there will be doubt cast—
With never a sign of any chaperone.

Instead Sarah sang, "With never a sign of any chapter one." When Ira listened to the record, he said, "That's kind of an interesting concept. It *almost* works." (Singers aren't the only ones who get the lyrics wrong, of course. I was once at a performance of a little show in Westwood cleverly titled *Let's Call the Whole Thing Gershwin,* in which the first act ended with "Bess, You Is My Woman Now." During intermission I heard a man with a very thick foreign accent turn to his friend and say, "That's the most wonderful music I've ever heard. I was so moved when he sang, 'Guess who is my woman now?' ")

In 1949, the radio performers Amos and Andy objected to singing the part of Ira's original lyric to "It Ain't Necessarily So" that went,

Methus'luh lived nine hundred years,
But who calls dat livin'
When no gal'll give in
To no man what's nine hundred years?

The Columbia Broadcasting System asked for permission on their behalf to change the last two lines to "Why that can't be livin', / To hold out for nine hundred years."

Even as late as 1960, radio censors could still be overly sensitive. I once played Ira a recording of a radio broadcast from that year of Bing Crosby and Rosemary Clooney singing a song Ira wrote with Harold Arlen in 1934 called "Let's Take a Walk Around the Block." One of the original lines was:

And then in Caracas,
On a jackass,
We'll sit and ride around the block.

In 1960 they had to change that, and suddenly we heard:

And then to Me-*he*-co,
On a burro,
We'll sit and ride around the block.

When Ira listened to that, he said, "Oh my God, they've ruined my song. I don't want anyone to think I wrote that!"

"Ira," I said, "this was broadcast once in 1960. Relax." Ira wrote one lyric called "Sing Me Not a Ballad" that was sung by Lotte Lenya in *The Firebrand of Florence*. There were no censors on Broadway, so he could get away with a lyric that said, in essence, Let's skip the preliminaries and just have sex:

> Romance me no romances;
> Treasure not my glove.
> Spare me your advances—
> Just, oh just make love!

But that lyric always vexed Ira because he felt it was "a little too on the nose," and any time the song came up, Ira got exasperated about it. Finally I said, "If it was so upsetting to you, then why would you write it that way?"

He threw his hands up in the air. "That's just the way it came out," he said. "I couldn't help it. That's where the song led me." And yet, of course, he chose to leave it that way.

A number of songs have been written with precisely such socially unacceptable thoughts in mind and with no intention of ever having them pass the censors. Page Cavanaugh made me aware of a song written by Joe Cook in the early '40s called "The Swelling of the Organ and the Coming of the Bride." And then there's "I'm Going to Give It to Mary with Love," recorded and sung by Cliff Edwards. The lyric went something like this:

> I'm going to give it to Mary with love.
> I've got a lot of what she's thinking of.

It went on about how Mary would take it in her hands and stroke it— but by the end of the ditty, we discover that what she's getting from the singer is a "little kitten."

Stereotypes of women were even more prevalent than racial stereotypes during the classic era. The singer Susannah McCorkle wrote a witty piece for the *New York Times* on the difficulty of being a politically correct chanteuse, having to jettison some old favorites from her repertoire because of their sexist connotations, including "I Got It Bad and That Ain't Good," "Diamonds Are a Girl's Best Friend," and "The Man I Love" ("And he'll be big and strong, / The man I love"). She even dropped Bessie Smith's apparently self-assertive "Ain't Nobody's Business If I Do" because of the couplet, "I swear I won't call no copper / If I'm beat up by my poppa."

Today, for instance, the second chorus of "Isn't It Romantic?" sounds impossibly chauvinistic. The only way I can sing it is by introducing it as such and explaining that Maurice Chevalier, who originally sang it, had such Gallic charm that he could get away with anything. Then I proceed to sing,

> Isn't it romantic?
> Soon I will have found
> Some girl that I adore.
> Isn't it romantic?
> While I sit around,
> My love can scrub the floor.
>
> She'll kiss me ev'ry hour
> Or she'll get the sack.
> And when I take a shower,
> She can scrub my back.
>
> Isn't it romantic?
> On a moonlight night
> She'll cook me onion soup.
> Kiddies are romantic,
> And if we don't fight,
> We soon will have a troupe.
>
> We'll help the population:
> It's a duty that we owe
> To dear old France.
> Isn't it romance?

Lorenz Hart wrote that tongue-in-cheek at the time, but today it's perceived as having been written out of total ignorance. Many songs may have a line or two that are politically incorrect today, but that will not keep me from singing them, because they are still works of art. It's that way with some of Stephen Foster's songs. Should we not sing "Massa's in de Cold Ground"? It is part of our cultural history, and to deny it is just as bad as ignoring the existence of it. Recently, I've taken to acknowledging the political incorrectness of certain songs when I do them, but I still *do* them. After one of my shows, one woman complained to me about the "tragedy" of political correctness and how unfortunate it is that one has to give a disclaimer before singing certain things anymore. "Swanee" is a significant song, as George Gershwin's first and biggest hit, even though it still is a "Mammy" song.

Susannah McCorkle also lamented the incorrectness of songs romanticizing cigarettes, from "These Foolish Things" ("a cigarette that bears a lipstick's traces") to "Smoke Gets in Your Eyes." I don't smoke but I think it's okay to sing a song about cigarettes. I was once hired to play a party for Philip Morris, which was donating a large amount of money to the Los Angeles Historic Theaters Preservation Committee. The party was essentially given to launch a new high-end cigarette called Cartier, which came in packs of ten in a designer box and was twice the cost of the average cigarette. I was briefed by a woman from the company who was a specialist in media relations and carefully explained to me how to deal with media, in case I got any calls about the fact that I was playing a party for a cigarette company. She also made sure that I knew that I did not have to say anything about cigarettes.

I may not have endorsed cigarettes, but that evening I sang an old song that was sung by Lanny Ross called "Two Cigarettes in the Dark." A man sees two cigarettes glowing in the dark and as the lights become clearer, he realizes that one of the smokers is his girlfriend, giving him a bad case of secondary smoke poisoning. The party was held at the St. James Club, where Bette Davis loved to go once a week to eat dinner. There was a huge photographic portrait of her in the lobby taken by Greg Gorman—a very elegant picture of Bette holding a cigarette. A day or two before the party, Bette Davis died of lung cancer and when the Cartier people arrived to set up for the party, they were dismayed to see that what would greet everyone as they entered the hotel was a photograph of Miss Davis holding a cigarette. They requested that the management remove the picture until after the party was over, which the management was happy to do. At the same time, however, Bette Davis's family was arriving to stay at the hotel for her funeral. They wanted to know what had happened to the famous portrait of their mother. So the picture went back up and stayed up. (Incidentally, my lawyer helped to catalogue her effects after her death and reported that he found a cassette of my *Isn't It Romantic* album in her tape player. Her secretary told him that Miss Davis loved that recording and sang along with it on occasion. What I wouldn't have given to hear *her* sing "Isn't It Romantic?")

There were several different lyrics for "Body and Soul," but they weren't changed because of censorship; the song just went through different incarnations. It was written in America by Johnny Green and Edward Heyman in 1930 but when it was later introduced in England by Gertrude Lawrence and initially published there, the lyric was altered by the British publisher, who also added names to the writing credits. Another version was written by Howard Dietz for the American premiere of the song, as sung by Libby Holman. Green was very specific about the lyric he wanted performed and he intensely disliked any other one. But because there were different editions of the sheet music, to this day performers still sing different lyrics.

"I've Got a Crush on You," originally written for *Treasure Girl*, was last used in the revamped *Strike Up the Band* of 1930, where the verse was presented as a duet and the lyric was split between two people. The male part went, "How glad the many millions / Of Annabelles and Lillians / Would be / To capture me."

When Lee Wiley first recorded it in 1939, she simply sang, "How glad the many millions / Of Toms and Dicks and Harrys / Would be / To capture me." But when the song started to get some attention from a Sinatra recording in the late '40s, the publisher, Herman Starr, without asking Ira, came up with a female lyric and actually printed in the sheet music: "How glad the many millions / Of Timothys and Williams." They sent a copy of it to Ira, who was furious because "millions" and "Williams" is not a perfect rhyme. He wrote a letter to Starr, in which he wrote, "I hate to say this to you, but that's not a good rhyme." He suggested two alternates; the one that was used was "How glad the many laddies, / From millionaires to caddies."

One day I played Ira a recording that someone had given to me of the San Francisco Gay Men's Chorus singing "The Man I Love." At first Ira thought it was a joke and he was laughing hysterically. But about halfway through, he said, "Wait a minute. Are they serious?" When I said yes, he got very embarrassed and said, "Would you t-t-take that off?" I asked him how he felt about it. "I never even considered that," he said, disconcerted. "I never thought of a man singing that lyric to another man." In the '50s, when Goddard Lieberson was making a recording of the complete score of *Girl Crazy* for the first time, he wrote a letter to Ira saying, "We are using all the lyrics for 'Bronco Busters,' including, 'On Western prairies, we shoot the fairies / Or send them back to the East.'" Ira approved it. Today, he certainly wouldn't have gotten away with that without Act Up or somebody protesting and picketing.

Ira himself was always willing to rewrite one of his lyrics if the situation or changing times called for it. "You Started It" was written in 1931 and intended for the movie *Delicious*, the first film George and Ira worked on in Hollywood. Maybe there was just cause for the declining box office of movie musicals prior to the surprise success of *42nd Street* in 1932. *Delicious* wasn't much of a movie. It starred those great singing talents Janet Gaynor and Charles Farrell and could have made anyone hate musicals. Leonard Maltin called it an "insipid romance." The lyric to "You Started It" was never used, although the accompanying music found its way into the background score of the film. Ira always felt it was one of the better unpublished Gershwin songs. When Ira and I were going through that material with an eye to possibly releasing some of the unpublished songs, Ed Koch was the mayor of New York. Of course, there were whispers then that he was gay. So when we played through the song and came to the lines "I once was gayer / Than the mayor / Of New York," Ira started laughing. "Well," he said, "we're going to have to change *that* line."

Duke Ellington was famous for writing parts or whole pieces for specific musicians in his orchestra, like Paul Gonsalves or Johnny Hodges. Ira and his contemporaries were attuned to writing the lyric not only in the context of the show but also for a specific type of character. In those days, the most important elements of a show were the stars, and the Gershwins knew that they were writing a vehicle for the Astaires or Gertrude Lawrence or Marilyn Miller. Lyda Roberti was a Polish comedienne, and she would pronounce the word "hot" as a guttural "cchhhot," so in *Pardon My English*, all Roberti's songs were specifically conceived with that in mind. "My Cousin in Milwaukee," for example, goes, "When she sings hot, you can't be solemn; / It sends the shivers up and down your spinal column." They made sure they had the word "hot" in there.

In the early days, George Gershwin and Buddy DeSylva wrote "Do It Again" for Irene Bordoni, who was known as "the French Doll." Ira and George later wrote a very coy song called "I Won't Say I Will (But I Won't Say I Won't)" that was specifically tailored to Bordoni's naughty French dame persona. In *Girl Crazy*, Willie Howard performed his role in Yiddish dialect that was a throwback to the days of vaudeville. Ira had seen his work and made sure that they tailored something that would show off his abilities, namely, "Goldfarb, That's I'm!" Interpolations of songs by other writers were still being added to shows back then. If the entertainer was a big enough name and wanted a special piece of material, he usually got his way. The biggest hit of the Rodgers and Hart show *Betsy* was a number interpolated at the last minute for star Belle Baker—"Blue Skies" by Irving Berlin. Often during a scene change, a performer would step in front of the curtain and do a song "in one," as it was called, to distract the audience. The songs weren't always related to the show, but sometimes George and Ira would create a specific kind of character song. The song "Little Jazz Bird" was created for Cliff Edwards—also known as "Ukulele Ike"—because it was just the sort of hot jazzy material that suited him.

In *Lyrics on Several Occasions*, Ira talks about a song that the comedian Bobby Clark sang called "If I Became the President." As an encore, Clark sang his own lyrics, which were funny but had terrible rhymes. Ira remembered one couplet that rhymed "homelike" with "Potomac." In a P.S., Ira added, "Imperfect rhymes or not, I am unhappy to report that his lines received as many chuckles as did mine."

Many of the ideas Ira preached in his lyrics appear simplistic on one level while on another level they are often rather profound. I can't help thinking that if he had embraced any number of the philosophies he expressed in his songs, he wouldn't have been so unhappy in his later years. For instance, the last part of "Shall We Dance?" goes,

Life is short; we're growing older.
Don't you be an also-ran.
You'd better dance, little lady!
Dance, little man!
Dance whenever you can!

It's very simple but also very wise. Set with the task of writing a title song for a Fred Astaire/Ginger Rogers movie, Ira delivered a classic restatement of the old theme of *carpe diem.*

Not all of Ira's songs about dancing were so profound. When he worked with Astaire in 1948 on *The Barkleys of Broadway,* Astaire had just opened a chain of Fred Astaire Dance Schools and wanted Ira to create a new dance song. To oblige him, Ira and Harry Warren wrote "Swing Trot." Ira agonized this time, trying to come up with another song about dancing, and the result was not particularly inspired or philosophical:

> It's bill and coo-y,
> Tea for two-y;
> Just watch your partner's
> Eyes grow dewy,
> *Entre nous*-y,
> You're slightly screwy
> But—irresistible!

This is pretty frothy stuff, and by comparison it shows up the relative depth of "Shall We Dance?" Of course, when you go through the canon of popular song, you find all kinds of interesting philosophies. Billy Rose once wrote a song called "Love Is like a Punch in the Nose," which has a certain flair. I don't know how the song goes, but it's a great title.

SOME popular songs have evolved from lyrics that were thrown out and replaced by other lyrics. For example, Burton Lane's "Old Devil Moon," with lyrics by Yip Harburg, was originally written for Lena Horne with the title "This Is Where I Came In" (also with lyrics by Yip). "You'll Never Get Away from Me" was originally called "I'm in Pursuit of Happiness" (lyric by Leo Robin) and was used in the TV musical *Ruggles of Red Gap.* And Rodgers and Hart's "Blue Moon" had three other lyrics before it found its current form. The first version was to be sung by Jean Harlow with a lyric Larry Hart wrote called "Prayer," which was never used. The same melody was later turned into "Manhattan Melodrama," and then was sung on screen by Shirley Ross as "The Bad in Every

Man." Jack Robbins, the publisher of songs for MGM musicals, went to Hart and said, "This is a good melody, but these lyrics are all wrong. I can't make a hit out of the kinds of lyrics you've been writing for it."

They started to argue and Larry finally said to Robbins, "I suppose you want some kind of stupid lyric like 'blue moon.' "

"That's exactly what I want!" Robbins said. So Hart wrote a lyric called "Blue Moon," and it was published in December 1934 as a single sheet, or popular song. It stayed in the Top Ten of the 1934–35 Hit Parade for eighteen weeks. Like certain other classic popular songs, "Blue Moon" had a second life in the rock 'n' roll era when a version by a group called the Marcels became a number one hit in 1961 with thirteen weeks on the Hit Parade—four of them in the number one spot. People who know the Otis Redding recording of "Try a Little Tenderness" may be surprised to hear that the song was written in 1933, as was the Jerome Kern/Otto Harbach song "Smoke Gets in Your Eyes," originally in a Broadway musical called *Roberta* but a huge hit for the Platters in 1959.

Harry Woods, who wrote "When the Red Red Robin Comes Bob-Bob-Bobbin' Along" and a number of other hits of the '20s and '30s, supplied both music and lyrics for many of his songs, yet he was a rough kind of guy who had lost part of his left arm in the navy in World War I. He played the piano, often banging on the lower part of the keyboard with the stump of his left arm. Harry used to frequent a bar in the Times Square area that was inhabited by "rough trade." Songwriters hung out there too, and one night Harry got into a fight with the bartender and started banging the guy's head on the counter with his good arm. Two of his cronies were sitting across the room and one turned to the other with a laugh. "See, that's Harry Woods," he said. "The guy who wrote 'Try a Little Tenderness.' "

In the endless debate over the relative merits of music and lyrics, Ira had a telling story about Sigmund Romberg playing in a card game at Jerome Kern's home with Kern and Otto Harbach. To let Romberg know what hand he was holding, Harbach started to whistle "One Alone," a song Romberg himself had written in 1926 for which Harbach had composed the lyrics along with Oscar Hammerstein. Romberg still made the wrong play and they lost. "Didn't you hear what I was whistling?" Harbach later asked Romberg in dismay.

"Yeah," Romberg said, "but nobody pays any attention to the lyrics."

The other side of that questionable truism comes out in a story often told about the wives of Kern and Hammerstein being introduced to some other guests at a party. "This is Mrs. Jerome Kern," the hostess announced. "Her husband wrote 'Ol' Man River.' "

"Not true," Mrs. Hammerstein interjected. "Mrs. Kern's husband wrote dum-dum-*dee*-dah. *My* husband wrote 'Ol' Man River.' "

The highest praise that Sigmund Romberg could give a lyric when it was handed to him was "It fits." He meant both that the lyric scanned properly and that it was appropriate to the mood of the melody. But Romberg was also considered a borrower by many people. It was said of him at the time, "Romberg writes the kinds of songs people hum going *into* the theater." Ira once worked with Romberg and George on a show called *Rosalie*. He spent a couple of hours sitting with Romberg while the Hungarian-born and -schooled composer took some of his own famous tunes and tried to turn them sideways—rework them into new melodies—but to no avail. That was a common practice, however, and hardly qualifies as plagiarism in any case. "For Me and My Gal" was such a big hit for George Meyer that six years later he wrote a song called "For Baby and Me" that is "For Me and My Gal" turned sideways. After Milton Ager wrote "Ain't She Sweet?" he wrote "That's Her Now," which is the same melody turned sideways.

Turning a melody sideways merely requires changing a few notes in the original melody while keeping most of the same rhythms and note values. In many cases it amounts to plagiarism, even though some of the notes may be different. One of the most notable plagiarisms ever committed involved Cole Porter's song "Be a Clown," which he wrote in 1948 for the movie *The Pirate*. In 1952, lyricist Arthur Freed, who produced the movie, came up with the idea for a song called "Make 'Em Laugh" and told Nacio Herb Brown to write a copycat melody. The last popular song of any significance Freed wrote, it was sung by Donald O'Connor in *Singin' in the Rain* and became very popular. But it had precisely the same rhythmic pattern, note for note, as "Be a Clown," with a different melody. Porter was a great gentleman about it and never acknowledged the fact that he had been plagiarized, but it was obvious to everyone else. At one point, Kay Thompson, the legendary vocal arranger and performer, went to Arthur and said, "How can you do that?" In characteristic Arthur Freed fashion, he replied, "What are you talking about?"

Roger Englander, who was a close friend of Leonard Bernstein's, once made me aware that one of the themes from a Vaughan Williams composition inspired the main musical phrase of "Cool" from *West Side Story*, just as a theme from Benjamin Britten's *Peter Grimes* became "A Boy like That." There's also a story about Bernstein from around the time his Mass was being premiered for the opening of the Kennedy Center in 1971. Apparently the last fifteen or twenty minutes of music were based on a theme that was clearly borrowed from his own *West Side Story*. Everybody recognized it except Bernstein but nobody could get up the nerve to tell him. One day, in the middle of a rehearsal, Bernstein stopped dead in his tracks and said, "Oh my God!" He disappeared for a while and returned with that section rewritten.

All sorts of plagiarisms have happened through the years. The Puccini Estate sued Al Jolson and Buddy DeSylva for taking the melody of "Avalon" from the aria from *Tosca* known in English as "The Stars Were Shining," and the Puccini Estate won. Fred Fisher sued Jerome Kern for stealing a bass line from "Dardanella" for an early hit in the Hawaiian mode, called "Ka-lu-a." Kern admitted he had borrowed it but felt that it was not something that was exclusive to Fred Fisher's song, because it had been used in classical music. The judge ruled that it was a borrowing but since it had been used previously, he didn't make Kern pay money.

Sigmund Spaeth was known as the "tune detective" because he was always called in to testify on behalf of one side or the other in plagiarism cases. In *The Facts of Life in Popular Song*, he wrote about Frank Silver and Irving Cohn's "Yes, We Have No Bananas," showing phrase by phrase from exactly which classical pieces Silver had intentionally borrowed. Jay Livingston and Ray Evans were sued for "Buttons and Bows" by a man named Fred Rich, who had a band in the '20s and had written songs at Paramount for early talkies. He claimed that Livingston and Evans had found an old song in the Paramount Music Library and plagiarized it to write "Buttons and Bows." At the trial, Fred Rich, who was very old and on crutches, gave an emotional testimony. Livingston and Evans got Sigmund Spaeth to come and testify that the theme had been used many times before in different forms; Spaeth demonstrated as much, and the case was dismissed. Livingston said that what scared him was that a couple of jurors had initially sided with Rich, thinking that they had really plagiarized it.

Harry Warren told me a story about being sued for "Lullaby of Broadway." He was informed by the studio that they were going to be sued by a composer alleging that Harry had stolen the melody of "Lullaby" from a virtually unknown piece this guy had written some years before. Harry went to visit Jerome Kern, who was a close friend of his. "Jerry," he said, "they are going to sue me for 'Lullaby of Broadway.' What'll I do?"

"Play me some of your tune," Kern said rather imperiously, as if he hadn't heard it before. Harry sat down and played the first eight bars, whereupon Kern said, "That's enough!"

Then he went over to a file cabinet, riffled through pages of old sheet music, and pulled out a dogeared score. "Here's your 'Lullaby of Broadway,'" he said, producing a song he had written twenty years earlier with the same melodic idea. Warren used that piece of music successfully to dismiss the case—claiming, in other words, that both "Lullaby" and this other fellow's song borrowed from the Kern piece. In 1924, Harry wrote a song called "The Only Only One for Me" which used the same basic theme as a now famous Vincent Youmans tune. Upon hearing Harry's song, a friend informed him that a very similar song, called "Tea For Two," was playing in the show *No, No, Nanette*, which was then in Chicago. Harry could not have heard the song yet—this was before the show came to New York and before it was famous. After his friend sang the melody for him, Harry turned his melody around a bit so it would not sound like "Tea for Two." Vincent Youmans's claim that George Gershwin plagiarized his ideas has to do with a similar phenomenon—that of ideas being in the air and coming out at the same time.

The fact is that there are only twelve notes in the scale and it's inevitable that unintentional borrowings will occur. Intelligent people recognize that some duplication is unavoidable when you are working with a finite universe; distinctions are achieved through tempo, rhythm, key changes, and other variables. Intentional or not, duplication happens all the time. Once, Harry Warren was going to be sued for his first published song, "Rose of the Rio Grande," by the publishers of "Sweet Georgia Brown," because it had the same chord changes. Then they realized that "Rose of the Rio Grande" had actually been written three years earlier, in 1922. He could have sued *them* if he'd wanted to.

When composers recycle their own melodies, it's intriguing to see how the new lyric often completely changes the character of the music. The best example I can think of is Stephen Sondheim's lyric for "Everything's Coming Up Roses" in *Gypsy*, the melody of which Jule Styne had saved from a number that was cut from *High Button Shoes*, his first Broadway success twelve years earlier. The original lyric was sung by Nanette Fabray as "Betwixt and Between," a namby-pamby kind of lyric in which she's saying, in essence, I'm betwixt and between, don't know which way to lean, and I just cannot make up my mind. The lyrics made the tune sound wishy-washy and indecisive, even singsong, but with Sondheim's new lyric, suddenly the music takes on depth and grandeur: "You'll be swell! You'll be great!" It becomes one of the great musical theater anthems and yet the music is identical; the only difference is the lyric. The musical phrase that had been behind the line "I just cannot make my mind up" was now under "Everything's coming up roses."

In most cases, although not always, I discovered that songwriters totally dismiss perfectly fine songs that happened not to be hits, saying that if the public did not like the song, then it wasn't worthy of recognition. Arthur Schwartz wrote a song for the movie *Dangerous When Wet*—obviously an Esther Williams vehicle—called "I Got Out of Bed on the Right Side," with lyrics by Johnny Mercer. I asked Arthur to play it one day.

"That's a terrible song," he said. He tried to play it but only stumbled through it. I was ready to push him off the bench and play it myself. "No, it goes like this," I wanted to say. "Don't you remember?"

Occasionally, I'd show Ira a lyric sheet to which his only response was, "I didn't write that." Yet it had clearly come from his typewriter and was written on his stationery. Along those lines, songwriters often appropriate their early material and rewrite it or use it again if it appeared in a project that didn't get much attention. For example, Burton Lane and Harold Adamson wrote a song called "I Want to Be a Minstrel Man" for the Nicholas Brothers to sing in the 1934 Eddie Cantor movie *Kid Millions*. The song was published but never did much because it was special material for the Nicholas Brothers. Years later, Burton contacted Harold Adamson and asked him if he would mind if he saved the melody and had a new lyric written for it. Burton had originally written the tune with Fred Astaire in mind and wanted it united with the man who had inspired it. Harold acquiesced and, with a lyric by Alan Jay Lerner, it became "You're All the World to Me" and was danced by Astaire in *Royal Wedding*. That's the number in which Astaire dances on the ceiling, although that visual image is so insistent that most people can't remember the music or the name of the song.

The Gershwin brothers occasionally resuscitated a melody with a different lyric. "Embraceable You" had been written a number of years earlier and George and Ira were just waiting for the right vehicle for that song because they knew how good it was. Ira Gershwin wrote a song with Vincent Youmans for *Two Little Girls in Blue* in 1921 that was called "You Started Something." In 1973, when Ira was listening to the cast album of *No, No, Nanette*, he discovered to his vast surprise that Youmans had recycled his old song. In the latter part of the '20s, Youmans had had Otto Harbach and Irving Caesar write a new lyric for that melody and it was put into the show, but Ira never knew a thing about it.

"I Can't Get Started" had an earlier lyric written by Yip Harburg called "Come Face the Music with Me." Before Ira wrote his stunning lyric for Harold Arlen's "The Man That Got Away," the song had a lyric by Johnny Mercer that was thrown out, but Ira never knew about it. David Raksin's song "Laura" had another lyric, by Irving Caesar, before Johnny Mercer wrote the current one. And Mercer's original lyric for "The Shadow of Your Smile" was thrown out by the producer and replaced by Paul Francis Webster's lyric. The Mercer lyric does exist and once when Johnny was asked what he thought of the new lyric, he said, "It kind of sounds to me like a woman with a mustache."

Mercer was a brilliant lyricist, having written words for songs as diverse as "Autumn Leaves," "Blues in the Night," "Too Marvelous for Words," "Moon River," "One for My Baby," and "I'm an Old Cowhand." But he was also legendary for his bouts of drunkenness. He had a serious alcohol problem and when he drank, he became anti-black, anti-Semitic (even though his wife, Ginger, was Jewish), anti-everything. A television producer named Jim Washburn told me he once took Mercer to see Miles Davis perform and in the course of the evening, Mercer got so drunk he started yelling at Davis and calling him a nigger. He was as obstreperous as he could be, but this was common behavior for Johnny when he drank. He was always filled with regret afterwards because he was truly a gentle soul. His was a classic Jekyll and Hyde case: he would get drunk and insult people and then send them flowers the next day. Once at a party I asked Gene DePaul, who collaborated with Mercer on the score of *Seven Brides for Seven Brothers*, what Johnny was like. His face turned red with anger.

"I'll tell you what Johnny was like!" he said. "If he was at this party, the first thing he would do is go over to the bar and have four or five drinks, one after another, because they're free. As soon as he got drunk he'd insult everybody in the room. And then he'd call me the next day and say, 'Who was I mean to? Who did I insult?' I'd say, 'Well, you could have been nicer to Rosemary Clooney. You were rude to Ned Washington and this one and that one.' And then he would send them all flowers."

One night Mercer was at a party with Jo Stafford and as he started getting drunk, he began to insult her. Stafford stopped him in midstream. "Johnny," she said firmly, "I don't need your damn flowers!" Yet all agree that, *sober*, there was no kinder or gentler soul than Johnny Mercer.

*M*OST music lovers get fairly indignant about the use of famous music in commercials with new lyrics added. I personally have a rather soft attitude about it, because as a kid growing up in the '60s and '70s, I learned a lot of songs for the first time when they were used in television commercials—and I still think of the advertiser's lyrics whenever I hear a particular song. The Johnny Mercer/Victor Schertzinger classic "Tangerine" will live forever in my mind as "Figurines," the diet bar that was advertised inordinately during the years I watched television. I can still recall a public service admonishment to wear your seatbelt, called "Buckle Up for Safety," sung to the tune of "Buckle Down Winsocki." It was many years before I learned that "Buckle Down Winsocki" was a real song and not just a tune written to help us remember to wear seatbelts. In fact, my first taste of the Dave Brubeck tune "Take Five" came in a public service announcement warning of the evils of cigarettes that was aired on a local Columbus television station.

I wonder how many people have learned their first classical pieces by hearing them used as theme music for television or radio shows. The classic example, of course, is the use of Rossini's *William Tell Overture* on *The Lone Ranger*. The famous 1940s radio serial *The Shadow* was accompanied by a Saint-Saëns piece called *Omphale's Spinning Wheel*. The "On the Trail" theme from *The Grand Canyon Suite* was appropriated by Philip Morris and I trust it brought the composer, Ferde Grofé, a huge amount of money. If you hear a song used for commercial purposes and the original songwriter is still alive, it's pretty certain that the advertiser had to obtain permission from the creator to use the song in that context—although not always. Sometimes a songwriter will sell the rights to a song for a small amount of money and retain no claim to the copyright. George Bassman composed "I'm Getting Sentimental Over You," which later became Tommy Dorsey's theme song, when he was eighteen years old and needed a few bucks. He approached the successful music publisher Irving Mills, offered to sell him the song for $30, accepted $25, and kissed the copyright of a huge perennial moneymaker goodbye.

Incidentally, Irving Mills was also known as the Great Cut-in Artist. He put his name on almost every Ellington song he published (including "Sophisticated Lady," "Mood Indigo," "Solitude," and "It Don't Mean a Thing") and quite a few by Count Basie, Benny Carter, and other jazz greats even though, of course, he had absolutely no part in their composition. But by attaching his name to the songwriting credits when he published them, he assured himself of a share of the royalties, completely unmerited. He even had the gall, about ten years before his death, to publish a catalogue of "Song Successes by Irving Mills," none of which he had anything to do with other than publishing them. When Duke Ellington died, some wit asked, "Does the tombstone say, 'and Irving Mills'?"

Being a cut-in artist was an easy way to supplement your income in those days. Lyricist, producer, and nightclub and theater owner Billy Rose cut himself in on a couple of Ira's songs in similar fashion. When Rose produced the revue *Sweet and Low* in 1930, for which Ira and Harry Warren supplied songs, Rose's own name was added to the publishing credits. I asked Ira specifically what Rose contributed; according to Ira, Rose would say, "I don't like the verse of that song. There's a word that's bothering me." He changed literally one word in the verse and had them put his name on it. That kind of thing was rampant in those days. Ross Gorman's name was added to Harry Warren's first published song, "Rose of the Rio Grande," because he was involved in the early performances of it. But then, George Bassman, who arranged and cowrote Benny Goodman's theme song, "Let's Dance," never got credit or royalties for it. Burton Lane told me that it was widely believed that Fats Waller wrote "I Can't Give You Anything but Love," which appeared in the show *Blackbirds of 1928* starring Bill "Bojangles" Robinson and Adelaide Hall. Jimmy McHugh, to whom it is credited, bought it from Fats. The song "Among My Souvenirs" has a lyric credited to Edgar Leslie, who wrote, among other things, "For Me and My Gal," but it was actually written by Al Dubin. My friend Fred Ahlert Jr. said to Edgar in the '50s, "I have to ask you something. Is it true that Al Dubin wrote the lyric for 'Among My Souvenirs'?" Leslie angrily and defensively replied, "I paid for it!"

Fred Astaire did not write his song hit "I'm Building Up to an Awful Letdown," which credits music to Astaire and lyrics to Johnny Mercer. The music was actually written by Fred's dance rehearsal accompanist, Hal Borne, who could produce a contract to prove it. Yet Astaire did legitimately write a number of songs and it was always curious to me that his name went on that one, because he seemed like such an honorable man.

Songwriters of Ira's stature, however, usually retained not only the credits but the rights to determine the use of their songs in every instance. When the International Ladies Garment Workers Union was trying to create a theme song for their ad campaign, they originally wanted to use the melody of Jerome Kern's "Look for the Silver Lining" with the lyric "Look for the union label," but the Kern Estate said no. Jerome Kern's daughter said, in essence, "My father's music will never be used for a television commercial." So the people creating the ILGWU song simply wrote a copycat melody with the lyric "Look for the union label when you are buying a coat, suit, or pants." The scan is the same as "Look for the silver lining, / Whene'er a cloud appears in the blue." Kern's daughter later regretted that she hadn't allowed them to use her father's melody because she would have made a good deal of money and, besides, the melody they used wasn't all that different.

Ira was less fussy; he sold the right to use "I Got Rhythm" for a TV commercial to Pathmark Supermarkets for a large sum of money. They

submitted it to him with the lyric "I got fresh fruits, / I got fresh meats"—
you get the idea. I asked Ira, somewhat incredulously, why he was
allowing such a trivial use of a great song. He said that it was only for
three states for a limited period of time and they were offering a substantial payment. He felt that as long as it followed the spirit of the original, it was okay. On another occasion, he was presented with a request
to use "Let's Call the Whole Thing Off" as a commercial for RCA Color-
trak Television. Ron Blanc, his lawyer, brought the request over when
Ira was upstairs, so I looked at it first. It was so bad, so tacky and corn-
ball, that I was certain he'd hate it as much as I did. The new lyric went
something like this:

> I like the football,
> And you like the movies,
> I like the cartoons,
> And you love Lucy.
> Football, the movies, cartoons, Lucy,
> RCA Colortrak's the one for us.

It didn't even scan properly. I looked at it and said to Ron, "This is
awful. Ira will never approve it."

"Is it really bad?" Ron said, with a big smile on his face.

"It's really bad," I said.

"Why don't you show it to Ira to get an official refusal?" he said. I
thought he'd at least get a kick out of it, so I took it upstairs. It came in
a storyboard format, with TV images above each segment of lyrics. Ira
looked at the storyboard. He read out loud, "I like the football, you like
the movies, I like the—" Then he stopped and said, "This is the worst
thing I've ever seen!" He denied them permission, but three months
later, on came that TV commercial, with a copycat melody but the same
lyrics and the same storyboard. It was unrecognizable as having been
inspired by "Let's Call the Whole Thing Off" because it was so bad. But
they tried.

The power of songwriters to squelch bad-taste attempts to use their
songs in commercials depends on the publisher. As a matter of courtesy, the publishers always came to Ira to ask his permission and then
abided by his decision. But not all publishers are as considerate or as

vigilant. According to Robert Montgomery, trustee of the Cole Porter estate, by oversight a Porter song was once licensed to the maker of a toilet-bowl cleaner with the lyric "I've Got You Under My Rim." Jack Lawrence, who wrote "All or Nothing at All" and the lyrics for "If I Didn't Care" and "Beyond the Sea," was once approached by an oven manufacturer with an idea for an oven that would signal when the meat was done by playing a few bars of his song "Tenderly." Jack declined.

Irving Caesar once said he would never ever allow anyone to use "Tea for Two" in a tea commercial. At one point, Lipton's was offering an exorbitant amount of money to use it, but he resolutely refused. Then about ten years ago, a Japanese company invented a teapot that actually whistled "Tea for Two" when the water boiled. Irving jumped on the bandwagon and they sold a great number of teapots. The only problem was that the pot was largely defective. It used such a fragile mechanism to create the melody that most of the kettles malfunctioned and had to be returned. I was offered one as a gift but I had to go through several before I got one that worked. I still have it, but it no longer whistles "Tea for Two." After that, Irving did sell "Tea for Two" to be used as a commercial, even though the man in charge of clearances at Warner Brothers Music showed me the memo from Irving saying that he would never allow it to be used.

According to Caesar, his lyric for "Tea for Two" was actually a dummy lyric. The song's composer, Vincent Youmans, liked to work at the piano hour after hour when he wrote a tune; he would take a melodic idea or phrase and play it and rework it until he found something he liked. Listening to him going through this process on home recordings becomes almost torturous because of the repetition of the melody, yet that's how he created things. Jule Styne said one of Youmans's devices was to take a small musical phrase and repeat it with slight variations. In fact, Styne acknowledged that he got the inspiration for "Just in Time," which has that same kind of repeated melodic figure, from Youmans.

In the case of "Tea for Two," Youmans had come up with a melody constructed of two- and four-note phrases, in which he used those same phrases again a few intervals higher. He was playing it for Irving, who had been taking a nap and was half-asleep. Youmans said, "What do you think of this, Irving?"

Caesar started to improvise in a sort of singsong voice: "Pic-ture you, up-on my knee, tea for two, two for tea, me for you, and you for me, a-lone. . . ."

"That's great!" Youmans said.

"No, no, it stinks," Caesar said. "It's a dummy lyric. I'll write you a good one in the morning, but at least now I know where the rhymes are."

"No," Youmans said, "go on!" And Caesar wrote the whole lyric that way, speaking it off the top of his head in his dazed state. That's a rare example of a dummy lyric becoming the final lyric and, if you examine it, you can see how silly it really is. The comedian Frank Faye used to do a routine about "Tea for Two" in which he sang little snatches of lyrics and then stopped and talked about how absurd they were. "The day will break, / And you'll awake, / And start to bake / A sugar cake, / For me to take / For all the boys to see. . . . Look fellas! It's a *sugar cake!*"

Dummy lyrics are a songwriting tool that has been around for quite a while. A working set of words that is not intended to be used as the final product, a dummy is created for the purpose of reminding the lyricist where he has to place the proper accents, how many rhymes he has to use, and things like that. It's helpful when the lyricist goes off by himself to work, so he'll have a reference on which to base the final lyric in case he doesn't remember the melody clearly. The dummy also saves the composer from having to sit at the piano and play the tune for hours on end when another pianist can't be hired to do that. Harry Warren used to complain that his lyricist Mack Gordon required Harry to play his tunes over and over so often that he used to get sick of his own melodies by the time Gordon had crafted a lyric. Frank Loesser, conversely, listened to a tune several times and then went away, only to come back a week or two later with a finished lyric. He was able to memorize the melody completely from a few hearings. Composers eventually started using home recordings on disc and, later, tape recorders to preserve the tunes for their lyricists.

Some dummy lyrics have become legendary among songwriters. Jonathan Lieberson, the son of Goddard Lieberson of Columbia Records fame, told me one line of a dummy lyric for "My Favorite Things." It went, "Cute little babies who fall out of swings, / These are a few of my favorite things." A side of Ockie Hammerstein we never saw! "It Ain't Necessarily So" began as a dummy title that Ira created as George played him the melody to help him remember where the accents fell. When Richard Rodgers played Lorenz Hart the melody for what eventually became "There's a Small Hotel," Hart wrote,

There's a girl next door
Who's an awful bore,
It really makes you sore
To see her.
By and by, perhaps she'll die,
Perhaps she'll croak this summer;
Her old man's a plumber,
She's much dumber.

What that lyric did, for example, was remind Hart that he needed triple rhymes in the bridge.

Lyricists like Hart and Hammerstein and Ira Gershwin didn't read music and didn't necessarily work very well from the lead sheet the composer would write down for them. (A lead sheet consists of the melody line, sometimes with chord symbols written above, but no piano part or full accompaniment.) Ira preferred to get the melody in his head, and then he played it in his mind obsessively until he found what he was looking for. I did find one lead sheet from the *Ziegfeld Follies of 1936* that Vernon Duke had written out for Ira's use, but he didn't normally work that way with George.

Ira once complained that Jerome Kern had been so impatient with him when he took a long time creating a suitable lyric for Kern's great melody that became "Long Ago (and Far Away)" that Kern sent Ira a dummy lyric of his own that began, "Watching little Nelly pee." According to a British friend of mine, actress Sandra Caron, who claims to have a copy of the lead sheet, the dummy title for Lennon and McCartney's "Yesterday" was "Scrambled Eggs." So now, whenever I hear "Yesterday," I think of breakfast.

When Ira was working on his lyrics, he would take a huge sheet of paper and spread it out on the desk. He would square off sections of the paper, one section for the first line, one section for the bridge, and so on, almost like a storyboard for cartoons. He would often start by working on the ending of the lyric first and then go back to the beginning. And when that page was filled up, he would go on to another sheet. In this way, he went through reams of paper. Before he started to write a lyric, he sharpened his mind by playing word games and doing whatever he could to get himself in the mode of verbal thinking. It was always torture for Ira to write lyrics, and he tried to avoid it unless he had to. The reason he was so prolific with George is that when George accepted a contract for a show or film, Ira was a part of it. But if it hadn't been for George's ambition, Ira wouldn't have produced nearly as much. As a matter of fact, in the '40s after George was gone, he used to accept two jobs at once so he could tell the first one and then the other that he was already committed and get out of both of them. Occasionally he got stuck and had to take one of the jobs. But he simply didn't want to work.

His last two Broadway shows, *The Firebrand of Florence* in 1945 and *Park Avenue* in 1946, were both huge failures. When *Of Thee I Sing* was revived in 1952, with Ira supplying some updated lyrics, that too was a flop. He worked with Harry Warren on the film *The Barkleys of Broadway* in 1949, starring Fred Astaire and Ginger Rogers, and that was successful, but *Give a Girl a Break* in 1953 with Marge and Gower Champion and Debbie Reynolds was another failure. Ira was always philosophical about his flops and considered himself lucky overall. When I mentioned the number of flops he had during that period of the late '40s and early '50s, Ira said, "Hey, I'm much luckier than Arthur Schwartz." Arthur had huge success with Howard Dietz in the late 20s and early '30s, but after *The Band Wagon* in 1931, his shows were mainly flops except for *A Tree Grows in Brooklyn* in 1951, which was moderately successful. After that he wrote three more Broadway shows that were all failures. Schwartz had a lot of hit songs through the years, but no other successful shows.

Oscar Hammerstein was considered washed up right before he got the job to write the lyrics for *Oklahoma!* Despite having helped revolutionize musical theater with *Show Boat,* he was thought of as a man who wrote operettas and old-fashioned material because he had worked with Romberg and Friml. By the end of the '30s, he had a string of flops and nobody wanted to hire him. He was at his lowest professional point when Richard Rodgers approached him about doing *Oklahoma!* Everybody said to Rodgers, "Why are you working with him? Don't do it." Of course, we know what happened after that. I'm not exactly sure why Rodgers picked Hammerstein at the low point in his career, although in retrospect the reason is clear. He must have seen something in his lyrics that attracted him and made him feel that he would be appropriate for a musical based on *Green Grow the Lilacs*. During that same time, however, Richard Rodgers asked if Ira would write the lyrics for the show and Ira turned him down. I don't know if Ira refused because he was working or because he just didn't want to do it. The latter reason is more likely. By the time he got around to working on *Cover Girl* with Jerome Kern in 1943, *Oklahoma!* had opened and had become a huge success. The publisher Max Dreyfus had sent the copies of the sheet music to Ira (music is usually published before a show reaches Broadway), and one day when Ira had them spread out on the piano, Kern happened to come over to the house. Kern saw the music sitting there, pointed to it, and asked, "What's that?"

"It's *Oklahoma!*" Ira said.

Kern asked if he could borrow it, collected the music, and took it home with him. He returned the next day and put the music back on the piano. "So, Jerry," Ira said, "what do you think of it?" Kern sniffed and said, "Condescending music!" He was very jealous of the success of *Oklahoma!* I'm not sure if Kern was jealous of Kurt Weill, but I know he hated the man and his music. In 1945, Kern asked Ira to work with him on *Centennial Summer* but Ira was working on *The Firebrand of Florence*. "I can't," he said. "I'm working with Kurt Weill." Kern said, "You'll be sorry." And Ira was, because *Firebrand* was a big flop, which probably cheered Kern greatly.

Flops come with the territory, of course, and even the best lyricists had to have a sense of humor to keep them in perspective. Oscar Hammerstein created one of the funniest testaments to both his failures and his wit when he placed an ad in the trade paper *Variety* on January 5, 1944, right after the triumphant opening of *Oklahoma!* A parody of the self-inflating ads regularly placed by prominent songwriters trumpeting their enduring prowess, it read:

❄ ❄ ❄ ❄ ❄ ❄ ❄ ❄

HOLIDAY GREETINGS

Oscar Hammerstein, II

author of

❄

Sunny River

(SIX WEEKS AT THE ST. JAMES THEATRE, NEW YORK)

❄

Very Warm for May

(SEVEN WEEKS AT THE ALVIN THEATRE, NEW YORK)

❄

Three Sisters

(SIX WEEKS AT THE DRURY LANE, LONDON)

❄

Ball at the Savoy

(FIVE WEEKS AT THE DRURY LANE, LONDON)

❄

Free for All

(THREE WEEKS AT THE MANHATTAN THEATRE, NEW YORK)

❄ ❄ ❄

I'VE DONE IT BEFORE AND
I CAN DO IT AGAIN

chapter 11

PIANO BAR MAN
(or, A Charisma of One's Own)

$\mathcal{I}$started playing in piano bars when I was sixteen years old, beginning with a restaurant on the west side of Columbus called the Warehouse. I don't know how far back in this century the piano bar originated, but by now it is a venerable institution. Piano bars range from the old and dear to the occasionally sleek and elegant, but many of them are just plain seedy. Which is fine by me, because a little seediness adds character— you almost *want* the carpet to be musty. All you really need is a piano (which is often as weathered as some of the customers), surrounded by a few swivel stools, preferably with backs to keep customers from falling off. The piano has a brass bar attached to its side to facilitate leaning (and, as the evening wears on, as a further aid to listeners to keep from falling off those stools). Then there's the requisite interrogation light pointed at the pianist (presumably so you can count the individual beads of sweat standing out on his forehead) and a sound system designed to announce airline arrivals and departures. But for all that, piano bars work because of the passion for music they seem to generate, the sheer energy that is the by-product of the joy of discovering a great song. Or a bad song.

You quickly learn that regulars have their favorite numbers, which, needless to say, are not always *your* favorites. When Eddie came in, he was going to sing "Delilah." Whenever Phyllis got drunk, sooner or later you were going to have to play "Misty" for her—and pray that Jessica Walter would stab you to death before you finished. In a piano bar, you live off your tips, so you don't often turn down requests; you learn how to ingratiate yourself with listeners and play requests even if you don't know them. If you can hum just a few bars to accommodate them, they'll be happy and give you a couple of dollars.

Still, I developed a list of songs I dreaded playing. My friend Page Cavanaugh, who shares my sense of dread, regularly announces to the room a list of songs he'd rather die than play one more time, along with the price he charges for each. If you just have to hear "Send in the Clowns," it will cost you $5,000; if you want "Impossible Dream," it's $8,000; "My Way" will set you back $10,000; "I Left My Heart in San Francisco" costs $12,000; "New York, New York," $25,000; and anything by Andrew Lloyd Webber is $50,000. "Feelings" isn't on his list because he doesn't even want to hear the word, and I'm with him all the way. I don't like to rejoice in the misfortune of others, but let's just say I was intrigued to learn that the song's composer, Morris Albert, was successfully sued for plagiarism by a French composer. Albert's publisher had to pay a large judgment to the Frenchman, whose name I've conveniently forgotten.

When I perform in concert halls today and people yell out requests, most of them are for songs that I've done, but inevitably someone will yell out "New York, New York." Then I just say, "Excuse me, but you have me confused with somebody else." When Liza Minnelli is performing and someone occasionally shouts out a request for "Over the Rainbow," Liza just says, "It's been done." It nettles her to hear anyone sing that song, especially Mandy Patinkin in his overwrought, excessively dramatic version.

It was at the Warehouse in Columbus that I began to encounter the Friends and Relatives of the Rich and Famous. One guy, for instance, claimed he was Nat "King" Cole's uncle and always insisted on singing "Mona Lisa." He felt his voice was indistinguishable from Nat's and he was half-right: it had all of the strange jaw-wrenching, mouth-expanding affectations but none of the glorious warmth and luxuriance of the original. Sometimes when I played a famous song, one of my customers would ruefully claim that he had actually written that song and sold it to the author many years ago. (I believed only one of them, a fellow named Martin Tuck, who claimed that he wrote "Mam'selle" and sold it to director Edmund Goulding, who used it in his 1946 film *The Razor's Edge*.)

After I left the Warehouse, I started playing at another Columbus spot called the Dell, which featured singing waiters with, for the most part, surprisingly good voices. This was fine for patrons until they wanted some sort of service, at which point they found that they had to wait for their server to finish the last chorus of "Ol' Man River" or some interminable operetta aria. When you just want to get your check and go home, that Ol' Man River really does keep on rolling and rolling *alonnng.*

The Dell was where they held the cast parties for the Kenley Players—the local summer theater circuit that was run by a man named John Kenley. He is a genuine physical hermaphrodite and spends part of the year as a man and part of the year as a woman. John put on summer stock versions of Broadway shows, which was where I first encountered many of the classic musicals and first learned the scores. The stars were frequently second- or third-tier players, like Pia Zadora in *Damn Yankees*, but that was big-time in Columbus. Kenley made very good money and could afford to bring in relatively big names, too. The most popular draw was Paul Lynde, riding the crest of his *Hollywood Squares* television success, and he *was* funny. At the end of the show he would leave the stage for a minute, then return in a caftan to answer questions from the audience (most of the performers did this or some kind of specialty at the evening's conclusion). One woman asked Paul rather coyly if he was married. He looked at her for a moment and then shot back in that characteristic voice, "Do you live in a cave?"

All the Kenley performers came into the Dell after the show and I got to meet many of them. I still remember how scared I was the first time a celebrity sat down at one of the seats around my piano. It was Harvey Korman, a regular on the *Carol Burnett Show,* and I stumbled through a couple of songs, feeling flustered at playing for a personality I recognized from TV. Korman sat politely for a few minutes and then left. It was obvious that his presence was impairing my performance to a great degree—my first experience of stage fright.

Things improved only moderately after I moved to L.A. Here's a typical entry from my journal when I was living there, working for Ira by day and playing places like the Toy Tiger by night: "Was terrible to start and then fabulous at the finish. Nobody applauded during my first set. I asked who gave the audience tranquilizers. I did this in a light, joking fashion. I think no one was offended by it. But then later, people who had seen me before came back to see me, and suddenly I had a huge cheering section. It was the best night I've ever had, as far as response goes. Only fifteen dollars in tips, however. The man who plays Mr. Whipple in the TV commercials was there. Great night!" At least by then, I didn't get flustered when Mr. Whipple came in.

You learn all sorts of tricks of the trade in piano bars. For example, the size of the brandy snifter that you use for tips is very important. The larger the bowl, the smaller the amount of money in it appears. That's good in the sense that people may take pity and give you more money. You salt the bowl with a dollar or two; putting in more than that will make people think you're doing too well. After some time, I acquired an enormous brandy snifter, which I eventually passed on as a memento to a friend who is currently playing in piano bars. Another thing you learn is how to deal with hecklers and drunks. It's the greatest training ground you can possibly have, because if you can get the attention of people when they're drinking and distracted in a situation like that, you can learn how to play any other room. But you have to find a way to get the offenders to stop doing what they are doing without being hostile. No matter how upsetting their behavior may be, if you show any signs of anger or irritation, it upsets the audience. So you deal with it in a humorous manner with an edge that will get the message across without alienating anybody else in the process. If someone is talking boisterously during the show, you learn to say things like, "If I'm singing too loud for you, let me know." If the audience laughs, that helps to defuse the situation and may give the troublemaker the impression that the crowd is on *your* side.

My friend David Ross wrote a song called "Talk," about a couple that had a fight and didn't talk to each other for years. Then one day, one sneezed and the other said "Gesundheit," and slowly they started to talk again. They realized they had a lot they wanted to talk about and, as the song goes,

> They looked for someplace quiet
> Where the lights were low
> To spill the million things they'd saved from long ago—
> They found a cozy spot that suited them—and so—
> They let their hair down and the words began to flow.
> They laughed and talked so loud and clear
> That you could hear them in Topeka or Tangier.
> I'm glad their quarrel's over, but I'd like to know
> With the world full of places they could go
> Why in the hell choose this hotel
> And bloody talk talk talk talk talk talk talk talk talk
> All through my show?

It was fun to do because by the end, it was directed at one particular couple that was sitting in the corner yakking away until they suddenly realized that they were the focus.

I soon found that the more money people have, the less polite they will be. They feel that they can afford to talk through your show because they can buy you and sell you. There's a line in one of the old Smith and Dale routines when they're having a fight. Smith says to Dale, "I can buy you and sell you." And Dale says, "I can buy you and *keep* you—I wouldn't have to sell you." It's the people who can buy you and keep you that you have to watch out for.

I discovered later in my career, playing at the Algonquin and other upscale places, that a rich, well-dressed drunk is still a drunk. One night at the Algonquin, a drunken woman at a table in the corner of the room kept talking very loudly about her affair with Talulah Bankhead. Much of the audience was riveted. I confess I was too. On another night when

I was playing there, Kay Swift came in. Knowing in advance that she was coming, I prepared her song "Can't We Be Friends?" Even though Kay was nearing ninety then, she drank quite a bit and was having a great time at my show. I sang "Can't We Be Friends?" and introduced her to the audience. She got up and took the applause very nobly, a great, classy woman. Then she decided to stay for the second show, which began at eleven, and by that time she'd had too much to drink. As I went into my second number, I glanced in her direction and saw that her head was down on the table. She was out like a light. I thought I'd better not introduce her. But later she seemed to rally and was awake for quite some time; as I got to the end of the set, I thought she might be offended if I didn't sing her song and introduce her again. So I sang another one of her songs and said, "Ladies and gentlemen, Miss Kay Swift!" She attempted to get up but found she was too drunk. All the patrons in the club assumed that she was so old that she must be infirm. So they continued to applaud as she tried heroically to push herself up from the table with both hands. She never quite made it; each time she started, she immediately slumped down in her chair. In the meantime the audience dutifully sustained their applause. Finally she just sat there and gave up.

A New York critic once came to see me with his wife, who unfortunately had some sort of sleep disorder. She fell asleep and snored very loudly during my set and people kept turning around and looking at her. They complained audibly, but the critic never budged or acknowledged his wife's disorder. Someone later explained to me about her problem, but I couldn't imagine why they would go to a nightclub under those circumstances.

Every once in a while, the gods seem to intervene and turn an awful situation into a triumph of sorts. One night I was playing at the Carlyle when a group of people arrived midway through my first song. "Where have you been?" I said. "We've been waiting for you." I was actually trying to ease their embarrassment at arriving late. But then I realized that they must have been drinking for some time before they came in, because they were quite drunk, and I watched as they proceeded to talk nonstop, ignoring the music and the people trying to hear me sing. The maître d' and the staff were hovering around their table but didn't say anything to them. I understood their position, not wanting to offend patrons who had paid a great deal of money to be there, yet wanting to keep order in the room and not upset the performer. So then I said, "Can you do me a favor and analyze the performance after I finish?" But they weren't fazed.

At one point I said, quite seriously, "How would you like to have your check comped tonight?"

"Oh," one of them replied, "we'd love that."

"All you have to do is leave right now," I said.

They all laughed, but they stayed through the rest of the set. For me to say something out of very thinly veiled anger like that was unusual, but I needed to get it out of my system in order to continue with my performance. Liza Minnelli was there and I saw her watching it all rather wide-eyed, wondering what I was going to do next. But then my savior appeared in the form of a guy at the bar who was tipsy but very jovial— the kind of drunk who's fun to deal with. For no apparent reason, he called out "Oklahoma!" I chuckled but otherwise ignored him as he kept requesting "Oklahoma!" after every song. At one point, I said I'd like to take requests for Gershwin songs, as I sometimes do. People were shouting out Gershwin requests and this guy yelled out "Oklahoma!" So I started to play "Oklahoma!" in the style of *Rhapsody in Blue* and got a big laugh out of the audience. After I finished the song, I started shouting "Oklahoma!" myself, which put the audience in stitches. Then somebody yelled out the name of some rap song. "You know," I said, "Oklahoma's starting to sound real good to me right now."

Liza talked to me afterwards. "You should pay that guy to come in every night," she said. "He was so funny, it was like he was a plant." She asked me if I wasn't afraid that he was going to turn on me, but that thought had never crossed my mind. Maybe that comes from all those years of playing piano bars.

Drunks aren't the only irritant. There are people who, by dint of some overabundance of ego, have to pretend that they know every song you're playing. One night in a piano bar, as I began each song, a woman sitting quite close would nod and smile and then mouth the words a half-second after I sang them, pretending she knew them all. So I started to play a song that I improvised on the spot. "Do you know this?" I said.

"Oh yes," she said, "I love that song."

"I'm making it up as I go," I said.

"Fuck you," she said. And she got up and pushed her drink across the bar and left.

And on occasion, I've gotten my own comeuppance. When I first met Liza Minnelli, I was playing at the Mondrian in Los Angeles. She came to my show and I was trying to impress her by playing the most obscure songs I could think of, starting with a Hugh Martin/Ralph Blane song called "You Are for Loving." I said, "Liza, do you know this one?"

"Yeah," she said, "it was written for me." That took me down a few pegs. Just as mortifying were those times when songwriters came into the club and asked me to play a particular song they had written. That was always frightening, because when somebody appeared out of the blue, I had to rack my brain to try to come up with some song of theirs; often I couldn't. You can't fake a song for the author. Unless it's Kay Swift at the second show—then *maybe*. I was quite pleased with myself one night at the Mondrian when I spotted the director Arthur Laurents, however. I started playing songs from *Anyone Can Whistle*, which he had directed. When I got no reaction from him, not so much as a nod or a smile, I started to play louder and louder until finally I saw him talking to the waiter. The waiter came over to me and said, "That gentleman would like to know if you would play more quietly." They were Sondheim songs, but the show had been a big flop and I guess he didn't like the memories those songs evoked.

When I was first starting out in piano bars, I mostly just played and didn't sing. Curiously enough, this gave me the opportunity to learn quite a bit from listening to other people get up and sing. That ranged from the singing waiters and waitresses at the Dell to the drunken guy at the far end of the piano late at night. I was aware that some of these amateur singers made a much greater impact on the crowd than others, but only gradually did I learn what it was about the different presentations that made one performance more effective than another. Sometimes it was just inebriation—a funny drunk could be entertaining—but other times the life experience of the singer lent the song great credibility. Some people were simply more connected to the songs and the words than others were, and that was rarely lost on the audience, even if the audience was just a few people sitting around the piano sipping their drinks and munching corn chips.

It was in piano bars that I first learned to sing and play at the same time. That sounds simple enough, but for the longest time I found it fiendishly difficult to do. I could play all right, but when someone asked me to sing one night, I was nonplussed. It took me a long time to develop coordination. Nat "King" Cole once said that he always felt both his playing and singing suffered when he did them simultaneously. When people ask me how I learned to do it, I have to say that it was a kind of baptism by fire.

The biggest problem a piano bar performer faces often isn't the audience at all but rather getting the management to provide and maintain a decent piano. Sometimes the pianos are completely unplayable and when you complain, the manager invariably says, "It sounds fine to me." At one of the first places I played in Columbus, the owner was a former music professor at a music school there. He had a grand piano in his club but it was just a piece of junk. I later discovered that he had inherited the piano from the university, which was disposing of it. So much for academic standards; it all came down to economics. (Well, at least they *had* a piano. I've been hired to play for parties only to discover that all they had was a mini electric keyboard or, God help me, an organ.)

Obviously, so much depends on the taste and sensitivity of the people who own and run the club. I have even encountered problems in England, and that came as a great surprise. It has been my pleasure and good fortune to play in London numerous times, but the ground rules are slightly different. Unlike America, there aren't many rooms to play and there isn't as much regard for performers, in certain instances. Even when you make an announcement that there's no smoking, people still light up cigarettes because smoking doesn't have the onus attached to it that it does here. I was once sitting next to Lord Charles Spencer Churchill, grandson of Sir Winston, who lit up a big stogie in the middle of Eartha Kitt's act on her opening night at a place called the Green Room. It's located in the Café Royal, an elegant old complex that goes back to the days of Oscar Wilde and has portraits of people like Rudyard Kipling on the walls. I believe Lord Churchill is part of the group that owns the Royal and other hotels, but I didn't care. I was very distressed by his lack of consideration and finally I said, "Would you please put out your cigar?" He did but then left a few minutes later. As he was leaving, I thought, I would have told your grandfather to put out his cigar, too.

Having said all that, I'm sorry to see that piano bars are disappearing so rapidly, because they are very important to the preservation of classic American popular music. When my father was a salesman, he could name all the piano bars you could go to in different cities, but over the last ten years, they have started to disappear, even in New York. A lot of them have been replaced by pianocorders and reproducing pianos, the modern version of player pianos. Some of the pianists playing those bars aren't very good, but many of them are excellent musicians. When the atmosphere is right and there's a decent piano, good lighting, and fine sound, it can be a beautiful experience.

But there's a curious ambivalence about piano bars that may keep them from being more widely popular. Bobby Short has always referred to himself as a saloon singer and, for that matter, so has Frank Sinatra, perhaps reflecting the slightly seedy origins of the clubs they've sung in. Yet even as piano bars are fading out, many of the remaining ones have become almost prohibitively expensive for the average fan who just wants to go and hear those classic songs. Certainly there are more new records (excuse me, CDs) being made of that material, and classic recordings are being rereleased aplenty. But a lot of my contemporaries can't afford to come to a place like the Oak Room, and until I started playing there, I couldn't afford it either. There was a long period when I felt uncomfortable putting on a tuxedo to perform at such places because I had never worn one before. It's not something that is natural to me. I once ran into a fan on the street who said, with genuine surprise in her voice, "Michael, you're not in your tuxedo!" Another time, I went to the theater casually dressed and unshaven. I saw a guy pointing at me and heard him say to his friend, "Look at that man. If you cleaned him up and put him in a tuxedo, he'd look *just* like Michael Feinstein."

I often think about Ira and some of the other songwriters I've met who were so unpretentious in their daily lives. It's terribly ironic on one level that this music has become associated with top hat and tails and white gloves and a certain kind of ritzy elegance from all those Fred Astaire movies, because so many of the people who created the songs were very simple guys. Ira hardly went out at all and didn't like to wear formal clothes. The same goes for Yip Harburg and Harry Warren. They just wanted to create songs that would appeal to the common man. Cole Porter is clearly a different story, of course, but he was atypical of the classic songwriters in so many ways.

Too many of the great pianists from the '40s, '50s, and '60s were unable to get other kinds of work and ended up playing in lounges and upscale restaurants. Yet rather than resenting it, they seemed happy to be able to work at all in such a changing world. Johnny Guarnieri was a wonderful pianist who spent the last years of his career playing in the lounge of a restaurant in North Hollywood called Tail o' the Cock. Guarnieri, who had toured and recorded with many jazz greats, was famous for playing everything in five-four time, including a piano concerto that he composed. I once went to hear him with my friend Peter Mintun, a fine pianist in his own right. Guarnieri played "Ol' Man River" and a couple of other standards in five-four time, which prompted Peter to ask him if he knew how to play "Two Hearts in Five-Four Time." Guarnieri was a bit of a curmudgeon; cigar clamped between his teeth, he said, without cracking a smile, "That's funny."

*M*OST of the people I knew fifteen years ago playing in piano bars are still doing the same thing. Some of them are jealous of me because I have stepped out of that world. I acknowledge that a good part of the reason for my escaping from piano bars is my connection to Ira Gershwin. But that connection is an integral part of my lifelong curiosity about the songs and songwriters, the scholarly, archival aspect of music that has always fascinated me. I have spent far less of my life as a performer than as an archivist—someone who for hours on end burrows through stacks of musty papers and manuscripts in libraries and private collections (and sometimes other locales too exotic to mention). My hope, of course, has always been to expand the general knowledge of the Golden Age of popular music and, in the process perhaps, to find some unknown treasure that would add to the limited storehouse of knowledge about show music. Somehow I was later able to integrate into my performances the historical knowledge I'd acquired in all my reading and rummaging, to talk about songs, tell humorous anecdotes, and educate the audience in a way that doesn't make them feel like they are being educated. (Of course, the motive is always entertainment, but there are other motives too—not just to educate but also to uplift people and even to heal them. The use of music as a healing medium has always been in the back of my mind, from the days I first began playing for people in convalescent homes.)

Somewhat to my chagrin, however, I find when I play a concert that a large part of my audience just wants to hear the most familiar standards. They will tolerate other songs but many of the older generation mainly want to hear the songs that they remember and can whistle or hum. This was a bit disconcerting to discover, especially since my own taste keeps leading me further and further back into the mists of American song history. For some time now, I've been collecting music from the aughts, the 1890s, and the 1880s. I've purchased a number of old books from the 1920s and '30s that were written about the music of those earlier decades because I feel that that body of material is worthy of revival and distribution. I recently met a singer who has more of an operatic than a theatrical or cabaret voice and who has been trying to find his niche in the world. He mentioned that he had heard a couple of songs that he liked by Oley Speaks, a concert singer who was born in 1874 and wrote hundreds of art songs in the aughts and teens, including "On the Road to Mandalay" (1907) and "Sylvia" (1914). I even found an old record made by Speaks's niece in the late '40s of some of his songs and I gave it to this singer, who has now embarked on his own search for the songs of Oley Speaks. He's having a hell of a time locating them—and I know just how he feels! It's not going to be easy, because that whole body of material is fairly obscure. If my audience is a little leery of a less familiar Gershwin song, what would they make of Oley Speaks? Nonetheless, I feel a responsibility to my audience, who made me successful, and so I try to give them a lot of what they like.

But that sort of thing was rarely a problem when I was appearing in the Oak Room at the Algonquin for the first time. Then I was too excited by the thought of certain celebrities and notables coming in to hear me. Once I was told that Paul Newman had made a reservation and I began trying to recall the theme from *Cool Hand Luke, The Hustler,* or something associated with Newman. But that night, a dentist arrived named Paul Newman. He later told me that it was his real name and that he never has trouble getting reservations anywhere. A couple of weeks later, there was a reservation for Joanne Woodward, and I thought, This is too absurd. But this time it really was Joanne Woodward. People have asked me if I was intimidated when Jackie Onassis or Elizabeth Taylor came to hear me. Once again, it's always the songwriters who intimidate me the most, and plenty of them came by the Algonquin: Harold Rome, Jule Styne, Jerry Herman, Cy Coleman. Playing in front of Stephen Sondheim was especially daunting because I had no idea he was going to be there. I sat down at the piano and at the first table facing me to my left, there was Sondheim. I gasped audibly at seeing that familiar face, which I had encountered previously only in photographs. Without thinking, I went into my opening number, which at the time happened to be "Wanna Sing a Show Tune." It ends with the lines, "From Cabaret to Carou*sel*, let me *tell* you how *fond* I'm / Of anything by *Ber*lin or *Rodg*ers or *Sond*heim." It's not a perfect rhyme—"fond I'm" and "Sondheim"—but it's close enough that I have no trouble singing it.

As I was approaching those lines, I was giving the song my all, but a certain part of my brain was saying, "What should I do? Do I want to acknowledge him and look at him when I sing this line, or should I ignore him altogether?" As the lines were getting closer and closer, they began to take on the momentum of an approaching train. In a situation like that, I've found, I end up doing what comes to me at the moment. So, as I got to the fateful lines, I turned to bow and acknowledge Sondheim. He was sitting there with both hands covering his ears, obviously not being able to listen to an imperfect rhyme involving his name. I was unnerved through most of the rest of the performance. Sondheim was very nice to me with his comments after the show and even sent me a piece of unpublished music of his that I'd heard of and asked him about. But man, it was a scary moment. Those sorts of things can make you lose your cool.

Much as I appreciate the classy atmosphere of the Algonquin, I sometimes miss the informality of the Mondrian in L.A. It's more casual yet you never know what famous face might pass by the piano. When Peter Allen was staying at the hotel, he was delighted to see Liza, to whom he was once married, and they had a very warm reunion. Then Peter got up and sang a number of songs he was writing for a musical called *Legs Diamond* that appeared on Broadway three years later to scant success. I remember being struck by the marvelous songs that he sang that night and I wondered why some of them didn't appear in the final show.

Madonna never came down to the lounge when she was staying at the Mondrian, although the hotel workers complained about how ill behaved she was. But I did often see people like Eve Arden, George Burns, Roddy McDowall, and others you don't expect to encounter, except perhaps in a place like that. Jean Stapleton came in one night and, before she sat down at a table, stopped at the piano to say hello. "I'm delighted to be here," she said affably, "but I beg you, please don't play the theme from *All in the Family*."

*B*ECAUSE of my experience playing in piano bars, it was relatively easy for me to put together a nightclub act. Since I didn't know how daunting the task could be, I was able to do it rather effortlessly the first time. Now that I know about all the complexities and the myriad pitfalls of assembling an act, of course, the task has become more difficult. But back then, it was a snap.

After years of playing the piano bar scene, I received an offer to play a club in San Francisco called the Plush Room. It had been newly renovated and whoever they had been after to reopen the room was unavailable. Someone who had heard me play at the Mondrian told the owners of the Plush Room about me. They flew down to see me and, by default, I was offered the gig. Suddenly I had to put together an act—as opposed to just playing requests and working my way through my repertoire at the bar. I wrote down many of the songs I knew, trying to pick the ones that I felt would go together in an hour's show. Then I figured out what I wanted to say about them and rather spontaneously put together an act that I ended up using, with variations, for quite some time.

In the course of performing nightclub shows over and over in that early period, I recognized that I had instinctively programmed the songs in the right way. It wasn't very different from a piano bar set, because even there you learn about emotional pacing. I sang a couple of songs up front that said different things about me that I wanted to express to the audience and I invariably said nothing myself until after the second song. The opening song is important because it's the first statement about who you are that the audience will hear. For a while, I sang "Wanna Sing a Show Tune," which was originally written by Ray Jessel for a musical episode of *The Love Boat*. That song told people in no uncertain terms what kind of music I like to sing and why I like to sing it, and it immediately explained who I was. After that got old, I began to open with the venerable Jolson anthem "Let Me Sing and I'm Happy," or maybe "Let Me Entertain You." When I saw Peggy Lee perform at the Ballroom a few years back, she actually opened her act with the Lieber and Stoller chestnut "Is That All There Is?" —the least upbeat, most inappropriate song I can think of to open a show. (She would have done better with Sheila MacRae's opener, "It Never Entered My Mind.") The lights went down, a voice excitedly announced, "Ladies and gentlemen, MISS PEGGY LEE!!" Lights up. There's Peggy sitting in her chair with her wan smile. The pianist begins to noodle in a Kurt Weill way and, barely opening her mouth, Peggy begins to recite, "I remember when I was a little girl. . . ." What an opener. But ya wanna know something? In spite of that, her show was great.

During those first years, my second number was another Lieber and Stoller song, "Feelin' Too Good Today Blues," a very funny song that lets people know that I have a humorous side, which isn't always apparent from my recordings. I try not to use cliché songs like "Get Happy" or "Nothing Can Stop Me Now" or "From This Moment On" or "You're Gonna Hear from Me" from *Inside Daisy Clover*. These are all great songs and that is *why* they have become clichés. I have, however, seen singers like Kaye Ballard take all the cliché songs and cut them up phrase by phrase and turn them into a comedic opener. There's a song I love to sing called "You," written by Stan Daniels for the ill-fated Broadway musical *So Long 174th Street*. The song consists entirely of short phrases culled from more than thirty popular songs of the '20s and '30s. It's on my *Algonquin* album—and copies are on sale in the lobby. . . .

Over the course of a show, I try to balance seriousness and comedy, which are the yin and yang of musical theater (or is it the yang and yin?). To do an entire show of upbeat comedy numbers or of heavy ballads could become intolerable. We've all seen enough bad cabaret acts to know. Several years ago, the late Bobby Gorman, a talented singer-pianist, put together an act called Bobby Gorman and his Mer-men. There were a half dozen guys on stage *all* singing like Ethel Merman. For the *whole* show. It was extremely funny for the first five minutes. After that, it seemed like cruel and unusual punishment.

The hardest thing for most nightclub performers to come up with is genuinely funny material. I always have some light comedy songs toward the top of the show to balance the heavier ballads that will come later. Even the ballads that I perform in the early part of a show are emotionally a little lighter than ones that I approach later, because I want to build up to something. Certain songs are just harder for the audience to recover from than others; their emotional freight takes a bit longer to throw off.

Then I try to balance material by songwriter, subject, and vintage, throwing in a certain amount of contemporary material to offset the classics. And when I sing familiar standards, I try to present them in a different way, by adding extra lyrics that I've discovered or emphasizing an aspect of the song that may have become overlooked or trampled down by countless perfunctory performances. Sometimes, of course, all people want to hear is a simple chorus of an old favorite, and I don't have to do a thing with it. I try not to give in to the temptation to overarrange or overorchestrate, which comes from simply not trusting the material. A sense of balance is essential.

Playing in New York later in my career was different from playing on the West Coast in that there was more pressure on me: I more closely examined the material I chose because there are more cabaret performers to listen to in New York, generating a higher level of expectation in audiences. I discovered when I started playing in concert halls that certain songs that I could play in cabarets didn't work in larger settings because they suddenly became "too important." Pieces that could be thrown away in a smaller setting suffered by having too much attention focused on them in a larger venue. One of the things I enjoy about playing in a nightclub is that I can toss off material, making it easier to try things out. The tradeoff is that in the larger hall, people are there specifically to listen to you and you have fewer diversions. (There's that yin and yang thing again.)

The positioning of the piano and making eye contact with the audience is a crucial element of my act. I have a way of letting everybody in that room know that I'm singing to them and I try to connect with every single person at least once (well, at Carnegie Hall I may miss one or two). I once did a series of exercises with Judy Blackstone, who taught a course at Esalen called the Subtle Self in Motion. Some of her exercises consisted of filling up a room with our energy by using a visualization technique. I realized that I had been doing that in performance for some time. When I play concert halls, I project my energy or my presence to the back of the hall and remain especially aware of the people who are the farthest away from me. After I first played the Hollywood Bowl, I was thrilled to find that practically all of the reviews mentioned that I had created a feeling of intimacy in that massive setting. That's something that cannot be learned. It is either there or not, like charisma or magnetism; it can be developed through awareness, and perhaps we all have it to a degree, but when it's there, it's there. It's an important element in cabaret because people want to feel that closeness and that connection. In the trade, we refer to this as having a good bench-side manner.

I've seen some wonderful singers whose reserve has kept the audience at arm's length and prevented them both from being as responsive as they could be. One of Harry Connick's great strengths is that he knows how to get an audience going. Sometimes, even when the interpretations are not my favorites, he still gets the audience involved, and that is a marvelous gift.

Talking to the audience should be kept to the point as much as possible, although I give myself the freedom to wander occasionally because spontaneous interaction can sometimes yield wonderful results. There is always the risk of going too far, or just going on too long, but that's part of the excitement of a live show. When I do talk I try to do it with humor, maybe by finding funny anecdotes that relate to the song or the songwriters. It depends where I am in the act; when I sing "Love Is Here to Stay" and I talk about that number being the last song that George and Ira Gershwin wrote together, it's not at all humorous. That anecdote also gives the audience a wider perspective on the song and helps re-create the intense feelings that make it such a powerful expression of love. After I've told an anecdote, I can give a little bit of the marginalia, maybe a brief history of the song or some archival tidbit, but first and foremost I want to be entertaining. You can feel the audience get restless or uncomfortable if you go on too long, or if you say the wrong thing. It can be especially hard to recover from such a slip. Nothing is more unsettling to a performer than experiencing the collective gasp of an audience suddenly undone by something he or she has said. Sometimes a quick saving line will pop into your head on those occasions, but in most cases you have to start over again emotionally and rebuild the trust. Something like that happened at my 1994 Carnegie Hall concert when I talked about Katharine Hepburn's palsy and did an impression of her that seemed to go too far. I felt a wave of disapproval from the audience so strong that I had to comment on it. (Nor was I imagining things; the following week, I received two letters of complaint from audience members who thought my impression of Kate was in bad taste.) Later in the performance, I made a crack about Pavarotti's girth and that got a laugh. Then I remarked that I guessed it was okay to tease Pavarotti but not Miss Hepburn. Little by little, I got back in their good graces, but it was touch and go for a while.

Patter is very hard to teach and yet it makes a big difference. On nights when my patter isn't as coherent as it is on other nights, I sing the songs the same way but I don't get the same audience response because the continuity is gone. Even though there may not be a logical connection between one song and another, your attitude as a performer and the choice of words between the songs affect the whole performance as much as the interpretation of the numbers themselves.

Liza Minnelli believes that you have to be completely prepared in what you're going to say. Even though she can appear extremely spontaneous, she always knows word for word what she's going to say. When Barbra Streisand returned to performing recently, I went to see her opening night in Las Vegas on New Year's Eve. I was startled to see that her entire act was on the TelePrompTer, including very specific stage directions like "Move stage right." Because this was essentially a stadium setting, many people in the audience could see what was on the TelePrompTer, which certainly removed a lot of the spontaneity of the performance for those people. When I perform, I *never* know exactly what I'm going to say. Even though I've evolved certain things to say by way of introduction, I purposefully will not go over the specific introduction of a particular song, wanting to retain the spontaneity and hoping that maybe something fresh will pop into my head.

One of my favorite nightclub performers is Andrea Marcovicci, partly because what she says to the audience about songs is always clever and insightful and up to date. She is a great interpreter of lyrics, sometimes so much so that the melodies are overshadowed. You could say the same thing for Mabel Mercer or Bobby Short, but the connection with the words is what always gets me. People say it about me too sometimes, but remember, the interpretation is the thing. Whatever sends you. . . .

I hate to buck popular opinion, but I'm not crazy about Billie Holiday as a singer. I've always felt too much of her pain in her interpretations and that has gotten in the way of my enjoyment of the songs. Her singing has always seemed to me to be more about her than about the songs, even though I have never doubted her sincerity in interpreting the material. Ira didn't like Billie Holiday either, because she strayed too far from the melody and the lyric. I even had to fire a masseur once because he insisted on playing Billie Holiday records when he worked on me. Sorry, but "Gloomy Sunday" and "Strange Fruit" do not relax my body.

And your response to the particular timbre and feeling of an individual voice is even more important in cabaret. In a club or boîte, you really get a sense of the voice, the being, and the soul of a performer. It's the real thing—forget Coke. The sound of live music when you enter a club is energizing and invigorating (sometimes) in spite of a setting that, especially in jazz clubs, is often dark, gloomy, and the visual antithesis of beautiful sound. But it doesn't matter. You're there for the music, and nothing will ever be able to replace it. Nothing!

*P*LAYING Broadway and Carnegie Hall and all the other large concert venues around the country may be exciting and profitable compared with hanging out for an indefinite run at the local piano bar, but it has one major drawback: having to travel. I don't think I've ever given a bad show, although there have been times when I got sick on the road or was so exhausted that it was difficult to play well. But I'm lucky in that no matter how tired I feel, when I get out onstage, the music will usually revive me in one way or another. It's something I have come to trust. (One time, Sammy Davis Jr. was giving a concert in a Las Vegas showroom and wasn't feeling up to par. He sang a few songs, stopped, apologized to the audience, and announced that he would not continue. Most stars of his stature would have muddled through with a less than top-notch performance and collected their paycheck; Sammy offered to refund everybody's money out of his own pocket. That was an extraordinary gesture.)

In general, though, it's no fun for me to be on the road and be tired, knowing that I am my business and that I constantly have to consider my most insignificant action in the context of how it will affect my ability to perform. This is particularly true of my throat. If I don't get enough sleep, for instance, the first place it shows up is my throat. If I eat a certain kind of food, my throat can be affected. Certain grains or improper food combining can cause mucus. Cold drinks aren't good for the throat, nor is alcohol. Carbonated beverages can make you burp onstage, and dairy is always dangerous. Sometimes I will open a bottle or jar of something and sprain my hand a little bit and I'll think, Oh my God, I have to play the piano. People frequently ask me if my hands are insured. I usually reply half-jokingly that they're not and that if something happened, how nice it would be to have a break for a while. I know I should not affirm that kind of thought, but sometimes it seems as if that's the only way to get some time off.

Whenever I happen to encounter other performers—whether it's at a party, in the studio, or at some big benefit concert—the topic that seems to dominate our conversation is Tales of the Road. There's nothing we love more than running our favorite horror stories about which hotels to avoid, the problems of getting decent room service, the alarm clock that woke you up in the middle of the night, or the wake-up call that didn't come at all. Once I was staying at a hotel in London and the management sent a complimentary bottle of champagne to my room—at eight in the morning! It was in an ice bucket, all chilled and ready to go, but having gotten to sleep at about three A.M., I had a hard time appreciating their thoughtfulness.

On the road, things sometimes seem to conspire against you every step of the way. For instance, once again because of my throat, I have to stay in hotels with windows that open. Internal ventilation can be hell on the respiratory system. But hotels with windows that open are becoming increasingly hard to find, particularly in a place like Cincinnati, where a city ordinance does not allow windows that open in tall buildings. They say it's because of fire department regulations, but I think it's really to keep disgruntled performers from jumping.

A less tangible but more pervasive problem is the deep well of loneliness in which I often find myself when I'm on the road. (By the way, this is not to be confused with the scandalous 1920s lesbian novel by

Radclyffe Hall entitled *Well of Loneliness*.) I try to incorporate those feelings into the performances, but that's not always easy. And they can be exacerbated by the insomnia that comes from a change of time zones or climates. Sometimes there just isn't time to find the things I need to give a good performance in the few hours I may have between checking into the hotel and getting to the concert hall. That's why performers have riders to their contracts that contain their specific requirements for their stay and for their dressing room. Some performers have lavish riders that involve a gourmet chef cooking meals for a dozen people, specific kinds of candy bars, or bottles of Dom Perignon. My rider is a little more contained, yet it may seem just as absurd to someone who doesn't understand the context. For example, I ask for bottled Evian water because I have to have good, clean water that won't affect my throat, and Evian is a national brand that I know I can get almost anyplace. I don't really care if it's not Evian, as long as it's some kind of decent bottled water. I need six whole lemons so I can cut them in half and squeeze them for juice in case my throat gets raspy. Often they give me those little wedges of lemon for tea, and I say, "No, no, it says I have to have whole lemons." They look at me like I'm Nigel Tufnel of Spinal Tap complaining about the size of the sandwich bread on the hospitality platter. "Well," they say, "what's the difference?" The same thing happens with my requirement to have herbal tea. Sometimes they bring me black tea with herbal flavoring. But black tea has tannins and caffeine in it that dry out the throat. So I say, "No, no—that's not herbal tea." And they roll their eyes and think, Oh God, look at this one.

But a bigger problem for many singers is just remembering all those song lyrics. One night in Oyster Bay on Long Island, for instance, my encore was a song I wrote with Bob Merrill called "Half of April." I had sung every lyric flawlessly that night until I got to the line "I have always had a problem with time." I couldn't remember the next line, so I played a few arpeggios until it became apparent that the lull between the first and second lines had gone on too long. Finally I said, "And that's not all." The audience started laughing. "Yep," I said, "I wrote this and I can't remember the next line. Bob Merrill would not be happy."

People were laughing but then it suddenly got kind of quiet and I said, "Does anybody know the second line? For the life of me I can't think of it." A woman yelled out, "I could swear you said forever and a day."

"Thank you," I said. "We're going to start this over."

On another occasion, I couldn't remember the lyrics to "Isn't It Romantic?" I sang the opening phrase and I thought, Isn't *what* romantic? I was trying to find the lyric but, for all the times I've sung that song, I had just lost it.

People ask me, "How do you remember all those lyrics?" As if it's by some miraculous gift of memory. I always want to say, in my best John Housman voice, "I remember lyrics the old-fashioned way. I *learn* them." There's no big secret. As dull as it sounds, the way I first learn a lyric is by rote. Before I start working on the interpretation and the meaning of the words, I have to get it in my head so that it comes automatically. The reason for that is to allow for nervousness. If I memorize something in a calm state, that doesn't mean that I will know it when I'm onstage. I have to go an extra mile and be able to remember it under pressure, which requires more work.

One technique that helps is that as I'm memorizing each line or sequence of lines, I include the first word of the next line or sequence. For instance, "Oh, the barnyard is busy, / In a regular tizzy, / And the obvious reason / Is because of the season, / Ma. . . ." The next line is "Ma Nature's lyrical, / For her yearly miracle, / Spring, Spring, Spring." If my mind goes blank, at least I'll know the first word of the next line to lead me in. That's one method that I've developed, but I also sleep with the lyrics under my pillow and sometimes I play a tape at night as I'm going to sleep.

But it can be agonizing to learn song lyrics. If a lyric makes logical sense, if there's some continuity to it, even though it is a long or difficult lyric, you can learn it. Certain sorts of songs that don't have continuity, especially "list" songs, can be extremely trying. The most notorious example is probably Ira Gershwin's lyric for "Tchaikowsky (and Other Russians)," which Danny Kaye introduced (and which more or less introduced him) in *Lady in the Dark*. The list, which Ira composed from ads on the backs of sheet music, begins:

There's Malichevsky, Rubinstein, Arensky, and Tschaikowsky,
Sapelnikoff, Dimitrieff, Tscherepnin, Kryjanowsky

and goes on to name over three dozen more Russian composers. Now that's a memory tester. How do you know what the next line is going to be if you don't have it in your head? I discovered that in my 1988 Broadway gig, for which Marshall Barer wrote a parody of "Tchaikowsky" using the names of Broadway composers; it was brilliant and funny and I never got it right. I did it opening night, tried it three times, stopped all three times, and never got through the song. And I never attempted it again. That's the only time I can recall that I just could not finish a song onstage. I worked overtime on that thing, and I just couldn't get it in my head.

"The Dressing Song," written by Dr. Seuss, is a close second:

I want my undulating undies with the marabou frills.
I want my beautiful bolero with the porcupine quills.
I want my purple nylon girdle with the orange blossom buds,
'Cause I'm going do-mi-do-ing in my do-mi-do duds.
I want my organdy snood and in addition to that,
I want my chiffon Mother Hubbard made of Hudson Bay rat.

And so on. If you don't have that down cold, you can forget about it. In fact, you *will* forget it entirely and make a total fool of yourself onstage.

But I don't want to give anyone the impression that touring is all heartache and insomnia. I've had some experiences that I wouldn't trade for anything, and some that were thoroughly incongruous but that still make me laugh just thinking about them. Take the time I did the Royal Command Performance in London in 1988 and shared a dressing room with Jackie Mason and Julio Iglesias. The whole time we were backstage, Jackie Mason kept saying, "What's all this crap about the Queen? The Queen this, the Queen that. I meet plenty of queens. I perform for the B'nai B'rith and they're all queens."

As you can see, Jackie in person is just like his stage persona. "What do you think about all this?" he asked me.

"I'm excited about being part of this evening," I said.

"What?" he said. "To sing for some yenta with a crown?"

"Yes, I think it's a great honor," I said, which must have sounded like the height of naiveté to Jackie. Meanwhile, in the other corner of the dressing room, Julio Iglesias was desperately trying to relearn the words to "Begin the Beguine," because the Queen Mother had requested that he sing it. Julio hadn't sung it for a number of years and he was standing in the corner, playing a tape of the song on a Walkman with the earphones in his ears, trying to sing along. As Jackie ranted on about the Queen, suddenly I'd hear Julio going, "When they begin—Shit! When they begin the—Shit! Goddamn fuck shit!" Then he would stop, light up another cigarette—he was chain-smoking the whole time—and start again. "Begin the—Shit!" But when he got out onstage he was fine. I may not remember exactly what I sang that night, but I'll never forget what happened backstage.

Of course, I don't have to remember what I sang because I have critics to do that for me. It's not that I don't like critics, it's just that I haven't read my reviews since 1986. Part of the reason for that is that I have almost never read a critic who wrote anything about me, pro or con, that I felt was useful or illuminating in any way, and I've found that most performers feel the same. Rarely do performers read reviews of their own work that contain something genuinely helpful to them as performers or that are written without any sort of bias. Having met quite a few critics through the years, I have decided that I really mustn't be attached to what they say about me. Even when reviews were good, they often skewed or colored my assessment of my performance by drawing attention to something that made me self-conscious about it. They might give me an inflated ego about some aspect of my performance, which I do not find helpful.

I don't even read feature articles about myself anymore. In 1986, after I'd been at the Algonquin for several months, a critic named John Stark wrote a piece about me in *People* magazine that stopped me from reading anything else written about me. He quoted several things I said and put them in a context that was very biased, like, "Feinstein said this bitchily," which hurt my feelings. Shortly after that, I was sitting in an optometrist's office waiting for an appointment when I opened *People* and read a review of a Harry Connick program in which the same writer referred to Connick as "the thinking man's Michael Feinstein." Just what does that mean, exactly? Would he say that I'm the moron's Mel Tormé?

Until I can read a review without attachment to the writer's praise or criticism, I will not read it. That means that I probably will never read another review of myself again, which is fine, because I feel relieved of the responsibility. I was quite happy to realize that it was at least a week after my San Francisco Symphony concert before even the thought of a review popped into my head. It was a full house, the audience seemed to love the performance, and I felt good about what I had done. And that's the thing that I think most entertainers carry with them; we know when we've done a good job and we know when we're not pleased with ourselves. We know when the audience is happy and when the audience isn't happy. Those two things are what are most important to the performer—our own assessment of our work and the response of the audience. It was Leopold Godowsky the pianist who once said, "When I haven't practiced the piano for one day, I know it. When I haven't practiced for two days, my friends know it. When I haven't practiced for three days, the audience knows it. And when I haven't practiced for four days, the critics know it."

Then there was the famous line I originally heard attributed to the pianist Artur Schnabel but that has also been attributed to H. L. Mencken. It was in a letter responding to a critic and it went, "I am sitting in the smallest room of my house with your review in front of me. Soon it will be behind me."

Many people who are longtime theatergoers and readers of theater criticism lament the demise of intelligent theater criticism. Walter Kerr, for instance, always talked about how the audience liked a particular show or performance, even if he didn't like it himself. Then he would attempt to give some sort of constructive criticism; he was not a malicious critic. It is so easy for critics to be malicious, like John Simon, who has built his career on being nasty. He says he's writing criticism for the ages, yet he is clearly a very disturbed and unhappy man—and I mean that quite seriously. I canceled my subscription to *New York* magazine in 1977 because of a negative review he wrote of Liza Minnelli, long before I ever knew Liza and certainly before I knew that he was going to savage me eleven years later. His review of Liza in *The Act* focused almost entirely on her physical characteristics. So many people wrote letters complaining about what he had done that three weeks later he wrote another piece defending himself and saying that he was writing for the ages, that he wanted someone to be able to look back and read what it was *really* like at this moment in history. And then he went on to savage Liza further. His piece was accompanied by a caricature exaggerating her features. I've never read *New York* magazine since then. I simply refuse to support it. People sometimes say to me, "Oh, that awful John Simon! Did you see what he wrote about so-and-so?" I always say, "No. If you don't like him, why do you read him? Why do you buy *New York* magazine?"

A critic who was a huge fan of mine once wrote glowing reviews of my work for the now defunct Los Angeles *Herald Examiner*. And then a couple of years later he panned me brutally for a performance in L.A. By then I had stopped reading reviews, but I heard about it from a friend. Now I refuse even to have people tell me about reviews, because I don't want to know anything about them. Still, I was curious to know what could make someone turn from total approval to total revulsion. A friend of mine who knew this writer called him up. It turns out that the writer had met and dated a woman to my music during the time he was writing all those wonderful things about me. But just before he saw my most recent show, he had broken up with his girlfriend, and they had been separated for perhaps a week when the assignment came to review the touring version of my Broadway concert. So I paid for his broken heart. Along those lines, there was a notorious critic in San Francisco whose review largely determined the success or failure of a show. This guy was single and it got around that whether you got a good or bad review from him depended on whether he got laid that night. Whether the story is apocryphal or not, the arbitrariness of so many reviews might as easily be explained by that hypothesis as any other.

The most byzantine experience I've had with critics occurred in connection with a touring version of my Broadway concert, when I played Ford's Theatre in Washington, D.C. I was reviewed by the major theater critic for the *Washington Post*, a man who, for a time, served as chief theater critic for the *New York Times*. (That's perfect, because he was always referred to as the Frank Rich of Washington and then he became the Frank Rich of New York. Recently he left the *Times* to return to the *Post*, although not as drama critic.) This critic had previously given me very good reviews when I'd done nightclub performances in D.C., but he gave my touring show a very bad notice. Again, I didn't read it but everyone told me it was bad—people seem to love doing that, don't they? Having read other reviews of his, I could only imagine how bad it probably was. (I did see the headline of Howard Kissel's review of my Broadway show in 1988, however, in the New York *Daily News*. I couldn't avoid it as I was leafing through: "He's Fine, He's Nice, But So What?" I refer to his writing now as the Kissel of Death. I got the Kissel of Death.)

Shortly before my Ford's Theatre concert, the *Post* also assigned a writer named Joe Brown to do a Sunday profile on me. He had come up to New York while I was working on my album with Burton Lane, hung out, observed sessions, and did interviews; he then saw the show in Washington and liked it. When he turned in his piece to his editor, the same fellow who had given me the bad review, he read the piece and said, "There's one problem with it."

Joe said, "What's that?"

Brown had included one brief paragraph describing the show in rather complimentary terms. The editor told him that he would have to change his opinion of my performance so it would jibe with his review.

"But I don't agree with you," Joe said. "I liked his performance."

The editor insisted that the opinion of the paper had to be consistent and that Brown change what he had written so that it was not complimentary. He threatened Joe, but to his credit Joe held his ground and the piece ran the way he had written it. When I tell my friends this story, most of them find it unbelievable. Fellow performers, however, don't find it so hard to believe.

Having said that, I should add that I don't envy critics. They have a tough job and, as with entertaining or any work that places one in the public eye, the ego can run rampant and leave one living in a vacuum. The power of theater and music critics has gotten out of proportion because of the dwindling number of influential newspapers. There used to be fifteen or twenty newspapers in New York, not just the *Times* or a particular magazine ruling the success or failure of a show. Even so, I do believe that critics are doing a service to the audience by educating them, and I do enjoy reading certain critics myself.

I believe that some critics consciously write in word bites because they know that what they say can be extracted for a blurb in an ad. Other critics, like Stephen Holden, consciously avoid writing phrases that can be extracted in that way. I have talked to him after concerts by other performers that he said he enjoyed a great deal or even loved, and yet his enthusiasm was not necessarily reflected in his review the next day because he writes in a restrained style. This is clearly my own postulation, but it seems to me that he doesn't want his reviews to be extracted for advertisements and I respect him for that.

My other problem with critics is that they are not as well informed as they could be. Oscar Levant's favorite story about a critic resulted from a time he was playing a concert tour in the Midwest. He finished his concert and breathlessly came back onstage to do an encore because he had to leave to go to the next city. "I've got to catch a train," he announced, and then he sat down and played the Gershwin Second Prelude. The next day, the local paper said that Mr. Levant was particularly moving in an encore titled "I've Got to Catch a Train." When I was still reading reviews of my concerts, I was often startled to find mistaken information presented as fact. One reviewer, writing about an early show of mine, criticized me for not mentioning Bix Beiderbecke when I played "I Can't Get Started." He meant to say Bunny Berigan, who had the big jazz hit with that song. Well, their initials are the same and they both played trumpet, I guess.

I advise all performers not to read their reviews. Most performers I know who have been in the business for a long time don't read them anymore either. We don't have any responsibility to read them and it's probably better that we don't, because they can change our focus. I even have to alert people around me to the fact that I don't want to know my reviews. After I did the Greek Theatre in Los Angeles, my manager called me up and said, "God, you got a great review in the L.A. *Times*."

"But I told you I don't want to talk about reviews," I said. "I don't want to know."

"But, Michael," he said, "if it was a bad review, I wouldn't have said anything."

"That's the point," I said. "That means that the next time I play, if you don't say anything, I'll know it was a bad review."

But it's hard to avoid. After I signed a new recording contract with Atlantic Records, I was at their offices for a meeting when the publicist told me that they would be sending out reviews of my Carnegie Hall concert. "We'll be mailing copies of the reviews in the *Times* and the

News along with the press release." So I immediately knew that the *Post* must have given me a bad review. (But at least I didn't get the Kissel of Death.)

If I don't feel a responsibility to read my reviews, I do feel, as I said earlier, a very strong obligation to my audience. Although it's not possible to please everybody, I at least make an effort to respect them. That respect goes up to a point, however. The chemistry between an audience and a performer is a curious one because the performer wants the audience to love him or her and to love the concert. And Lord knows I'm grateful for my fans, because without them I'd have no career. But when you get offstage, you want to be left alone. I'll see the fans at the stage door, but then I want to say, "Okay, see ya later." So many people cannot separate the two, and I mean both performers and audiences. Lee Gershwin talked about visiting Judy Garland when Garland was staying at the Waldorf in New York. Lee said, "Let's go out and take a walk."

"I can't," Judy said. "I'll be mobbed."

"Oh, stop it, Judy," Lee said. "Don't be silly." They went downstairs and, sure enough, Judy was mobbed in the lobby. People started gathering and she couldn't get away from them. That's one thing that Liza *can* do, because she has grown up with celebrity. As she put it, "I was born and they took a picture." But Liza can go out anywhere and get through crowds. She has a kind of radar that allows her to zip by and get away from people and live her life, so she can go to the market, the theater, restaurants. When someone does come up to her, she's as slippery as a fish. She says, "Thank you," and she's nice and she moves on. If someone comes up to me, I can't get away. They start talking and I engage with them and I can't seem to detach. But if I'm with Liza, she'll just say, "Come on, Michael." And she moves on. That's a talent I admire.

*W*HEN anyone asks me who my earliest vocal influences were, the answer is always very easy: Al Jolson and Bing Crosby. As I listened repeatedly to the Jolson 78s in the basement of our home, his voice came through the grooves of the records in a way that electrified me at that young age. He died six years before I was born, and yet he remains one of the most vibrant and living figures I have ever encountered. When I first heard his voice, I was overwhelmed by the bravura and nerve and mournfulness, by the vaudevillian theatricality, and by the Jewishness of it. Even though Jolson didn't connect with his own Jewishness, it was a palpable presence in his voice. I knew that the Mammy songs he was singing were make-believe and a bit hokey, but the vitality and energy of the performances got to me in a visceral fashion. Even today, although the songs sound cornier still, I believe that people respond to them and forgive them because of the memories they evoke. The Jolson persona is so resilient that almost any singer can put a Jolson medley in his or her act and know that it will work—and we almost all do some Jolson, including me. Eddie Fisher was particularly carried away by an obsession with Jolson and patterned much of his career after him.

Jolson was a powerful influence on me beginning with the records he made in the late '40s after his comeback, when his voice was very deep. It wasn't until a number of years later that I discovered the early Jolson recordings that he had made in his prime and that sounded quite different. After I graduated from high school and was working as a dance accompanist at Ohio State University, one of the modern dance students approached me looking for something unusual with which to choreograph a dance sequence. I played her the Jolson records from the '20s and she created an entire sequence around them to great success with the students, who were captivated by a voice most of them had probably never heard before. Jolson persists because of that magical chemistry in his voice.

Everyone I've spoken to who saw Jolson live has said that, as amazing as he sounds on record, the recordings just don't compare with the live experience. Here's what humorist Robert Benchley wrote in *Life* magazine during Jolson's prime in the mid-'20s: "When Jolson enters, it is as if an electric current has been run along the wires under the seats where the hats are stuck. The house comes to a tumultuous attention. . . . He trembles his underlip, and your heart breaks with a loud snap. He sings a banal song and you totter out to send a night letter to your mother. Such a giving off of vitality, personality, charm, and whatever all those words are, results from a Jolson performance." George Burns and

Milton Berle said much the same thing, as did many people who had reason to despise the man personally but still could not resist what Jolson could do on the stage. Beyond his vocal power, his onstage movements were also very sexual; he swiveled his hips in a way that presaged Elvis Presley by a good forty years, something that is documented on the few films he made, as weak as most of them were. Electric, charismatic, ego-driven, Jolson was the epitome of the high-powered performer.

At the other end of the spectrum was Bing Crosby, cool, laid-back, the ultimate crooner. Bing remains an enigmatic character to most people. Louis Armstrong talked about how Bing never invited him to his home, although they had a very cordial relationship. Personally, I don't care if Crosby was a terrible father—I still love his records. His voice was like an instrument in the orchestra, the way he could bounce on top of a note. His rhythm was impeccable. In fact, I believe he was the greatest rhythm singer of the century. Just listen to the phrasing on any of the hundreds of records he made with jazz backing; the natural way he felt the tune was unparalleled. Crosby fooled with the melody more than many other singers, and yet it rarely bothers me, because it never seems forced or merely for the purpose of bravado as it does with Sinatra. The records with all the pickup bands and studio bands of the early '30s can sometimes be over the top, but they are also among my favorite recordings because they are unfettered by the affectations that came upon him later.

The thing that most intrigues me about Crosby is his change of style through the decades, his ability to survive and to sing every kind of song by adapting it to suit his voice. He recorded everything from hillbilly songs to Victor Herbert operetta, from opera to children's songs, Hawaiian and Irish songs, and songs for every holiday known to humanity. The trashiest pop songs he sang were often hits on the radio. He made it a point to look and sound like everything was off the cuff, yet he worked extremely hard. Jimmy Cagney discovered that one time when they were working together. Bing seemed to be hardly exerting himself at all, until Cagney put his arm around him and realized that Crosby was drenched in sweat.

Crosby's early recordings, the ones from the '20s with Paul Whiteman, are different from the ones he was making in the early '30s, just as *those* are different from his recordings at the end of the '30s. He kept changing with the times and I don't even think that it was a conscious decision. He just took each song as it came. He was largely regarded as the first singer to use the microphone in a way that was intimate, becoming the first real crooner and, in that respect, an important figure in the evolution of male popular singing.

For me as I was growing up, Jolson and Crosby divided the world between them. I don't recall being aware of any other voices in the same way that I was of those two. Later, of course, I was influenced by Fred Astaire, although when I first heard his voice, it was rather uninteresting to me. As I discovered more about interpreting lyrics, though, he grew on me, especially his way of delivering a lyric clearly. Later still, Ethel Waters was a genuine revelation. She had a rare combination of theatricality and blues feeling; her performances of standards blended the two elements so that one was never a detriment to the other. And like Astaire, Waters enunciated every lyric in a way that brought out the meaning of whatever she was singing. You got it the moment she started singing it. That fusion of clarity with an almost ferocious energy was extremely captivating.

As I continued to grow musically, I began to relish the other flavors and colorings in the world of song, like the bluesy voices of Ella Mae Morse and Margaret Whiting. Even as I worked my way toward the more mainstream singers of the genre—Tony Bennett, Jack Jones, Andy Williams, Perry Como—I continued to be influenced mainly by the older style of singers, not only Jolson and Crosby but also Buddy Clark and Russ Colombo. Maybe it's because the recordings that I first listened to, which are the ones I still enjoy the most, were all from the '30s and '40s. Whatever it was, I've never lost my deep-seated connection to the singers and the songs of that era.

But as a relative newcomer to the world of cabaret, it's fitting that I say a few words about some of the modern legends in the field. Perhaps because of his longevity, Bobby Short is considered the father of modern cabaret performing. He was championing the obscure songs of the great songwriters as well as singing the great standards in respectful and authentic versions long before it became fashionable to do so. Bobby started performing as a child in Hollywood clubs, where he gained plenty of experience; he still has an encyclopedic knowledge of popular song that is equaled by very few people. Beyond that, he's an extremely nice man who is quite generous with other performers.

I had not heard Bobby Short's albums in my teens, but when I was twenty or so, a friend discovered some in a record shop in New York and brought them back to Columbus. At first, Bobby's voice sounded rather peculiar to me, as it probably does to most people on first hearing. But then I began to warm to its unique quality, largely because of both the intelligence of the interpretations and the jazz influences in his singing. He's a terrific pianist to boot, something that is greatly underestimated because people are so busy listening to his voice that they usually don't hear his piano.

One thing that confuses me about Bobby, though, is that he puts up with often intolerably noisy audiences at the Carlyle Hotel. I don't understand why. When George Shearing or Eartha Kitt or any number of top-flight performers play the Carlyle, the audience is quiet and respectful. But when Bobby is there, people frequently chatter away and he never says a word about it. He has a charmingly self-deprecating way of calling himself a saloon singer, and so maybe the audience takes him literally. Or maybe it has just been that way for so many years that he's used to it and it doesn't bother him. Mind you, it never affects his performance.

The other side of the coin is that Bobby has enjoyed great longevity with the jet set and the swellest of swells. The richest folks have always adopted Bobby as their own and, indeed, he still is very much a part of those circles and a very important element in their social lives. He certainly went through a bit of a shaky period before becoming a fixture at the Carlyle, but he has endured, not only because of the songs but also because of his integrity. He is a rare human being.

I met Mabel Mercer on only one occasion and found her to be a very sweet woman who seemed vexed by the constant references to her having a queenly aura. She was not at all like that in person. Early recordings of Mabel Mercer reveal her to have had a high soprano voice, which I was staggered to discover. Most of her more recent recordings are half-sung, half-spoken interpretations that are very effective but, like Bobby Short's, take some getting used to. It was rather disconcerting to come upon those later records first, not having heard her live, and to wonder how she got such a grand reputation. Frank Sinatra, of course, always credits Mabel Mercer as one of the major influences on his ability to interpret a lyric. I asked him about that one night and he acknowledged that he used to go hear Mabel regularly, adored her work and was greatly affected by her. Liza Minnelli told me that when she was just a little girl, her father took her to hear Mabel. Liza turned to her father and said, "I don't understand, Daddy. I don't understand." And he said, "Shhh, listen to the words." That's how Liza learned to listen and to interpret lyrics. Her father always treated her as an adult in certain fundamental ways.

Yet many people are not fans of Mabel Mercer—a famous Broadway composer among them. When Mabel had a milestone birthday coming up, her manager, Donald Smith, sent a letter to the composer, asking if he had something that he'd like to say about Mabel Mercer, who at that time was giving what was considered the definitive interpretation of the composer's most famous song. He responded, "I have absolutely nothing to say about Mabel Mercer." I admit that I don't always enjoy listening to her records myself if I'm not in the proper mood. They can be pretty rocky going, but Mabel still has the rare ability to take a very familiar song and make it fresh again. My favorite album of hers is the Cole Porter songbook with Stan Freeman and Cy Walter at the piano.

Julie Wilson has a similar ability to make me hear anew some Cole Porter songs that I thought I hated until she sang them. For many years, Julie was considered essentially a singer of spicy material. She was one of those sexy broads who was supposed to sing only a certain kind of sultry and suggestive song lyric. But years later, she started to sing ballads and got into the songbooks of the great composers; now she is hailed as one of the great interpreters of classic American songwriters. That is something none of her early audiences could have possibly predicted.

It's no secret to anyone who knows me that my favorite living interpreter of American popular song is Rosemary Clooney. Some people ask me why, as if they just don't get it. Why Rosie above all others? Just listen, I say. I try to explain that there is something about the sound of her voice that touches me deeply, that affects me in a way that is not intellectual but goes right to my heart center. She has the quintessentially warm and comforting sound and I stop being fully rational when I talk about her. It wasn't until the age of twenty-one that I first became an admirer of hers; before that, I had known only some of her hits for Columbia, like "Come on-a My House," "Botch-A-Me," and "Mambo Italiano," songs that made very little impact. But once again as I became more aware of lyrics and lyricists, I began to understand why she was so great. During the time I worked for Ira, I became personally acquainted with Rosemary, who happened to be Ira's next-door neighbor. Frequently after I left Ira's house at the end of the day, I would stop by Rosemary's to visit. "What did Ira say today?" she would ask. And then she would proceed to amplify his suggestions and comments about my singing, allowing me to get a more rounded picture of how songs could be interpreted. Rosemary was particularly helpful to me when I started recording. On my first album, she joined me for a duet of George and Ira's obscure but wonderful "Isn't It a Pity?"

"Honey," she said, "smile when you sing. You'll hear it on the recording."

That made a huge difference in my approach. But I've also learned a lot about interpreting songs just from listening to Rosemary perform. One night, she was singing "Bewitched (Bothered and Bewildered)," which I'd heard a million times. There's a couplet in the verse that goes, "Love is not a new sensation, / I've done pretty well, I think." Those lines are always more or less thrown away, but this night, Rosemary sang it and took a little pause toward the end of the phrase: "I've done pretty well . . . I think." The freshness of the idea bowled me over, the way she discovered an element of ambiguity that may have always been lurking in that lyric but that I'd never heard before. When a singer does something like that—as Julie often does and Mabel Mercer did—they help you more fully appreciate the richness of the material.

Experience is the best teacher when it comes to interpreting lyrics, although I remember Liza Minnelli telling me that she grew up listening to all of the Ella Fitzgerald songbooks of different composers' works. Those songbooks were her constant companions as she traveled with her mother from place to place, and so by the age of eleven or twelve, she was relating to the lyrics expressed in many of those songs simply based on hearing them over and over. Although Liza's experience is somewhat atypical, most of us have probably been captivated by songs that had a lyrical impact on us before we were old enough to have experienced what the lyrics were actually describing.

Yet experience isn't always kind, I'm afraid, and plenty of fine performers have retired to Florida or otherwise removed themselves from the spotlight rather than continue the touring grind. Among my favorites are Murray Grand, Charles DeForest (who wrote "When Will the Bells Ring for Me?"), and Bart Howard, who used to play piano for Mabel Mercer (and wrote "Fly Me to the Moon"). It's always thrilling to hear them play. Stan Freeman is in a dazzling class by himself and won't play unless the situation is artistically exciting for him or he's getting a ton of money. Between retirement and death, many of the legends of cabaret have disappeared. For some of them, retirement *is* death but others have just had enough and given it up. The burnout rate can be very high.

Fortunately, the ranks of cabaret continue to be refreshed with new recruits who are wise enough not to listen to people like me who tell them what a hard row they'll have to hoe. Among the more recent arrivals, I especially love Weslia Whitfield, who struggled for years in San Francisco and couldn't get a gig in New York because of the snobbism of the cabaret world there (something I learned firsthand when *I* tried to land a job). I finally helped get her a gig at the Algonquin and hosted her opening night. She has since had great reviews and now plays there regularly. It's wonderful to see that happen and it's gratifying that other people recognized her talent right off. Nancy LaMott is another very talented singer who should be more widely known. She can invest a lyric with all kinds of emotional depth and richness without taking liberties; if anything, she simplifies a piece until the essence of the song emerges.

And what about Jeff Harner and Philip Officer and K. T. Sullivan and many, many others? I wonder what's going to happen to them. There are so many gifted performers and, unfortunately, fewer and fewer places for people who do cabaret exclusively. Cabaret singers are becoming an endangered species, despite the fact that people still want to experience that sound. San Francisco used to have plenty of clubs; now it has only a couple. L.A. is hopeless and even New York, which remains the world capital of cabaret, is becoming somewhat dicey. Curiously enough, although the remaining cabaret rooms tend to be rather expensive, most people in the field have to struggle to survive. There's good money at the top but the audience there is not large enough to support anything like the hundreds of performers who make a comfortable living playing rock 'n' roll or country music. Maybe as the baby boom generation grows older and less tolerant of loud music, they will discover cabaret and its economics will improve. Meanwhile, I've had to accept the fact that the music I love makes up a very small slice of the marketplace.

And that is shameful, because the intimacy of cabaret is unbeatable. I love playing large venues, but there's something about the closeness of cabaret that is wonderful when it works. If you can handle the drunks and the people making noise and the waiters banging glasses and plates on the table, the bad sound systems, poor lighting, and lousy pianos—if, as performer or listener, you can get past all that to the right club on the right evening, then there is little you will ever find to compare to the pleasures of a night of cabaret. Maybe life isn't a cabaret, but cabarets certainly have brought a lot of life and joy to those lucky enough to inhabit them.

*M*AYBE it's all George Gershwin's fault, but for some reason whenever a pianist is invited to a party, people expect him, or her, to perform. At least, the hostess often does. Nobody would dream of asking Baryshnikov to toss off a few entrechats for their amusement or demand that Jason Robards deliver his famous soliloquy from *The Iceman Cometh.* Saxophonists don't face the same problem because there usually isn't a spare horn lying around. (Have you seen the Gary Larson cartoon about Why Accordion Bars Didn't Work? It shows a guy playing the accordion surrounded by patrons sitting on stools in a circle holding their drinks in their laps.)

But if there's a piano in the house, I can be pretty certain that the hostess will ask me, either directly or indirectly, to "play a little." "A little" means an hour or two, including requests. In those situations, I resolutely refuse to play unless I actually want to. I admit that I've been intimidated into playing on occasion because the hostess was so insistent or had set it up in a way that I couldn't refuse, but it always makes me extremely uncomfortable. (And I somehow don't feel even the slightest twinge of guilt for entertaining visions of the host or hostess sinking forever in a pool of quicksand or being devoured by piranhas. They deserve to, dammit.) Stan Freeman told me that if he's going to a place where he's certain to be asked to play, he often bandages one of his arms. ("Oh, I had a slight accident. My razor slipped when I heard you were going to ask me to perform.")

It's always the ultrarich who ask you to play unexpectedly; they're the ones who won't take no for an answer. I just say, "No, thank you. I really don't feel like it." Sometimes they lose their edge of politeness and say, "All these people want to hear you play." Then I raise my voice and say, "NO, I DON'T FEEL LIKE IT. THANK YOU!" I was at a party at the home of Ann Getty when she came up to me and said, "We'd love it if you'd play tonight."

"You know," I said, "there's a time and a place for everything, and this is neither the time nor the place." She was very nice about it and retained her composure, always the perfect hostess, but I don't know if she understood how I felt. Some people invite you under the pretense that they want you to be there for your own scintillating self, but all the time they want you to play for them without going through the inconvenience of actually *hiring* you. Then they probably complain to their friends at lunch the next day how ill-mannered you were in refusing. And I agree; it's just so hard to get good help these days.

When I started to play Beverly Hills parties professionally, I was frequently asked to use the service entrance. "We want you to be a surprise for our guests," was one hostess's rationalization, but it was still about being hired help. In those days, people often invited me in the hopes that I would bring Ira Gershwin. "Can Ira come to the party, too?" they would ask casually. This at a time when Ira was lucky if he made it downstairs.

I once played a party for a Hollywood producer who had a grand piano made entirely of Lucite. He was very proud of his piano. "It's one of a kind," he said.

"Are you sure Liberace doesn't have one?" I asked, but the joke went over his head. This man gave A, B, and C list parties with very different guest lists, and this particular party was strictly B list. He paid me very little money, but I agreed to play because he was so influential. I had also heard that his house was extraordinary and I was anxious to see it. I wasn't disappointed. He had a disco on the lower level that was decorated in Egyptian motif, with gold statues everywhere. He also had an alarm system rigged in such a way that if terrorists tried to kidnap him, he could push a button and security doors would go up and he would be hermetically sealed in his bedroom. Which, as I think about it now, probably would have been to the betterment of humanity. At the end of the party, he put me through my paces, asking me to play Rachmaninoff, then some Spanish music, some Ellington, and so on down the list. I managed to fake my way through the things I wasn't quite sure of and he bought it all. Finally he said, "I've enjoyed very much the way you played tonight. As you know, I throw a lot of A list parties and I would like you to be the pianist at all my parties. But, of course, because it would be so good for your career, I'd expect you to do them for free."

My response was that I had done enough things that were good for my career, and now I was working for money. He never hired me again.

I used to play for one philanthropist who donated money to different charities for tax purposes. After I had finished playing for one of his parties, he said, in front of his guests, "Michael, I'd like to remind you of one thing: Man does not live by bread alone."

"Obviously not," I said as I gestured at all the valuable objects surrounding us, including paintings by Cézanne, Degas, and Manet. This man later became angry after I raised my regular price by a hundred dollars. On another occasion, I had to play a party for Burger King's top executives—in their flagship restaurant, the largest Burger King in America. Unfortunately, it was located in the skid row area of downtown Los Angeles, so hundreds of people were emerging from their limos in formal dress in the worst part of town. I did my concert variations on "Hold the Pickle, Hold the Lettuce." At least they didn't serve burgers. ("I'd like a Whopper with everything on it and, oh, Michael, do you know 'Mad Dogs and Englishmen'?")

I often play at parties at which the host has had some elaborate musical centerpiece created. When I finished playing at one gathering a couple of years ago, the hostess offered me the dessert, which was a chocolate grand piano. I refused to eat it because it wasn't a Baldwin, and I'm an exclusive Baldwin artist.

One night I was playing at the home of a well-known society matron who shall here go nameless. As a matter of fact, she'd be better off if she always went nameless. The year was 1983, and *La Cage aux Folles* had just opened. "Oh, *La Cage aux Folles* is simply marvelous," she gushed to me when I sat down at the piano. "You must play some songs from it!" She started mingling with her guests and then came back over to the piano a half hour later. "Have you played any of the songs from *La Cage* yet?" she asked.

"Yes," I said, "I've been playing them for quite some time."

"Oh, I haven't heard the score," she said, "so I wouldn't know them." She just knew that it was the big hit of the moment and, therefore, she had to have songs from *La Cage* played at her home. When people want to seem sophisticated, they generally request Cole Porter. "Will you play some Cole Porter?" they ask. "Sure," I say. "What Porter song would you like?" And many times they can't name one. They just like the *idea* of Cole Porter. (But hey, it could always be worse. I could have grown up showing a talent for, say, cross-dressing. My best friend in junior high school did and, come to think of it, he's now a successful lawyer and very happily married. I wonder if his wife knows.)

After playing a lot of Beverly Hills parties early in my career, I began to get a little jaded and wasn't so easily impressed by lavish homes and big-name celebrity gatherings. And then, of course, there are the Annenbergs. Walter Annenberg, who made his fortune publishing *TV Guide*, the *Philadelphia Inquirer*, and the *Daily Racing Form*, among others, and his wife, Lee, give some of the all-time most lavish parties for the Beverly Hills power elite. Their two-hundred-acre estate in Rancho Mirage, California, near Palm Springs, is equipped with its own golf course and landing strip. Where the Annenbergs live, most of the streets are named after famous entertainers; it's the only place where, when you hear people mention celebrities, you don't know whether they're dropping names or giving directions.

The first time I was invited to play for the Annenbergs, it was during the Reagan presidency and Ron and Nancy were staying there. I was to play cocktail music from six until dinnertime, and after dinner I was to come back to play some solo numbers and entertain, followed by a sing-along. I started to play the theme from *Dr. Zhivago*, which was not a particular favorite of mine but which Annenberg forcibly requested, as he did most songs. As I played it, President Reagan drifted over to the piano. "You know," he said in that affable drawl of his, "I think that that theme song had a lot to do with the success of that film."

I nodded sagely. "I would have to agree with you, Mr. President," I said. When I finished it, I said, "Do you know this one?" I immediately launched into the theme from *Kings Row*, his 1942 Warner Brothers movie. It's not that I've made a study of Reagan movie themes, but that one is by Erich Korngold and I happen to love his music. As I started to play it, Reagan looked at me with his trademark blank expression. I played it for quite a while and then, as if he were on *The $64,000 Question*, he snapped his fingers and said, "That's *Kings Row*." Then he yelled across the room, "Nancy, he's playing *Kings Row!*"

After that, Reagan couldn't get enough piano music. He stayed around and I played some Irving Berlin songs, whereupon he repeated the Irving Berlin anecdote I related earlier about recording "Oh, How I Hate to Get Up in the Morning" for *This Is the Army*. Reagan claimed that he was actually present at the recording session and had observed that exchange firsthand. I doubt that very much because there's no reason for an actor to have been at a recording session for Irving Berlin, especially since Reagan didn't sing in the movie.

If I had any lingering doubts about who was really running the country, they were cleared up the second time I played at the Annenbergs'. After the show, I needed to call a car to pick me up because they had not provided transportation for me. I asked Walter if I could use the phone and he said sure. I walked in the direction he pointed and stopped when I came to an old-looking phone with a rotary dial on it. I thought, Walter Annenberg can't afford a touch-tone phone? I picked up the phone and before I could dial, I heard a click and a ring and someone at the other end picked up. A serious voice said, "White House." I had mistakenly picked up the hot line to the White House. "Excuse me, wrong number," I stammered, and hung up the phone. That's when I saw the touch-tone phone that I was supposed to use on the next table. I wonder if the line is still connected to the Clinton White House.

However, my most memorable evening at the Annenbergs' is one I'd rather forget. I arrived around two in the afternoon, preparing to play for their New Year's Day gathering. Ronnie and Nancy were there, of course, among other celebrity guests. Lee Annenberg greeted me and said, "Michael, guess who's coming to dinner tonight?"

"Sidney Poitier?"

"No, no," she said. "Andrew Lloyd Webber."

"Oh," I groaned.

"What's the matter?"

"I'm not a huge fan of his work," I said. "Some of his early things were very good. I liked *Jesus Christ Superstar*, but I think a lot of his later stuff is not top-notch."

"Well," she said, ignoring this, "we want you to play something of Andrew's for him."

"Honestly," I said, "I don't know anything of his, so I couldn't play it."

"Can you do anything from *Phantom of the Opera*?" she asked. It had just opened in London but hadn't yet come to the States.

"No," I said, relieved. "I haven't heard it."

"That's all right," she said. "I'm going to play you the tape so you can learn something." It was still several hours before the party would begin. I explained that it doesn't work that way, that I could not just listen to the tape and learn a song of his by ear in a few hours.

"I insist," she said. "There's one song that you'll love. It's a wonderful song and I'm sure you'll be able to pick it up." Nancy Reagan was sitting nearby, observing this exchange. When Lee Annenberg went into the house to get a cassette player, Nancy turned to me and said sarcastically, "Oh, great. Now we have to listen to *this* epic."

Lee returned and played me one of the songs from *Phantom*. "Well?" she asked eagerly.

"I don't think I'm going to be able to do it," I said. "Please don't ask me to play anything of his tonight, because I don't want to create an embarrassing situation." If I had been told in advance that he was going to be there, I might have been able to prepare something at the hosts' request, but even then I doubt I would have done it with much enthusiasm.

Later that night, after dinner, I played a set of songs. Webber's former wife, Sarah Brightman, is a delightful woman and couldn't have been nicer when I was playing. She sat right by the piano and applauded and nodded encouragement to me all the way through my little performance. Lloyd Webber, on the other hand, was in the back of the room with his arms crossed, pretending I didn't exist, until Walter Annenberg got up to make an announcement. "Ladies and gentlemen," Annenberg said, "we are very delighted to have the distinguished company of

Andrew Lloyd Webber and his wife, Sarah Brightman. And in their honor, we would like Michael Feinstein to play a song of Mr. Webber's."

Oh shit, I thought, what am I gonna do? Lloyd Webber had walked slightly forward but still kept a respectable distance from the piano with his arms crossed, looking at me rather imperiously. He was probably angry that I hadn't been playing his songs earlier. Then I remembered that in my piano bar days, I used to play "Don't Cry for Me, Argentina." So I announced with relief, "I would like to play 'Don't Cry for Me, Argentina' from *Evita*. But I'd like to apologize in advance if I 'go up' on some of the words, because it's been a long time since I've played the song."

I started to play and got through the first verse and chorus all right. I got into the second verse—"And as for fortune and as for fame. . . ." I couldn't think of the next line. I vamped a little, then I looked over at Lloyd Webber and said, "Can you help me?"

And he said very angrily, "I didn't write the lyrics!"

That night at the Annenbergs' was rivaled for sheer deflation only by a party I played one Christmas at the home of Marvin Davis. Marvin and his wife, Barbara, have always been very kind to me and they really know how to throw a party. Their Hollywood Christmas party is usually *the* party to be invited to, and I was the entertainment that year. As I arrived, I learned that the previous year, Peter Allen had entertained and had stormed off the stage because everybody talked through his entire performance. Undaunted, I sat down at the piano and began to play. Everywhere I looked, I saw familiar faces—from Johnny Carson to Bette Midler to Dinah Shore to Clint Eastwood to George Burns. Anyone you can imagine in show business was there in that room. And almost all talked through my entire performance. It was the worst feeling I have ever had, sitting down in front of everyone I'd ever dreamed of meeting and entertaining and barely being able to make myself heard above the din.

I decided to stay focused on the music and just sing the songs, which turned out to be the right thing to do. Mrs. Davis had specifically asked me to play certain songs and she sat up close and was happy. But I have found that in many instances, a Hollywood industry gathering can be the worst audience because they have the attitude that they've seen it all before and so they don't have to listen. Entertainment? That's for the masses. These folks have a heightened awareness of the process of performing; for them to sit and listen and applaud at the end means that in some way they've been taken in by the artful deception that they spend their lives trying to perpetrate on others.

I should add that most of these people can be quite civil when I meet them offstage, although even then they find little ways to let me know I'm not as famous as I might prefer to imagine. Like the night I hosted a gala tribute to Alan Jay Lerner and ran into Gary Collins at the party afterwards. "You were wonderful tonight, Harvey," he said.

Yes, it's true. Many people, even celebrities, frequently think that I wrote *Torch Song Trilogy*. Or they have some skewed idea that *Torch Song Trilogy* was a musical and that I sang in it. I once even got flowers that were intended for Harvey Fierstein. Sometimes a young man will come up to me and tell me that he took his parents to see *Torch Song Trilogy* and thank me for having given him the opportunity to expose them to it.

This happens frequently, even though Harvey and I couldn't look or sound any more unalike than we do. Harvey even pronounces his name Fire-STEEN—which brings up another common occurrence. A flight attendant once came over to me with the manifest of passengers' names and smiled broadly.

"Mr. Fein-STEEN?"

"It's Fein-STINE," I said.

"It's usually pronounced Fein-STEEN," she said. "Isn't it?"

"No," I said. "My name's Michael Fein-STINE."

"But it's spelled just like the entertainer, Michael Feinsteen," she said.

"I *am* the entertainer," I said.

"Michael Feinsteen," she said conclusively.

"No. Michael Fein-STINE."

"So you don't pronounce it the same as the entertainer," she said.

"I *AM* the entertainer!"

"Well, I'm a big fan and I have all of his tapes," she said triumphantly, "and it's Fein-STEEN." She got a little huffy and walked away. Later in the flight I was somehow able to communicate to her that I was the entertainer she loved so much and that I pronounce my name Fein-STINE. "I'm so sorry," she said. "I've never seen you in person before. You're sure it's not Feinsteen?"

Fans sometimes say very strange things to me or have memories of things that did not happen. Like the woman who came up to me and said, "Oh, we saw you for years at the Algonquin. We went there every year you were there. We must go back ten years with you."

"Thank you," I said, "but I only played there twice, in 1986 and 1987."

"Oh, no," she said. "We saw you at least ten years ago the first time. And we went every year."

You can't even argue with someone like that. I used to try to set them straight and then I realized that it was futile. Not long ago after a concert, two women approached me at the stage door. "Hi, remember us?" they said. I didn't.

"Can you refresh my memory?"

"We met you at the St. Moritz. Remember? You were playing there and we kept asking you to play 'New York, New York' and you said, 'I don't play "New York, New York." ' "

"I've never played at the St. Moritz," I said.

"Oh, of course you did," one of them insisted. "Don't you remember? That's why we came to the concert tonight—because you said if we ever saw you playing somewhere, to come backstage and say hello."

"I've never played at the St. Moritz," I repeated.

She looked at her friend and winked, as if to say, "Oh, he doesn't want to admit that he played there."

"Maybe it was the Algonquin," I offered.

"No, no, no. This was the piano bar at the St. Moritz."

"Fine," I said. "Then you met my twin, but I was never there."

Richard Deacon, the character actor, used to tell me that people often came up to him with that gleam of recognition in their eyes and ask his name. He would reply, "Richard Deacon."

"No, no," they would say. "That's not it."

Worse than that is when someone says, "I saw you, now let me think where." And they hold you captive while they try to remember where they saw you perform. "It was at . . . well, was it 1987 or 1989? I know it was in Chicago and I think it was. . . ." Until they remember where they saw me, I have to stand there and wait for their memory to improve. That's when I wish Liza were there to say, "Come on, Michael. Let's go!"

But maybe these folks are just mistaking me for Larry Brendler. A

friend once sent me an ad from a newspaper showing a picture of a
guy with a multicolored bow tie and, underneath, the following:

LARRY BRENDLER
the Michael Feinstein of Miami Beach.
Album available now.
Selections include "Great Balls of Fire,"
"Memory" from *Cats*, "The Wind Beneath My Wings,"
"New York, New York."

Some piano bar performers have told me that people frequently go up
to them and say, "Do you know any Michael Feinstein?" They don't ask
for Gershwin, they want to hear Feinstein. I believe them because people often come up to me and say, "Do you know any Bobby Short?"
One night I was talking to a guy who said, "Boy, that Bobby Short. I
hear he has a lot of charisma."

"Yes, he does," I said.

Then the man added, with the assurance of a broker offering a solid
stock tip, "I understand that you have charisma of your own."

*B*UT what good is charisma if you never get to spend it?

Every once in a while, as I'm racing around from job to job, something happens in my life that reminds me where all this musical knowledge fits into the workaday world outside the rarefied confines of the
Oak Room and the Café Carlyle. One event that stands out in my memory took place a few years ago as I was driving back to my home in
the Hollywood Hills. It was about two o'clock on a Sunday morning and
I was absorbed in plans for my impending trip to New York later that
day. I wasn't at all prepared to make the trip—I had too many things still
left to do at home and too many loose ends to think about. As all the
various bits of chatter spun around in my brain, I grew more and more
irritated. For one thing, I didn't have any travel money in my pocket
and had barely enough time to get home, sleep a few hours, and be up
in time to get to the airport. Then I remembered the ATM located in a
7-Eleven on my route. Of course. What could be simpler?

A few minutes later, I pulled into the parking lot and suddenly felt
very conspicuous. Half a dozen street people in various states of alert-

ness were hanging out in front of the store, and the ones who seemed most awake were also most intent on observing me as I drove up and parked. They were all in pretty bad shape—a couple asleep on the sidewalk, another squatting sullenly against the wall, one guy poised with a squeegee and a bottle of nondescript liquid, talking and singing to himself. My knee-jerk response was to pull away and avoid the peculiar urban mixture of danger, sympathy, and guilt implicit in the whole tableau in front of me. But I needed to get cash and I didn't know of another ATM on the way home. Practicality dictated that I just be cool and hang in there.

I tried to let my paranoid thoughts wash past me and drift away, even as my logical mind devised a game plan to enter and leave the store with a minimum of contact. I would glide quietly and nonchalantly by, looking somehow alert yet absorbed in thought, making no eye contact. Drawing a deep breath, I exited my car. Alas, my game plan dissolved immediately, as the guy with the squeegee fixed me in his hollow gaze and asked if I'd like my windows washed. Glancing back nervously at my car, a beat-up '82 Mazda, I saw that the windows were filthy indeed. (Lately, I had been neglecting my car, which was in serious need of replacement. Every time I was tempted to have it washed, I'd tell myself not to bother because I was going to get a new one any day now. This had been going on for months.) Squeegee was ready to go for the windows but I just didn't see the point. "No, thank you," I said with a smile. "But I'll give you something on my way out." If the car's still there, I thought. He smiled back with a distracted "Cool, man."

I strode purposefully to the cash machine, looking back over my shoulder to see if any of the crowd outside were watching me. They all were. The possibility of robbery now loomed. My fatigue only added to my nervousness, and my hand was trembling as I gathered in the pile of bills that spewed from the machine. I walked to the cash register and got change for a twenty. Securing the rest of my money in an inside front pocket, I kept a dollar bill in my hand as I made my move outside. I walked straight up to Squeegee and handed him the buck. He seemed overwhelmed and his whole demeanor changed. He offered a grateful thanks and drifted away smiling. I quickly opened my car door as I looked around for other denizens of the night.

I was feeling marginally more relaxed now and it was at that moment that an amazing thing happened. I've described my car as being rather dirty and ordinary looking, but it does have one distinguishing feature: a vanity license plate that reads SWNDRFL. It was given to me by Ira Gershwin in 1982. I had asked him if he'd mind my getting a plate with those letters on it and he had laughed and said that if I could find three people who even knew what it meant, he'd buy the plate for me. As it turned out, the first three people I asked—a couple of friends of mine and one of Ira's—got it immediately, and I got my gift license plate. But few people outside of Ira's circle have any idea what it means or else they misread it altogether. I was visiting Elizabeth Taylor one day and my car was parked just inside her gate. While I was there, a Bel Air security guard phoned Liz to see if she was all right. He said he was concerned because he had spotted a car parked in her driveway with a license plate that read SWINDLER.

As I was about to close the door and put my key in the ignition, the guy I'd seen earlier squatting against the wall came over with a curious look pointing to the front of my car. I braced myself. "Your license plate says ' 'S Wonderful,' don't it?" he said with genuine surprise. "That's a Gershwin song."

I did a double take. This guy, who from all appearances was living on the street and begging for money and who, a moment ago, had appeared more than a little crazy and menacing, suddenly transformed my experience of paranoia into one of connection with another soul. My fear and anxiety dissipated in that moment. I got back out of the car and closed the door behind me.

"I can't tell you what it means to me that you said that," I said. He smiled at me and I smiled back. We stood there for a moment, silently enjoying the chance connection. As I pulled out of the parking lot a moment later, I waved to the guys, who now seemed friendlier and a lot less frightening. A couple of them waved back and I drove home feeling like a very lucky man.

Ira had once again provided a bridge for me to the rest of the world.

epilogue

SOUNDTRACK

When you're dealing with songwriters, I think you're dealing with the most intuitive kind of guys. None of them can explain where the hell their stuff is coming from. They're all a little nuts—and it comes out. See, everybody forgets that the purest example of abstract art in our world is music. Music gives you all of those things, love, hate, anger, fear, all of it in abstract form.
—ABE BURROWS, QUOTED IN MAX WILK,
They're Playing Our Song

I've spent most of this book discussing the great legacy of songs left to us not only by the Gershwins but also by Porter and Berlin and Kern, by Harry Warren and Harold Arlen, by Duke Ellington and Andy Razaf, by Rodgers and Hart and Comden and Green, by Vincent Youmans, Yip Harburg, Johnny Mercer, Dorothy Fields, by Jerry Herman and Stephen Sondheim and Burton Lane. But how can I do right by the astonishing wealth and beauty of that legacy in all its variety and richness? For openers, it represents the endowment of hundreds of composers and lyricists, men and women, Jewish and Italian and Irish and African American and even a handful of White Anglo-Saxon Protestants (is that multicultural enough for you?). Constituting a vast treasury that lies hidden beneath daily consciousness much of the time, these songs are a ground source that continually sends wellsprings to the surface, suffusing my life—and yours, I hope—with a lavish array of gorgeous melody, beguiling visual images, crystallized emotions, and rhythms for every conceivable mood and activity, from the softest ballad to the most passionate and frenetic dance tempo.

I have been told by some people of a certain generation rather close to mine that those "old songs" all sound alike, with their cliché 32-bar AABA form and their bridges that are alarmingly similar. And so it is—many of them do sound alike. I prefer to think of their similarity in terms of the sameness amid infinite variety of something as common as the snowflake. Popular songs were not meant to last much longer than snowflakes. Evanescent and plentiful, they were created for commerce, yet the best of them were also imbued with an eternal life force that transcends their 32-bar form as well as the creaky stage or film scenarios that provided their reason for being. They were unwittingly built to last—not all of them, but the ones encoded with a strong enough strain of divine DNA. It is that miraculous connection with infinity, an inherent part of any great music, that I feel every time I experience a great popular song. "Popular"—the word itself seems to militate against any claim to timelessness, as if something created with mass acceptance in mind couldn't possibly be art. As if art hadn't so often served the populace, from African sculpture to European cathedrals to Hollywood films themselves. I have seen firsthand how popular songs heal the masses, how they give joy and hope in a very personal way to those who don't even know how badly they need them.

They're just songs, you say. Yes, but that's the point: they're just songs that work on many levels, from the mundane to the magical. Egocentric old Irving Caesar becomes a divine messenger when he opens his mouth to croak out "If I Forget You" for the umpteenth time. In spite of everything, the truth somehow resides in these apparent confections, along with clarity, hope, and, most of all, joy.

And so I'm not concerned about the circumstances surrounding the creation of any particular song, whether it was written for purely commercial purposes, to create a hit, to cash in on a catch phrase or craze of the moment, or any of the other mercenary excuses that have caused popular songs to spring into being. Even the creators themselves, in many cases, were not aware that they were creating great art, that something was coming through them to serve a purpose beyond paying next month's rent. Ira always said that he wrote the songs merely for a moment in time, for a plot in a show, and often a fairly mindless one at that. I have repeatedly been amazed to see one of these old songwriters get up to perform and talk about his songs—at performances once aptly called "And-then-I-wrotes"—with a mixture of egotism and insouciance. "Yeah," he would croak, "and then I wrote the song in twenty minutes." As I've watched them, I have sometimes asked myself, How could something so lovely and artful have come out of these cranky, rather expressionless, even emotionless people? At times they appear to be almost caricatures of themselves. Do they no longer feel what they once wrote? Did they ever?

Songwriters are often the last to know whether one of their songs is any good or not. Richard Whiting, who wrote "Louise," "My Ideal," and "Hooray for Hollywood," among many others, once contemplated entering a war-song contest at the Michigan Theatre in Detroit during World War I. According to his daughter, the singer Margaret Whiting, he wrote a waltz and Raymond Egan wrote a very simple lyric to fit the melody. Contemplating the finished product, Whiting decided that a song like that could never win, so he didn't bother to enter it. Instead, he tossed the music and lyrics in the wastebasket. His secretary found it as she was emptying his basket and, suspecting what had happened, took it to Whiting's boss, Jerome Remick, who ran the only major music publishing house with offices in Detroit. Without Whiting's knowledge, Remick entered the song in the contest; it won three nights running, sold millions of copies of sheet music, and went on to become the quintessential World War I song, "Till We Meet Again." Like today's Hollywood studios, songwriters often succumbed to the temptation to cash in with sequels to their big hits. Whiting wrote a waltz sequel to "Till We Meet Again" a few years later—a blatant copycat of the same song—but no dice. Whiting didn't strike twice. Likewise, Irving Caesar tried to follow his huge hit "Just a Gigolo," actually his translation of a preexisting German lyric, with a more humorous sequel called "Spanish Jake." Few songs today are more obscure than "Spanish Jake." The famous team of DeSylva, Brown, and Henderson wrote "Sonny Boy" as a joke, a compendium of sentimental clichés. Jolson sang it seriously. The public seriously bought it by the millions—but not their sequel titled "Little Pal." Surefire often became sure fizzle.

But maybe we shouldn't blame the songwriters. After all, who can say why certain songs survive and become indelibly imprinted in our awareness while others do not? Some songs have endured not by virtue of any inherent greatness but because they're connected with a certain moment in theater or film history or with the person who sang them. For instance, I think that "As Time Goes By" has a rather peculiar lyric. What exactly did its author mean by "The fundamental things apply"? And while we're at it, what else did Herman Hupfield ever write of any lasting value? He was talented, yes; he even had several Depression-era hits. But how many people remember "When Yuba Plays the Rhumba on the Tuba"? (It was later on the flip side of the Spike Jones 78 of "Laura.") In fact, Hupfield wrote "As Time Goes By" in 1931 but it didn't become an all-time standard until it landed in *Casablanca* eleven years later. The pungency of memory and nostalgia, and its association with the romance of that film, makes "As Time Goes By" just as insistently significant as the greatest Gershwin song—not in a critical but an emotional sense.

Luck also plays a part in it. Gerald Marks, who wrote "Is It True What They Say About Dixie?," "All of Me," and many less notable songs with Irving Caesar, likes to tell how "All of Me" became a hit through a series of fortunate coincidences. In 1931, Marks came to New York from his hometown of Saginaw, Michigan, with just enough money to stay for a week while he peddled "All of Me," but there were no takers. Returning home, he played it backstage in Detroit for vaudeville singer Belle Baker, who happened to have a piano in her dressing room. "When I got to the line 'Your good-bye left me with eyes that cry,'" Marks has said, "she became hysterical. Later, I learned it was the anniversary of her husband's death. From then on, she plugged my song and made it a hit all by herself." (The last time Marks told that story in public, by the way, was at an "And-then-I-wrote" at Lincoln Center in 1994—on the eve of his ninety-fourth birthday.)

Fortunately, the bad songs have for the most part disappeared, something you can ascertain by looking at the Hit Parade lists of any given year and counting the vast majority of songs that did not survive the test of time—a figure that has been estimated at ninety-seven percent or more. Some of them are campy or so silly that they're fun to sing, like "When It's Sweet Onion Time in Bermuda, I'll Breathe My Love So True," or "When It's Apple Blossom Time in Orange, New Jersey, We'll Make a Peach of a Pair," or (my current favorite) "If I Can't Have Anna in Cuba, Then I'll See Esther in Spain."

The songs that have persisted, many hundreds of them, have done so on the basis not of nostalgia but of quality, craft, and inspiration. They make up a seemingly inexhaustible underground stream of music that sustains me even as it serves as a constant reminder of the incomparable richness of human creativity and, by extension, of the universe itself. The melodies of countless songs play continuously on the soundtrack of my heart and mind—sometimes, I admit, with infuriating tenacity. For at times, to my chagrin, fragments of the least desirable and, one would presume, least memorable songs get stuck in a baffling tape loop that momentarily evades my sternest efforts to switch it off. Some of the great musical creators have complained about the dogged way their gray matter fiendishly repeats a musical phrase that should rightly have been forgotten. The famous theater orchestrator Robert Russell Bennett, who worked side by side with Gershwin, Porter, Rodgers, Berlin, and other greats, was known to walk around his little office constantly and mindlessly whistling a minor tune by Robert Emmett Dolan from a 1949 show called *Texas, Lil' Darlin'*. Why, of all the hundreds and hundreds of great songs he orchestrated, did this one staple itself into his brain? I don't know, but I certainly understand. Happily, my soundtrack is more often composed of threads from the most delightful melodies that appear unbidden and are then woven and spliced into a carpet of many colors.

But I have to be careful what I hum in public sometimes, because it can be like passing a virus. Years ago, I was taking a picture to be framed and in the car on my way to the framer's, I was listening to a tape of Bing Crosby's greatest hits. Bing sang a lot of great songs, but he also sang some that were intrinsically mediocre yet became "great" by his performance of them. One such song was an early '50s duet with his son, called "Sam's Song," which goes in part, "Nothing on your mind, / Suddenly you'll find, / Now you're singing Sam's Song." It's an idiotic kind of thing, but it has a countermelody that his son Gary sang, a very rapid patter that's kind of catchy. Anyway, as I went into the frame store, I was humming it under my breath, barely aware of it. I showed the picture to the guy behind the counter, who then took all the measurements. I thanked him and left and just as I opened the door to walk out, I heard him singing, "Nothing on your mind, / Suddenly you'll find, / Now you're singing Sam's Song." I didn't know whether to laugh or apologize.

So the lyrics can be just as insistent as the melody, and can just as easily catch in your head. For Ira's sake, let's not forget the words. Lyrics, apart from their inherent charm, can be a hotbed of Freudian analysis. When I'm in the company of playwright and actor George Furth, he'll stop me several times in the course of an afternoon to ask me, "Okay, what were you humming now?" And then he'll make me analyze the title and the lyric for the purpose of pointing out what I'm really thinking or feeling at that particular moment. If I pay attention to some of the lyrics I'm humming in the context of a specific activity, they can be quite revealing—whether I'm on my way to a date, humming "The Thrill Is Gone," or joining my parents for an anniversary celebration and discovering with no small amount of guilt that the tune running through my brain has been "You Always Hurt the One You Love."

Some songs, as I've said, are frankly silly, even ridiculous. Others are merely pedestrian or cliché-ridden, mechanically produced as if turned out by some rusty, clunky piece of machinery in a sub-basement somewhere in the corroded end of Tin Pan Alley. Some are workmanlike, serviceable, even catchy, but not inspired, not transcendent; others are pleasantly quirky and oddball and never came close to being hits or standards. Yet they've carved themselves a place in my heart, too, and without them, the repertoire might not be as rich and varied as it is. Just as some metaphysicians insist that without suffering we cannot know what true joy is, perhaps without the lesser songs we couldn't fully appreciate the sublime ones. But it's for those sublime ones that I live, those divinely inspired songs that happen when melodic inventiveness and harmonic depth meet with a genuine profundity of thought and emotion. Feelings and insights are converted into words so apparently simple and streamlined that they almost bypass the intellect, conveyed in the velvet carriage of melody, until they catch somewhere between the heart and the gut. (And the feeling is quite different from heartburn.)

Music, after all, is not intellectual. Maybe the lyrics are, to some extent, but the best lyrics, combined with the music, always go to the heart more than the head. What neither music alone nor the spoken word alone could accomplish, a song can do. The work of a few hours, days, or even months, often the collaborative efforts of two people with very different minds and hearts and sensibilities, is compressed into a three- or four-minute piece of art that has the power to change our mood, inspire us, perplex us, or send us into reveries from which we may actually emerge transformed. That possibility of transformation is what keeps me energized and propels me to play and preserve this music and to treat it as the great irreplaceable treasure it is. My debt to this music and to the men and women who have created and continue to create it is entirely unrepayable. Through them, my life has been enriched materially—no small feat in itself—but it has also been expanded and fulfilled in a way that no financial endowment or inheritance of any kind could possibly have done.

I used to get embarrassed when people said, "Look what you're doing for Ira! Isn't it wonderful that he has you in his life?" That always made me feel uncomfortable because no matter what I did for him, I could never repay him for the gift he gave to the world with his lyrics, or to me by sharing his treasury of knowledge and experience. So I continue to try to find ways to pay a small portion of my debt. I'm on the installment plan, and I imagine that plan will take the rest of my life to pay off. I doubt that very many people wake up every morning thinking, How can I let more of the world know who Harry Warren was? How can I find some way of getting "You're My Everything" into the Top 40? But I do, because I feel I owe it to Harry, once again, for what he gave the world and for what he shared with me. When I feel that I haven't given a proper interpretation to a song or that I've been unable to get across what that song has to say, melodically or lyrically, I sometimes feel guilty. (Okay. Maybe, having been born Jewish, I'm just looking for things to feel guilty about.) And I feel unsettled because I imagine that the songwriters are somehow watching me—those ghost writers in the sky. I feel a distinct responsibility to preserve and present their work, however long it takes to get it out there and get it right.

But that's okay. I'm not in any hurry, because I'm already where I've always wanted to be. The genie that appeared to me all those years ago and showed me the way into the magic cave of Ira Gershwin's work-room has been lavishly and inexplicably kind to me. And when all else is said and done, the songs will remain. The soundtrack will always be there, playing in the minds and hearts of generations to come. Maybe, if I'm lucky, I'll be reborn in a place where I'll get to hear the music I love all the time, perhaps as librarian in the Cosmic Music Archive of Rhythm and Rhyme. (But please, no whole-tone scales or Scandinavian folk music.) I'll just be happy for a chance to help plant the seeds for the next generation to enjoy. And I'll probably be tending the fields of the Gershwin Plantation for a long, long time.

index

Photo Credits

Section I: pages 1, 2 (top), 4 (top)—courtesy of Mazie Feinstein; page 2 (bottom)— © John Livesay; page 5 (top)— © Robert Millard; (bottom)—courtesy of ASCAP; page 6—courtesy of the Donald Smith Collection; page 7 (bottom)—used by permission of Turner Entertainment Co. All rights reserved; page 8 (photos of Oscar Levant)—courtesy of June Levant; all others—from the collection of Michael Feinstein.
Section II: page 2 (top)—courtesy of Tita Cahn; (bottom)—courtesy of Mabel Mercer Foundation; pages 3 (bottom), 4 (bottom)— © Alan Berliner/Gamma Liason; page 4 (top)—Official White House Photo; page 5 (top)— © Greg Gorman; (bottom)— © Academy of Motion Picture Arts and Sciences; page 7 (top)— © Marc Bryan-Brown; (bottom)— © J. Greg Henry; page 8 (top)— © Janet Macoska/Starfile; (bottom)— © William Claxton; all others—from the collection of Michael Feinstein.

Song Permissions and Credits

"Ach Du Lieber Oom Pah Pah" by Ira Gershwin and Burton Lane © 1953 (Renewed) Ira Gershwin Music and Chappell & Co. All rights o/b/o Ira Gershwin Music administered by WB Music Corp. All rights reserved. Used by permission. Warner Bros. Publications U.S. Inc., Miami, FL 33014.
"Alexander's Ragtime Band" by Irving Berlin © 1911 by Irving Berlin. Copyright renewed. International copyright secured. All rights reserved. Used by permission.
"All Dark People" by Richard Rodgers and Lorenz Hart © 1937 (Renewed) Chappell & Co. (ASCAP) and Williamson Music (ASCAP). All rights reserved. Used by permission. Warner Bros. Publications U.S. Inc., Miami, FL 33014.
"Anything Goes" by Cole Porter © 1934 (Renewed) Warner Bros. Inc. All rights reserved. Used by permission. Warner Bros. Publications U.S. Inc., Miami, FL 33014.
"Aren't You Kind of Glad We Did?" by George Gershwin and Ira Gershwin © 1946 Gershwin Publishing Corp. Renewed and assigned to Chappell & Co. All rights administered by Chappell & Co. (ASCAP). All rights reserved. Used by permission. Warner Bros. Publications U.S. Inc., Miami, FL 33014.
"The Babbitt and the Bromide" by George Gershwin and Ira Gershwin © 1927 (Renewed) WB Music Corp. All rights reserved. Used by permission. Warner Bros. Publications U.S. Inc., Miami, FL 33014.
"A Bar on the Piccola Marina" by Noel Coward © 1955 (Renewed) Chappell Music Ltd. (PRS). All rights administered by Chappell & Co. (ASCAP). All rights reserved. Used by permission. Warner Bros. Publications U.S. Inc., Miami, FL 33014.
"The Begat" by E.Y. Harburg and Burton Lane © 1952 (Renewed) Chappell & Co. (ASCAP). All rights reserved. Used by permission. Warner Bros. Publications U.S. Inc., Miami, FL 33014.
"Bewitched" by Richard Rodgers and Lorenz Hart © 1941 (Renewed) Chappell & Co. (ASCAP). All rights reserved. Used by permission. Warner Bros. Publications U.S. Inc., Miami, FL 33014.
"(What Did I Do To Be So) Black and Blue" by Andy Razaf, Thomas "Fats" Waller, and Harry Brooks © 1929 (Renewed) EMI Mills Music, Inc. All rights reserved. Used by permission. Warner Bros. Publications U.S. Inc., Miami, FL 33014.
"Blah, Blah, Blah" by George Gershwin and Ira Gershwin © 1931 (Renewed) WB Music Corp. (ASCAP). All rights reserved. Used by permission. Warner Bros. Publications U.S. Inc., Miami, FL 33014.
"Bojangles of Harlem" words and music by Jerome Kern and Dorothy Fields © 1936 Polygram International Publishing, Inc. Copyright renewed. International copyright secured. All rights reserved.
"Brigadoon" by Alan Jay Lerner and Frederick Loewe © 1947 (Renewed) Alan Jay Lerner and Frederick Loewe. Rights assigned to EMI Catalog Partnership and Warner/Chappell Music, Inc. Worldwide Print Rights controlled and administered by EMI U Catalog Inc. All rights reserved. Used by permission. Warner Bros. Publications U.S. Inc., Miami, FL 33014.
"Bronco Busters" by George Gershwin and Ira Gershwin © 1930 (Renewed) WB Music Corp. (ASCAP). All rights reserved. Used by permission. Warner Bros. Publications U.S. Inc., Miami, FL 33014.
"Brother Can You Spare a Dime" by Jay Gorney and E.Y. Harburg © 1932 (Renewed) Warner Bros. Inc. (ASCAP). All rights reserved. Used by permission. Warner Bros. Publications U.S. Inc., Miami, FL 33014.
"But Not For Me" by George Gershwin and Ira Gershwin © 1930 (Renewed) WB Music Corp. All rights reserved. Used by permission. Warner Bros. Publications U.S. Inc., Miami, FL 33014.
"By Strauss" music and lyrics by George Gershwin and Ira Gershwin © 1936 (Renewed) George Gershwin Music and Ira Gershwin Music. All rights administered by WB Music Corp. All rights reserved. Used by permission. Warner Bros. Publications U.S. Inc., Miami, FL 33014.